CONTENTIOUS POLITICS
IN BRAZIL AND CHINA

CONTENTIOUS POLITICS IN BRAZIL AND CHINA

BEYOND REGIME

DECEMBER GREEN

WRIGHT STATE UNIVERSITY

LAURA LUEHRMANN

WRIGHT STATE UNIVERSITY

WESTVIEW
PRESS

A Member of the Perseus Books Group

Westview Press was founded in 1975 in Boulder, Colorado, by notable publisher and intellectual Fred Praeger. Westview Press continues to publish scholarly titles and high-quality undergraduate- and graduate-level textbooks in core social science disciplines. With books developed, written, and edited with the needs of serious nonfiction readers, professors, and students in mind, Westview Press honors its long history of publishing books that matter.

Published by Westview Press,
A Member of the Perseus Books Group
2465 Central Avenue
Boulder, CO 80301
www.westviewpress.com

Westview Press books are available at special discounts for bulk purchases in the United States by corporations, institutions, and other organizations. For more information, please contact the Special Markets Department at the Perseus Books Group, 2300 Chestnut Street, Suite 200, Philadelphia, PA 19103, or call (800) 810-4145, ext. 5000, or e-mail special.markets@perseusbooks.com.

Designed by Pauline Brown

Library of Congress Cataloging-in-Publication Data
Names: Green, December, author. | Luehrmann, Laura, 1969- author.
Title: Contentious politics in Brazil and China : beyond regime / December
    Green, Wright State University, Laura Luehrmann, Wright State University.
Description: Boulder, CO : Westview Press, 2016. | Includes bibliographical
    references and index.
Identifiers: LCCN 2015043547| ISBN 9780813350042 (pbk.) | ISBN
9780813350080
    (e-book)
Subjects: LCSH: Brazil—Social policy. | Brazil—Politics and government. |
    China—Social policy. | China—Politics and government. | Social
—policy—Cross-cultural studies.
Classification: LCC JL2431 .G74 2016 | DDC 320.951—dc23 LC record available at http://lccn.loc.gov/2015043547

10 9 8 7 6 5 4 3 2 1

CONTENTS

Preface   *ix*

Acronyms   *xiii*

1   **Brazil and China: Contention in Comparative Perspective**   **1**

Introduction   1

Regime Type and Contentious Politics: Beyond Regime   4

Democracy as Regime Type   *5*

Authoritarianism as Regime Type   *6*

"The Messy Middle"   *7*

Contributing Factors Beyond Regime   *9*

Our Approach to State and Society: Receptivity and
Resistance in Brazil and China   11

"The Messy Middle" in Brazil and China   *11*

The Advantages of an Eclectic Approach   *13*

State-Society Dynamics in Brazil and China   *14*

How Political Opportunity Structures Shape Contentious Politics   *19*

Emerging Political Cultures and the Power of Social Media   *23*

Fitting All the Pieces Together into a Frame   *25*

Why These Cases   27

Outline of Book   30

Discussion Questions   35

2   **Heritage and Culture**   **37**

Introduction   37

Brazil   39

Approach to the Past: "The Brazilian Way"   *40*

Revolution/Not   49
The Partido dos Trabalhadores *(PT): From Society to State*   59
China   64
Approach to the Past: "Middle Kingdom" Complex   64
Revolution(s)   72
The CCP: State Management of Society   79
Analysis   83
Discussion Questions   87

3   **Human Security**   89
Introduction   89
Brazil   92
Migration: "The Rights to the City"—or Not   96
Criminality and the Rule of Law: High Crime and Official Impunity   104
Health Care and HIV-AIDS: Citizens Lead the State   112
China   118
Migration: Registered Rights—or Not   121
Criminality and the Rule by Law: Low Crime and Official Impunity   128
Health Care and HIV-AIDS: State Tolerates Society   135
Analysis   140
Discussion Questions   148

4   **Politics of Social Diversity**   149
Introduction   149
Brazil   150
Layers of Identity: Color in Brazil   151
Sexual Politics and LGBT Rights   159
China   172
Layers of Identity: Religion and Ethnicity   173
Sexual Politics and LGBT Rights   179
Analysis   191
Discussion Questions   200

5   **Environmental Politics**   201
Introduction   201
Brazil   202
Pollution: Oil, Water, and the Valley of Death   202
Deforestation: Trees vs. People / Trees Plus People   206

China   218
   Pollution: "Smogapolypse" Plus Water Shortages   220
   Deforestation: Cracks in "The Green Great Wall"   230
Analysis   233
Discussion Questions   240

6   **Leadership from Brasilia and Beijing**   **242**
    Introduction   242
    Brazil   244
       The Regional Arena: Is Brazil Too Big for the Room?   246
       The Transnational Arena: Diplomacy as "The Beautiful Game"   249
       Case in Point: Climate Change   255
       Types of Power: Soft over Hard   260
    China   264
       The Regional Arena: Crowded by History and Resources   265
       The Transnational Arena: Reluctant Reemergence   271
       Case in Point: Climate Change   276
       Types of Power: Soft with Hard   279
    Analysis   281
    Discussion Questions   288

7   **Conclusions: Beyond Regime**   **289**
    Dissolving Dichotomies   291
    Postscript   298

Bibliography   299

Index   353

PREFACE

"Brazil and China? Why would you ever compare those two countries?"

Many cocktail parties and professional receptions have been peppered with conversation along these lines these past few years as we developed this book comparing state-society relations in one of the world's largest democracies (Brazil) and the largest authoritarian state (the People's Republic of China, or PRC). At a time in which the global center of gravity is rapidly shifting beyond Washington, DC, we believe it is more important than ever to understand dynamics between the governed and the governing in these two ostensibly most different states.

The initial idea for this project began in the winter of 2008, born of officials' concerns within both Brazil and China about the political impacts of the growing gap between the rich and the poor within their countries. As students of the developing world with a special interest in social movements, we were intrigued by the creative ways in which state-society interactions were playing out in these two states. The initial structure of the book was drafted (and redrafted) over multiple working sessions at a local pizza place close to our university, a little bit of New York City in the middle of southwestern Ohio. Throughout these planning sessions, the importance of this unlikely comparison of these two fast-emerging states became more and more apparent to both of us.

We believe that a close comparison of these two states highlights issues that analysts would otherwise miss in a single state (or single region) view. For example, leaders and citizens in both countries frame themselves as exceptions to the paths followed by others. Both states have a record of cultural dilution—in Brazil with social "whitening," and in China, with Han migration to Tibet, Xinjiang, and other minority-populated regions. Brazil is much more sexually liberated than the PRC, yet Brazil has some of the most restrictive abortion laws in the world (and still high rates of abortion), whereas China leads the world in virtually unrestricted access to abortion. Think of the headline-grabbing issues of our time, including economic, gender, and racial inequalities, urbanization, climate change. Both public servants and private citizens in Brazil and China increasingly have much to say about the resolution to these tough issues. Image and "face" often motivate decisions in both states, even if, for the most part, Brazil is open and oriented more toward the international audience, with Chinese leaders warily watching the lid of social discontent at home. Both states claim to be engaging in ongoing, seemingly far-reaching attempts at reform, and "change" is a catch-all phrase for both. Just underneath the surface, though, the level of continuity in both states is striking.

In this book, we aim to show the utility of unorthodox comparisons: we contend that some things become clearer when two unexpected cases are placed next to each other. The reveal can, at times, be flattering (e.g., the state's support for alternative energy sources), and at others, damning (e.g., the prevalence of gender inequality and the mistreatment of sexual and gender minorities). Because of the size and diversity found in both Brazil and China, it is tempting for scholars to claim exceptionalism and limit their claims to within-state comparative analysis. However, we call on readers to push these boundaries, to consider the benefits of viewing Brasilia and Beijing not in isolation, but in a comparative light.

This is a book for anyone interested in the tension between state and society in China and Brazil (or emerging powers generally), or anyone just intrigued by the overall messiness of politics. However, we wrote it to fulfill a more specific need. Most required texts for graduate and undergraduate Comparative Politics courses tend to fall into one of two categories: either they are very broad or they are very narrow. As a result, it is common for professors teaching these courses to adopt a textbook and a supplementary reading (often a case study). In some of the most commonly used textbooks as many as thirteen countries are presented in (largely) consistent format, but there is little actual comparison of them, and often the various cases are written by as many different authors. This results in a cacophony of voices and there is rarely much attempt to tie them all together—or to actually compare the cases.

Hence the need for a supplement. The reason professors turn to these additional readings is to add richness and depth to the breadth of the assigned text. However, most of the books currently used as supplements make the opposite mistake of the big texts and go too narrow. Despite a consensus among comparativists on the need to include attention to contentious politics and civil society, the supplemental readings routinely fail to include chapters on the ways in which citizens challenge the state—despite the fact that this is perhaps the aspect of politics that students find most compelling. Yet contentious politics is our focus. As a supplementary reading our book competes with monographs that are too narrow; they fix on a single issue or type of activism in one or maybe two cases, and they rarely compare cases outside a single region. We break this mold with a book that endeavors to be none of these things. In it, we encourage students to challenge dominant theory and conventional thinking. And by offering two unexpected cases on a range of issues, our book does what a supplementary reading should do: it serves as an innovative counterpoint to the text.

WE HAVE MANY INDIVIDUALS AND GROUPS to thank for their support and assistance in bringing this project to fruition. Both of us have benefited enormously from generous professional development leave granted by the Wright State University College of Liberal Arts, which freed us each to focus on various stages of this project. Our colleagues in the Wright State University Department of Political Science, especially Donna Schlagheck and Charlie Funderburk, served as helpful sounding boards in the earliest stages of this project and offered sage advice. We also appreciate the feedback and suggestions of our colleague Margaret P. Karns, professor emerita at the University of Dayton. Our wonderful administrative assistants, Joanne Ballmann and Renée Harber, provided moral and technical support, always with a great sense of humor. We also want to thank Nickki Webb for her assistance with the bibliography. Conversations with many of our students, undergraduate and graduate alike, have helped shape our approach to the importance of unexpected comparisons as well as the most useful ways of approaching the "messiness" of our findings. We want to formally acknowledge the adage that professors often learn more from their students than the other way around. We have especially drawn on the experiences and insights of many of the fine graduate students in our Master of Arts Program in International and Comparative Politics, most notably alums Pablo Banhos, Fabiana Hayden, and Rafael Ranieri. Of course, the views presented are our own and do not necessarily represent theirs.

We want to thank our editors at Westview Press who believed in the wisdom of this unconventional comparison and guided us throughout the process, especially Kelli Fillingim and Catherine Craddock. They have been great to work with, and we appreciate their patience, responsiveness, and attention to detail. We also extend our gratitude to the anonymous reviewers who offered fine suggestions for improving the manuscript.

As with any lengthy research project, it is our families who have often endured the most hardships throughout the process, and this book is no exception. For their understanding of late nights at the office, marathon weekend writing sessions, and the proverbial highs and lows of the publishing process, we thank our sons Luke, Jakob, and Andrew. They have grown up with front-row seats to the (sometimes unappetizing) processes of academic writing and publishing, and we hope they each continue to gain an understanding of our commitment to international awareness. Our greatest source of support continues to be our wonderful partners, David and Joe, who have been with us through it all, sometimes serving as helpful critics but most often being rocks for the both of us: encouraging us always, and nudging us away from the computers and libraries when necessary. As a small expression of our heartfelt gratitude, it is to these two that we lovingly dedicate this book.

DG and LML
Dayton, OH
June 2015

ACRONYMS

AIIB	Asian Infrastructure Development Bank
ART	anti-retroviral therapy
ARV	anti-retroviral
BCE	Before the Common Era
BOPE	Special Police Operation Battalion (Brazil)
BRIC	Brazil, Russia, India, China
BRICS	Brazil, Russia, India, China, South Africa
CCP	Chinese Communist Party
CCT	conditional cash transfer
CCTV	Chinese Central Television Station
CE	Common Era
CIMI	Indigenous Missionary Council (Brazil, *Conselho Indigenista Missionario*)
CPPCC	Chinese People's Political Consultative Conference
CUT	Central Workers' Union (Brazil)
CYL	Communist Youth League (China)
DC	developed countries
"Eagles"	Emerging and Growth-Leading Economies
EPA	Environmental Protection Agency (Brazil)
FHC	Fernando Henrique Cardoso
G8	Group of 8
G20	Group of 20
G77	Group of 77
GDP	Gross Domestic Product
GMD	Nationalist Party (*Guomindang*)
GPV	Group for the Affirmation, Integration, and Dignity of People with AIDS (Brazil, *Grupo Pela VIDDA*)

HDI	Human Development Index
IBAMA	Brazilian Institute of Environment and Renewable Natural Resources
ICTs	Information Communication Technologies
IMF	International Monetary Fund
IPEA	Institute for Applied Economic Research (Brazil)
KTV	Karaoke Television
LDC	less developed country
LGBT	lesbian, gay, bisexual, and transgender
MAB	Movement of People Affected by Dams (*Movimento dos Atingidos por Barragens*)
MNU	Unified Black Movement (Brazil, *Movimento Negro Unificado*)
MP	*Ministério Público*
MST	Landless Workers Movement (Brazil, *Movimento dos Trabalhadores Rurais Sem Terra*)
MTST	Homeless Workers' Movement (Brazil, *Movimento dos Trabalhadores Sem Teto*)
NAACP	National Association for the Advancement of Colored People
NAP	National AIDS Program (Brazil)
NATO	North Atlantic Treaty Organization
NGO	non-governmental organization
NPC	National People's Congress (China)
NPT	Nuclear Non-Proliferation Treaty
P-5	Permanent Five (members of UNSC)
PAP	People's Armed Police (China)
PCC	First Capital Command (Brazil, *Primeiro Comando da Capital*)
PFLAG	Parents, Families and Friends of Lesbians and Gays (China)
PLA	People's Liberation Army (China)
PRC	People's Republic of China
PSB	Public Security Bureau (China)
PT	Workers' Party (Brazil, *Partido dos Trabalhadores*)
RTL	Reform through Labor (China)
SCO	Shanghai Cooperation Organization
SUS	Unified Health System (Brazil, *Sistema Único de Saúde*)

UN   United Nations
UNAIDS   Joint United Nations Programme on HIV and AIDS
UNASUL   Union of South American Nations
UNDP   United Nations Development Program
UNICEF   United Nations Children's Fund
UNESCO   United Nations Educational, Scientific, and Cultural
          Organization
UNSC   United Nations Security Council
UPPs   Police Pacification Units (Brazil)
WHO   World Health Organization
WTO   World Trade Organization

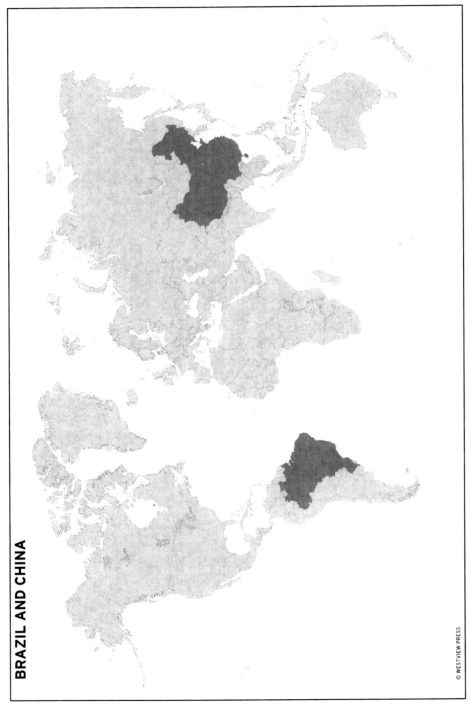

BRAZIL AND CHINA

© WESTVIEW PRESS

MAP 1.1

1

BRAZIL AND CHINA: CONTENTION IN COMPARATIVE PERSPECTIVE

God is a Brazilian.

—A common saying in Brazil

China is a 3,000-year-old civilization in the body of an industrial teenager: a mega-rich, dirt-poor, overpopulated, under-resourced, ethnically diverse mass of humanity that is going through several stages of development simultaneously.

—Jonathan Watts, *When a Billion Chinese Jump: How China Will Save Mankind—or Destroy It*

INTRODUCTION

Open a newspaper, or follow a blog on world affairs, and you won't get very far before there is some discussion about the role of either China or Brazil in regard to any major world issue—economic growth, biodiversity, clean energy solutions, health care, inequality, urbanization—you name it. Discussions of politics, economics, culture, even sporting events are more and more likely to include these countries. In some of the most serious challenges facing the world

1

community today, Brazil and China are burgeoning nations, and (equal to their size and aspirations) each play significant roles as path breakers, problem makers, and sometimes both. Neither is anyone's "yes man," and neither Brazil nor China is going to conform or hop into line just to please the United States—or anyone else, for that matter.

Such a stance is based in the view that US hegemony is in gradual decline and there is a shifting balance of power.[1] Both Brazil and China are known for their independent attitudes, and both are to varying degrees—and in varying ways—challenging the United States on a number of fronts in what they view as a new, increasingly multipolar order. Grabbing the headlines, neither of these big states is willing to stand on the sidelines; both want your attention and respect. But do they want the responsibility that often comes with it? That's a tougher question. As different as they are, this is an exciting time for both the Brazilians and Chinese.

Clearly, each country has something very different to offer the world. Sharma (2011) coined the phrase "Brazil is the 'Un-China,'" but he focuses on the two countries' different approaches to economic policy—particularly in regard to the value of their currency, rate of savings, and investment. However, in some ways Brazil is more the "un-China" for its unique worldview and the way it presents itself. As we will see throughout the following chapters, Brazil appears to be quite the package; its flamboyance, its fearless cultural dynamism, and the way of life it projects is undeniably attractive to much of the world. Brazil seeks to capitalize on its reputation as cordial, accommodating, and conflict-free, and a national identity that is easy-going, open-minded, and tolerant. Brazilians are famous for their optimism, and Brazil is perceived as a friendly country—the friendliest in the region, according to a 2011 Latinobarómetro poll. When respondents to that same poll were asked what country would they most like to emulate, Brazil ranked fourth in the world—interestingly, just ahead of China ("Latinobarómetro Report" 2011).

Surely the two countries made this list of role models for very different reasons. Due to its well-known human rights violations and prickly regional

---

[1] One striking example of the possible emergence of this shift is the formation of the Asian Infrastructure Investment Bank (AIIB) in 2014. Led by Beijing, this project, set to fund development projects throughout Asia, is perceived as a rival to the US-dominated World Bank and Asian Development Bank. When Beijing revealed the official founding members list in mid-2015, it included all four BRIC (Brazil, Russia, India, and China) states and 14 out of the Group of 20 (G20) members. The AIIB is expected to be fully established by the end of 2015.

ties, one might have a hard time seeing China win a popularity contest. But the Chinese are deemed worthy of emulation; citizens are known as resourceful survivors who, in the face of tremendous limits enforced upon them from above, craft solutions that have played a large part in China's truly amazing economic success story. China's narrative is compelling, and therefore one of its attractions. It is considered a model for many developing countries because of its history as one of the world's oldest civilizations, its reemergence after humiliating Western domination, and its approach to economic development. China's experiences trading items, ideas, and culture across borders has run in fits and starts, even pre-dating the famed Silk Road begun in the Han Dynasty (206 BCE–220 CE).

Although there are some major differences between them, we also suggest that the two are very much alike. Their behavior in the global arena is a reflection of a number of factors, including state-society relations back home. But often the differences between them are more about style than substance. For example, as emerging nations, Brazil and China are not interested in conforming to preexisting norms or expectations. Guez (2014) has described Brazil's dynamic, aggressive, and exciting style on the soccer field as a survival tactic, the product of the poor having to play on rough turf. Similarly, Brazil and China perceive the international fora, dominated by Western, industrialized countries, as necessitating similar adjustments. The two are thus alike in that—to some degree—they seek to make, not accept, the new rules. As such, Brazil very much wants a bigger say in the world. It has outsize aspirations, it longs to be taken seriously, and one way of confirming its status would be permanent membership in the UN Security Council (UNSC) ("The Brazilian Model" 2011). On the other hand, China is secure in its status as one of the five permanent members of the UNSC and is not eager for more company. As we will discuss later, neither is seeking radical change, but both want the West to move over and make room. What can we expect from these states on the world stage? Look at how they interact with their citizens. We believe that, regardless of whether it is democratic or authoritarian, the way that state and society interact tells us a lot about the role states will play in the global arena.

As fast-emerging powers that will not be ignored, what will these states and their citizens bring to the table? What political priorities, domestically and internationally, do leaders of these two states have? How engaged and active is their citizenry? What difference may this make for international relations in the coming decades? If you want to know how countries will lead on what are likely to be the most compelling issues of the near future—climate change, poverty, or religious, ethnic, and other divides—perhaps the best way of knowing this is to ask about how they deal with issues—such as inequality, identity, and the environment—internally.

REGIME TYPE AND CONTENTIOUS POLITICS: BEYOND REGIME

We're interested in using comparative politics to understand both domestic dynamics and international relations, but our primary concern is what McAdam, Tarrow, and Tilly (2009) term "contentious politics," (or calls for action and the resulting interactions of citizen and state) and the multiple forms political encounters take. "Contentious politics," also known as non-routine politics, focuses on efforts by non-elite actors to engage and influence the state. Such efforts run the gamut from non-violent to violent, routine to extraordinary, and conservative to transformative. While the term "contentious politics" was originally used to describe politics inside countries, it can also be used in reference to how society influences the state's foreign policy. Cognizant of these linkages, comparative politics scholars are "extending the boundaries" to examine transnational contention and social movements as well (McAdam, Tarrow, and Tilly 2009, 282–284).

Contentious politics is a related set of theories that seeks to trace the role of collective action and explain state-society relations. It is a field of study that is interdisciplinary, but at times it has been characterized as fragmented and disconnected, especially since its rebirth as a thriving subfield in the 1990s (McAdam, Tarry, and Tilly 2009, 260). Assumptions about regime type fare prominently in this literature, as two of the founders of the field argue: "In mainly democratic regimes, the repertoire of contention leans towards peaceful forms of contention that intersect regularly with representative institutions and produce social movement campaigns; in mainly authoritarian regimes, the repertoire leans towards lethal conflicts and tends to produce religious and ethnic strife, civil wars and revolutions" (Tilly and Tarrow 2007, 161).

This view, which draws distinctions between authoritarian and democratic political systems, has so dominated the field that it has come to be assumed that regime type plays a major role in shaping contentious politics and state-society relations. Many studies argue that different forms of contention dovetail with different types of regime. This view, also held by O'Brien (2015), Schmitter and

Karl (1993), and others, is that the degree of democracy in a country shapes the fundamental forms of contentious politics operating there. Democracies "promote freedom as no feasible alternative can" (Dahl 1989, 88). The more democratic a state, the more open, receptive, and responsive it is to society's demands (O'Brien 2015). As Foweraker and Landman (1997) contend, the very essence of democracy is that it reflects this people power and not simply the choices of enlightened elites.

Democracy as Regime Type

Democracy, widely known as the institutionalized competition for power, is defined by Schmitter and Karl as "a system of governance in which rulers are held accountable for their actions in the public realm by citizens, acting indirectly through competition and cooperation of their elected representatives" (1993, 40). There is no one form of democracy, as democracies vary in a variety of ways, including levels of citizen participation. However, most analysts expect democracies to meet certain minimum criteria and allow regular, free, and fair elections; citizenship rights, which include personal freedoms; and civil freedoms of speech, press, association, and assembly. In democracies, citizens have the right to redress grievances through petition, protest, and other channels through which they hold government accountable. Moreover, in democracies the rule of law is respected; all citizens are equal before the law and no one is above it. Citizens have the right to form independent organizations, to express themselves politically without fear of severe punishment, and are protected from arbitrary action by governmental agents (Schmitter and Karl 1993; Diamond and Plattner 1993). Taken together, the various components of democracies foster tolerance, dialogue, negotiation, and compromise. Although competition within democracies can become intense, this regime type is based in institutions that channel conflict through regular procedures (Schmitter and Karl 1993). Not all democracies make it to this point, but those that consolidate (or mature) have a much better chance of facilitating distinctly cooperative repertoires (or patterns in state-society relations), thus creating an attractive arena for relatively peaceful varieties of contention (McAdam, Tarrow, and Tilly 2009; Diamond 1999).

The existence of a lively civil society is seen as a fundamental component of democracies. According to McAdam, Tarrow, and Tilly, "Democracy results from, mobilizes and reshapes popular contention" (2001, 269). In other words, civil society shapes democracy and democracy shapes civil society. Diamond

(2008) agrees, adding that without the broad mobilization of civil society, we wouldn't have seen what is known as "the Third Wave" of democratization (Huntington 1991) in the 1990s. Once democracy is established, civil society checks and limits abuse of state power. A virtuous circle is assumed to be at work in democracies, as civil society contributes to democratization and democratic states are assumed to be more responsive than resistant to civil society, which makes it more likely that they will consolidate and deepen (McAdam, Tarrow, and Tilly 2009; Linz and Stepan 1996). Still, not all contentious politics is necessarily good for democracy (Kasfir 2004; Diamond 1999; Abrahamsen 2004). Civil society varies in type and social activism that is illiberal and uncivil and can undermine or detour democracies. Cavatorta (2013) takes this argument further, maintaining that civil society doesn't necessarily lead to democratization and it isn't necessarily good or bad, it's neutral.

Authoritarianism as Regime Type

Civil society may be good, bad, or neutral, but the relationship between state and society in authoritarian regimes has long been assumed to be the opposite of what it is in democratic ones. Authoritarian regimes come in many forms. Juan Linz highlighted the key characteristics of this political system: limited pluralism,[2] low levels of social mobilization, and leadership by a single party or small group of leaders (Linz 1970, 255). In such a system, society has little or no protected consultation in its engagement of the state, as undemocratic regimes restrict many or most of the freedoms listed above (Stepan 1993). Unlike democratic systems, there are no—or few—checks on state power or rule of law. As a consequence, the arena for political contestation is highly circumscribed. Whereas civil society shapes democracy and democracy shapes civil society, it is assumed that civil society plays little role in shaping authoritarian systems. Rather, the state shapes society. Because they more ruthlessly repress, they often effectively suppress civil society (McAdam, Tarrow, and Tilly 2009). For years this view, which framed state-society relations based

---

[2] Pluralism is the existence (and affirmation) of the diversity of values within political systems. Pluralistic systems are marked by competition among convictions, usually expressed in terms of interest groups, parties, and civil society organizations. One of the first articulations of the centrality of pluralism within democratic systems was Robert Dahl's classic work, *Who Governs? Democracy and Power in an American City* (New Haven: Yale University Press, 1961).

on a strict, black-and-white view of regime type, dominated discussions of contentious politics.[3]

"The Messy Middle"

However, developments in the real world have led to an evolution of the field (McAdam, Tarrow, and Tilly 2009). As authoritarian systems fell (or were remodeled) in the late 1990s and since, the mainstream view has been faulted as overly broad and democratization scholars criticized for making "unwarranted use of dichotomous measures" (Rosato 2003), or simple either/or categories. In response, the study of contentious politics has broadened, with analysts calling for more nuance as many of the old assumptions about state and society based in regime theory have sometimes fallen flat. This is because on more than one occasion society has shown itself capable of engaging even undemocratic states in ways that veer from the script—and regimes have crafted limited participation as a way to increase their legitimacy (Nathan 2003). Analysts agree now that activated citizenship is not the exclusive preserve of democracies. Studies from several regions of the world have demonstrated that there is a range of ways in which society expresses itself in authoritarian regimes, from individual writings (sometimes called "complaint-making"), to mass participation in seemingly non-political events, to outright political engagement (Henry 2012, 2010; Nathan 2003; Rosato 2003; Stepan 1993).

Similarly, in regard to state behavior, democracies and authoritarian regimes may usually engage with civil society in different ways, but there are differences among authoritarian regimes in the ways in which they engage civil society. Using various terms, analysts such as Levitsky and Way (2010), Joseph (1993), Diamond (1999), Hoelscher (2015), and others introduced a variety of terms for "the messy middle," a large, wide-ranging category of hybrids. The recognition that both liberalized or electoral authoritarian regimes and illiberal, semi-, or pseudo-democracies exist adds several shades of gray to old black-and-white dichotomies of authoritarianism and democracy. According to

---

[3] Tilly and Tarrow (often with McAdam) point out that they were always dealing with ideal types, into which few political regimes fit perfectly (Charles Tilly and Sidney Tarrow, *Contentious Politics* [Boulder, CO: Paradigm Press, 2007]; Doug McAdam, Sidney Tarrow, and Charles Tilly, "Comparative Perspectives on Contentious Politics," in *Comparative Politics: Rationality, Culture, and Structure,* ed. Mark Irving Lichbach and Alan S. Zuckerman [New York: Cambridge University Press, 2009], 260–290).

Levitsky and Way (2010), often it's not simply a matter of "good" regimes versus "bad" ones. Democracies vary in their responsiveness, and not all democracies consistently live up to their pledges in regard to freedoms and rule of law. Conversely, not all authoritarian regimes are run as tightly as their rulers might wish. Similar to democracies, authoritarian states vary in quality: some regimes of either type are vulnerable and unstable, some more resilient and enduring than others. It can't be surprising, then, to learn that what we long assumed to be true of society under authoritarianism isn't necessarily uniform. The varied forms of authoritarianism have a profound impact on how society is structured.[4] This variation and its effect on society may be true of democracies as well.

Thus, the literature now recognizes that within authoritarian regimes and democracies alike, state and society are capable of exhibiting a wider range of behaviors than once understood. Increasingly, it is now accepted that under all sorts of regime types, state and society aren't necessarily always separate and in opposition. Rather these relationships should be understood as dynamic; state and society may cohabit a continuum in which the two come to meet and cooperate and/or come into conflict. In democracies and authoritarian regimes alike, governments may turn to professional associations to provide important functions otherwise relegated to the state (Cavatorta 2013; D. Lewis 2013). In both democracies and non-democratic systems, we can find examples of symbiotic relationships formed between society and state, a compact of sorts in which the two are enmeshed in a network of linkages so that society may not push nor the state repress as soundly as either could. And although such cooperation sometimes ends up reaffirming and legitimizing the state, not all synergistic relationships should be read as signs that it is society that has been compromised. State—even an authoritarian one—and society can develop mutually advantageous modes of cooperation that serve important social functions or marginalized groups (D. Lewis 2013). O'Brien (2015) sums it up succinctly: democracies vary widely—as do authoritarian systems—in the degree to which they permit and engage with public participation. All kinds of regime types utilize a variety of instruments in dealing with society, including repression, co-optation, and divide and rule. Of course, the arena in which society seeks to engage an authoritarian state is more severely limited than it is in democracies. Certain core issues are out of bounds; any effort to raise them is likely to

---

[4] One example is "competitive authoritarianism," in which rulers allow multiparty elections but engage in other forms of democratic abuse and rig the system to their benefit (Levitsky and Way 2010).

be met with the full range of oppression (D. Lewis 2013).[5] However, as long as society stays away from these issues, analysts are discovering that sometimes the state—and not just democratic ones—allows itself to be led.

Thanks to these findings, analysts have gradually moved away from simple dichotomies based on regime type. In general, democracies are expected to be more responsive than resistant to society—and authoritarian leaders are more likely to prove resistant than responsive to citizen demands—but more and more, analysts are recognizing that state-society relations under democratic and authoritarian constructs are very complex. Compared to the research on civil society in democracies, the research is still limited, but more and more studies are finding that non-democratic states today frequently coexist in various relationships of coercion and cooperation with a range of civil society actors (D. Lewis 2013; Brown 2012; Steinberg and Shih 2012; Göbel 2011; He and Warren 2011; Levitsky and Way 2010). Analysts are finding that state-society relations do not always line up quite so neatly, with democracies always responsive and authoritarian leaders always resistant. Perhaps regime type has less explanatory power than we long assumed (Cavatorta 2013).

Contributing Factors Beyond Regime

Those who subscribe to this view call for a deepening of our understanding of contentious politics. This requires attention to much more than political regime type; it calls for a synthesis of approaches into a new model that considers how different conjunctions of regimes, political opportunity structures, and repertoires explain the differences in state response to society's demands. For example, variations in the strength of institutions or state capacity (or the ability of the state to enforce its will) may explain some of the differences that we see (Hoelscher 2015).[6] Or, it may be that international factors or "contingent

---

[5] Core issues are likened by David Lewis to what has been called "the lie that is the very core of a political system" (quoted in D. Lewis 2013). We identify and discuss Brazil and China's core issues in our framework and subsequent chapters.

[6] As an example of a theory that mixes attention to regime type and capacity, McAdam, Tarrow, and Tilly (2009) hypothesize that high capacity authoritarian governments exert such extensive controls that society is rarely capable of summoning much influence. In such a context, when they do occur, contentious encounters between state and society will typically involve large disparities of force. On the other hand, low-capacity governments—authoritarian or democratic—are more likely to face challenges from society that the state lacks the means to suppress.

historical events," random or not, may explain shifts in behavior—by society or state (Acemoglu and Robinson 2013). However, for many analysts, the difference between the two regime types is still quite clear. Whether a state is democratic or authoritarian is still widely accepted as the strongest predictor of the ways states behave—and of the ways in which society is shaped. In terms of state-society relations, most analysts continue to maintain that the character of the state has everything to do with receptivity and resistance: what the state defines as the limits of accepted behaviors, the boundaries it sets—and its ability to enforce them. McAdam, Tarrow, and Tilly (2009) encourage analysts to consider a variety of episodes of contentious politics so as to compare the range of contention as it exists in different places and times. They also urge us to take regime type explicitly into account in explaining contentious politics.

We take them up on this suggestion, but attempt to look at the conventional wisdom differently. In fact, we offer what some might characterize as a "theory-infirming" comparative case study (Lijphart 1971). Although we can't disconfirm the conventional thinking on contentious politics and regime type, we raise doubts about it. As of 2015, the consensus view in the literature on contentious politics is this: regime type is not the only variable associated with different levels of state responsiveness to society—nor is regime type determinative in shaping society—but it is a strong indicator of these things.

Now, among political scientists, the idea that leaders act to preserve power is accepted as established truth. But it is relatively rare to hear them go further, as Bueno de Mesquita and Smith (2012) do, to argue that all successful leaders—democratic or not—are best understood as almost entirely driven by their own political survival. In other words, states—in their origins, in the ways in which they operate and interact with society, how they evolve and adapt and still manage not to change—often turn out to be more alike than different, regardless of regime type. As you might expect, for a variety of reasons this is a transgressive view and one that sparks debate. But what nearly everyone can agree on is the need for what the elder statesmen of the field have called for: "a synthetic approach that combines the search for common mechanisms and processes with knowledge of specific forms of contentious politics—like social movements and civil wars—in particular contexts" (McAdam, Tarrow, and Tilly 2009, 273). That is the task we take up in the pages that follow: a richly contextual, comparative study of contention that illuminates similarities and differences in state and society relations—in two ostensibly most different cases.

OUR APPROACH TO STATE AND SOCIETY: RECEPTIVITY AND RESISTANCE IN BRAZIL AND CHINA

Emphasizing the complexity of contentious politics, we argue that contention is not necessarily shaped by degrees of democracy in the ways most would expect. Dictatorships can have fuller and more changeable repertoires than is commonly recognized, and sometimes even they behave in ways that can be described as receptive (some would say that Iranians being allowed to elect Hassan Rouhani to the presidency, a moderate whose campaign promised reform, is an example of this). Moreover, even states that most would characterize as democratic have shown that they are capable of behaving in ways unbecoming to their status, resorting to repression to protect what they consider dangerous, core, or "redline" issues (consider, for example, the way the South African government has handled miners' protests in recent years). We encourage others to determine the robustness of our theory, to see whether it holds up or can account for the same phenomena in a variety of other places. In the meantime, what we are trying to do is to refine and elaborate on established theory with a closer examination and comparison of two cases. Our study challenges the conventional thinking as a theory-infirming case study because although we can't disconfirm the conventional thinking on contentious politics and regime type, we raise doubts about it (Collier 1993).

"The Messy Middle" in Brazil and China

Therefore, we will demonstrate that Brazil, touted as one of the world's largest democracies because it has met certain benchmarks, appears open, but still has some work to do. Technically, it is considered a consolidated democracy, but in many ways it has weaknesses that render it a shell of democracy. Toward the other end of the spectrum, China is the world's largest authoritarian state. But it too suffers from fault lines or weaknesses that render its authoritarianism not quite as "consolidated" or as closed as many assume. In other words, just as Brazil falls a bit short of the democratic ideal, there are signs that China is one step from a full-on authoritarian regime. China appears closed, yet we note relatively unexpected areas of tolerance for contention and expression, most notably in the environmental movement, but in other areas as well. There are major limits to how far it is willing to go, but the Communist Party has made reforms aimed at addressing grievances and responding to public opinion (Gewirtz 2014). On certain issues, it's actually the Chinese state that has been willing to engage society and Brazil that resorted to repression. In the end, what elites in Brazil and China have in common is that neither is willing to "play" when it comes to core issues, but both can be accommodating on other issues, particularly if it will offset threats to their continued power and help protect what they hold most dear. Gewirtz (2014) said it about Party elites in China, but it's true of Brazilian elites as well: they've come around to the idea that they need to constrain some of their power in order to keep it. If such behavior is true of states as different as Brazil and China, then it can't be viewed necessarily as congruent with regime type.

As we will see, the two countries are very different in some important ways besides regime type. Most notable among these differences perhaps is that China had a revolution and Brazil did not. But a closer look at context reveals some unexpected similarities. There are two striking parallels in their histories that shape the countries that they are today. Historically both have had (for centuries in Brazil, a millennium or two in China) centralized rule (albeit weak capacity in the vast hinterland) and a marked concentration of wealth in the hands of a small elite. Fast-forwarding to the 1960s, both countries were dictatorships (Brazil's authoritarian; China's totalitarian), that had turned on their own citizens (in Brazil it was the "Dirty War," in China "the Cultural Revolution"). By the 1970s and 1980s, a variety of events combined to set both countries off on transitions (top-down in China; bottom-up in Brazil) and the two veered off in dramatically different directions. Brazil began its democratic transition, opening up politically, while China moved from a totalitarian system to an authoritarian one, opening its economy. Today, Brazil and China are identified as at opposite ends of the democratization spectrum. But for all their differences—and they are significant—the two share at least one remarkable similarity: fault lines that have their origins in one particular critical juncture, during the transitions of the 1970s and 1980s.

In this book we will show how critical junctures can have as much of an effect on politics inside these countries as it does on their international relations. Outwardly the two states—and countries, for that matter—couldn't seem more different. But comparative historical analysis, which is crucial for understanding context, allows us to see that not far beneath the surface, Brazil and China are strikingly similar, sharing serious problems of corruption, inequality, and repression. Therefore, we take on the conventional view that states belonging to the same regime type will behave in similar ways and that those at the opposite end of the spectrum will behave very differently. But it is possible that states—and citizens—have a much larger repertoire (or list of actions regularly performed) than is usually acknowledged, and which goes beyond regime (type). This examination of state-society relations in Brazil and China will reveal that the distance between them, while significant, is not as great as some would suppose.

The Advantages of an Eclectic Approach

To do this, our study of state-society relations takes an eclectic approach. We base our analysis in the political science literature on contentious politics but combine it with public health policy analysis on the resistance and receptivity of state elites to citizen demands. With this synthesis, we aim to look at politics in a new way, and add nuance and complexity to the dominant representations of the way state and society interact.

As leading analysts of state-society relations, political scientists McAdam, Tarrow, and Tilly (2009) encourage such an approach. They support the construction of a comparative political science of contentious politics that compares different forms of contention and their relationship with different regime types. The best way to do this, they argue, is to pay close attention to context and focus on specific episodes of contention, identifying the dynamics of contention as well as the different forms of contention (McAdam, Tarrow, and Tilly 2009). In the chapters that follow, we will attempt to do just that. To explore the dynamics of contention regarding a wide range of issues, for each issue we will analyze episodes marking critical junctures in the contentious politics of Brazil and China.

We also borrow from Gómez (2009), a political scientist who focuses on health policy and whose work in many ways parallels that of McAdam, Tarrow, and Tilly. His study of contentious politics utilizes different terminology, but in many ways he's doing what McAdam, Tarrow, and Tilly recommend. However, instead of identifying mechanisms such as brokerage (or striking deals or horse-trading), co-optation, repression, et cetera, Gómez proposes a framework using the terms "receptivity" and "resistance" to explain how Brazil, Russia, India, and China interact with the international health community to strengthen domestic HIV-AIDS programs. Gómez characterizes "receptivity" as state openness to influence and compromise. On the other hand, "resistance" is characterized by the state's lack of willingness to change norms or policies. What we like most about Gómez's study is his recognition of the possibility of states' simultaneous receptivity and resistance to external influences. Both receptivity and resistance are present in each of the three major policy areas we observe: identity, human security, and the environment. However, our focus is on domestic influences and the interchange between state and civil society, non-state actors making claims against the state. In order to understand the puzzling and often conflicting results of the strategic give-and-take between state and society, we create a hybrid, adapting Gómez's approach to study McAdam, Tarrow, and Tilly's contentious politics.

State-Society Dynamics in Brazil and China

Our interest is in the state-society dynamic in that it is not just the state but also society that can wield power and shape outcomes. In this book we identify the many different ways individuals work alone or with others seeking to extend the community's rights and broaden the public agenda, often—but not always—by creating political will, building relationships, and recruiting a champion within the state for their cause. We also observe how activism changes over time. According to Levy, there is a demonstration effect, as early initiatives trigger a variety of responses (an extension, imitation, or an attempt to avoid repeating the same mistakes) in later groups. Known strategies become part of a list of actions or repertoire that is repeated; institutional memories shared between different groups serve as a guide to action (Levy 2010; Hochstetler 1997).

The groups that compose civil society often learn from each other. According to Gómez (2009), when individuals or society demand greater input in social welfare policy and it results in modifications of the way in which health care is provided, for example, we observe a high level of receptivity on the part of state actors. Such a "win" can have a catalyzing effect; society may revel in their newfound power, triggering further efforts to shape policy. But it is just as important to observe how society recalibrates in the face of resistance and how the state attempts to manage engaged individuals. The state can facilitate the development of certain groups in unexpected ways. State receptivity doesn't always result in a synergistic partnership between state and society; rather, receptivity can effectively demobilize activists by bringing them into the fold. On the other hand, as Levy (2010) points out, a highly resistant state can inadvertently produce collective actors by blocking the development of certain groups and drive them to resort to non-institutional means as a way of having their concerns heard.

So keep in mind that as much as the state will attempt to "manage" the relationship with society, it doesn't always have control over the outcome. Moreover, in the chapters that follow we are careful not to treat "state" or "society" as monolithic entities; rather, each is constructed of diverse interests, preferences, limitations, and aspirations. As state and society, these diverse interests may sometimes combine as factions or movements—or they may divide and serve as countervailing pressures. In fact, one of the biggest challenges in state-society analysis is disaggregating the state, or, instead of viewing the state as a unitary actor, understanding that at different levels state authorities may have varying priorities and therefore play different roles. For example, in Brazil and China there are sometimes strains between central authorities and state and local actors, in Brazil over deforestation, in China over population policy. Although we are not working at this level of analysis and do not provide detailed analysis of its inner workings, we recognize not only the power and competing interests of various bureaucratic entities within the state. Given its prominent role in both Chinese and Brazilian politics, we will often focus on the executive (and in Brazil, to some degree, the judiciary), but it is also important to recognize that the "state" rarely speaks with a unified voice; it is riddled with internal contradictions, competing interests, multiple actors, and often conflicting goals. Although the legislature and judiciary have significantly more power in Brazil than they do in China, civil society in both countries tends to focus on the executive. Therefore, when we refer to the "state," in most cases we mean the executive.

By "society," we refer to civil society, which is commonly defined as voluntary associations of individuals or formal and informal organizations independent of the government and business. Civil society runs the gamut from small volunteer groups and social movements (whose protests are—with some important exceptions—often shorter term, more spontaneous, and protest oriented) to large, professionalized non-governmental organizations (which are more likely to have the skills and expertise, and financial and institutional resources to undertake longer-term projects). Although civil society is composed of much more than just NGOs, it is important to note that the number and power of these organizations have grown in the last few decades, as international NGOs often provide funding and other support to domestic NGOs and social movements. NGOs should be viewed as a complement to, not a replacement of, social movements (since they often work together). On the other hand, NGOs may compete with each other and with social movements for resources and media attention. As is the case elsewhere, civil society in Brazil and China is hardly monolithic; as we will see, factions often vie for the state's attention and view each other not just as rivals, but as enemies. In addition, as Hochstetler (1997) shows for Brazil, civil society can suffer from the failings of the state, such as a tendency to clientelism, exclusion, and self-interested behaviors.

Rivalries and divides within civil society are interesting and important, and certainly affect its development, but our focus is on the leading edge of society's dynamic interaction with the state. For example, in China, it is some religious groups that have taken an oppositional role and been among those most willing to confront the state demanding economic and some social reforms. Religious activists are not only speaking out for their right to assemble, but also for marginalized groups, especially migrants, orphans, and street children. Meanwhile, in Brazil, conservative religious groups, which have historically partnered with the state, often seek to enforce the status quo or turn back the clock. They demand the state's attention when the issue is sex, whereas when liberal religious organizations have confronted the state, they have taken the lead on issues such as poverty, the treatment of indigenous peoples, and the environment. Thus, in Brazil and China it is not just the relationship between society and state that is fascinating, it's also the interchange within society. As we will see, on any given issue there is often more than one group of activists taking very different positions and working at cross-purposes, vying for the attention of the state.

For example, although unions can be a leading branch of civil society, they are so closely tied to the government of China that they can't be considered as such there. On the other hand, unions have a long history of activism in Brazil. The Workers' Party (PT, which stands for *Partido dos Trabalhadores*) grew out of the labor movement and the largest unions (such as the Central Workers' Union, the CUT) in Brazil remain very close to (and are, some say, co-opted by) the PT government. However, strikes are common in Brazil. Sometimes they are "managed" by the cooperation between union leaders and the government to act as safety values. On other occasions the CUT and the other larger unions have joined the state in opposing strikes and demonstrations led by a rank and file that doesn't obey the bosses or by splinter, opposition unions (Kiernan and Jelmayer 2014; Costa 2014). Generally these countermobilizations occur between groups on different ends of the political spectrum. However, those with similar ideological inclinations but with different priorities may also find themselves at odds (for example, at times leftists who prioritize environmental protections line up against leftists whose priority is poverty reduction and job creation, and vice versa). In each of the chapters that follow, we'll detail the complex negotiations involved in moving the relationship between state and society from resistance to receptivity, and consider why in other cases it appears impossible to move from here to there. It is often said that sometimes society leads and sometimes it tails the state. This is true both in democratic and authoritarian systems. But it is perhaps more accurate to say that when the magic happens and "society" leads the state, it's actually a small segment that does the heavy lifting: the rest of the population gets dragged along. In the chapters that follow, we will provide a series of vignettes about how, in these two very different countries, when certain issues have come to a head, society has tried to lead the state—and whether (and when) the state has allowed itself to be led.

Our interest is the process by which citizens get their concerns (which are mostly domestic but include foreign policy) onto the agenda. In other words, how do citizens contribute to broader processes of social change? Society tries to lead the state through a variety of means; some are confrontational and some are polite. Two of the most common nonviolent means that citizens use to promote change worldwide are 1) using the legal system or 2) defying it, through direct action or civil disobedience. While the former often takes place inside formal institutions of power, the latter often involves higher-risk forms of concentration (occupations, invasions, flash mobs, etc.) or lower-risk methods of dispersion (boycotts, stay-aways, go-slow demonstrations, etc.) (Chenoweth 2012). Civil disobedience, which often employs creative tactics, seeks to disrupt routines to create a crisis. As a subcategory of civil disobedience, artistic protest creates a stir with provocative entertainment; often it confronts with flamboyance and humor. To some degree, any civil disobedience is performance; the goal of such protest is to force the observer to choose sides and join it, thus adding greater pressure on the government (Seltzer 2012). In this sense, the display is as much for society as it is for the state. This is important because it is widely recognized that mass participation by diverse groups is crucial to any movement's success, as it suggests the existence of a vision with legitimacy (Swiebel 2009). And it doesn't take everyone to come out; according to Lichbach, few governments—dictatorships or democracies— can resist the demands of a sustained, coordinated disobedience campaign that engages more than 5 percent of the population (cited in Chenoweth 2012). This is what we mean about *part of* society leading the state and the rest being dragged along.

In our two cases and around the world, protesters use many of the same activities (petitions, demonstrations, and occupations, just to name a few). But analysts of civil society often draw distinctions between protests intended to pressure a government and those that represent opposition to the government. Both types of protest can employ the tactics mentioned earlier (using the law or defying it, ranging from the diplomatic to the muscular), and both (protest as pressure and protest as opposition) can be disruptive. Groups that use protest as pressure are integrative: they assume that the organization and the state have similar goals. But they are autonomous, propose policies independently, and assume that the state just needs to be prodded to do the right thing. In this circumstance, protest as pressure simply enables the government to make the right choice. On the other hand, groups that protest as opposition aren't seeking to work with the state; they openly oppose the government policies with which they disagree. As we will demonstrate, these groups aren't static. They may move back and forth along the spectrum over time. And it is important to keep in mind that all but the most oppositional groups seek to develop a dialogue with the state. They consider the political support or regular channels of access necessary for seeing their demands become policy (Swiebel 2009). On the other hand, groups moving from using protest as pressure to using protest as opposition are those that have become discouraged or disgusted with the process. They have decided that change can only come from outside the system, not within it.

Of course, success within the system depends on the attitudes of elites within the targeted organizations—and it is important not to underestimate their role. States provide different kinds of access to different sectors of civil society. It is the state that controls the form and scope of access; states choose to exclude or ignore some groups altogether or to direct the process from the top down. They generally seek to co-opt and deal only with those that obey their rules (Friedman and Hochstetler 2002). However, even in authoritarian states it is not unheard of for activists with the right resources to gain institutional access and be brought in to work with the government. For example, many Brazilians who started out as critics of the government's AIDS policy were eventually hired to redesign and lead those programs. Often these relationships become institutionalized, as these protesters became bureaucrats, outlasting any particular administration. Formally or informally, on a permanent or temporary basis, the goal of these groups is to form instrumental coalitions and "infiltrate" the government in key decision-making positions or as consultants (Swiebel 2009; Foller 2010; Hochstetler 2003). It should be noted, however, that analysts disagree about who is being "infiltrated." They also disagree about whether the result is co-opting, in which the state effectively neuters and absorbs the movement, or synergistic, a win-win relationship achieved through complementarity, interdependence, and embeddedness in which the state and society mutually influence and transform each other (Evans 1997; Guidry 2003).

Who's co-opting whom? Is "synergy" really possible? Let's just say then that this is a question that will not be resolved here, but as we will see, civil society is highly pluralistic in Brazil and China. Consequently, a mix, or variety of arrangements, exists in these countries. Similarly, it is wrong to assume that the relationship between NGOs and the state is always contentious; many NGOs in Brazil and some in China receive funding from the state (Hochstetler 1997). Certainly some groups have more clearly been able to maintain their autonomy from the government and political parties than others. From civil society's perspective, the litmus test for synergism is whether the relationship moves the group toward achieving their goals for policy. But the fact remains that once they are in a position to make decisions, these new policymakers often find themselves limited by budgetary and other constraints. As a result they disappoint and become divided from those still on the outside (Avritzer 2009; Hochstetler 2003). As Hochstetler and Keck (2007) contend, activists labor inside and outside the state, and both are sites of struggle. Therefore, perhaps it is best to conceptualize these different positions—from working in the government, to protest as pressure, to protest as opposition, to seeking the government's ouster—as points existing along a continuum rather than a simple "inside the state" vs. "outside the state" dichotomy. And the impetus is hardly unidirectional; this is not simply a story about society seeking to leverage the state (Friedman and Hochstetler 2002). Rather, the state is trying to leverage society, too. Often the relationship between them is like a tug-of-war—albeit one in which the state has the advantage of weight.

How Political Opportunity Structures Shape Contentious Politics

Much of the success—or failure—of any particular group (or actors) within society depends on the political opportunity structures or broader environment (at home and in the world) that affect the likely outcome of this interaction (Tarrow 1994). The political opportunity structure varies by actor (not all actors face the same access or constraints) and it can change for actors over time. It is important to keep this in mind as we trace how the various episodes of contentious politics unfold. For each we will ask the same questions: Are elites friendly? Were issues linked? Did there exist countervailing protests blocking or impeding government action? All of these things—and more—can work together to determine receptivity or resistance. Another factor influencing this is that today social movements can be pretty ephemeral. The Internet facilitates activism, but often groups mobilized by social networks around one or several causes resemble flash mobs; they often have diffuse and horizontal modes of organization and lack permanent leadership (Sola 2013). Consider their precarious resource and personnel basis and it is easy to see how the political opportunity structure (whether it is welcoming or not) can make or break a movement (Swiebel 2009; Hochstetler 1997). The more institutionalized NGOs are generally less vulnerable, but they also must deal with the fact that the political opportunity structure (in other words, the context they're working in) plays a large role in whether their interaction with the state results in repression, reform, revolution—or nothing at all (Tarrow 1994).

In other words, in predicting outcomes, context is everything. Understanding a country's history is key to assessing its political opportunity structure. Brazil, for example, has never had a revolution—in part because of the state's willingness to use repression, but more commonly it has been the case that the state has made just enough reform to maintain the status quo. Today's Brazil is a consolidated democracy and there is no serious talk of outright war in the country—even by the most disgruntled elements in society, although one could argue that gang violence amounts to a low-simmering civil war. In China it is only the most disgruntled individuals—rarely groups—who employ violence. There, because political violence is a such a potent tool of the state, it is used by citizens more sparingly, although since the mid-2000s, there have been multiple violent attacks in schools and train stations (often using knives or axes), usually pinned on the "psychologically disturbed" or so-called "splittist" elements within society. Interestingly, the choice of weapon reflects the Chinese state's strict gun control laws—and monopoly on the use of force. This couldn't be more different than the situation in Brazil, where—despite some attempts to restrict the purchase of firearms—the state has proven unable to control access to guns. In some parts of Brazil, including major cities, the result is gunfights in the streets. But in neither country is there a major armed oppositional movement seeking to overthrow the state. Political violence perpetrated by members of the state and society certainly exists in Brazil and China, but instead of flaring into war, in both countries this violence is better characterized as set at a low boil (Ahnen 2007).[7]

To citizens in both countries it may seem that out of all the possibilities, society's interaction with the state results most commonly in nothing at all. Certainly, out of our menu of options regarding state-society interaction

---

[7] According to Chenoweth (2012), the limited use of violence is just as well, as violent protests (vandalism, assassination, armed insurrection) frighten, annoy, and/or turn off citizens and diminish participation. Moreover, aggressive citizen actions often work to build support for a state's policy of resistance, as regime supporters who feel personally threatened by violent protests unify and resolve to defeat the movement. We have seen this happen around the world time and time again.

(repression, reform, or revolution), revolution is the rarest result. It is much more likely that change—if it comes at all—will be more piecemeal, and specific issues will cycle on and off the political agenda—and perhaps that's why it appears to many that the result is nothing at all (Hochstetler 1997). One might expect this in authoritarian China, but just because a country is democratic does not guarantee it will provide welcoming political opportunity structures. Similarly, political opportunity structures in repressive, authoritarian states may be more open than one would assume (Tarrow 1994). On some issues, gay and lesbian rights, for example, authoritarian states (as opposed to democratic ones) may be able to afford to ignore social conservatives and offer greater prospects for progressive political reform. However, authoritarian—and even revolutionary—governments have often found it necessary to assuage the concerns of these groups.

As Chua (2012) points out, in authoritarian systems, where an oppositional approach can be too risky, activists must make their way through countless restrictions in a carefully choreographed "strategic dance." Such groups, which are often categorized as conformist, tend to adopt a form of pragmatic resistance. Theirs is a "strategic adaptation" that challenges power only in highly specific and limited ways. Taking into consideration cultural norms, they carefully prioritize demands, and then subtly apply pressure—not in public, overt protests—but in a way that avoids direct confrontation. They survive by doing whatever they can to avoid being seen as a threat to the existing power arrangements, and they create a way for the state to see the change as in its interests (e.g., to augment its international legitimacy) or act on their demands with its dignity intact (e.g., the state may act like the policy change was its idea all along). The question is, Do such groups achieve change by pushing norms while adhering to them? Or, by accepting their confines and making choices within them, do they actually help to validate and reinforce the boundaries drawn by the state, thus strengthening the existing order (Chua 2012)? Such questions again illustrate the importance of political opportunity structures, and we will return to them in later chapters to consider how well this explanation fits the Chinese, and, for that matter, the Brazilian cases.

Another factor that helps to shape the political opportunity structure given any particular issue is whether the issue is considered "safe" or "dangerous" (one that the state considers a "core interest" and is extremely sensitive about) (Tarrow 1994). Both Brazil and China have core interests, which we will identify in the chapters that follow. Although it may use reform or repression to protect these interests, these are the most highly contested issues, and ones on which the state will not budge. One litmus test for whether an issue ranks as dangerous, and a useful predictor of whether the state will be receptive or resistant in regard to an issue, is how the state characterizes protesters. For example, the state's use of labels (such as vandals, drunks, traitors, terrorists, etc.) for what many would simply call citizenship is obviously a sign of trouble ahead.

Often when the state's reaction to a mobilization is expected to be violent, society will dial it back and join less threatening forms of protest to air grievances against the regime while reducing the risk of a repressive response. Yes, atrocities (notably, the murder of Brazilian activist Chico Mendez) have occurred even then, but according to Hochstetler (1997), back in the 1980s, protecting the Amazon and the rights of indigenous people were relatively safe issues to raise with the state. Today, these are two of the most dangerous issues to protest in Brazil, along with calls for agrarian reform. Unknown numbers of activists have been killed for their efforts, usually by non-state agents (thugs hired by moneyed interests, with state agents usually only participating indirectly, complicit in the violence but not actively perpetrating it). But it's not only environmentalists and indigenous rights activists whose lives are at risk, and sometimes state actors are directly involved. In response to 2013 protests against government priorities and spending on the World Cup, Brazil's president, Dilma Rousseff, first characterized the demonstrations as proof of the energy of the democracy. But within a few days she sent police with clubs to use pepper spray, tear gas, and rubber bullets against citizens (Strange 2013). The Chinese government behaves similarly, but it is more often the size of the protest rather than the cause that determines the regime's reaction. And, although there are cases of hired thugs roughing up activists and journalists who try to promote their cause, house arrest and detention are Beijing's favored tools to preemptively limit unrest.

As mentioned earlier, we should keep in mind that any particular movement's relationship with the state is capable of shifting over time. Not only are movements dynamic (their membership, tactics, and strategies changing), but participatory opportunities are episodic (and may be linked to the larger, international context and events outside the country) (Friedman and Hochstetler 2002). For example, the 1960s marked some of the darkest days for human rights in both countries. Moreover, Brazil's democratic transition coincided not only with the end of the Cold War, but with a time of tremendous upheaval in China. The Brazilian military dictatorship ended in 1989, just as the Chinese regime faced its greatest political, social, and ideological challenge in the widespread protests throughout that spring and early summer.

Emerging Political Cultures and the Power of Social Media

Emerging with efforts to force out the dictatorship, a new political culture has since emerged as civil society in Brazil that is unusually active, participating in developing, implementing, and co-managing public policy (Friedman and Hochstetler 2002; "BTI 2012" 2012; Foller 2010). In China, an increasingly deeper moral vacuum pervades much public discourse, as the ideology espoused by the Chinese Communist Party (CCP) appears increasingly irrelevant—even within the CCP itself. Citizens continue to improvise, innovate, and adopt new forms of performance (petitions, press statements, demonstrations, lobbying, etc.) with which to engage the state, and each year we observe tens of thousands of major demonstrations against pollution, corruption, and illegal land grabs. But society tends to develop and repeat a particular repertoire because it is often limited by the feasibility of different types of performance. In some places this is more true than others because states attempt to exert control over various types of performance, prescribing, tolerating, or forbidding them (McAdam, Tarrow, and Tilly 2009).

While Chinese have always—even in Imperial times—had channels to communicate grievances to the government (including officially sanctioned complaint bureaus where masses of aggrieved citizens vent their frustration), these avenues and their volume have become amplified with social media. New media have greatly energized protests in Brazil and China—especially social media, blogs, and Web 2.0 technology. In China and Brazil the old (or established) media isn't trusted because it is monopolized by the state and/or established interests and believed by many to be biased in their favor. To counter media bias and get their issues on the agenda, more and more social movements (and individual acts of defiance) are making their voices heard by going digital or becoming "networked": as elsewhere, Brazilians and Chinese are finding alternative, new forms of participation by turning to social media and using information communication technologies (ICTs), including mobile phones, micro-blogging services, and tablets to get their arguments heard and to mobilize and organize protest much more quickly and efficiently than ever before. With the new media, Brazilians continue to push the limits of freedom of expression in their democracy—a preferred method is videos of satire and biting humor. Activists have a ready audience in Brazil; the country is second only to the United States in the number of Facebook users and Twitter accounts (Romero 2013d). China is now home to the world's largest population of Internet users, with an approximate Internet penetration rate of nearly

49 percent and growing annually—Brazil is number five on that list of total numbers of users, but its penetration rate in 2014 was 57 percent (China Internet Network Information Center 2013; "Data: Internet Users" 2015). But it's not just society that is using this tool; technology can be used both to mobilize populations and to contain them. For example, both democratic Brazil and authoritarian China censor, and both use technologies as a means of control. Through the Web they conduct online surveillance and seek to sow disunity in movements. Despite attempts to restrict online communication (Facebook, Twitter, and YouTube are each blocked on the mainland), Twitter-like microblogs in China are unruly and contentious, often driving national discourse on even some sensitive topics, including forced abortions and consumer safety issues. Social media, sometimes perhaps more accurately termed "antisocial media," has prodded the formation of a variety of forms of activism, including digital mobs and cyber manhunts spawned by everything from marital infidelity to attempts to mediate between pro-Tibet and pro-China demonstrators. The millions of Internet monitors are kept busy taking down unauthorized photographs of disasters—natural and not—sensitive discussions that have been banned by local or central authorities, and even items that are seen to simply be attracting too much attention, because they have the potential to incite instability, a serious crime.

Brazilians also do a lot of their politics online. Virtual activism is now recognized in Brazil as proving more effective than political parties and trade unions at uniting diverse groups and for its ability to convene tens of thousands of people in flash mobs to protest. Called to action by Twitter, they are tweeted where and when to meet (Tavener 2011). Cell phone videos from deep in the rainforest of indigenous peoples' clashes with police are posted on Facebook or YouTube in real time, showing Brazilians a side of the story they're not getting from the old media. They are making headlines across the world, and prompting the government to promise investigations (Fellet 2013). If, as Ackerman puts it, "the mixture of confrontation, creativity and social media becomes a volatile cocktail for an authoritarian regime" (Ackerman 2012), you can imagine how it could put a democracy under the table. As Friedman has warned us, smartphones, Twitter, Facebook, and the rest have brought people into the streets with the independent means to get their stories across faster and at higher decibel levels than ever before. Sure, this may mean that authoritarian governments—like China's—are less sustainable now, but it also means that democracies—like Brazil's—will be more volatile than ever (Friedman 2013).

Fitting All the Pieces Together into a Frame

Of course, it takes more than such tactics to produce change. It takes leadership, clear goals, and the ability to follow through on an agenda. In this study, we will consider a variety of the tools (from the very old to the very new) as well as tactics, strategies, and the diversity of participation used by society in its push and pull with the state. Due to limitations of space, this book cannot recount every action, include every group, or apply the receptivity-resistance model to every contentious issue the two countries face—nor is every issue contentious for both countries. After a chapter on the history of this give and take—as well as the factors that gave rise to it—we examine contentious politics and the (sometimes surprising) strategies employed by a variety of actors over a period of time in both countries in three areas: human security; social issues and social diversity; and environmental politics. These chapters are structured the same way: for each issue the cases are presented, and then analyzed and compared to reveal parallels and patterns. Although our narrative follows the stories over longer periods of time (sometimes decades) to illustrate the dynamic nature of contentious politics, conceptual frameworks near the end of each chapter freeze the frame to condense and recap our findings. First, we sort the issues by how highly contested they are: "less contested," "moderately contested," and "highly contested." As claims against the state, all the issues we discuss are contested, but some are more dangerous than others. The most highly contested of them are core issues, ones that the state—or powerful political forces behind the scenes, namely elites— considers to be non-negotiable. From the state's perspective, challenges regarding such issues amount to an existential threat. Then, in association with each issue, depending on the tactics employed to make its claims heard, we categorize each societal approach as "conventional" (which ranges from seeking to work with the government to using protest as pressure), "confrontational" (not seeking to work with the government, opposing it, and seeking its overthrow), or "hybrid" (representing the mix of approaches).[8] Society can adopt a conventional approach and still be highly critical of the state; the distinction is whether it seeks to reform the system or replace it. Next, we classify the state's response as "receptive" (open to influence and compromise), "resistant" (unwilling to change norms or policies), or "both"

---

[8] This analysis focuses on those seeking to change the status quo, as opposed those who support it, although we recognize the role both groups play in contentious politics.

(indicating elements of both receptivity and resistance). This third category is necessary since Gómez's (2009) receptivity-resistance model allows us to see the realities of "both . . . and" rather than a simple "either . . . or." Finally, we assess the outcome of the political encounter between state and society as one based in "reform" (acceding to society's claim and adopting change, which can include working synergistically with or co-opting society) or "repression" (rejecting society's claim and refusing change, which runs the gamut from stonewalling to various uses of coercion, including violence). A third possible outcome we identify is "indeterminate," when there is no clear outcome.

FIGURE 1.1 CONCEPTUAL FRAMEWORK

Issue	Less Contested (consensus on need for some action; safe to discuss)
	Moderately Contested (tense, but not a core issue)
	Highly Contested (linked to a core issue; dangerous to discuss)
Societal Approach	Conventional (works with government or uses protest as pressure)
	Hybrid (a mix of conventional and confrontational)
	Confrontational (opposed to government and seeking its overthrow)
State Response	Receptive (open to influence and compromise)
	Both (a mix of receptivity and resistance)
	Resistant (unwilling to change norms or policies)
Outcome	Reform (acceding to claim, possibly adopting change)
	Indeterminate (no clear outcome; a mix of reform and repression)
	Repression (rejecting claim and refusing change)

Of course, what we're describing is an unfolding social process; no outcome is permanent. It is important to stress that these figures merely abbreviate our findings and encapsulate the story of the push and pull of state and society by issue. To paraphrase Migdal (2009), in these figures we are offering a snapshot of what is actually a moving picture. We "show" the moving picture in chapters 3–5. We don't attempt to apply the framework to chapters 2 or 6 because these chapters don't serve the same functions as the rest. Chapter 2 provides the historical context for understanding all that follows. Chapter 6 is almost an epilogue. It rounds out the book, linking contentious politics to international relations. In it we consider how contentious politics at home shapes our cases' foreign policies, which are also more similar than most would expect, largely a difference of style over substance.

WHY THESE CASES?

Our argument, that contentious politics in countries at opposite ends of the spectrum is more similar than many would assume, could be applied to any of the large variety of states found in what Schedler (2013) and other analysts call "the messy middle." But why choose Brazil and China, such apparently disparate cases, at opposite ends of the "middle"?

One easy answer is that they are late developers and another is because they are commonly linked as emerging powers. In 2001, Goldman Sachs economist Jim O'Neill popularized the association of Brazil, Russia, India, and China as "BRIC" states as rising economic powers. Debate lingers as to whether the grouping should be expanded.[9] As one observer quipped, "It must be the beginning of a new week: a new emerging market acronym is doing the rounds" (Mance 2010). Thus, there are several emerging states vying for leading roles on the shifting world stage, but Brazil and China are the two that are always in the mix. Brazil and China are contenders because they enjoy many of the classic components of power: large populations, large land masses, and large and fast-growing economies. Even with its post-boom slump, in 2014 Brazil was the seventh-largest economy in the world—and it is projected to be the world's sixth-largest by 2030. By then, only the economies of China, the United States, India, Japan, and Indonesia will be larger ("The World in 2050" 2015).

But India and Russia, with many of the classic components of power, fit the bill as well. Why not include them? Because we agree with those who argue that political phenomena are best understood through the careful examination of a small number of cases (Collier 1993). It would be a mistake to attempt a comparative historical analysis, studying a small number of countries over

---

[9] BRICS includes South Africa; BRICK adds South Korea; BRICET incorporates eastern Europe and Turkey; and BRICA includes the Arab states of Saudi Arabia, Qatar, Kuwait, Bahrain, Oman, and the United Arab Emirates, etc. More recently, the Spanish bank BBVA proposed the image of the "Eagles" ("Emerging and Growth-Leading Economies"): states that will soon be increasing international demand to the global economy, to include China, Brazil, India, South Korea, Indonesia, Russia, Mexico, Turkey, Egypt, and Taiwan. These are also the states that are likely to account for nearly half of all global growth between now and 2020 (Wassener 2010).

long periods of time, of all four BRIC states (Brazil, Russia, India, and China) because of the concomitant loss of depth. In other words, we can see more by just focusing on two. As Collier put it, "The close scrutiny of each country limits the number of national cases a scholar can consider" (Collier 1993, 105).

We also agree with Collier that even more is revealed with a comparative light. And part of the appeal of comparing just Brazil and China—and not all the rest—is because they are the two cases least likely to be analyzed side by side. Comparisons of Russia and China or China and India abound. And, arguably, in any mix of the four, at least at face value Brazil and China are the most different. We believe that a most-different case analysis, which moves beyond regime type—and beyond region—will produce the most unexpected and the richest results. Let's be clear: by our use of the term "beyond," we are not arguing that regime type and region are irrelevant. Rather, we use it synonymously with "over and above": beyond differences of regime and region, there is a resemblance between these countries. Obviously, regime type shapes state-society relations. And within-region comparisons are standard in the field. But we're hardly renegades to break with this convention. Over four decades ago, Rustow (1968) called on scholars to move beyond case selections based on region, and instead consider "cross-area" studies, but it is relatively unusual to find accessible, in-depth comparative case analysis across single cases in Asia and Latin America. This is surprising, given that countries are rarely defined by regional cultures anymore, and partnerships across borders, cultures, and governing types are less unusual than they were before.

We readily admit that our adoption of the alternative, "cross-area" approach— and the use of Brazil and China as our cases—does put us in something of a predicament. As mentioned earlier, ours is a theory-infirming case study because we counter the dominant view by contending that regime distinctions may not be as significant as is often assumed. As a result, we end up making an argument that undeniably causes us some discomfort: just beneath the surface, for two countries at opposite sides of "the messy middle," the parallels between Brazil and China can be striking. Let's be crystal clear: no one is arguing that China is Shangri-La and Brazil is an unmitigated hell, but neither will this be a story of "good state" vs. "bad state." Brazil, a democracy, has often—but not always—worked in partnership with civil society to do great things. Sure, such a partnership in authoritarian China is a rarer find, but the government has at times worked with civil society—which is more than one might expect. As we will demonstrate in the chapters that follow, authoritarian China does not always resort to the use of repression, whereas the Brazilian state has at times behaved in ways unbecoming to a democracy. Yes, usually democracies reform and non-democracies repress, but despite their very different political, economic, and social systems, both our cases have used reform and repression for much the same reason—to protect core interests and offset real, significant change.

In other words, even most-different case designs require that the cases be comparable, that they share a number of common properties. For all their differences, Brazil and China fit this bill: they both straddle the line between weak and strong / developing and developed country because, as many analysts have pointed out, they are both. And these two countries are alike in other, more important ways as well. This assessment can, at times, be flattering (e.g., their support for alternative energy sources), and at others, embarrassing (e.g., their deforestation and treatment of protesters). It is thanks to this unusual juxtaposition of cases that this pattern emerges. In effect, we're offering "most different, similar outcome" cases to see what the two have in common that might explain these outcomes (Guy 1998). Like a feat of prestidigitation manipulates an object to produce an effect, an analysis of these two countries side by side reveals their contradictions, their dynamics, and their realities more clearly and vividly than a regional or regime type comparison ever could. As you will see, it is the unexpected juxtaposition of these cases that is illuminating.

As mentioned earlier, this study is theory-infirming: while regime type has a role to play, it is the issue under contention that best predicts the likelihood of state receptivity or resistance to citizen demands. We maintain that this is true for all states. In particular, when it comes down to core issues, countries existing at opposite ends of "the messy middle," democracies and non-democracies, can—and do—behave in strikingly similar ways. As you will see, it's not just the dictatorships that have redline issues that are sacrosanct for them. Democracies aren't always receptive to civil society; on certain matters the Brazilian state has shown itself willing to resort to brutal repression. And, yes, authoritarian China often does live up to all our expectations of dictatorships—but not always.

Issue salience goes far in explaining why dictatorships can sometimes appear surprisingly pliant. This study suggests that regardless of regime type, all states are to some degree concerned about legitimacy. As you'll see in the chapters to follow, Brazil and China are more willing to "give" on some issues than others. We argue that dictatorships and democracies alike are more willing to negotiate the disputes that are less important to them; both are willing to engage society on some things to deflect attention and better protect their core interests. And, as you'll see, contrary to popular assumptions, it's not useful to try to peg society by regime type, either. In the chapters that follow, we will discuss the impressive variety of ways in which Brazilian and Chinese citizens seek to engage the state.

In other words, in contentious politics it's more about issue than regime. It is only by going beyond assumptions about regime type—and considering the complexity of state-society relations instead by issue—that the largest determinant of state behavior comes into focus. It then becomes clear why, despite their differences, state (and society) at opposite ends of "the messy middle" can be more alike than many would suppose—or wish.

OUTLINE OF THE BOOK

We promise to highlight issues that others might miss with a single case. In our first feat of prestidigitation, we will examine these countries' histories side by side, to reveal their contradictions, dynamics, and realities more clearly. This is a needed context that will help with understanding state-society relations in the chapters that follow. Therefore, in chapter 2, we compare a number of legacies, the imprints of the past on the present that set the stage. We do this not by attempting a full recounting of history, but by highlighting the events and processes that have made these countries what they are today. For example, despite its acclaim on the world stage, some analysts have characterized Brazil as an incomplete democracy or low-quality democracy in which new and old forms of exclusion exist side by side. Perhaps most obviously associated with its long history of slavery, social hierarchies and traditions of deference hang on. This is in part due to Brazil's preference for conciliation and accommodation, and its history of evolutionary change. The foundations of its inequitable system, based in land concentration and a slave economy, were never smashed, as Brazil never had a revolution, or even a civil war. Of course, China can claim one of the major social revolutions of the twentieth century, but despite its revolutionary heritage, social hierarchies and traditions of deference thought to be abolished have come roaring back. Although the Chinese leadership is promising to make amends, change is likely to come slowly after the fog and mirrors subside.

We reveal another intriguing juxtaposition in chapter 3: despite their differences in revolutionary experience, both countries have been identified as some of the world's most unequal: China has its luxury-item audience (including many CCP officials), while Brazil has its rich, too (old money and new). This chapter's focus is on how both states and societies struggle with disparities of wealth, despite—and sometimes because of—concerted efforts to promote economic growth. Within the last fifteen years, both Brazil and China have made significant strides combating poverty within their borders. Both countries bask in the early achievement of halving extreme poverty five years ahead of the 2015 deadline ("Millennium Development Goals Report 2012" 2013). Nonetheless, as we discuss in chapter 3, important disparities continue to challenge ordinary citizens and haunt a leadership whose legitimacy is closely connected to a record of improvement.

Another question we consider in chapter 3 is change—and the illusion of it. Brazil is on the verge of eliminating absolute poverty. Its approach to HIV-AIDS and *Bolsa Familia*, the Brazilian program of conditional cash transfers, are widely considered huge successes and emulated worldwide.[10] As a result, Brazil has garnered a reputation as a human security superpower. Still, it could be argued that at home, Brazil is only "minimizing the exploitation," and has only made enough change to keep everything in place. The reforms the government has made are offered up and celebrated, while structural changes such as agrarian reform are put aside and declared—even by the PT government, the leading leftist force in the country—as no longer necessary or relevant. Chinese leaders pride themselves on their significant rates of poverty reduction, and the big buzz now is how Beijing is taking on significant economic reforms—vowing to reduce the government's influence on the economy—under the "Fifth Generation" of leaders, Xi Jinping and Li Keqiang. Yet it seems once again to be more about appearance than genuine change, and bold agendas are again likely to become bogged down in bureaucratic muddle and much of the same.

Any consideration of inequality must also include the push and pull of state and society over the issue of crime. Beijing maintains a covert system of detention centers (labor camps and extrajudicial "black jails") designed to hold petitioners and other individuals who threaten to expose political problems. Here, people are held incommunicado without trial. However, China is pressured to build a more reliable system of laws and judicial independence—seen as necessary to promote long-term financial and investment stability—and it has responded with limited reforms, thus developing the veneer of a more gentle authoritarianism. Meanwhile, Brazil, a consolidated democracy ranked

---

[10] Conditional cash transfers are safety net programs (large or small) that are popular because they have proven successful at reducing poverty by making access to welfare conditional on a receiver's actions. They vary in how they are used, but often require parents to invest in their children's health and welfare (Fiszbein and Schady 2009).

as "free" by Freedom House, has a homicide rate three times the global average. Fearing for their safety, citizens have voted for a tough approach to crime. As a result, human rights have deteriorated since the return to democracy and Brazil has some of the most abusive security forces in the world ("Brazil: Freedom in the World 2011" 2011). Embarrassed by attention to this fact, the state has attempted to rehabilitate its image by mixing its counterinsurgency tactics in poor neighborhoods with community policing aimed at engaging and winning over hearts and minds. The big surprise in this analysis is in the levels of violence: citizens in democratic Brazil are much more likely to witness or be a victim of violence than those in authoritarian China, but majorities in both countries want the state to take a tougher line on crime.

Chapter 4 is all about social contradictions and struggles over identity. Its focus is religion and ethnicity, sexual politics and the rights of sexual and gender minorities. Brazil is so diverse that it's often said to comprise five countries, a point of pride for citizens and leaders alike. But Brazil is full of contradictions. For much of the twentieth century it was upheld as a model for the world, a racial democracy uniquely harmonious and conflict-free. UNESCO (United Nations Educational, Scientific, and Cultural Organization) representatives even traveled there in the 1950s to learn what Brazil could teach the world about racial tolerance. Until recently most Brazilians, including many blacks, argued that there was no racism in Brazil. Most agree now that what existed was a myth of racial democracy. An extremely asymmetric access to resources is no doubt tied up in race and class, but for years many people believed the fiction that Brazil has somehow transcended racism because its manifestation in Brazil was more subtle than Jim Crow. Those used to its harsh expression in the United States had a harder time recognizing it where social status and hierarchies coexisted with a culture of cordiality in which people who are not social equals could mingle and relate (Adelman and de Azevedo 2012; Philippou 2005). Brazil had the world's largest slave population and it was the last country to abolish slavery in the Western hemisphere, but until recently most Brazilians argued that it was a more tolerant, gentler slave system. China is equally (if not more) diverse, but this variation is often viewed as threatening by elites, who recognize only officially sanctioned ethnicities, officially fifty-six of the over four hundred groups that submitted applications to be recognized as a national minority (Blum 2010), and only the official discourse of ethnic identity is welcomed. However, individuals and groups routinely push the envelope. But both official discourses have largely fallen apart, as both states have a record of cultural dilution—in Brazil with social whitening, and in China with Han migration to Tibet and state-orchestrated migration to Xinjiang, one of China's Muslim-majority provinces. Thanks to the efforts of civil society, most Brazilians recognize now that what they had was a myth of racial democracy; it is a new generation of activists that is pushing the state to do something about it.

It is also in chapter 4 that we point out other social contradictions, as well as some of the important differences between the two countries. When it comes to religion, China is recognized as a majority non-religious state; the ruling CCP professes atheism and actively discourages family members of cadres from participating in public religious or spiritual rituals. Still, tens of millions of individuals are flocking to a wide range of organized religious services, practicing spirituality in both official and unofficial channels. The government views such organizations as a potential threat, and officials who belong to religious organizations can be expelled from the CCP.

Brazil, on the other hand, famous for its sensuality and eroticism, is much more sexually liberated than China. At the same time, it has the world's largest Catholic population, and a fast growing number of evangelical converts. This contradiction is why Brazil has some of the most restrictive abortion laws in the world, but still high rates of abortion. Meanwhile, China leads the world in virtually unrestricted access to abortion, largely due to state enforcement of population-control initiatives. As one might expect, religious morality has little influence on policy regarding sexuality in China, yet the lesbian, gay, bisexual, and transgender (LGBT) and sex worker movements are in their infancy, still largely closeted due to both social and political conservatism. Sexual politics in China also provides an alluring window on the precarious status of laws and legality in the country, and how even an authoritarian state can suffer from impotence. For example, even though prostitution is officially illegal in China, it is rampant, with deep connections to the growing problem of human trafficking. Conversely, sex work is legal in Brazil, but human trafficking is a major problem there as well.

When it comes to other forms of sexuality, China is still in the closet. Its socially conservative mores compel many gay men to marry women and have children—due to family and social pressure—but continue to seek same-sex partners behind closed doors. And although conservative religious groups have been able to hold the line on maintaining highly restrictive abortion laws, they appear to be losing their battles against the LGBT and sex worker movements in Brazil, which have won on the legislative battlefield in recent years, as same-sex marriage and adoption is now legal.

Another surprise comes in chapter 5, in our discussion of the interchange between state and society over the environment. On one hand, as a state-socialist regime, the People's Republic of China (PRC) limits expression and participation in many areas of life, namely any topic deemed "sensitive" by the national elite. Still, at the same time, there are areas of expression where openness is more permissible—most notably efforts to curb water pollution—albeit with an eye toward the safeguarding of social stability. We discuss the surprising finding that some forms of environmental activism are more dangerous in Brazil—witness the murder of Dorothy Stang by entrenched ranching interests—than in China, where the national bureaucracy has invited limited input from environmental activists on limited issues. The Amazon is as much a core interest for Brazil as issues of territorial integrity are for China—both countries have made it abundantly clear that they'll not tolerate any interference with their sovereignty when it comes to these issues.

We conclude the book by projecting out from this examination of state-society relations to consider the styles of leadership emerging from within these two fast-emerging powers. In chapter 6 we analyze lessons from the preceding discussion to forecast the kinds of powers—regionally and globally—Brazil and China are likely to become as the twenty-first century unfolds. As Nye (2013) reminds us, soft power is based in culture, values, and foreign policy, in other words, the ways states seek to set the global agenda. Foreign policy is the focus here, and based in their pasts, their own experiences, and worldviews, state leaders within Brazil and China chart a new path for their states in the early twenty-first century. They engage in strategic receptivity to and resistance of international pressures, norms, and proposals in order to carve influence in an increasingly multipolar and contested international arena. Brasilia and Beijing see themselves as leading actors at center stage in many of the significant policy challenges of the early twenty-first century. They see themselves as no one's co-star and they're not just players in a supporting role. Like other actors, they seek to advance their own agendas. For example, by promoting solidarity and South-South cooperation, Brazil and China are known for staking out counterhegemonic or antihegemonic policies. Some examples of this include the Beijing Consensus, which—unlike the West—doesn't make any claim of linking human rights performance to foreign aid and investment, or the Brasilia Consensus, which calls for the West to also play by free trade rules. Both Brazil and China take leadership roles challenging Western orthodoxies, agreeing, for example, that rich countries should make the biggest sacrifices in cutting carbon emissions. China expects and Brazil hopes that the South will repay its efforts with support for the causes it cares most about. For China, that means toeing the line on Tibet, Taiwan, and Xinjiang. For Brazil, it is support for a permanent seat on the UN Security Council.

While analysts disagree over whether Brazil and China will seek to reform and preserve the existing international order—or subvert and provide alternatives to it—at the very least these rising powers are determined to put their mark on it. They both want recognition; they want respect. And increasingly they're demanding it. Each country is following a different trajectory, and they are likely to find themselves, like all states, continually frustrated in their efforts. However, there is no doubt that these two countries—Brazil with its reciprocal multilateralism, China in seeking a new hegemony—are playing a large part in shaping the next world order.

Sure, the comparison of state-society relations in Brazil and China that follows is likely to exhibit some of what you'd expect—but it also reveals some real surprises. A juxtaposition of these two states exposes some striking contradictions and gaps between rhetoric and reality, in how these countries present themselves and how they are presented. More importantly, our findings invite a cautious approach to generalization across regime types. In their interactions with their citizens and on the world stage, democratic and authoritarian states can be more alike than most expect. To understand two dynamic states and to help forecast the kind of presence they will reveal on the world stage, it is useful to pay more attention to state-society relations. As we think you'll agree, behind all the smoke and mirrors there are some real eye-openers.

DISCUSSION QUESTIONS

1. The authors contend that Brazil and China each have something very different to offer the world. Do you expect them to be more different than alike? Why? Do you expect their differences to be more about style or substance? Explain.

2. What's the dominant paradigm in explaining contentious politics? Why is it the dominant paradigm and why do you think it has been so enduring? Are the authors right to challenge it? What other variables might be associated with different levels of state responsiveness to society?

3. This study seeks to challenge assumptions about how democracies and authoritarian governments engage with public participation. Can you think of any other cases in which dictatorships have displayed fuller than expected repertoires, or responses to civil society? What are some examples of democracies "behaving in ways unbecoming to their status"? Does this leave all states in "the messy middle"? Explain.

4. Part of what is unique about this study is the unexpected case selection and the hypothesis that these ostensibly most-different cases are more alike than many of us might assume. What might be some other unexpected, interesting cases to compare? What's your hypothesis?

5. The authors contend that, regardless of the differences in regime type, Brazil and China are alike in the ways in which they engage civil society. They're receptive on what they deem "safe" issues, but on "dangerous" issues that threaten core interests, both have proven fiercely resistant. Is this true of all states? And what kinds of issues are more likely to be regarded as "safe" vs. "dangerous"? What do core interests have in common?

2

HERITAGE AND CULTURE

In Brazil, either you give orders or you plead.
                                    —A common saying in Brazil

As any good revolutionary will tell you, there are three
choices for dealing with the past: rejection, transformation, or invention. At any given moment, Mao and his
followers have tried all three.
                        —Rubie Watson, "Afterword," in *Faiths on Display:*
                        Religion, Tourism and the Chinese State

INTRODUCTION

Few things are as controversial as history. Every country has parts of its past
that many people would like to forget, as well as aspects of the story that are
exaggerated, often in order to justify a particular set of circumstances. Brazil
and China both have lengthy, complicated, and contentious histories. Official
histories are just one version of reality, but it is one that plays a crucial role in
crafting any country's image and socializing its citizens. Every country has a
national mythology, and the best source of it is the "official history" contained
within its textbooks. All countries have a talent for self-invention, and official
versions of history shape national identities by defining norms and dissemi-
nating values. Common understandings of history serve as tools of political
socialization, which, in non-revolutionary states, promote continuity (Niemi
and Sobieszek 1977). The Brazilian and Chinese states are hardly unique in that

37

they have drawn from the past (a significantly doctored-up version of the real thing that rejects the less savory details of the record) to bolster their images and promote their agendas at home and abroad. But for all their differences, the similarities in these official histories are striking—as is the fact that it is not just the state that has found a reading of history useful. They may be using a different version of it, but Brazilian and Chinese social movements have also looked to the past to inspire.

We make no attempt here to provide a comprehensive, beginning-to-end narrative of these vast and complex stories. Rather, this chapter on history is only included to provide some context for understanding the relationships between state and society described in chapters to follow. Toward that aim, our focus is on what we believe to be these countries' most significant historical legacies. It is in this chapter that we identify perhaps the most influential political opportunity structure of all: how the past shapes contemporary debates and alliances.

As you read on you may find that it is easy to contrast the two countries' histories. Brazil's is marked by more continuity than change; any change in Brazil over the last five hundred years has been evolutionary, whereas China's long history of evolutionary change was interrupted by one of the major social revolutions of the twentieth century. Clearly, in many regards the two cases are more different than alike. However, one can't help but be struck by the ways in which certain patterns repeat themselves and run parallel in the two countries. Particularly over the last fifty years, the coincidence of events in Brazil and China is remarkable; this includes crackdowns by hard-liners in the 1960s, transitions of power and openings (economic in China / political in Brazil) in the 1970s and 1980s, followed by rapid economic growth and recognition of each as rising powers in the early 2000s.

On the face of it, where their experiences diverge—such as in 1989, when Brazilians had elections marking a return to democracy and Chinese rulers made it clear that they were having none of it at Tiananmen Square—it is most often concerning the tug-of-war between state and society and the manner in which political alliances (inside and outside the state) have determined the tenor of state-society relations. But nothing is as simple as it seems. As you will see, in relatively slow-changing Brazil, these relationships are more dynamic than one might assume. Brazilians have periodically made attempts to speed up the process of change. On the other hand, revolutionary China is known for the dramatic changes it has experienced since 1949. But despite its revolution and phenomenal economic growth, the CCP is just a new emperor; power remains centralized and state-society relations continue on as they have for thousands of years. Before we dive into this, let's be clear: the sections that follow are not comprehensive histories that recount the full breadth and depth of the past. Rather, what follows is an attempt to direct your attention to broad themes and repeated patterns of receptivity and resistance in state-society relations in Brazil and China, as it is this history that sets the stage (or provides the political opportunity structure) for contention and collaboration down the road.

BRAZIL

Brazil's perception of itself as exceptional dates back at least one hundred years. This is a view held by elite and non-elite actors. It is as true of society as it is of the state: Brazil's long-term goal has been aspirational. Brazil very much wants to live up to its grand expectations, to achieve its enormous potential as "the country of the future"—and, one day, to be recognized as such. How did Brazil come to see itself in this way? And what explains state-society relations today? What are the longstanding political opportunity structures native to Brazil? What patterns of protest do we see again and again, and how do they shape— and how are they shaped by—state responses of receptivity and resistance? Like

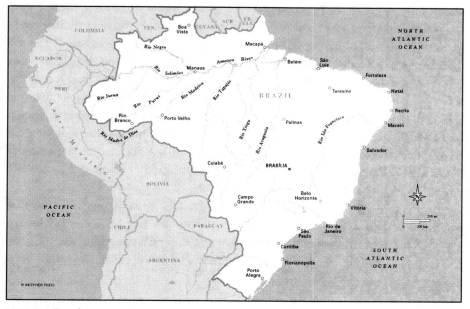

MAP 2.1 Brazil

any country, Brazil is a product of its history. There are aspects of this history that are (and should be) celebrated because they have made Brazil what it is today: pragmatic, flexible, and relatively peaceful and stable. These qualities will serve it well as an up-and-coming world power. However, in order for Brazil to realize its potential and gain the international recognition it so desires, the country will have to come to terms with the other side of its history. As we will see, slow change or no change explains Brazil's festering problems with inequality and violence.

Approach to the Past: "The Brazilian Way"

As mentioned earlier, one way of understanding states is to categorize them by how they deal with the past: do they invent, reject, or transform it (Niemi and Sobieszek 1977)? Clearly, Brazil falls into the first category; it has been much more likely to invent its history than to reject or transform it. Brazil is hardly alone in this; every country uses history to do a bit of self-invention. In terms of invention, there are several myths that are bedrock to Brazil's official history: that it is a racial democracy, that slavery there was largely benevolent, that the country is uniquely stable and peaceable. Certainly the celebration of conciliation as a national trait or collective identity, known as "the Brazilian way," confirms its non-revolutionary heritage and sustains the status quo, promoting at best incrementalist, evolutionary change. Since early in Brazil's history elites demonstrated an extraordinary preference for conciliation, or a muting of conflict and agreement to avoid controversial issues. Brazil does not have a revolutionary history. In fact, its history is characterized by the remarkable continuity of its economic and social structures. The dominant narrative in Brazil has largely applauded this; the country is exceptionally peaceful and a rare example of stability. But while the body count in wars is relatively low for Brazil, perhaps it is too soon to celebrate, since this story ignores the casualty rate from structural violence and the good possibility that some of this stability is due to a persistent authoritarian tradition.[1]

Many students of Brazil wonder why it is that Brazil never had a revolution, given that there has been plenty of fodder for one. The most common answer to that question is that it's just not part of the DNA of Brazil, that Brazilians are different. What are we to make of this? Certainly some clues can be found in its

---

[1] Structural violence includes racism, classism, and sexism, and refers to the harms caused by inequality, which impairs people's ability to meet their basic needs.

history. We can tell a lot about countries by their heroes (and the stories told about them). Arguably, Brazil's greatest hero is King Sebastian of Portugal, who disappeared fighting the Moors in 1580. Every Brazilian knows his story and is familiar with Sebastianism, the folk belief that this "sleeping king" is prophesied to come again, to save the country and lead Brazil into a glorious future. Interestingly, some believe he took the form of Lula, who is certainly considered by more than a few as a savior.[2] Not everyone agrees with that assessment, but Sebastianism is indicative of the popularity of messianic movements over the course of Brazil's history. And to some degree it may partially explain the Brazilian proclivity for strong executives and, until recently, passive civil society (Vincent 2003). Some might say that Brazilians would rather wait than fight. What major events in Brazil's history have shaped this particular trajectory? And what are the legacies of Brazil's history? What vestiges of it continue to have a formative impact on its future? To answer these questions, let's begin at the start with perhaps the biggest relic of them all: the violence perpetrated by the colonizers against indigenous people (and later Africans). Slavery and the decimation of Amerindians helped to create and entrench social inequality in Brazil. The disregard for non-European life is evidenced by the belief—which, curiously, has been widely accepted by most Brazilians—that Brazil is a young country and its history began as recently as just five hundred years ago, when whites arrived. However, when Portuguese explorer Pedro Álvarez Cabral's ships veered far off course and he "discovered" the territory now known as Brazil by accident in 1500, Brazil's indigenous populations had been living there for twenty thousand to forty thousand years (Skidmore 1999).

Although it is now estimated that the indigenous population of the enormous swath of eastern South America in 1500 ranged anywhere from five hundred thousand to eight million, the first Portuguese arrivals described the territory that would be known as Brazil as strikingly under-populated (Skidmore 1999). One group, the Tupí-Guaraní people, scattered in small tribes and living along the coast, were foragers and semi-sedentary horticulturalists. Less was known of the semi-nomadic groups living inland, but historians describe this diverse group as self-sufficient but not wealthy; the indigenous people of Brazil were believed to have produced no cities or complex political systems, and no monumental culture. In comparison, the Aztec and Inca populations numbered in the tens of millions (Eakin 1998).

---

[2] Luiz Inácio "Lula" da Silva, a former steel worker and union leader, helped bring down the dictatorship and was elected to two terms as president (2003–2011).

Even for the centuries since 1500, remarkably little is known of Indian perspectives or voices on those earliest exchanges. Instead, the official history is told by European travelers. For the most part these accounts represented the indigenous people they first came into contact with as friendly, childlike, and primitive.[3] In recent decades, however, archaeologists have made dramatic advances in our understanding of Amazonian societies (Heckenberger and Neves 2009). The long-held view of Brazil's Indians may be changing, but largely negative stereotypes of them were (and are) used to rationalize non-Indians' treatment of Indians—the effect of which can be summed up as devastating (Schwartz 2000).

Regardless of the claim's veracity, most Brazilians have been brought up believing that theirs is a young country and that this is a positive attribute. Ideas of Brazil as new, vibrant, and oriented to the future have certainly shaped Brazilian exceptionalism. Because most Brazilians were taught that 1500 was the first year of the country's history, that history began with colonialism. The colonial experience in itself is nothing unique; the whole hemisphere was colonized and had some shared experiences stemming from it. However, Brazilian history makes much of two distinguishing characteristics: 1) Brazil was the largest colony in South America, and 2) it was the only territory in the Americas to be colonized by Portugal. Portugal's own unique experience, given that it was colonized for hundreds of years by the Moors of North Africa, meant that it was exposed to other cultures and religions (Islam). This experience is widely believed to have engendered in the Portuguese national character high levels of tolerance and appreciation of the benefits of blending with other cultures (Neuhouser 1999). These two traits would be passed on to Brazil and are said to be reflected in its history, time and time again.

Another legacy the Portuguese passed on to Brazil was a penchant for the decentralization of power. From the earliest days of colonialism, the Portuguese crown, which was far more interested in the Orient than this new land they had happened upon, left the Portuguese elites to their own devices, with control over vast lands, powers, and a great deal of autonomy (Paquette 2011).

---

[3] More recent studies have upended these accounts, characterizing Amazonian societies as more varied and complex than previously thought. Although it does not appear that these indigenous groups developed large bureaucratic states or empires, they were hardly the "primitive" tribes depicted in the history books. Rather, archaeologists have found evidence of large-scale transformations of the natural environment and regional political economies based on the trade of prestige goods. Deep in the forests they only recently discovered late prehistoric settlements that included large walled towns and ceremonial plazas (Heckenberger and Neves 2009).

Members of this landed aristocracy eventually became known as *fazendeiros* (masters of plantations known as *fazendas*), and most of their wealth was based on sugar (and over the generations later estates producing coffee and other cash crops such as today's soya). Brazil's kings and emperors depended on the cooperation of local authorities, who were and are a power base to be reckoned with. For hundreds of years, much of the countryside has been run in a semi-feudal fashion. The heads of landowning clans were the law of the land, backed by private armies. The system has become known as *coronelismo*, in which *coronels* (or local bosses) rely on patronage to assert enormous influence over their rural domain—and all who live in it (Neuhouser 1999).

Coronelismo also forms the basis of the social authoritarianism, the unequal and hierarchical social relations that pervade Brazil today. Remember, with the Portuguese authorities relatively absent, decentralization was the rule, as local bosses and governors acted (and act) with unchecked power as patrons. Only the mechanisms of power the coronels wield has evolved over the years. Today, in large expanses of the countryside they produce the votes and thus still call the shots. This patronage, and social stratification based on race, class, and gender, put everyone in their place. Underlings were expected to submit to cultural rules that defined them as objects, not citizens. In what has been called "the culture of gift," the only rights most people had were favors or gifts from the powerful. Although there are examples of the poor acting as agents, struggling against their economic inequality and political subordination, this social authoritarianism remains pervasive. The maxim "In Brazil, either you give orders or you plead" sums up this oligarchic tradition (Dagnino 2005, 152).

Throughout its history, much like the master-slave relationship, Brazilians have been socialized into the passive acceptance of hierarchies. According to Skidmore, "Monarchy combined with slavery created an atmosphere of deference that was powerfully transmitted to the non-elites. The inculcation of this attitude of subservience that must be shown toward any superior was by and large successful in convincing non-elites there was no way to change their world" (Skidmore 1999, 39).

Therefore, the system's effect on the national psyche is believed to have been powerful, and the resulting passivity helps to explain the continuation of one of the most highly concentrated systems of landownership in the world. There were certainly valiant (and even sustained) acts of resistance, but for most Brazilians for hundreds of years the most common way to survive was to find a powerful patron. Until recently at least, collective action has not been a rational option in this world. Brazil's system of landownership dates back to the captaincy system of the sixteenth century.[4] In Brazil, land continues to be the principal source of wealth (Skidmore 1999). As of the late 1990s, 1 percent of landowners owned 44 percent of all the farmland (the average farm was over seven thousand acres) while 53 percent of farmers worked less than 3 percent of the land and six million people lived as *sem terras*, working other people's land as renters, squatters, sharecroppers, or migrant day laborers (Neuhouser 1999). Therefore, a small white elite of large landowners dominated not only the economic but also the political system, and a non-white majority. This continues to be the story in much of the countryside today. To paraphrase Eakin, it is a pattern from the past that continues to intrude on the present (Eakin 1998).

Another pattern from the past that continues to intrude on the present is Brazil's slave economy, which was the once the world's largest. Sugar is famously labor intensive, but the Iberians disdained manual labor and the Indians fled or were decimated by war and disease early on. Some Indians were forced into labor, but by the 1570s the Portuguese slave industry was filling the gap. Over the years it brought in an estimated 3.6 million Africans to Brazil as slaves— more than any other country in the world (Baranov 2000).[5] Slavery provided the principal source of labor, mostly but not exclusively for its sugar plantations, and it lasted longer than in any other country in the Americas.

As we will see, slavery is arguably the most important of all Brazil's historical legacies. Associated with it is *para inglês ver* ("for the English to see"), a practice that has endured and is widely recognized in Brazil today. The term goes back to the early to mid-nineteenth century, when, after it abolished its own slave trade, Britain prevailed upon Brazil to do the same. However, Brazilian elites considered slavery to be the foundation of their economy, and once they realized that they could not persuade the British to back down on the issue, they found back channels to bring in nearly one million more slaves. They made just enough adjustments so that it would appear as if they were acceding to British demands when, in fact, nothing at all had changed (Zimmerman 2008). The term *para inglês ver* perfectly sums up what many characterize as a Brazilian preference for keeping up appearances—even if they are deceiving.

---

[4] This system of patronage and nepotism was based on royal land grants. Without the interest or resources to invest in its colonial project, the Portuguese king divided the territory among fifteen Portuguese noblemen, known as *donees*, who in exchange administered the colony on behalf the crown, each donee amassing vast responsibilities and power (Vincent 2003).

[5] It is estimated that of the 9.6 million slaves brought to the Americas, 38 percent entered Brazil (4 percent went to the United States) (Neuhouser 1999).

Because the practice involves putting up a formal edifice to maintain harmony, *para inglês ver* often helps to explain the chasm between reality and the law or, as it is known, "the real and the legal Brazil"(Carter 2010). *Para inglês ver* is a perfect example of the importance Brazil places on its image of cordiality and accommodation, even if it is feigned. This way of operating may help to explain why things change so slowly there. In the end, the Brazilian state created the appearance of change so as to placate the British in order to avoid conflict with local elites. It only ended the institution of slavery gradually, in stages. Brazil was the last country in the Americas to abolish slavery, which didn't come until many decades later, in 1888. Depending on whom you ask, this gradual approach worked: Brazil emancipated the slaves without a bloody civil war. Perhaps one could also argue that by the time it occurred the abolition of slavery amounted to *para inglês ver*, since it allowed the system of large landholdings to continue to go unchallenged (Skidmore 1999).

However, the institution of slavery is said to have been different in Brazil than in the rest of the world. The country's historians long argued that the Portuguese were less racist than other Europeans and the masters ruled with a lighter touch—that this was a uniquely benevolent, even compassionate form of enslavement. In Brazil extensive miscegenation (sexual relations between Europeans, Africans, and Indians) contributed to the growth of a large mixed race population; it is said that the masters and slaves were a family, often literally so, as many children were born from such unions, consensual or not. Whereas in other slave economies it was not uncommon for the children of slaves to be sold away from their parents, the separation of families was highly unusual in Brazil. Slaves in Brazil were given one day a week off, and the money they earned on their own could be used to purchase their freedom. Freedmen could rise to social prominence in Brazil, as the color bar and segregationist laws that followed slavery elsewhere never existed there. Certainly discrimination against bi- and multiracial people existed, but compared to the United States, a degree of social acceptance existed in Brazil that formed the basis for the racial democracy long touted there. This is discussed in greater detail in chapter 4.[6]

---

[6] This characterization of the Portuguese as less racist and the Brazilian institution of slavery as benevolent, noble, and less degrading was part of the long-held official history (see Freyre 1933). Other historians have provided ample evidence to counter this view, pointing to Portuguese prejudices and their reliance on the use of violence to terrorize populations into obedience, the high mortality rates and low life expectancies for slaves, and multiple examples of rebellions (as well as the existence of *quilombos*, or communities of runaways) to demonstrate that slavery in Brazil was not significantly different than anywhere else (Skidmore 1999).

Similarly, the Catholic Church ruled with a lighter touch in Brazil as well. As elsewhere in Latin America, Catholicism (in this case, specifically the Jesuits) went hand in hand with colonialism, imposing European languages and cultures. Unlike the Spaniards, for the Portuguese colonialism was clearly more about trade than religion. The priests and brothers of the Society of Jesus weren't the only religious order in Brazil, but they played a major role in running the (very limited) education system under colonialism and converting the Indians, and there was no separation of church and state. However, in 1759 the crown expelled the Jesuits, who were distrusted for their independence, secrecy, and wealth, and who came into conflict with landowners for opposing the enslavement of Indians. The Church was taken down a notch then, and again under Pedro II in the 1880s, when the emperor sought to restrict the development of the Church and the two came into conflict. Still, the Church remained the state religion in Brazil even after independence; there was no separation of church and state until 1892, with overthrow of the monarchy and the establishment of the Republic (Skidmore and Smith 2005). It certainly was the dominant religion there and it is powerful (as we will see in later chapters), but the country is often described as "soft Catholic." With its access to resources and organizational characteristics, it is arguably the most powerful branch of civil society in Brazil. It has influence unlike any other institution, but it has never had the same degree of power in Brazil that it has in neighboring countries. Some analysts have suggested that this more laissez-faire approach to religion contributed to the thriving syncretism that we see there. For example, it is not uncommon for those who consider themselves good Catholics to visit Afro-Brazilian spiritual advisers. The mix of Catholicism with indigenous and African religions is hardly unique to Brazil, but it arguably goes further than most. Such flexibility may be derived from the high levels of tolerance originally attributed to the Portuguese.

Whatever the case, the Portuguese soft touch, and relative lack of interest in the colony, was replaced by a more ardent pursuit of colonial interests once the mercantilists found that there were indeed resources to exploit. Two hundred years after Cabral's arrival, the Portuguese crown was no longer willing to leave Brazil's bounty to private interests and was now intent on reaping it all for itself. The first extractive industry was brazilwood, lucrative for its scarlet dye so fashionable in European courts. After that resource was fully stripped, sugar in the northeast dominated the economy until it too was replaced, through endless rounds of boom and bust. What really piqued colonial interest, though, was in the southeast: the discovery of gold in the late seventeenth century.

This led to a reassertion of control and by the eighteenth century, Brazil was the world's largest gold exporter, a major diamond exporter, and Portugal the richest monarchy in Europe. Closer control of the mining industry left Portugal flush with cash but its colony saw little of the benefits. Mercantilism was operating at full throttle, and Brazil became known as "the king's plantation" (Skidmore 1999). The colony was paying taxes through the nose, but the colonizers were unwilling to make any investments, in education or infrastructure, that would form the basis for future growth. The Portuguese allowed none of this capital to help Brazil industrialize; rather, the colony was to continue as an exporter of raw materials. Meanwhile, the Portuguese went on a binge buying manufactured goods, and even as the money flow continued for a few more years (thanks to Brazil's discovery of diamonds), Portugal had acquired tastes that it could never sustain on its own. As Portugal found itself dependent on its colony, it became evermore rapacious, falling into debt (to the British, financing their industrial revolution) while producing little more than wine and cork back home (Eakin 1998).

As the Portuguese crown sought to squeeze even more wealth out of the territory by centralizing control, more Brazilians began to question the relationship. But there were several factors working in the colonizer's favor. One was distance. Rebellions, revolts, and conspiracies were much more common than official histories have recognized. However, given the colony's size, these uprisings never coincided or were coordinated to pose a significant threat to the government. Brazil was too wide open to have developed much of a sense of nationalism until much later in its history. Just as notably, the relatively flexible Portuguese approach to administration helped to assuage tensions. Although it must be noted that when charm failed, the Portuguese did not hesitate to bring the gauntlet down hard. The Portuguese proclivity for tolerance described earlier was coupled with what is also characterized as a unique flexibility and preference for compromise over confrontation. For example, the Spanish colonizers actively discriminated against their "creole," American-born subjects, giving favors and plum appointments to their subjects born in Spain. As you might imagine, such a policy spurred nationalist, anti-colonial sentiment, and this was a mistake that the Portuguese sometimes made. Brazilians resented what they saw as the arrogance of Portuguese administrators, but not to the extent we see elsewhere in the hemisphere. Rather, the Portuguese were generally careful to include elites, co-opting them, American-born or not (Paquette 2011).

For many years this conciliatory approach mostly worked, and, as opposed to their counterparts in the Spanish colonies, American-born Portuguese elites were far less restive than their Spanish American counterparts. By the late eighteenth century, however, this was all changing. But one thing in particular did help to contain republican fervor. Brazil was the largest slave-owning economy in the world at this time. Despite any grievances that they might have with Lisbon, Brazilian elites lived in fear of the slave insurrections that they saw in Haiti and elsewhere. In Brazil, where whites were greatly outnumbered by slaves (in 1800, 37 percent of Brazil's population were slaves and another 30 percent were free persons of African descent or of mixed race), elites agreed to put aside their differences and unified to ensure that radical change was not an option (Paquette 2011). Even before *para inglês ver*, Brazilian elites proved adept at compromising without endangering their own position. This approach has worked quite well for them (Skidmore 1999).

Thus the patrimonial hierarchies described earlier—paternalistic systems in which fatherlike figures rule and everyone is expected to know and accept his own place in the established order—have been maintained. According to Eakin, in Brazil, everything is about who you are. Everyone knows their place. The good ole boys club, in effect, social authoritarianism, doles out patronage, keeps the masses in check and the system intact (Eakin 1998). Elites (whether old money or new, sugar planters or real estate moguls) have put aside their divides to maintain cohesiveness and stuck together out of the shared fear of rebellion by the impoverished majority. Throughout Brazil's history, elites have improvised a largely effective way to defuse the threat posed by what is known as "the dangerous classes" or "marginals." Here's how they did it: they maintained the system by dulling its sharp edges. Former president Fernando Henrique Cardoso sums this up with an example of the elite preference for conciliation, arguing that traditionally the ruling class treated people as if they were closer in rank than they really were. The rich would maintain differences without provoking a strong reaction, by being mild, saying "please," and not ordering ("Fernando Henrique Cardoso on Brazil's Future" 2012). In a variety of ways over its history, elites have used compromise, creativity, improvisation, flexibility, pragmatism—anything to stave off significant change. These traits have become known as the bedrock to the Brazilian national character.

One other historic contributor to Brazil's exceptionalism is the *hegira*, the flight of the Portuguese royal family (the Braganza dynasty), which took refuge from Napoleon's advances in Rio de Janeiro in 1808. At precisely the time that Spanish America was falling apart, when Napoleon's invasion of Spain led to a power vacuum that encouraged wars for liberation, Brazil remained stable. In fact, this is a period when its self-image bloomed. No royal family had even set foot in the New World prior to this time, let alone set up court there. Nonetheless, the Portuguese royal family made Brazil their new home and delighted in it, developing Rio as "a tropical Versailles," a true court in exile. For thirteen years the Portuguese crown spent money in Brazil, investing not only in a palace and government buildings, but also world-class theaters, an opera house, university, a press, and a botanical garden. Most notably, Rio replaced Lisbon as the capital of a global empire. Prince Regent Dom João went on to declare Brazil a kingdom in 1815; from 1808 to 1821 its ports were opened to the world (ending the Portuguese monopoly), and Brazil's stature in the world skyrocketed as it went from being a lowly colony to coequal with Portugal (Schultz 2001). The significance of this relatively sudden change in status cannot be overstated. It is said to have been formative in Brazilians' political culture, changing the way that Brazilians think of themselves, and their potential.

Revolution/Not

Brazilians pride themselves on their reputation for conciliation, pragmatism, and flexibility, but that was not always the route taken in Brazil. And, for that matter, the image of Brazil as exceptionally pacific does not quite stand up to closer scrutiny, either. When comparing their history to others, Brazilians are very proud of the fact that their country has never had a revolution or a civil war.[7] Some Brazilians explain their country's relative lack of turmoil by arguing that cordiality is intrinsic to the national character. They point out that (unlike its neighbors) Brazil won its independence with virtually no bloodshed.

The latter is a fact that can't be denied, and the way that it happened serves as another good example of the use of accommodation to offset transformative change. Brazil's independence came on September 7, 1822, through a declaration, the *Grito de Ipiranga* ("the Cry of Ipiranga"). Here's the backstory: Prince Pedro, King João's heir, had been left behind after his father and the royal court were compelled to return to Portugal in 1821. A year later, Pedro too was being pressured to return home by the Portuguese parliament, which planned to restrict the king's power and return Brazil to colonial status. Pedro resisted, knowing that Brazil would never accept this demotion. After receiving an order for him to return to Portugal immediately, while traveling near a brook known

---

[7] Brazil has had a number of regional revolts, but none of them threatened the viability of the central government, which employed grisly reprisals to successfully defeat every one (Skidmore 1999).

as the Ipiranga, Pedro preempted revolution and maintained the kingdom and monarchy. By declaring "Independence or Death," he played to Brazil's desire for self-rule and rejected Portugal's demand. The Portuguese blinked: a deal was made and Brazil agreed to cover their former colonizer's two million pound sterling (approximately US$10 million) debt to Britain. In return Britain backed Brazil's independence, and Britain replaced Portugal as the dominant foreign actor in Brazil's economy. It was all very tidy; Brazil's liberation was virtually bloodless and it became a stable, relatively unified "empire" (Eakin 1998).

And it has remained relatively unified. For all its diversity, Brazil has cohered culturally and politically as a nation. Brazilians even consider themselves to have their own civilization (Skidmore 1999). Therefore, Brazil's independence offers a good example of how the country's leaders have used the illusion of change to neutralize it. Brazil was "independent," but Pedro had kept power in the family. Brazil was "independent," but Brazil had really only traded a Portuguese monarch in Portugal for a Portuguese monarch in Brazil. On paper it was the end of an absolute monarchy and the beginning of power-sharing with a parliament, but there was already a difference between the real and the legal Brazil. As Paquette (2011) notes, at "independence" there was no overhaul of politics, society, or the economy.

Therefore, instead of forging an independent nation out of a break with the colonial past, independence (and all that has followed) was fused with that past (Eakin 1998). As we will see, despite all the turmoil on the surface and the appearance of change, very little of substance has altered. This practice has been maintained ever since. Brazil's elites are hardly homogeneous or monolithic, but they have kept challenges from below from forcing fundamental change or allowing truly representative politics. Continuity has been maintained as elites remained firmly in control of the instruments of power (such as the electoral system) through their extraordinarily creative use of accommodation. As evidence of the consensus around this understanding, in the nineteenth century power shifted back and forth between the two (elite) parties twenty-six times in a forty-nine-year period, indicating a remarkable degree of cooperation. At least until 2002 (and some would argue even since then), the only real question has been which group of elites would control the lion's share of political power at any particular time (Eakin 1998).

As a result, most major political transitions in Brazil have been pulled off as accommodations between elites. It is the reprisals that have been gory (Skidmore 1999). *Inconfidencia Mineira*, Brazil's first serious plot for independence, is a good example of how the state has managed threats when charm fails. In the late 1780s, inspired by the American and French Revolutions, a group of elites led a revolt. This would be no social revolution; it was a movement led by oligarchs for oligarchs (merely seeking a regime change). When the Portuguese authorities discovered the plan, its leaders were put on trial. Interestingly, the way the government handled the rebellion is telling, and indicative of how it would deal with later challenges. It first promoted its conciliatory image and sought to pacify with soft power by pardoning the elites who surrendered or having their death sentences commuted. It also sent a message of deterrence to anyone who might have similar ideas. Moreover, it brought down the hammer on the only non-aristocratic leader of the conspiracy: an amateur dentist named Joaquim José da Silva Xavier. Known by all Brazilians as Tiradentes (or "Toothpuller"), the rebel was to serve as an example to others: he was hanged, his body torn apart and displayed in his home state for all those who had heard his revolutionary ideas to see (Eakin 1998).

The "Tiradentes treatment" was hardly a one-time affair (Skidmore 1999, 34). On multiple occasions Brazil has shown itself capable of severe, violent responses; it is said that the "unrestrained might of the military combined with the soft power of the monarchy" to pacify unrest (Paquette 2011). For example, the period following independence (1830–1845) was one of Brazil's most turbulent, with rebellions, revolts, and conspiracies that involved the active participation of slaves, the lower classes, and Indians. Most of these uprisings were not revolutionary, some of them were even pro-royalist, and none of them produced widespread upheaval. Still, Brazil's leaders made it clear very early on that there were limits to the range of permissible social protest; those who promoted disorder were met with a crushing response (Skidmore 1999). In the Cabanagem uprising (1835–1840), a liberal, multiethnic alliance of rebels (many of them poor) seized a provincial capital and controlled it for nine months, calling for the rights of citizenship. In response, the government, surprised at the success of the attack, sought annihilation: 30,000 out of a population of 120,000 were killed; many of them were civilians starved to death or hunted down and executed (Paquette 2011).

But because the story was retold as *Os Sertões* (Rebellion in the Backlands), by Euclides da Cunha, one of Brazil's foremost writers, the Canudos Rebellion (1897) is Brazil's most famous example of resistance. It started with an itinerant, millenarian preacher who formed a community in the dry, hardscrabble *sertão* (or backlands) of the northeast in a town known as Canudos. This preacher, a critic of the new republic named Antônio Conselheiro, was a Sebastianist character for the faithful whom he promised an alternative social, political, and religious order if they lived by God's Commandments and awaited the Day of Judgment. Described as an immensely compelling figure, Conselheiro taught an anti-tax message and protested the extreme poverty and official neglect suffered by the population, including the lack of compensation provided to freed slaves. The community, composed of the poor of all colors, eventually grew to fifteen thousand inhabitants. Whereas the problem began when Conselheiro got into a scrap with the local bosses, the state and federal governments were eventually brought in. Threatened by the protests against the dominant culture and the prospect of genuine social transformation, the authorities considered Conselheiro a fanatic, the community part of a plot, and declared war. After a rude shock when the peasants defeated two army expeditions, the military eventually cracked down hard and the rebellion was brutally suppressed as thousands of men, women, and children were massacred. The siege lasted for two years; by the end there were only two survivors. The government had adopted scorched earth tactics; many of those who surrendered suffered the *degola*—their throats cut like cattle (Vasconcellos 2002; Vincent 2003).[8]

It could be argued that this approach is indicative of Brazil's authoritarian tradition, which dates back to colonialism and the decimation of indigenous peoples. Still, the institution of the *poder moderador* (moderating power), established by Brazil's first (1824) constitution after independence, is emblematic of Brazilian authoritarianism. Under the constitutional monarchy, the emperor was the poder moderador. The emperor served as a corrective influence; his job was to rise above petty politics and moderate crises. In this capacity, the crown was in effect a fourth branch of government. Claiming his right and responsibility to enforce the constitution, the poder moderador was expected to serve as a moderating influence. He prevented abuses by serving as final judge and arbiter in disputes and it was he who had the authority to dissolve the legislature, veto legislation, appoint provincial presidents, and name ministers—and even bishops (Freyre 1955; Skidmore 1999; Vincent 2003).

But eventually the balance of power shifted. Prior to 1860, the Portuguese emperors had kept the military small and weak (Brazil didn't even really have a national army), fearful that it might adopt the role taken in the Spanish American republics. But during a five-year war with Paraguay in the 1860s the military was built up and transformed as an institution. And as much as

---

[8] Similarly, between 1912 and 1916, nearly half the Brazilian army was sent in to crush 15,000 peasants led by another prophet critical of the republic in what turned out to be the very bloody Contestado Rebellion (Diacon 1990).

the emperor wanted to return to the status quo ante, the military made it clear that it was never going back. When a small group of conspirators stepped in to depose Emperor Pedro II in 1889, replacing the constitutional monarchy with a republic, the armed forces assumed the role of moderating power (Skidmore 1999).

It should be noted that, as at independence, the shift from constitutional monarchy to republic occurred in the Brazilian way—without much upheaval. But an important pivot had occurred: the military's role had forever changed and it would become the most prominent power broker of the twentieth century. With the 1889 coup, the precedent was set for officers' involvement in politics. Based in the Positivist teachings of Herbert Spencer and Auguste Comte that were popular with elites at the time—the Positivist motto, *"Ordem e Progresso"* ("Order and Progress"), is emblazoned on Brazil's flag—the military sought to reshape Brazil on the European model. This included promoting progress, which was defined as conservative modernization guided by science and based on state action, and enforcing order by putting an end to social conflict and what the military saw as excessive freedoms that might weaken the country (Skidmore and Smith 2005; Eakin 1998). Positivism and the authoritarian model were considered key to the industrialization and modernization of Brazil, and the military considered itself the rightful savior of the nation. Although social movements calling for a variety of new rights (the right to pensions, to education, women's suffrage) were also active in Brazil of the 1920s and organized labor was the strongest of them, it was the military that ushered in and out the corrupt oligarchy that had replaced the monarchy. It was also the military that in 1930 ushered in—and eventually out, twice—Getúlio Vargas, the country's longest-serving president. Typical of Brazil, this was done with little or no violence (Dagnino 2005).

Interestingly, the events of 1930 are commonly referred to in Brazil as "the 1930 Revolution." That year marks a turning point in Brazil's history. However, this was more a revolt against a rigged election than a revolution. Yes, Vargas is widely touted as the most influential Brazilian leader of the twentieth century, but the country was hardly transformed under his guidance. When he could not run again legally, the president canceled elections in 1937, in the name of law and order, and established the *Estado Novo* (New State), Brazil's own authoritarian experiment. His dictatorship was populist and corporatist; he was an economic nationalist, supporting state intervention, specifically import substitution industrialization and nationalization to reduce the country's export dependence and diversify the economy. His regime is said to have resembled the German and Italian fascist states at the time, but most would not characterize it as totalitarian. Sure, there was repression (extraordinary police powers, rule by decree, censorship, torture), but it was carried out in a characteristically Brazilian way, relatively accommodating, allowing limited dissent. For much of his rule this enigmatic strongman centralized power while working hard to appear to be accommodating diverse interests. Vargas was an opportunist more than anything else; his regime survived as long as it did because it played to the Brazilian audience by avoiding such extremes (Eakin 1998).

Vargas not only exemplified "the Brazilian way," he played a leading role in shaping Brazil's image and exporting it to the world. Besides being more opportunist than ideologue, one of Vargas's most notable talents was the use of propaganda, as Vargas was the penultimate conjurer of image. A nationalist, he scorned those who wanted to remake Brazil in Europe's image. Rather, with samba, soccer, and Carnival he celebrated popular (including Afro-Brazilian) culture and firmly established Brazil's image abroad—and its exceptionalism (Roett 1999).

It is important to emphasize that Vargas, who ruled as a dictator from 1930 to 1945 and served as president from 1951 to 1954, unified Brazilians and re-created the country without transforming it. He mobilized the urban masses to win their support. Recognizing that with urbanization, Brazil was changing rapidly and that the old politics were unworkable, (for a while, at least) Vargas pulled off a realignment of politics, setting off diverse interests against each other while appeasing and neutralizing resentments.[9] And although elites felt threatened by his popularity with "*o povo*" ("the people"), he was actually protecting established interests. His social welfare programs and interventions for labor were just another form of patronage. According to his critics, they succeeded mostly in co-opting the masses and keeping them passive since Vargas never fundamentally dealt with growing income inequality (Eakin 1998). Instead, this pragmatic politician found other ways for managing grumbling from below.

---

[9] A populist (but a staunch anti-communist), Vargas cast himself as "father to the poor." However, analysts characterize him as more appropriately "mother to the rich" because Vargas played both sides, and for all the talk, the largest numbers of the masses (rural dwellers, who composed 80 percent of the population at the time) were left to their own devices. Most crucially, Vargas managed to hold sway without touching (or, rather, because he never touched) the third rail of Brazilian politics: land reform (Eakin 1998).

But Vargas had a more difficult time managing the military, which, fearing that he had amassed enough power as a populist to threaten the established order, forced him out of office. Vargas eventually made a political comeback and returned to the presidency. But as president, besieged from all sides and facing a corruption scandal, he ended it all with a self-inflicted bullet to the heart in 1954 (Eakin 1998). His suicide turned out to be perhaps his shrewdest move of all: such an exit not only generated a massive outpouring of grief, it guaranteed Vargas's influence beyond the grave—and an indelible place in Brazilian history (Dagnino 2005).

It could be argued that the military's fear of Vargas's power in death provoked the coup of March 31, 1964. After a democratically elected president abruptly resigned, he was replaced, as required by the constitution, by his vice president, João Goulart. Goulart was a former minister of labor under Vargas, who had championed raising the minimum wage by 100 percent and called for abandoning literacy requirements which restricted suffrage. While in office, he dared to touch what in Brazil is the third rail of politics: directly appealing to the masses and raising the issue of land reform. Perhaps just as risky, Goulart was accused of encouraging insubordination, telling sergeants that they should disobey their superiors if they believed their orders were not in the best interests of the nation. As one might expect, the military and elites converged against him as Goulart struggled for three years to hold on to power. Conservatives operating with a Cold War lens regarded the president and his followers as evil (anti-business, anti-Christian, and anti-family). The country went into crisis as economic growth averaged near 0 percent and inflation quadrupled—to nearly 100 percent a year. Now even the centrists had turned against him as half a million Brazilians marched in São Paulo, urging the military to "do something" (while foreign investors and the US government cheered them on). This was enough for the military to decide to pull the trigger, and Goulart was promptly shut down as a communist radical threatening to bring a revolution like Cuba's to Brazil (Eakin 1998; Neuhouser 1999).

When the military overthrew the civilian government in 1964, it was not the first time that it had stepped in as the political arbiter (*poder moderador*)—it had "moderated" crises in 1930, 1937, 1945, and 1954. Until 1964 the Brazilian military had been considered relatively tame; except for the establishment of the republic, it never stepped in and stayed in power—until 1964, that is. But that's not all. In 1964 Brazil set the precedent for others. Brazil's military takeover was the first in a chain of coups that followed in South America (and Brazil was last of these countries to come out of its dictatorship) (Eakin 1998).

Brazil's longest-lived democracy had been crushed, and except for some limited violent resistance in the northeast, civil society was incapable of forcing the military back to the barricades. If anything, civil society had egged the coup on.

Starting in 1964, the next five presidents of Brazil were all generals, and although the dictatorship was certainly comparable to those in Argentina and Chile, the difference was that for the Brazilian dictators it was important to at least appear legitimate. More than any other Latin American dictatorship, it continued the tradition of *para inglês ver* and went through a variety of legal acrobatics to present a democratic façade to the world. For example, to maintain a civilian face it kept Congress open throughout most of the dictatorship (although only two parties, described as the party of "sir" and "yes, sir!" were allowed to participate in elections) (Skidmore 1999). As we have seen is so often the case in Brazil, efforts were made to keep up appearances and to dull the sharp edges of what had become a persistent authoritarian tradition (Skidmore and Smith 2005).

However, the façade couldn't hide the fact that the military was governing by fiat, purging the government of "undesirable" elements, creating a secret police, disbanding civil society groups, arresting and imprisoning opponents (Eakin 1998). This period became known as Brazil's "Dirty War," and, according to Vincent (2003), this was a time when citizens felt that they had to either submit or join open revolt. Nearly fifty thousand resisters (and anyone suspected of being a subversive) were harshly punished. During the most intense years of repression, between 1968 and 1973 (with assistance from the US military and CIA), thousands were tortured and hundreds killed; some of them disappeared (Neuhouser 1999).[10] Such behavior wasn't new to Brazil—but the targets were. Some analysts contend that this violence is a legacy of slavery, born out of a disregard for human life. It came as a shock to the nation when the military started targeting the children of the middle class (and sometimes elites): students with the time, education, and financial resources to organize and oppose the dictatorship (Eakin 1998; Skidmore 1999).

As more and more of their young were savaged, even many of the relatively advantaged who had supported the dictatorship turned against it. After a decade in power, there were divides within the military over how to proceed. The soft-liners were able to eventually initiate the *abertura* (or "opening") because

---

[10] According to Brazil's national truth commission report released in 2014, more than 400 people were killed or disappeared during the 1964–1985 dictatorship ("Brazil Truth Commission" 2014).

they were able to persuade the others that they didn't have any solutions to the country's problems—and that the transition to democracy could be carefully controlled. The decision to return to the barracks was also in part due to Brazil's desire for international respectability; the regime was discredited and Brazil wanted to return to the democratic world. With triple-digit inflation, the economy was in a free fall and Brazil's debt was ballooning. After the 1973 and 1979 oil shocks, the government continued to borrow, trying to buy its way out of the crises. As a result, foreign debt grew—from US$3 billion in 1964 to more than US$100 billion in the early 1980s. As interest rates rose, the country became the largest debtor in the developing world—and came perilously close to default (Skidmore 1999).

It is in this context that a long political transition, orchestrated by elites and described by General Ernesto Geisel as "slow, gradual, and certain," began in 1974 and took fifteen years.[11] Civil society pushed for and took advantage of this opening and forced a reconfiguration of state-society relations. According to Dagnino, new parameters were set for the relationship of state and society, as citizens demanded direct participation in shaping the new democracy and expanding what citizenship would mean in Brazil. Citizenship was redefined and previous notions associated with "the culture of gift" (the idea that the only rights most people had were bargains or favors the powerful had granted them) were thrown out (Dagnino 2005). A wide-ranging and unwieldy civil society poured out into the streets: the Church, labor, professional associations, as well as organizations of Indians, blacks, feminists, homosexuals, and students broke with the traditional ethos that had for so long favored individual and family over collective action and was blamed for the problems of strong leaders and personalist politics (Skidmore 1999). In an unprecedented show of force, more than one million people turned out in 1984 as part of the *Diretas Ja!* movement to demand direct elections for president. This was perhaps the culmination of oppositional politics in Brazil's recent history.

But in the end, deals were made in backrooms, and the first president of the new democracy was selected by an electoral college handpicked by the military. This is just one of the many traumas of Brazil's democratic transition, which was not transparent or inclusive. In fact, some analysts consider the democracy to be suffering from a number of birth defects that imperil its quality, if not its longevity. Controlled from the top, the military distorted and delayed the

---

[11] As cited in Skidmore 1999: 186.

democratic process (Skidmore and Smith 2005). The clearest example of this is the general amnesty declared by the military in 1979. Political prisoners were pardoned and their torturers were let off the hook.[12] The military never apologized or atoned for its acts. Brazilians let it go because they feared another military crackdown. More than a decade after the end of the dictatorship, President Lula was careful never to go there. Out of fear of antagonizing the military, he resisted reopening the past.[13] In this way Brazil is unique among its neighbors; Argentina and Uruguay overturned the amnesties that allowed the generals to walk free. Until now, Brazil has never addressed this part of its past; there has been no national process of reconciliation and, many would argue, no healing of Brazilian society. In fact, in its report, the truth commission concludes that illegal arrests, torture, executions, and forced disappearances continue today because the crimes committed under the dictatorship were never denounced, investigated, or punished ("BTI 2012" 2012; Filho 2012; "Brazil's Truth Commission" 2014).[14]

However, analysts contend that a decade ago, such a report would have been unthinkable, and that even if no one is ever held accountable, the release of a report like this is "a historic development in the consolidation of Brazilian democracy"(Romero 2014). Perhaps this accommodating approach makes sense for Brazil. It may be what allowed the democracy to survive and grow. As mentioned, Brazilians value adaptation, creative solutions, agility, and managing change. Instead of the rigid enforcement of rules, Brazilians prefers a *jeito*, a "fix" or pragmatic solution that is helpful to both sides (Eakin 1998). The people got a democracy, and the military will never have to answer for its sins. But this flexibility, this culture of bending the rules, which exists at every level of society and in every branch of government, contributes to a significant problem with impunity ("Fernando Henrique Cardoso on Brazil's Future" 2012). Compromise is necessary for democracy, but so is accountability. If the rules are bent so much that they're nearly useless, the result can be a low-quality democracy.

---

[12] A similar collective amnesia occurred after the end of slavery, as nothing was done to compensate former slaves for their treatment.

[13] Although a truth commission was finally convened by Dilma Rousseff's government in 2011, she made it clear that the amnesty deal would hold and there would be no prosecutions.

[14] The commission identifies 377 people as responsible for human rights abuses. It maintains that the amnesty is invalid because of the grave nature of the crimes and contends that 100 of those still alive should be brought to trial ("Brazil's Truth Commission" 2014; Romero 2014).

The *Partido dos Trabalhadores* (PT): From Society to State

It is ironic now, but before it became the state, low-quality democracy, particularly in the form of corruption, was exactly the problem that the *Partido dos Trabalhadores*, the PT, promised to fix. As a political party, the PT was long considered unusual because of its base in the unions and its history of alliances with social movements. There were always doubters, but many Brazilians respected it for being democratic in its internal organization and relatively "clean," or uncorrupt. It has lost much of that luster since winning the presidency more than a decade ago, but it is (arguably) the dominant party in Brazilian politics and it is the only one with a strong and specific ideology.[15] Although the PT has changed over time, its two major priorities have been 1) a commitment to socialism and redistributive policies that favor the interests of the poor, and 2) an effort to institutionalize popular participation in decision making, namely inclusion of citizens in consultative processes that create social consensus and build civil society "ownership" of government policy (Hochstetler 2003).[16]

The PT got its start in Brazil with the unions and it was one of an array of groups, including the Catholic Church, that joined together during the period of political opening (known as the *abertura*) in the 1970s. A lively, highly inclusive civil society formed in defiance of the decade-old military dictatorship and in the midst of an economic crisis. Many different groups that had often been on opposing sides coalesced into an oppositional movement that demanded citizenship and the right to participate in decision making (Hochstetler 1997; Foller 2010). With the reestablishment of democracy in 1989, many of these groups supported the PT in subsequent elections and were thrilled by Lula's eventual election to the presidency in 2002.

But many feared that under the façade of democracy, Lula's win would fall in with the elite tradition of accommodating just enough change to neutralize

---

[15] Since it won the presidency in 2002, PT politicians and party officials have been caught up in a number of corruption scandals and several of President Lula's closest aides were found guilty of misconduct. Lula survived the scandals and managed to be reelected and at first Dilma worked hard to rebuild the PT's reputation, sacking several corrupt ministers. Not all Brazilians have been persuaded. They disagree over whether the PT is different than the rest, whether the system has changed the PT, or whether the PT is doing the best it can under the circumstances (and given the prevailing political culture) (Bourne 2009).

[16] It should be noted that for many years there have been divides within the PT over how fast and how far to go in promoting change. Some leftists have broken away from the PT to form their own parties and challenge it.

the possibility of real change. Lula was elected—but was it because elites *let* Lula win? Was he co-opted? It took this former metalworkers' union leader, long considered a radical firebrand, four tries (1989, 1994, 1998, 2002) before he was elected president. Lula knows his history and surely recalls Goulart's political demise as a cautionary tale. Just before the 2002 elections, as Lula was rising in the polls, the stock markets teetered. The candidate, who had campaigned to end dependency on the International Monetary Fund (IMF), attended meetings with its representatives and ended up promising to honor the country's commitments to calm the markets (Muello 2002). In the end a pragmatist, Lula made a deal (and has been excoriated by the left for it, the resulting policies derided as "Lula lite"). But part of Lula and his party's calculus had to be the worry that if the poor did make use of their political power, it might not be tolerated by elites—Lula could suffer Goulart's fate—and the democracy overturned. Lula and his advisers were certainly aware that even though the democracy appeared to be consolidating, this was a risk, since over the course of Brazil's history, any significant change in the status quo has always been blocked (Neuhouser 1999).

People disagree about what actually happened behind the scenes in 2002 in Brazil. We do know that Lucky Lula (as he is known) went on to accommodate internal and external elite concerns while presiding over one of the greatest periods of economic expansion in the country's history. As president he went on with social welfare programs that lifted millions out of poverty. This is a huge triumph for Brazil and perhaps a sign that change is possible. But was he permitted to extend this assistance because elites recognized these reforms as a means of co-opting (and quieting) the masses—and thus offsetting larger, structural change?[17]

At least at the highest levels of government it appears that much has changed; every Brazilian president elected since 1994 had at one time been considered by the dictatorship an enemy of the state: Fernando Henrique Cardoso was forced into exile, Luiz Inácio "Lula" da Silva was arrested as a union leader, and Dilma Rousseff was imprisoned and tortured at age twenty-two for being a member of a guerrilla group (Peixoto 2012).[18] Fifty years ago, no one would have ever expected anyone like them to be president. And today, the only parties that have a shot at being elected to the presidency in the foreseeable future

[17] Some wonder if the limited reforms the PT government has enacted can be sustained. Perhaps the best test will come now that times are lean.

[18] Brazilians commonly refer to politicians by their first names or nicknames; Lula and Dilma are both widely used tags for the presidents.

are center-left or left (social democratic and democratic socialist) that would likely maintain Lula's social welfarist programs. Therefore, despite all the talk about the ingenuity of elites or complex, "multiple political and social forces," it would go too far to say that Brazil is unchanged (Shifter 2014). Although a 2014 poll showed that most Brazilians want improvements in the way the country is being managed, it is more democratic than it has ever been (Watts 2014a). The middle class has grown, and poverty and inequality have declined. But massive inequality persists, old patterns of corruption such as clientelism remain (in which politicians and clients trade favors), and structural trans- formations (such as agrarian reform) that would deepen the democracy have largely been avoided. There have been changes, but those that we are seeing have not greatly impinged on the prerogatives of elites (Eakin 1998). Although they've made a real difference in many Brazilians' lives, one could argue that these changes amount to an alteration that has only staved off substantive, transformative change and shored up the status quo.

Besides dealing with elites, another part of the challenge for the PT has been dealing with society. Upon Lula's election, leftist civil society had high expectations; they believed they shared the same agenda as the state and used protests as pressure to help him stick to that shared agenda in the face of con- servative opposition. A new political culture has emerged as civil society in Brazil has been unusually active, participating in developing, implementing, and co-managing public policy (Friedman and Hochstetler 2002; "BTI 2012" 2012; Foller 2010). In many ways, it would be hard to find a state more recep- tive to society than that headed by the PT.

But the relationship between parties and their allied social movements of- ten becomes more conflictual once the party is in power, and this is true of the PT and one particular organization. For years Brazil's Landless Workers Move- ment (*Movimento dos Trabalhadores Rurais Sem Terra*, or MST) had a close rela- tionship with the PT, as forces of the opposition joined against the dictatorship. Using confrontational tactics such direct action, the MST demands agrarian reform, the most highly contested of all issues in Brazil. The MST has never sought to become a traditional party; rather, it has always prided itself on its autonomy and has consciously rejected the idea of becoming imbedded within the state, or trying to influence it from within (Fernandes 2009). This modern peasant movement is seeking not just agrarian reform, but much more than this: a wide-ranging social revolution. At its peak it had one to two million members throughout nearly every Brazilian state and was considered the largest social movement not only in Brazil but probably on the continent ("Introduction:

Lula's Legacy" 2011; Carter 2010; "Mass Favela Eviction Highlights Squatters" 2012). The MST has become powerful for its ability to mobilize people and its long-sustained mobilizations, as well as its "unruly" tactics. These include direct action in the form of high-profile protests and acts of civil disobedience such as land occupations (Carter 2010; Landertinger 2009).

As one might expect, the MST has had a confrontational relationship with every Brazilian government—and this includes its old ally, the PT. To be clear, the PT is still on the left, but its repertoire has changed and its shift to the right not only alienated the MST, but it has radicalized some environmentalists and others who have turned to open opposition against many of the government's plans. Few would have guessed it fifteen years ago, but the most oppositional groups today facing down the PT are not on the right, but on the left: those who feel abandoned by the PT government (Fellet 2013). The PT was supposed to be different, "cleaner" than all the rest.

In many ways the PT's problems are Brazil's problems. Many people who thought the PT and democracy offered the solution are increasingly disillusioned with both. The democracy has survived several blows—including an impeachment and a debt crisis—but the PT has turned out to be like all the other parties and has survived multiple corruption scandals. The scandals of 2015 are said to be some of the worst yet. It's not a surprise that Brazilians display widespread cynicism about politics and distrust institutions, but what is interesting is that the number of Brazilians who say that democracy is preferable to any other form of government has risen steadily, from 35 percent in 2003 to 49 percent in 2013 and since ("The Latinobarómetro Poll" 2013). Despite its problems, Brazil's democracy is considered "locked in," consolidated. But is it deepening, improving in quality (Diamond 2014)?

Advocates of democracy are gladdened to see the steady improvement in these numbers, but the poll also indicates that more than half of those surveyed are clearly unhappy with democracy in its present form—and they're probably not all far-right-wingers. For the millions of Brazilians that turned out into the streets in 2013, the issue was actually non-partisan—it was a crisis of legitimacy. It is because there had been a long-festering crisis of legitimacy that what started out as a localized and specific demand to reduce the price of public transport rapidly became a nationwide movement with a long list of demands all targeting the quality of the Brazilian democracy—no doubt aggravated by the slowing of the economy (Sola 2013).

In many ways, the period leading up to the World Cup may well be recognized one day as a critical juncture for Brazil; the interchange of state and society during this period may well have altered the country's political trajectory in ways that we can only surmise. Despite the furor associated with the World Cup, the PT managed to hold on to power (Shifter 2014). The 2014 election for the presidency was cast as an ideological battle drawn along class lines, but it turned out to be a bitter race for the presidency between parties that have only become more alike over the years. Both the center-left incumbent and the Brazilian Social Democracy Party's Aécio Neves, her center-right rival in the runoff, promised to maintain popular anti-poverty programs. With both parties smeared by corruption allegations, the biggest difference between the two was economic policy, and investors made it clear that they blamed her for the country's economic woes and much preferred Neves's pro-market approach. In the weeks leading up to the election, markets dropped precipitously whenever she rose in the polls and rebounded whenever Neves took the lead. Feeling the pressure, Dilma found herself in the position her mentor Lula had encountered in 2000, pledging reforms to open the economy and keep investors happy (Shifter 2014). In the runoff election, Dilma just squeaked by, winning 51 percent of the vote. But in the end, many Brazilians were asking themselves whether it matters who wins elections ("Brazil Elections" 2014). Brazil doesn't have to worry about a democratic breakdown or failure per se, but the democracy is showing signs of wear and corruption is a big part of it.

Does the passing of another election just amount to politics as usual? Now, after more than a decade in power, the question remains whether the PT has changed politics in Brazil as much as it has been changed by them. Some might call it accommodation, but just as the PT absorbed what were leading oppositional groups, the state machinery may have absorbed the PT. As we have seen, this accommodation is an identifiable pattern in Brazil's history, it is a hallmark of elite survival, and as we will continue to identify this tendency in the chapters to follow. That's the common denominator behind the shared frustration expressed in the demonstrations since 2013; it is an aversion to politics as usual—and democratic decay—that is bringing so many disparate individuals into the streets (Sola 2013). Today's lively civil society is perhaps the saving grace of the democracy; it serves as a counterbalance to the social and political forces that stand in the way of a democratic deepening. This is just the latest iteration of a long standoff. As we go on to assess the push and pull of state and society in Brazil, we must keep in mind the patterns that run through the country's history and that continue to shape it.

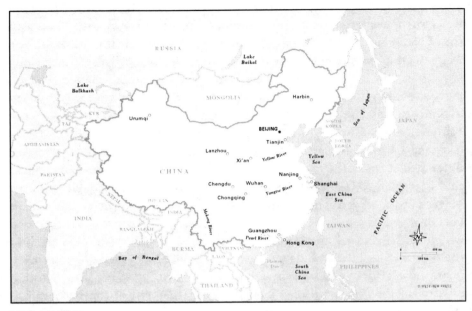

MAP 2.2 China

CHINA

China is marked by centuries of grandeur and achievement, followed by periods of significant upheaval, change, and contention. The Chinese narrative centers on its status as a unique mix of ancient and modern. It points to the country's longevity as one of the world's longest continuous civilizations and in the same breath highlights China as an example of what "modern" can mean in the early twenty-first century. As the 1949 Chinese communist revolution nears its seventh decade, its legacy, in many ways, becomes even more carefully defined by those most vested in promoting its gains.

Approach to the Past: "Middle Kingdom" Complex

The Chinese pride themselves on being recognized as the world's longest continuous civilization, dating back, depending on how you measure it, nearly five thousand years and encompassing not only one of the world's greatest ancient civilizations, but also one of the world's three classic social and political revolutions (Skocpol 1979). China is often celebrated as a mixture of young and old, most visibly highlighted in the hyperbolic opening ceremonies of the 2008 Summer Olympic Games. The grand event, orchestrated by China's famed film producer Zhang Yimou, and initially supported by American producer Steven Spielberg (who later withdrew as an artistic adviser to protest China's role in Darfur, Sudan), emphasized the official narrative of cultural diversity and achievements of Chinese civilization.

The celebrated accomplishments of China's official history include the unification of prior defense systems into what became known as the Great Wall of China, the creation of the Grand Canal (during the Sui Dynasty, 589–618), and the formal linkages established with peoples west of China by way of the Silk Road, during the subsequent Tang Dynasty (618–907). As the so-called Middle Kingdom (*Zhong Guo*), China dominated regional affairs, expanding its influence in Korea, Vietnam, Mongolia, and Central Asia as suzerain states: they maintained internal autonomy while having the bulk of their foreign policy significantly influenced by the Chinese Empire. This system, referred to as the "tribute system," involved complex rituals of exchanges of goods and loyalty pledges, meant to broker relations with foreigners in ways that would support Chinese political worldviews. It had mutual recognition (and, at least for a while, benefits). For example, as Britain was attempting to limit Russia's expanding influence in East Asia in the late 1880s, they negotiated with Chinese, rather than Korean, authorities, on the status of Korea (Chu and Liu 1994). Diplomatic protocol called for the performance of the *kowtow* (literally "knock head") by anyone approaching the Imperial staff with a request—even between heads of state. In 1793, Lord George Maccartney, the ambassador designate from King George III, stubbornly refused to kowtow, but rather agreed to bow on one knee to the Emperor as he would to King George (all of his requests on behalf of the British crown were denied and he returned home with no concessions). Maccartney observed that the Chinese Empire, though strong at the time, faced significant internal weaknesses that would be its undoing (Spence 1990). The Chinese imperial system stretched from approximately 221 BCE to 1911 CE. Imperial China crafted a legacy of self-importance and brutality from the beginning—the self-proclaimed "First Emperor of Unified China," Qin Shihuangdi (c. 260–210 BCE), ordered servants and artisans responsible for building his tomb, the famed terra-cotta soldiers in Xi'An, buried so as to guard the secret of its existence. It worked—the artifacts remained mostly undisturbed until 1974.

Chinese imperial society was vastly unequal: the emperor was framed as the son of heaven (with authority stretching wide and vast, incorporating *tian xia*, "all under heaven"). A small minority held economic, legal, and political dominance over the vassals who worked the land in exchange for meager subsistence. Socio-economic divisions bred resentment and anger that spilled over into support for the uprisings and, later, revolution. It was also used to help justify brutality in the name of breaking the backbone of resistance as well. Imperial China was marked by rebellions—many local, some more widespread—that were symbolic of deep underlying discontent. The eruptions often lacked stated grievances or goals, but indicated both distrust and empowerment. The Qing Dynasty was marked by ever-increasing rebellions, especially in the later eighteenth century, made worse by the foreign presence of the British and others after 1840.

Throughout Imperial China, the vast majority of individuals lacked any rights to land ownership, a custom that continues today as even home owners only lease the land upon which their structure is built. The unequal social, economic, and political relations that persist today in modern China—despite CCP rhetoric to the contrary—are re-created manifestations of the deep divisions that have long marked Chinese society. Although the economy was not nearly as dependent upon it as in other places, slavery in China dates back to the Shang Dynasty (c. 1600 BCE–1046 BCE) and was often used as a punishment for rebellion. Slaves were either privately held or viewed as property of the government, with the former being concentrated in domestic labor as a form of status for their owners (Watson 1976). Eunuch labor was used for many of China's massive public works projects, from the terra-cotta soldiers in Xi'An to the Grand Canal. Slave trading was prominent along Silk Road markets, and foreign expeditions captured prisoners, men and women alike. It was also common for debtors to repay their arrears by offering themselves or their children as payment. Chinese "coolies" (*ku li*, literally "bitterly hard use of strength") were sent to Peru, Cuba, and British colonies throughout the late 1700s and early 1800s, especially after the opening of the Treaty Ports following the Opium Wars, discussed below. They were often abducted or deceived by dishonest labor agreements, and many endured a grueling Pacific Passage journey during which death was common (Yun 2008). After 1865, coolies worked on both the US Transcontinental Railroad and the Canadian Pacific Railway. The law abolishing slavery was passed during the last dynasty of China, in 1906, and took effect in early 1910, although slavery persisted throughout the following half century and continues today. Estimates are that there are nearly three million individuals living in slavery or slave-like conditions today in China (thirty million worldwide), facing domestic servitude, forced begging, and sexual exploitation, including forced marriage ("2.9 Million Trapped," 2013).

Social stratification was also reinforced by a widespread system of landlord control over crops that existed for much of China's imperial period, with the employment of peasant laborers to cultivate the fields. Although some scholars have hesitated to call this a feudal system, it is clear that mobility, access to wealth, and prestige were structurally defined throughout the Chinese imperial period. Not all peasants, however, were landless or poor. Millions of peasant proprietors owned more than they needed, turning often to seasonal laborers for support, and due to great diversity in rural China, it was often difficult to distinguish between landlords and peasants (Spence 1990).

However, politically, for all of the images of central control that we may hear about in Imperial China, a truer expression of power relations is captured in a common saying from the time, "The sky is high and the emperor is far away." This slogan conveys the lack of capacity for the center to be able to control affairs far away. Through the years, the impact of this reality has been the legacy of local interpretation of central mandates, subnational power brokers, and emphasis on local conditions that were highlighted by the CCP in its early years, especially in the base areas it used to be able to gain early experience in governing. This focus on local conditions and local interpretations of central mandates continues to dilute central leaders' initiatives to attempt to resolve vexing social and political challenges (i.e., corruption).

China's global stature as the Middle Kingdom was significantly enhanced by its maritime technology, especially the reach of its navy into Arabia and East Africa. However, it was during the middle of the Ming Dynasty (1368–1644), that the Chinese Imperial system began to erode, in large part, torn apart by corruption, infighting, and epidemics of disease (Spence 1990). The descent of the Middle Kingdom accelerated as rulers lacked a clear vision forward in the face of a rising West, and subsequent dynasties failed to foster a strong sense of legitimacy. As the Western world began to advance deeper into Asia, incorporating advanced weaponry and "modern" scientific ways, China's perch at the top of the international spectrum significantly slid. This led to the view that is widely held today—China suffered unjustly at the hands of Western imperialist powers.

China was never a formal colony; Sun Yatsen (the first president and founding father of the Republic of China) called it a "hypo-colony," and Mao Zedong referred to China before the 1949 revolution as a "semi-colony" (Hayford 1996, 140). Yet the creation of so-called "treaty ports" after two humiliating losses to the British in the late 1800s separated a significant portion of China's commerce-generating region from Beijing, placing these concessions under the legal authority of Western powers and establishing a system of legal extraterritoriality, essentially the application of foreign laws on Chinese soil.

Combined with the political separation of Taiwan, Hong Kong, Macau, and portions of Manchuria, the Chinese experienced a palpably decreased ability to control their own fate.[19] The dominant concession powers (Australia, Britain, France, Japan, Russia, and the United States) created enclaves of influence in major Chinese cities, treating the Chinese as second-class citizens, at best, in their own country. China as "Middle Kingdom" had long been sought after for its luxurious silk, jade, porcelains, and silk, and as Western empires sought a foothold in Asia, China's ability to resist outside pressures began to collapse, inaugurating China's so-called "Century of Shame" (or humiliation) in the mid-1800s, during which Imperial Chinese leaders were forced to concede territory and authority to outside countries, including Japan, Britain, France, Russia, and others.

Even though Christian missionaries had a long-established presence in China (the famed Jesuit missionary, Matteo Ricci, lived in China from 1583–1610), as we have seen in Brazil and elsewhere, religion became an important tool for the cultivation of influence across the country. Foreign Christian missionaries, especially because of their dominance within the publishing sector, ended up being a primary conduit of modern knowledge in the late 1800s. Christian missionaries were also the main providers of health care and modern medicine until the early 1920s, and were active in the discussions about women's rights, including calling for the end of concubinage,[20] foot-binding, and infanticide (Hunter 1989; Spence 1990).

The missionary presence became indelibly associated with the treaty ports (viewed by most Chinese as unequally imposed on a weak and ineffectual government), extraterritoriality (foreigners living in China were immune from Chinese laws and enjoyed the protections and exemptions of their home

---

[19] The term "treaty ports" implies that outside control over major cities of China was established by formal diplomatic treaties and that the locations were commercial towns along waterways. Some of these areas, however, included remote inland towns in the northeast, and not all jurisdictions were established by formal treaties. In addition to the more than forty cities that were designated as formal "ports," there were formal "possessions" of territory that had been ceded in perpetuity, as well as multiple areas that were formally leased from the Chinese government (but which nominally remained under the sovereign control of Beijing). See Hutchings 2001, 436–439.

[20] Concubinage refers to an ongoing sexual relationship outside of marriage, usually between two people who cannot be married due to differences in social class. Concubines were common throughout Imperial China, and some, including Empress Dowager Cixi, rose to political prominence (although most always remained subordinate to wives and many were treated as prostitutes).

country), and China's decline. Anti-Western sentiment became closely connected to anti-Christian views, to very violent ends. The Boxer Rebellion of 1899–1900 serves as a symbol of how weak and disunified China had become. Foreigners rushed to partition China, drought increased the popular sense of crisis, and self-proclaimed "Boxers," one of many secret societies flourishing at the time, mobilized to vanquish foreign missionaries and restore order, in an attempt—supported by the Empress Dowager Cixi at one point—to rid China of all "foreign tormentors" (Spence 1990: 47–48).

Mao Zedong was known to favor a popular slogan from the Qing Dynasty (1644–1912) that captures the official approach to China's long history: "*Gu wei jin yong, yang wei zhong yang*," ("Make the past serve the present, make foreign things serve China").[21] In a nutshell, this has been the official Chinese perspective on the past. Chinese government and society are very conflicted about the history of the People's Republic of China and the periods that predated the People's Republic. The official version includes the glories of the CCP and its triumph over warlords, imperialism, and the Nationalist Party (GMD), as well as the much-vaunted "liberation" of the people since 1949.[22] As we discuss below, China's revolutionary heritage and its status as one of the three classic social revolutions are fundamental aspects of its identity and political culture, both in acquiescence and rejection. Citizens have digested the official version of history and, especially since the age of the Internet, reconcile their understanding of history and contemporary events with that of the official record. As the opening line at the top of this chapter suggests, the Chinese have—uncomfortably at times—invented, rejected, and transformed competing versions of past achievements and challenges.

The status of heroes in China is again one of official versus popular, although it is difficult to overstate the importance—both positively and negatively—of Mao Zedong as a domineering figure. One journalist referred to Mao as "George Washington, James Dean and Che Guevara wrapped in one" (Barboza 2006). Mao's legacy is still a delicately sensitive topic in official circles

---

[21] Cited in McGregor 2005, 20.

[22] *Jiefang*, or "liberation," is a very loaded term within official Chinese circles, and is commonly used to express the official view that the CCP removed the shackles of feudalism, capitalism, and corruption that imperial powers and the GMD had imposed upon the Chinese people. It is common within Chinese discussion of history to refer to the period after 1949 not by year but by the phrase *jiefang yihou*, or "after liberation." The military forces of the CCP, known prior to 1949 as the "Red Army," became formally known as the People's Liberation Army (PLA), terminology that is continued today.

today. His body continues to lie in state along the edge of Tiananmen Square for all to view, and his official portrait hangs below the point where the Chairman, once an unimportant librarian at the rear of the room during the early CCP discussions in the 1920s, declared that the Chinese had "stood up" to the evils of imperialism and announced the commencement of the People's Republic of China.[23] Mao's legacy has proven vexing at best for the CCP, as he not only led his people to moments of great achievement, including the defeat of the GMD, victory over Western forces in Vietnam, and eventual opening with the United States, but also to periods of nearly unspeakable horror. This includes the devastating human-made famine and aftermath of 1958–1962, which claimed anywhere between twenty and forty-five million deaths (Dikötter 2010a). It also must include the scourge of the so-called "Great Proletarian Cultural Revolution" that launched China into a ten-year internal struggle that at times mimicked a civil war, with revolutionary youth empowered to overturn party elders and all forms of authority, zealous "Red Guards" preaching the virtues of the Chairman's wisdom, and families separated for years, some never to reunite. After Mao's death in 1976, the country was plunged into official mourning, and an imposingly massive memorial hall was built to house his remains—citizens traveled from all across China in order to join the "voluntary labor" brigades that were designed to help with the rapid construction, and materials from every region of the country, including sands from the Taiwan Strait, were included in the final product. The mausoleum was built on the old central axis radiating from the Forbidden City. The CCP Central Committee, embroiled in fierce succession battles to replace the Chairman (since his first anointed successor, Lin Biao, had been killed in an airline crash that remains shrouded in mystery, and Mao had purged his second in command, Deng Xiaoping, twice during the Cultural Revolution), formally declared in 1981 that Mao was 70 percent correct and 30 percent incorrect, with most of the mistakes being made during the latter years of his life (Spence 1990).

If there is another hero to be considered within the reaches of China's lengthy history, it would be Confucius, known within China as Kong Fuzi, or Kongzi. Similar to other great sages throughout history, his impact was not realized until long after his death, but his ideas on the proper relationships

---

[23] While Mao has long been credited with these words on October 1, 1949, most accounts are that he had actually delivered this part of the famed speech in June 1949, at the opening of the Chinese People's Political Consultative Conference, during which the CCP was formally "elected" as the ruling country. See Chen 2009.

between individuals within society, the importance of morality, benevolence, and reciprocity, and the centrality of promoting harmony within society emblazoned an indelible mark on Chinese society and much of East Asia. Many of the commonly cited characteristics of Chinese political culture have their roots in Confucian principles, including respect for family, elders, and authority; the tendency to foster personal relations rather than relying primarily on rules and regulations; and the dominance of hierarchical relations and rank. Policy impacts of Confucianism included the creation of civil service exams for public service, effectively opening up careers in government to individuals from all walks of life as long as they had the intellectual capacity to pass rigorous exams, with quotas for the number of candidates designated at each level (district, provincial, and metropolitan). Throughout society, the values and ideals associated with Confucianism—as an approach to life—gradually became informally adopted as a metric by which personal and social relationships should be evaluated. After being declared the state philosophy in the Han Dynasty (206 BCE–220 CE), Confucianism, as an ideology that glorified achievements of the past, was criticized during the intervening years between the collapse of the imperial system and the commencement of the PRC as being one of the sources of China's relative backwardness. It was even more formally denounced as feudal and counterrevolutionary—largely because of the CCP emphasis on struggle and conflict—by the CCP after 1949. Regime leaders approached Confucianism inconsistently through the years, violently condemning it during the Cultural Revolution in the late 1960s, then cautiously embracing it as a tool to help unify overseas Chinese and "Taiwanese compatriots" in the 1970s and 1980s. More recently, some leaders welcome Confucian images as evidence of China's grand civilization, couching the major "soft power" efforts to promote a kinder, gentler image of the Chinese abroad through the officially government-sponsored "Confucius Institutes." This is akin to similar government efforts such as the British Council, Alliance Française, and Goethe-Institut, yet housed within universities, colleges, and some secondary schools.[24] Still, even this more recent embrace was cautionary. The seventeen-ton bronze Confucius

---

[24] Confucius Institutes are formally affiliated with the PRC Ministry of Education and the Office of Chinese Language Council International, and are established to promote Chinese language and culture, as well as other forms of educational exchange. Founded in 2004, within their first decade 440 Confucius Institutes have been established in 120 countries—with the United States hosting the greatest number. For more information, including some of the controversy surrounding their operations, see Chen 2014.

statue that was erected on Tiananmen Square stood for less than four months in 2011 before it was removed in the cover of darkness. This exemplifies the unease with which current CCP leaders approach this great hero of Chinese civilization (Jacobs 2011a).

Violence and turmoil are firmly ingrained in China's past—even prior to the civil war and revolutions that marked the early twentieth century. One observer stated, "Viewing the history of China in the past two centuries, one is struck by the turmoil, disorders, violence, and destruction Chinese people have endured" (Nie 2005, 252). The Chinese have long accepted the reality of *chi ku*, or "eating bitterness," and there has been much hardship to swallow. This is especially true for peasants and ethnic minorities, despite the claim of every Chinese government in the modern era labeling China as a unitary, multinational state. Although less numerous than the dominant Han ethnic group, national minorities in China inhabit approximately 60 percent of China's total land area, albeit in much less dense concentrations than we find in the areas populated by the majority Han (Hutchings 2001). As we discuss in chapter 4, ethnic harmony continues to be more of an aspiration than a realization within contemporary China, especially when these boundaries intersect with religious and economic cleavages.

Authoritarian traditions marked China's history—throughout the dynasties and in modern times as well. Social, family, and interpersonal relations in China were long hierarchical and unequal, with rigid senses of how best to promote harmonious relations among groups. Economically, China has been influenced by millennia of uneven sharing of resources, a feudal history that the Chinese Communist Party of today likens to caricature, despite the lasting nature of the divide between the landed and the landless. China has always struggled with population-land pressures, and, despite the many promises of elites of all stripes who saw the challenge before them, the problem has mostly worsened, even today. Social stratification based on gender, race, and ethnicity dominated most of China's modern history, and individuals lacked any sense of rights. As we discuss throughout this book, the struggle to gain rights continues in earnest.

Revolution(s)

With China, we can talk not of one but rather multiple revolutions: the 1911 revolution that overthrew the Qing Dynasty, the 1949 revolution that ushered in the People's Republic of China, and the devastating internal revolution known as the Great Proletarian Cultural Revolution, from 1949–1976. Each has left an indelible mark, especially in terms of interactions between rulers and ruled.

The first of these revolutions, known as the Republican Revolution of 1911, succeeded in eventually uniting many of the disparate groups opposed to the Qing Dynasty to declare the commencement of the Republic of China on January 1, 1912. This revolution brought together everything from secret society organizations to nascent political parties, merchant groups, and local militias to overthrow a weakened and decaying monarchy. Political structures changed more rapidly than social structures, especially as unity became a lofty aspiration that was evermore challenging to achieve. The country devolved into regional and provincial blocs, dominated by warlords and local armies and widespread rural unrest. In the Republican period that followed the 1911 revolution, many alliances and parties rose to the fore—most notably the GMD (formed in 1912 out of Sun Yatsen's United League—that began in 1905) and the CCP (founded in 1921). The socio-political climate of China after the 1911 revolution was one of chaos and dislocation, combined with grinding poverty; many believed the renowned Middle Kingdom would simply cease to exist, and one of the world's grand civilizations would splinter, as all that had held the Chinese order together seemed to wither away (Lieberthal 2004, 26), launching a "period of political insecurity and unparalleled intellectual self-scrutiny and exploration" (Spence 1990, 271).

The 1949 revolution that gave rise to the People's Republic of China was a significant upheaval calling for the remaking of basic social, political, and economic relationships throughout society. Odd for a Marxist-inspired revolution, it invoked nationalism and ended up relying on the peasantry for its base of support. The latter was largely a tactical decision by Mao Zedong, a decision that led to a divisive split within the CCP over its course and future direction. The revolution—which crafted a new state and propelled into power a group of activists who were sorely inexperienced with bureaucracy and governing—led to over three decades of ideological zeal and restructuring that impacted more than one billion people's lives. Even though revolutionary rhetoric may be lost in the twenty-first century, the structures of power and backbone of leadership within the CCP remain indebted to the political currents of the 1940s and 1950s for their source of legitimacy and power.

Mao was nothing if not a revolutionary. Major gains, such as the establishment of the PRC in 1949, only heightened the need for greater vigilance and fervor. Mao believed that every aspect of China, from the most grassroots level up, needed to be completely redone, and in a continuous fashion—the revolution must never end. By 1956, he ordered an end to family farming that had resulted from early CCP land reform policies, setting up massive communes that were supposed to be self-sufficient units of production and administration. The country was plunged into desperation by the late 1950s, after efforts to enforce rapid industrialization produced severe food shortages and the worst human-made famine on record (Dikötter 2010a, 2010b).

Rather than being deterred by the disastrous impact of these excesses, the Chairman ordered the country to "continue the revolution" in which so many people had suffered so greatly. Ideological purity, a shrinking sense of privacy, and paranoia combined with some of the already risk-averse attributes of traditional Chinese culture to produce significant constraints on actors, including many elites. The country was plunged into what would become a decade-long cataclysmic experiment known as the Cultural Revolution.

The Chinese Cultural Revolution, generally dated from 1966 until Mao's death in 1976, is difficult to succinctly characterize. For our purposes here, its importance is in the complete upheaval of all institutional structures and social relations. Mao's original target was the institutional base of the CCP, which he feared had become too bourgeois in the time since the initial revolution. Nonetheless, the impact of turning the party on itself, of promoting an ideology of "it's right to rebel!," and of smashing the organizational base of life throughout the country was a legacy of upheaval, chaos, and distrust that, in many ways, endures today. Some have argued that much of the hardships of the Cultural Revolution, during which many urban youth were sent to the countryside to live and work with peasants, is responsible for planting the seeds of ingenuity and entrepreneurialism that is behind China's rapid modernization in the 1990s and 2000s, as this generation mastered the importance of frugality and craftiness. Society experienced cruelty and oppression on a scale the country had never before seen, and family ties, the most basic social relations (especially in a Confucian-influenced society), were severed in ways that were nearly irrecoverable. Children watched as their parents were paraded in front of jeering groups, and students placed dunce caps on their teachers, humiliating them in front of crowds of onlookers in stadiums and public squares. Suicide was common and very public during the Cultural Revolution, including the joint actions of well-known intellectual couples, faculty members at some of China's most prestigious universities, as well as musicians, artists, and others who were driven to absolute despair, including one of Deng Xiaoping's brothers

(Lester 2005; Coonan 2006). Some accounts estimate that hundreds of people a day took their lives in Shanghai during the early days of the Cultural Revolution (Lester 2005). In terms of historical imprints, it's hard to exaggerate the lasting nature of the cruelty of this lost decade, which not only left China in economic and political shambles but had inflicted deep fissures throughout Chinese society as well.

Recovering state-society relations after the Cultural Revolution is, in many ways, an ongoing task, evidenced in part by the muted national debate about whether or not there should be a central-level museum honoring those lost during the ten-year period.[25] Having nearly destroyed all educational institutions—from primary through post-graduate—for a decade, a generation of young people in China faced a permanent disruption to their formal education. Fields that required technical training were clearly saddled by the absence of properly trained personnel or research. Party elites faced a particularly vexing challenge: attempting to rectify Mao's legacy as the founding father of the state with his commanding role in the chaos of the period.

For all of their differences, the first two generations of PRC elites turned to the masses for support of their policies: Mao by calling on their support for continuous revolution in 1966, and Deng by riding in the wake of a movement that became known as the Democracy Wall. During the winter of 1978–1979, brave individuals, representing a wide swatch of Beijing society, posted essays and testimonials on city walls around Beijing. This became the only outlet by which many blue-collar workers and educated youth could vent their concerns about China's backwardness, and the postings drew large crowds eager to discuss the end of tyranny after Mao and envision a better political future.

At first, the ascendant Deng Xiaoping welcomed the outpouring of popular expressions, as they tended to support his campaign against CCP conservatives who sought to resurrect Maoist forms of struggle. As the calls for change became too bold—one set of posters, penned by Beijing Zoo electrician Wei Jingsheng, argued that China needed to democratize in order to overcome its most basic

---

[25] Even though PRC leaders have rebuffed multiple efforts to establish a national Cultural Revolution museum, a local museum was opened in 2005, led by a former vice-mayor in southern China's Guangdong Province. Although the museum was built without official backing, it receives nearly 1,000 visitors daily (Coonan 2006). A "Virtual Museum of the Cultural Revolution" is maintained online by the editors of China News Digest, http://www.cnd.org/CR /english/.

problems[26]—Deng ordered the posters torn down, with Wei and others arrested as counterrevolutionaries.

If Mao can be characterized as a revolutionary, Deng is best labeled a reformer, in the sense that he called for the end of many of the personalist policies and the cult of leadership that surrounded his predecessor, and attempted to move the country in a more institutionalized fashion. This is not, by any stretch of the imagination, to say that Deng was attempting to democratize Chinese politics. As a Leninist, he firmly believed in the elite character of the party, and of its important role as an unchallenged sense of power. These attributes were most clearly visible during his response to the Democracy Wall, as well as to confrontations between state leaders and demonstrators in Tiananmen Square in the spring of 1989.

Deng was a pragmatic leader who was keenly aware of the exhaustion of Chinese society with the fits and starts of the decades-long revolution and internal strife. As such, he sought to improve people's lifestyles through economic reforms, starting with household farming. Combined with farm irrigation policies and increased payments to farmers, agricultural productivity began to increase, leading to a significant decrease in poverty across following decades. "Reform" became the catchphrase of the period, but it was clear from the outset that reform would be constrained within a limited framework. Much of the political reform initiated during the Deng years—especially attempts to separate CCP and government functions—was thrust into doubt by the massive and widespread demonstrations that gripped China's major cities in the spring of 1989, the most serious challenge to CCP rule since 1949. What made the events so threatening—from the perspective of Party and state leaders—was the range of citizens who participated in the demonstrations in Beijing and nearly every other provincial capital across the country. It wasn't, as many popular accounts tend to emphasize, confined only to rebellious student demonstrators; rather, the protestors included factory workers, doctors, even journalists working for the flagship *People's Daily*, published under the tutelage of the Central Committee of the CCP.

---

[26] Wei's essay, known as the "Fifth Modernization," was a direct challenge to the policy priorities that had been recently announced by the nascent regime, known as the "Four Modernizations" (agriculture, industry, national defense, and science and technology). Wei provocatively signed his essay with his real name and address—rather than anonymously—contending that without the so-called "fifth modernization" of democracy, the other achievements could never be sustained. Wei was arrested and detained from 1979–1993, serving jail time after a brief respite in 1993, until he was exiled to the United States in 1997.

Similar to the Cultural Revolution, CCP leadership has arduously confined the degree to which people can reflect on the reach of the 1989 protests, both in terms of the numbers of people mobilized as well as the wide-ranging nature of their grievances. On mainland China, Internet searches for "Tiananmen Square" or "Tank Man," as the famed lone protestor who challenged the column of tanks advancing on the crowds in Beijing became known, are scrubbed of any unapproved images of the carnage. Even organizers in Hong Kong, a special administrative region of the PRC that is supposed to maintain autonomy over its domestic matters, have had to curtail some of its Tiananmen commemorations, which draw tens of thousands annually. Nevertheless, shortly before the twenty-fifth anniversary of the crackdown in 2014, a tiny museum commemorating the victims—believed to be the only one in the world—opened in Hong Kong (Chan 2014).

Despite attempts to delete all references to the event, individuals and groups remain vigilant in their quest to provide an accurate accounting of deaths from the events, as well as attempts to change the government's official position on Tiananmen. One of the most prominent is the "Tiananmen Mothers" group, co-founded by retired philosophy professor Ding Zilin and Zhang Xianling, whose teenage sons were shot and killed during the massacre. They formed the association, which brought together parents, friends, and relatives of the deceased, in September 1989, when repression remained fierce. They have maintained a steady repertoire of actions that included campaigning, public petitions, even lawsuits against the government. In return, they have received heavy surveillance, police escorts for any travel around Beijing, and travel bans beyond the capital. Some members of the Tiananmen Mothers have been arrested, although such actions have done little to deter their crusade.

Although, as we discussed in the prior section, economic and social groups were often pitted against each other throughout the imperial period, there was little awareness of class consciousness, and class lines were blurred (Spence 1990). In the early to mid-twentieth century, however, the importance of class struggle emerged as a legacy of the Chinese revolution. Contrary to the Confucian emphasis on harmony, Mao highlighted the values of tension and even tense public relations—which went very much against Chinese social convention—as a way to challenge what he perceived to be the passive nature of Chinese society. For Mao, struggle awakened the latent power of Chinese society and mobilized citizens to face injustice. Struggle became a core part of individual and group identity in Maoist China, especially a sense of class struggle that was integral to the revolutionary aim of creating a new identity. Public struggle sessions were known for their violence—during Mao's rule, millions of people died as a direct result of struggle sessions—sometimes pitting family members against each other to test loyalty (Lieberthal 2004).

Even though traditional Marxist class analysis did not really fit the conditions on the ground in China—capitalism was virtually non-existent, and there was little sense of a proletarian class—Mao attempted to force a new, Chinese-style class system that elevated the peasants, who constituted the vast majority of the Chinese population in the 1950s, to the vanguard. He also bypassed the traditional Marxist emphasis on relations to the means of production as the defining aspect of class identity, replacing it instead with political attitude. Again, this led to disastrous consequences, as hundreds of thousands of individuals were labeled in terms that effectively ruined their careers, often significantly impacting their family's well-being as well (Spence 1990). Within the first three years of the establishment of the country, the CCP launched a series of campaigns that established hereditary class and political labels—including the disastrous signifier as a counterrevolutionary—of nearly every rural and urban resident (Lieberthal 2004). Many of the most damaging labels were only formally "lifted" from the dossiers of hundreds of millions of Chinese after 1978, when the significance of "class background" was significantly reduced (Harding 1987, 176).

Another legacy of China's revolutionary heritage is the mobilization of society in order to accomplish defined tasks. The CCP elevated the amorphous "masses" of the country to a preferred position within the revolutionary regime, drawing on popular uprisings in order to significantly reorganize and restructure the entire political, social, and economic order of the state (Pines 2012). The communist revolution aimed to empower precisely those who had become most adept at popular uprising in earlier eras, and then, with the party's guidance (under Maoist principles broadly known as the "mass line") they would become politically active. The mass campaigns that became a hallmark of the first two decades of the PRC were the politicization of citizens on an unprecedented scale (Pines 2012), including the most wide-ranging, and often involuntary involvement of the population in state affairs. After the chaos of the Cultural Revolution, through the Tiananmen Square uprising and even including the contemporary period, mass mobilization—especially in organized ways—has been actively discouraged. As we discuss throughout this book, Beijing has expressed limited receptivity to feedback from citizens, allowing it in carefully approved areas.

Bloodshed, violence, and a mobilized—but largely depoliticized—society have clearly left their mark on contemporary China, and are legacies inseparable from the history of both the revolutionary foundation of the modern state and the CCP. China today maintains an official narrative of a revolution that, in many ways, is not owned by the society in whose name it was crafted.

The CCP: State Management of Society

Authoritarianism has marked the Chinese experience from the dynasties through the contemporary period, with the creation of a one-party state enforcing severe limits on expression and assembly. In most ways, the priorities of the CCP, as both the founding and the ruling party of the PRC, have not significantly changed over the last sixty years: maintain the unity of the nation-state, achieve economic growth, and reinstate China's prior greatness on the world stage. The social alliances fostered by the party, however, have shifted. During the Maoist years (1949–1976), at least in rhetoric, the most important alliance was that between the CCP and the peasants, the standard bearers of the revolution. Loyal CCP members were encouraged and ordered, in the later years of the Cultural Revolution, to emulate the peasants, who, in Mao's view, had never lost their sense of revolutionary zeal. After the tumult of the Cultural Revolution, party leaders had a difficult task rebuilding the fractured country and party, as Deng Xiaoping encouraged the Chinese people to adopt a more pragmatic approach to daily life, boldly proclaiming, "Let one part of the population get rich first." They did and, as such, political and social alliances with the CCP became economic alliances. Looking back on it, it should surprise no one that, in the summer of 2001, in one of last major speeches as CCP general secretary, Jiang Zemin advocated (with the support of even the most conservative members of the powerful Politburo) that private entrepreneurs be permitted to join the Chinese Communist Party (Fewsmith 2002). In many ways, CCP leaders court the most necessary allies to accomplish the tasks before them: peasants made up the majority of the Chinese population in the 1940s (and continued to until 2011) ("China's Urban Population" 2012), as the young country was attempting to transition away from decades of internal strife and chaos. By the time the old revolutionaries were passing the proverbial baton to the younger leaders, China was well on its way to occupying the number two position in the world, at least economically, and capitalism became the blueprint for the party's longevity. As one dues-paying businessman observed at the time, "Our party is doing what it takes to survive. It is attracting the people who have the social status and the economic clout to govern" (Kahn 2002). Class distinctions that had been the primary fuel of the CCP for decades took a backseat to entrepreneurship and financial wherewithal, and the bigger tent of a CCP continued to adapt in order to remain relevant.

This new alliance and embrace of capitalist entrepreneurs by the monopolistic CCP has significantly worsened a challenge that has faced Chinese leaders since long before the 1949 revolution: corruption. Few issues ignite the rage among citizens as the corruption conundrum, yet few issues remain so omnipresent. It may seem surprising that complaints about the corruption of individual leaders are permissible and even encouraged by the regime, as it presents an opportunity for leaders to demonstrate the responsiveness of the system. The challenge becomes where to draw the line, how to keep plucking out the rotten apples without perpetuating the perception that the entire Party is corrupt. Current president and general secretary Xi Jinping, who quickly launched his own anti-graft campaign months into his regime, has reportedly been warned by both of China's living presidents (Jiang Zemin and Hu Jintao) that the campaign Xi has placed at the center of his political consolidation better not reach too deeply into the top tiers of the party, lest it become too destabilizing (Keck 2014).

One aspect maintaining the stability of the single party system in China has been the intimate relationship between the party and the military. Mao's dictum that "the Party commands the gun; we must never allow the gun to command the Party" (Meisner 1986, 72) is as true today as it was during the 1940s. The Tiananmen protests presented the biggest challenge in understanding the role of the military; the open defiance by a major-general who refused to lead troops to clear the square sent tremors through the CCP establishment, which believed a military revolt was at hand (Jacobs and Buckley 2014). Despite, and in part because of, the challenges of 1989, the military's loyalty to the CCP remains staunch—the PLA still mandates classes on "Mao Zedong Thought" for its members (Mu Chunshan 2012).

China never projects the maintenance of a depoliticized military, but rather a party-army. Alignment between the PLA and the CCP maintains stability, and, by all accounts, the PLA exists in order to serve as the guarantor of CCP rule. That is part of the reason why soldiers dedicate time to both military training and "political work," such as study sessions, and all new soldiers swear allegiance to the CCP, rather than to the PRC. All career officers are members of the CCP. Even if many join the CCP for personal gain, the CCP, with more than eighty-two million members, ranks as the largest political party in the world, with membership increasing year after year, even as ideological purity wanes (Yuen 2013). Over 45 percent of the total population, including almost all high school graduates, are members of the Chinese Communist Youth League (CYL), a mass organization in which membership serves as prerequisite for entering the CCP (Yuen 2013).

While in other countries with multiparty systems—or at the least alternations in power—we may talk of shifting alliances with various groups within society, what we can observe in the case of China is the importance of various leadership factions. Recognizing the salience of competing worldviews—even if within a single political organization—is critical to grasping the diversity that exists within this commanding organization. Some factions lean toward the traditionally conservative side of the spectrum, valuing Party orthodoxy and Maoist roots, while others tend toward more business interests or the plight of those left behind in the rush for China's economic growth. Most analysts speak of two significant factions dominating the upper levels of Chinese politics, coining the phrase "one party, 2 coalitions" ("Viewpoint: The Powerful Factions" 2012; Lai 2012). These groupings within the CCP are based less on ideology than patron-client networks, and they maintain their cohesion more for personal advancement than because of policy agreements (Cohen 2012). The so-called "populist" clique of former leaders Hu Jintao and Wen Jiabao (also affiliated with current premier Li Keqiang) is known for advocating for those who have been left behind in China's reform and opening. Generally, the populists have come from less privileged families (although, as was famously reported by both *Bloomberg* and the *New York Times*, their families have certainly benefited from their political rise),[27] and tend to be associated with the influential CYL. The second dominant faction in the contemporary CCP is often referred to as the "elitist" clique, most closely associated with former president and general secretary Jiang Zemin, as well as current president and general secretary Xi Jinping. This clique is sometimes split into the so-called "Shanghai gang" of Jiang and the "Princelings" (those with famous parents who

---

[27] In 2012, both *Bloomberg News* and the *New York Times* were blocked in China after both published reports on the wealth of families of leaders and well-connected individuals, including former prime minister Wen Jiabao, disgraced former leader Bo Xilai, and the then presumptive leader Xi Jinping. Multiple foreign journalists were also denied visas and deported following these incidents, and local agencies were barred from using Bloomberg data in their financial reports.

were influential in the 1949 revolution) of Xi. It can be challenging to discern the dividing lines of these factions, as well as their relative strength at any given time: citizens are not supposed to see possible cracks in Party cohesiveness. Maintaining the appearance of a united front in public has been elevated to the highest importance, especially after visible splits among Party leaders seemed to embolden demonstrators and create a positive political opportunity structure for protest in the spring of 1989.

Despite significant incentives to "play by the rules of the game," the CCP faces more than a few challengers, from a variety of angles. As we will discuss throughout the book, there are many areas in which the regime welcomes citizen input and feedback, as ways not only to demonstrate the legitimacy of Beijing, but also to provide more informed feedback than government bureaucrats themselves would be able to muster (this is especially true for much environmental mobilizing). Still, on sensitive topics—especially related to regime change or independent rights of minorities—protagonists work underground or are forced into permanent exile abroad. Activists who do shake things up in country are viewed as a menace (the architect/artist Ai Weiwei) or as a threat (Liu Xiaobo). In the latter's case, the famous intellectual, who returned to China from abroad at the height of the demonstrations in Tiananmen Square during the spring of 1989, crossed the line by participating in an effort that was seen as a direct challenge to the CCP's monopoly on power. By joining the petition that became known as Charter 08,[28] Liu was arrested at home and honored abroad. He was named the recipient of the 2010 Nobel Peace Prize, which he was not able to personally receive. Liu was one of over 350 signers of the charter, among them individuals from inside the government, as well as former CCP leaders. As this book goes to press, Liu remains in prison and his wife is under house arrest, terms that become more strident as significant anniversaries approach.

Structurally, the regime has attempted to co-opt possible anti-system actors by providing various institutions, most notably the Chinese People's Political Consultative Conference (CPPCC), in which to house the loyal

---

[28] Released on the sixtieth anniversary of the Universal Declaration of Human Rights, this document, initially signed by over 300 activists and intellectuals within China, called for competitive parties, separation of Party and state, and accountability, among other changes. Modeled after the Czech Charter 77, some of the signers included former government officials (Ramzy 2009). It has since been viewed as one of the most broadly based and intellectually sophisticated challenges to CCP dominance since the movement in 1989.

non-opposition parties that exist "in parallel" with the CCP. The CPPCC, which includes representatives of officially recognized national minority groups, religious associations, and various professional groups, meets annually in tandem with the three-thousand-delegate-strong National People's Congress (NPC) meetings each March.

To most observers, both within and outside of China, the impunity of the Party—even after the stains of the Great Leap Forward famine, the Cultural Revolution, Tiananmen Square, and pervasive corruption—is surprising, especially in the era of Web 2.0 social networking. Some of the regime's resilience is in the perceived lack of possibilities for a better model, although this is certainly diminishing as more and more Chinese travel to, study in, and work with democratic countries. The CCP's attempt to broaden its membership to be inclusive of entrepreneurs and capitalists has worked. The lessons of Tiananmen—avoid politics and pursue business—have not been lost on many, including some of the students who initially served as protest leaders (Barboza and Forsythe 2014). And some of it is certainly due to the sense of pragmatism with which many citizens approach the ideologically bankrupt CCP these days: if they want to get ahead, especially in business or politics, the Party is their path.

ANALYSIS

Even for two countries that at face value couldn't seem more dissimilar, history serves as a frame for understanding state-society relations. Two stories compete for our attention, but in each we see the basis for political opportunity structures that have been established over the years, which at the very least will affect—if not determine—outcomes. Sure, Brazil and China are from opposite sides of the globe. One is a relatively young five hundred years old; the other—at five thousand—is perhaps the world's oldest continuous civilization. One, a mélange of American, African, and European cultures, is known for its fascination with the future; the other, with at least an official narrative of homogeneity, has long considered itself the center of the earth.

Brazilians and Chinese both frame their history (and contemporary experiences) in exceptionalist terms. Both states have been significantly impacted by outside control: Brazil by the Portuguese for hundreds of years, China at the hands of European and limited American powers that coincided with the collapse of the imperial system. The social psyche in both cultures has long embraced—or had imposed on them—social hierarchies, with the concomitant acceptance of inequalities. Like arguably every other country on the planet, both have myopic views of their own history; most Brazilians don't recognize their history prior to the arrival of Europeans, and Chinese are woefully ignorant of other cultures, as the official narrative for so long considered non-Chinese to be barbarian. It's hard for outsiders to imagine, but many Chinese today remain extremely unaware—mostly due to censorship—of the brutality of the CCP. Perhaps more than any other social institution or practice, Brazil's lengthy and violent history of slavery left a mark on the country and led to patterns of enduring social inequality (Freyre 1955). This is manifested most distinctly in the myth of racial democracy, but also in its exceptionalist status as Portugal's prodigy. It was, after all, the only colony in the Americas to host its royals, and the only one to be catapulted from status as colony to kingdom, and then empire. China's history of suzerain control throughout East Asia also led to a sense of cultural and moral superiority that was smashed by China's humiliating losses—first to Japan (a former vassal state) and later to Great Britain, resulting in loss of prestige, self-worth, and land. When the Middle Kingdom collapsed and the treaty ports were established, Chinese citizens' supersized sense of identity tumbled with it. This created fertile ground for the rise of nationalist sentiment and pride that continues to gloss over social divisions today.

Likewise, for all their shared history of authoritarianism, hierarchies, and patron-client relations, the lived experience in both states is much more decentralized than most would expect. For hundreds of years in Brazil and thousands in China, the center rarely mustered the capacity needed for control of the interior, and this pattern continues today in both countries. Part of this is perhaps due to their sheer sizes, as well as their diversity. Brazil is often said to be five countries in one and China, unwilling to embrace more than an officially defined diversity, stretches to control and incorporate its distant reaches in Tibet and Xinjiang.

Another similarity is that neither is quite what it professes to be. Brazil claims a uniquely cordial, harmonious, and peaceful history that was actually wracked by spasms of violence. China owns up to the importance of violence in its revolutionary history—Mao, the so-called "Great Helmsman" viewed it as one of the important characteristics of true revolutionaries—but stifles discussion of more contemporary episodes. Both countries have been characterized as historically having passive political cultures—and perhaps with good reason, given that rebellions in both places have been so ferociously crushed. For example, both countries—both in the 1960s—had their witch hunts. Brazil had its Dirty War and China its Cultural Revolution. Unknown numbers were killed, though certainly more in China than in Brazil. But even in the face of state violence, what society in the two countries actually share is the appearance of submission. The give and take between state and society can take a variety of forms, and it has always occurred to a larger extent than the official story allows. So it is misleading to paint society in either country with such a broad brush; we must remember that it may have been orchestrated, but China did have a peasant revolution, and it was ordinary Brazilians who risked their lives to bring down a dictatorship and bring on a democratic transition.

As we will see in the pages to follow, citizens in both countries face and have faced down the state, including the Tiananmen Mothers who try to inform others of the true death toll at the hands of the PLA and militia. These women are placed under house arrest, sent to jail, or otherwise muted. At least in Brazil a national truth commission investigated the crimes of the military dictatorship. It found that illegal arrests, torture, executions, and forced disappearances were performed systematically ("Brazil Truth Commission" 2014). But its report came nearly fifty years after the fact, making Brazil exceptional in that it was the last in South America to unearth the ghosts of its Dirty War. Chinese officials continue to parrot the line that the Party has reached a clear conclusion on the events of 1989, and reject calls to overturn the controversial "counterrevolutionary" verdict on participants and the movement as a whole. The CCP can't risk public discourse on past violent events—including the Cultural Revolution—because the official narrative of the Party may begin to unravel. As mentioned earlier, regardless of the truth commission's findings, no one will ever be prosecuted in Brazil, due to the amnesty law passed by the military government. But there was at least some public recognition of the crimes by the state. President Rousseff (who was tortured by the regime back in the day, as you recall, when she was a young opponent of the government) was willing to go further than her predecessors, who had also been mistreated by the regime. She supported the investigation. But even Dilma didn't protest that this reckoning came with no strings attached. Such restraint suggests the enduring power of the military, even in this consolidated democracy ("Brazil Panel Delivers Report" 2014). Still, it's hard to imagine that a Chinese demonstrator who was officially punished by the regime could ever become a leader of the country. Conversely, it's a sad commentary on the state of affairs that a Brazilian demonstrator tortured by the regime would become the country's president—and change would still come so slowly.

Ultimately, for all the talk about change in these two countries, continuity is the rule in both of them. Brazil's pace of change has been evolutionary—but it has evolved into a democracy that many would argue has only been able to make enough change to keep the most important things as is. China's history, on the other hand, is revolutionary. It claims one of the great social revolutions of the twentieth century, but the gap between rich and poor is perhaps as big—or bigger—than ever. Democratic Brazil ranks even higher than China as one of the most unequal societies in the world. This is particularly ironic in that both Brazil's PT and China's CCP share an identity; in their earlier lives they were oppositional social movements that brought down dictatorships. Today, both countries are led—and are likely to continue to be led—by dominant parties mired in corruption and betting it all on better economic times.[29] Around the world, in dictatorships and democracies, too, we see that parties that stay in power for long uninterrupted periods of time tend to suffer from the same kinds of problems (Altman 2014). But let's be clear: they might have resembled each other when they were society, but otherwise the PT and CCP, in their role as state, could not be more different.

In terms of coincidence, 1989 was a critical juncture for both Brazil and China. For two countries that share so much in common, it is striking how far the two countries have parted ways since then. That year in Brazil, citizens reestablished a democracy and went to the polls to directly elect their government; that year at Tiananmen, in putting down the largest popular movement since the 1949 revolution, the Chinese government made it crystal clear that its citizens would not be afforded the same luxury. Today the dissimilarities between the two states stand clear. Brazil is widely recognized as democratic and China as authoritarian for good reason: in Brazil a variety of institutions limit the powers of the party and government elites, including a lively and increasingly autonomous new media able to expose the government's deficits and a judiciary that has demonstrated its independence on more than one occasion (Sola 2013). That's simply not the case in China.

Therefore, for all our talk about the correspondences between them, we recognize that these are two very different countries. Yes, it is frustrating for many of Brazil's citizens that even with a democracy the most important things

---

[29] No one would argue that the PT and CCP are dominant in the same way, of course. It says a lot about the two parties' differences when one considers why they're dominant. Brazil is not a dominant party democracy; Dilma narrowly won the runoff election in 2014 and not even a year later she had a popularity rating of 8 percent—the worst of any president since 1992—and he was impeached (Winter 2015; Zainulbhai 2015). But her win allowed the PT to continue on for a near-twenty-year hold on the presidency, which may be extended if Lula returns to run for a third term.

continue to go unchanged. Perhaps one could argue that the PT has done all that it can, given its constraints. As we've seen over its history, Brazilian elites have done an impressive job of at staving off real change—and in the long run, perhaps even more effectively than those of the CCP. As hard as it is to imagine, a reading of history suggests that China is more likely to experience transformative change than Brazil. With *para inglês ver*, *jeitos*, and a proclivity for finding an accommodation, Brazil's rulers have proven to have had more success in offsetting change than China's. Although Brazil's history is about reinvention while China's is arguably more about transformation, in many ways the CCP has become just another dynasty, a status quo power fighting to hold on in a country with a history of bringing down even formidable powers. In the meantime, keeping in mind how the past provides the political opportunity structure for all that has happened since, let us turn next to a more contemporary comparison of state-society relations in Brazil and China and consider, now a quarter century on, how the events of 1989—when one state opened the door to democracy and the other attempted to slam it shut—may have had significant, long-term consequences in these countries.

DISCUSSION QUESTIONS

1. Both Brazil and China are said to have lengthy, complicated, and contentious histories. Which aspects of their histories are the most complicated and the most contentious? Explain why, offering examples. How has the past shaped contemporary debates in the two countries?

2. If countries are products of their histories, what would you expect relations between state and society to be like in Brazil and China today, given those histories? Compare the role of elites historically in the two countries, as well as the role of society and state-society relations. Has either (or the relationship between the two) changed substantially over time? If so, when—and how?

3. What has—and hasn't—changed in Brazil and China over the years? In other words, what are these countries' most significant historic legacies? Are they significantly different? Are they interchangeable? Explain.

4. Especially over the last few decades, Brazil and China have experienced a remarkable coincidence of events. Both Brazil and China experienced upheaval and violence in the 1960s, transitions in the 1970s, and reforms since the 1980s. The year 1989 marked a critical juncture in the histories of both countries. Identify and discuss the significance of the events of 1989 as well as major turning points in each country's history. Could it be argued that these events serve as prequels, necessary for understanding state-society relations today?

5. Compare and contrast the Workers' Party (PT) and the Chinese Communist Party (CCP) on their origins as society and transformation as state. How much have they changed? Are they living up to or betraying their ideals? How would you characterize their relationships with society, the military, and elites? What are their biggest concerns and needs? Ultimately, how different are they?

3

HUMAN SECURITY

When your son is ill, take him to the stadium.
> —A sign protesting Brazil's priorities
> (Vanessa Barbara, "Brazil's Vinegar Uprising")

My parents left home when I was very young. Their faces are fading away.
> —A middle-school-aged child of migrant parents in rural Hubei (Aris Chan and Geoffrey Crothall, "Paying the Price for Economic Development: The Children of Migrant Workers in China")

INTRODUCTION

They're far from twins, but on some matters related to economics and human security, Brazil and China share a striking resemblance. From other angles, however, they are mirror images of each other; they are identical—in reverse. As you will see in this and every chapter, on a variety of issues China and Brazil are following parallel trajectories—although they don't necessarily run in tandem; one is often several years behind the other. The comparison offers surprises; in some of the ways we expected Brazil and China to be opposites they turned out to be duplicates.[1]

---

[1] For the first decade of the new century, Brazil's economic growth was on a similar trajectory as China's. While the speed of economic expansion certainly couldn't compare to China, whose growth rates during this period ranged between 8 and 12 percent, Brazil's economy boomed from 2000–2011, with rates averaging an impressive 4 percent from 2002–2008 and peaking at 7.5 percent in 2010. Reversing course in tandem, both economies weathered the Great Recession relatively well but have since slowed.

As an example of their similarities, China, despite slowing growth rates, remains an economic powerhouse, recognized for its might as the world's second-largest economy. Brazil, coming out of an economic boom that peaked in 2010, had fallen into recession by mid-2015.[2] Both China and Brazil continue to be recognized for their potential, but both economic models are showing strain, especially in light of rampant inequalities throughout society. Brazil's rapid economic expansion in the first decade of the twenty-first century was based in a commodities boom. Its strong growth rates held on through the Great Recession, but the economy was stalling by 2011 ("Brazil's Coming Recession" 2015).[3] Meanwhile, Chinese growth rates—while still high compared to the rest of the world—slowed as well, with the gap between rich and poor little changed ("World Development Indicators" 2015).

For many years both China and Brazil have also been ranked as two of the most unequal countries in the world (Roberts 2014). They both remain on that list. But here's where the two become mirror images of each other—in reverse. Brazil has actually reduced its levels of inequality; China, with a weak record on redistributive efforts, has not (Ravallion 2011; "World Development Indicators" 2015). Brazil's Gini coefficient, the most commonly used measure of income distribution, fell by 5.08 points between 2000 and 2009, while China's increased by 2.8 points (Colitt 2014). In other words, human security has been expanding in Brazil as it has been contracting in China. In China there is a larger income gap between rural and urban areas now than at any other time since the government launched its reform and opening policy in the late 1970s (Fu 2010). As is clear in both countries, growth alone is necessary but

---

[2] As another illustration of their similarities, the mood was souring, but even as their economies slowed, 60 percent of Brazilians and 66 percent of Chinese citizens responded that they were better off financially in 2014 than they were five years earlier ("People in Emerging Markets" 2014). And of all emerging economies surveyed by the Pew Research Center in 2014, China and Brazil ranked as the second and fourth most optimistic about their children's future (Vietnam was number one and Chile number three). That year clear majorities (72 percent in Brazil / 85 percent in China) expected their economies to improve in the near future ("Emerging and Developing Economies" 2014). But by 2015, Brazilian optimism had turned to anger as the country grappled with major corruption scandals and a plummeting economy (Zainulbhai 2015).

[3] China's economy continued to outpace Brazil's, which took a nosedive, to just over 1 percent growth from 2011–2015. As of 2015, many analysts expected Brazil's economy to continue its decline, and dip into recession before bouncing back ("World Development Indicators" 2015; "Brazil's Coming Recession" 2015).

insufficient to reduce inequality. This has ramifications for contentious politics in Brazil and China.

As illustration of this, more Brazilians may be freer from want, but the overall state of the economy may do more to explain why a higher percentage of Brazilians than Chinese report dissatisfaction with their country's direction (55 percent versus 10 percent) ("Economies of Emerging Markets" 2013). However, this is something leaders in both countries are concerned about; as their economies slow, both states are increasingly engaging in a "tight-rope walk" (Fisher 2012). Moreover, both states have faced mounting citizen protests in recent years, particularly over corruption. Beijing is finding itself forced to respond to the contradictions introduced by its rapid ascension—economic inequality lies at heart of much social unrest in China that threatens to destabilize CCP rule. With its economic slowdown, many worry that any progress in its war on poverty would soon be lost. Economic inequality is nothing new in Brazil, but if the protests of recent years offer any clue, more Brazilians than ever are fed up, turned off by politics as usual.[4] In March 2015, nearly 1.7 million citizens from across the country, frustrated with the economy and a massive corruption scandal, demanded the president's impeachment or resignation—some went as far as to call for a "constitutional" military intervention—in some of the biggest demonstrations since the country's return to democracy in 1985 (Romero 2015b). The larger protests in China do not dare call for anything like this, but as we will see in the sections to follow, economic growth has only raised expectations, and regime type seems to make little difference, as both Brasilia and Beijing clumsily grapple with citizen discontent over three challenges for human security: migration, crime, and health care.[5]

---

[4] Given its success in growing the middle class and reducing poverty, the Brazilian government was stunned in June 2013, when citizens demanded more: what started out as a protest against an increase in bus fares turned into something much bigger. For several days more than one million people poured into the streets in eighty cities to protest—mostly peacefully—high taxes and corruption and call for a "World Cup" quality of public services (Rohter 2013).

[5] Human security is defined in the UN Development Report as "protection from sudden and hurtful disruptions in the patterns of daily life"—whether in homes, in jobs, or in communities—and safety from such chronic threats as hunger, disease, and environmental degradation, to which we devote a later chapter. It is usually associated with "freedom from want." In recent years, however, analysts have broadened the definition of human security to recognize that freedom from want cannot exist without "freedom from fear," such as repression, or threats to personal safety. For these reasons, we include violent crime, including state violence such as police abuse, as a human security concern (Jolly and Ray 2006; O'Brien 2015).

BRAZIL

Not long ago it appeared that Brazil was a rising economic power. Fresh off a major oil discovery and flush with wealth from a commodities boom, by 2011 Brazil had risen through the ranks to displace the United Kingdom as the world's sixth-largest economy. But it also had the dubious distinction of being the second-most unequal society in the world ("Gini: Out of the Bottle" 2013).[6] The gap between rich and poor is so glaring in Brazil that during his 2013 visit Pope Francis warned against the ephemeral idols of money, success, and power (Barchfield and Winfield 2013). By 2014, Brazil held neither of these titles; Brazil's economy had clearly reversed course. The gap between rich and poor had closed somewhat, but the country remained highly unequal ("Inequality-adjusted Human Development Index" 2014). Hundreds of years of slavery and colonialism, the exploitation of indigenous peoples, and land concentration are the foundations of a system that has contributed to problems of severe inequality and rampant violence that have proven resistant to change. Brazil's richest 10 percent control approximately 42 percent of the country's wealth, whereas just over 3 percent remains for the poorest 20 percent ("World Development Indicators" 2015). But, remarkably, Brazil has made some headway in raising people out of poverty in the last decade. It has been able to reduce poverty by half since 2003 ("How to Reduce Poverty" 2014). According to the World Bank, in 2012 less than 7 percent of the population remained in poverty (earning less than US$2 per day) and 3.8 percent lived on less than US$1.25 per day ("World Development Indicators" 2015). These numbers reflect a real improvement from even just a decade before, when over 30 percent lived in poverty ("Brazil Overview" 2013). But there remain significant regional disparities between the more developed southeast and south, which has been compared to southern Europe in terms of living standards, and the disadvantaged northeast and north—where living standards are comparable to sub-Saharan Africa (Croix 2012a; Hargis and He 2009). In recent years, economic growth rates in Brazil's northeast have outpaced those of the southeast, but it would take much more than this for these desperately poor areas to catch up with Rio de Janeiro and São Paulo.

---

[6] By 2013 Brazil had fallen behind Britain to place as the world's seventh-largest economy ("GDP Ranking 2014" 2015).

For years Brazil, an upper-middle-income country, has been embarrassed on the global stage by international attention to the miserable conditions of its poor, particularly its street children.[7] However paradoxically, on that same stage Brazil is on its way to being known as a human security superpower, thanks to its innovative approach to poverty reduction and social development. This relatively recent turnabout began in the early 1990s and is largely due to the joint efforts of civil society and Brazilian governments. Civil society prodded elected governments that aren't threatened by the idea of partnering with such groups. The resulting policy, based in collaboration and experimentation, makes good on the promises of the 1988 constitution, which recognizes such things as food and nutritional security as human rights.

To earn its reputation as a human security superpower, the Brazilian state intervened to promote social welfare, most notably the reduction of poverty and HIV-AIDS. Being a world leader in this regard has become an essential part of Brazil's national identity (Amar 2009). There is still work to do, particularly in regard to health care, but the country has met its Millennium Development Goal of cutting poverty in half, and much of that progress is due to the combination of Brazil's impressive economic growth over the 2000s, low inflation, and the inclusive development promoted by government programs designed to benefit the poor ("BTI 2012" 2012). Brazil continued to sustain decent growth rates during the Great Recession, but, as mentioned earlier, as of 2015 they had slowed significantly. Growth is necessary for reducing poverty; over the years, as Brazil's economy has had its ups and downs, the Cardoso, Lula, and Dilma governments have acted pragmatically, promoting this new developmental model with the view that there can be little justice without growth to pay for it ("What the US Can Learn" 2011).

Because Brazil's last three governments designated fighting poverty as a strategic priority, as of 2014, a total of more than fifty million Brazilians (a quarter of the population) were registered for government social programs (Colitt 2014). One of the most innovative and effective of these initiatives is *Bolsa Familia* ("The Family Stipend"), which grew out of *Bolsa Escola* ("The School Stipend"), a program federalized under the Cardoso administration in the late 1990s. Both are examples of conditional cash transfers (CCTs). Whereas Bolsa Escola was simply tied to school attendance, Bolsa Familia goes further and reduces poverty in the long and short run by paying poor families with children

---

[7] There is no agreed-upon estimate of the numbers of street kids in Brazil; guesses run from the 100,000s into the millions ("Street Children of Brazil" 2007).

under age fifteen to keep their kids in school and vaccinated. Bolsa Familia covered 3.6 million families in 2003 and was expanded on an unprecedented scale over ten years, reaching nearly 14 million households ("BTI 2012" 2012; Colitt 2014; Khazan 2014). Because of its record in improving well-being, this CCT has been emulated in countries around the world as a model of how to improve public services.

Another factor in Brazil's status as a human security superpower is President Lula's signature initiative, *Fome Zero* ("Zero Hunger"). Fome Zero seeks to end hunger—which has long been widespread, even in this food-exporting country—by guaranteeing every Brazilian three meals a day. Private businesses, churches, and other civil society groups helped to design and implement this joint effort with the government, which relied on locally grown food, thus aiding small farmers. Brazil is now recognized as a world leader in food security because of this program, which is based on social participation to boost food production, consumption, and distribution ("Rio +20" 2012).

Continuing in this tradition, in 2011 Dilma launched *Brasil Sem Miseria* ("Brazil without Misery"), a multibillion-dollar social welfare program that extends the very popular Bolsa Familia. At the time, the president had set a high goal for the program, declaring that by 2014 extreme poverty would be extinct in Brazil. As of 2015, the percentage of Brazilians living in absolute poverty is under 3 percent, the cutoff at which the World Bank considers the problem eradicated (Colitt 2014; "World Development Indicators" 2015). Dilma's government helped to achieve this goal by increasing the cash payments provided by Bolsa Familia to approximately US$35 per person per month. This cash payment alone has brought many families out of absolute poverty. But the comprehensive Brasil Sem Miseria goes further, increasing access to health care, housing, and sanitation, and providing credit and skills training to the poor ("Brazil: Freedom in the World 2012" 2012). Sure, Brasil Sem Miseria is still a work in progress, and improving the quality of health care—and access to it—will be a particular challenge. In fact, after the economy, Brazil's health-care system is commonly identified by citizens as the biggest problem the country faces ("Brazilian Discontent Ahead" 2014). But with the assistance of community groups the state is taking on the problem of access, reaching out to include over 2.5 million people not currently in the system because of lack of information, geographic isolation, or other barriers ("Social Spending in Brazil" 2013; Croix 2012a; Boadle 2013).

Of all of these anti-poverty efforts, Rousseff's pet project is *Minha Casa, Minha Vida* ("My House, My Life"), a public-private partnership that promised to build and subsidize nearly three million homes, helping low-income families afford to buy them. Critics argue that the program suffers from a variety of deficiencies: there are complaints about the quality of the homes, their remote locations, and that the program has not benefited the poorest families (Barbara 2014). The government's belief is that Bolsa Familia, Fome Zero, and Minha Casa, Minha Vida will stimulate consumption and the economy while promoting social justice, since demand will rise for products needed for construction, home furnishings, et cetera, thus creating jobs (Barbara 2014; Verbeek 2012).

These programs, the product of state-society collaboration, have undoubtedly improved the lives of many Brazilians. It is thanks to a confluence of events that Brazil may have turned a corner: since the 1990s nearly forty million Brazilians have entered the middle class, which for the first time represents over half the population, and the living standards of many more have improved. It's all about growing the middle class as opposed to trickle-down economics. As a result, the advocates of these programs argue that the social pyramid, a long tradition in Brazil, with a large base of poor at the bottom, is being replaced by a diamond-shaped distribution of wealth, with a growing middle class spanning the center, with few rich at the top and a few abjectly poor at the bottom (Ituassu 2011).

However, critics point out that these gains are tenuous; those newcomers to the (lower) middle class could lose their footing, and many of those who no longer live in absolute poverty live just above that line and are still poor, also at risk of falling back (Hinchberger 2012). What happens to these welfare programs if the economic growth that paid for them doesn't rebound soon? To stop the loss of investor confidence and turn the economy around, Dilma in her second term has been compelled to adopt pro-business policies. But will she be willing to hurt the poor and middle classes by adopting austerity—obliterating these safety nets?

It is likely that future Brazilian governments—PT or not—will manage to avoid a return to the status quo ante for a variety of reasons, and that the state will maintain these social programs credited with reducing poverty—unless the economic slowdown continues for several years without respite. Sure, *assistencialismo*, or welfare, has its critics in Brazil, but it is a widely accepted view among voters that the state is responsible for reducing inequality and that the government's welfare programs, and the government's decision to raise the minimum wage, have promoted a more equitable income distribution that has in turn benefited the economy. According to a 2013 poll conducted by the Institute of Economics at the Federal University of Rio de Janeiro, three-quarters of the Brazilians surveyed said the program has been good for the country and should be continued (Jordan 2013). For nearly two decades Brazilians have voted in governments that view the state as having a responsibility to the poor. Although their critics from the left contend that they are only making enough reform to avoid larger, structural changes, the Lula and Dilma governments are fighting poverty and inequality by playing the long game. The result is a virtuous circle: social protection programs that provide a way out of poverty promote further economic growth because as GDP per capita rises, larger numbers of people have become consumers, strengthening the domestic market. Sure, old-school economic growth is an imperative, and it's easy to be generous when times are good, but all the major parties in Brazil at least give lip service to the argument that the engine of growth is decreasing inequality (Font 2003; "The Brazilian Model" 2011; Creamer 2012; Jordan 2013). If Brazilian governments put their money where their mouth is and Brazil is proven right about this, it could set economic policy on its head in countries—rich and poor—worldwide.

Migration: "The Rights to the City"—or Not

For many years in Brazil, because of the concentration of land ownership, migrants have poured from the countryside to the cities, looking for opportunity. One hundred years ago, over 70 percent of the country's population lived in rural areas. Although there were waves of migration to the cities in the late nineteenth and early twentieth centuries, Brazil's population remained predominantly rural until the mid-twentieth century; there was a mass exodus from the countryside to São Paulo and Rio de Janeiro from the 1950s to the 1970s (Wagner and Ward 1980; Martine and McGranahan 2010). By 2010, more than 85 percent of the country's citizens were city dwellers ("Brazil: The World Factbook" 2015). Brazil's transition from rural to urban society was particularly rapid. People built their houses themselves on whatever land was defined as the periphery at the time. Land was bought cheap—and often illegally—from con artists /developers who failed to abide by city regulations. There was little or no planning by the state; rather, the process of urbanization operated while the state looked the other way. As a result, *favelas* (low-income, precarious illegal settlements scattered through the cities) exist alongside exclusive neighborhoods in what is known as "the legal city." But tension exists between these communities. Whether driven by concerns about crime or the desires of real estate developers, Brazilian governments have periodically forced those with fewer resources out of central areas of the cities and further onto the margins. With their homes designated as slums, occupants are resettled into areas on the outskirts that lack even minimal so-cial services such as sewage, electricity, and transportation—while their former neighborhoods are gentrified (Martine and McGranahan 2010; Caldeira 2003).

Residents of these communities resisted their eviction over the years through various means. According to Kathryn Hochstetler (1997), at least as early as 1912, urban social movements used street protests. By the mid-1970s, toward the end of military rule, residents of these neighborhoods started some-thing earlier generations facing the same problems had for the most part not done: they organized themselves into hundreds of neighborhood associations, forming an urban reform movement. Often guided by liberation theology and protected by the Catholic Church, citizens fought against their social exclu-sion and for structural reforms. They demanded inclusion—not only rights as citizens but "rights to the city." As such, they demanded that the state pro-vide access to housing and other public goods (including education) that were available in "the legal city," the city centers (Avritzer 2009). Unlike most in-volved in the movement today, these activists were not seeking to work with the state; rather, they sought to replace it. In this they joined the larger, diverse pro-democracy movement, which was clearly oppositional. After the return to democracy in 1985, most of these urban popular movements declined. Some activists went to work for the state; some developed clientelist relationships with local politicians and lost all credibility, while others were displaced by the rise of drug gangs and Pentecostalism, both newcomers to the neighborhoods and looking for recruits (Hochstetler 1997; Erickson 2011).

To the disappointment of many, care of the cities lapsed while problems grew. At the turn of the twenty-first century it was estimated that over ten million Brazilians lived in illegal or substandard housing. Urban popular social movements concerned about issues of everyday life were resurrected and began pushing the state for a national policy on informal land and housing markets ("Mass Favela Eviction Highlights Squatters" 2012). Unlike their predecessors, this generation of activists sought "the rights to the city" by working within the system; they made connections with political parties, particularly the PT but also with more conservative leaders, lobbied political leaders, and pushed through new legislation. The most notable of these laws, the City Statute of 2001, created mechanisms for long-term residents to gain legal title to land and required popular participation in the design and implementation of urban reform (Souza 2009).

Its advocates argue that this collaboration is an example of how civil society can negotiate successfully with key political actors to manage urban growth in a more inclusive way. In this case, although the state's receptivity and responsiveness to society can be read as an auspicious sign for democracy in Brazil, not everyone is so enthused about this approach. The reforms enacted are faulted for being state-centered—and therefore limited—and as appeasing rather than contributing to more radical, deeper change (Souza 2009). Still, critics and supporters agree that, for better or worse, the effect of the reforms has been stabilizing. The state has worked with civil society to legalize more urban land. It has invested in urban infrastructure such as sanitation and public transport, which has meant improvements in the conditions of life in some areas of the periphery. Of course, there is room for improvement; many programs have never lived up to expectations. Some initiatives haven't been implemented or approved at all levels of government and therefore much remains to be done ("Submission Prepared by Centre on Housing Rights and Evictions" 2008; Caldeira 2003; Avritzer 2007).

Impatient with this legalistic, technocratic approach, a grassroots-based urban reform movement recalibrated and began using a new repertoire of insurgent practices to demand more affordable housing and access to infrastructure and services (Souza 2009; "Bringing the State Back" 2012). This was unusual in Brazil, as urban popular movements had never been especially politically contentious (Levy 2010). Unlike activists seeking land reform in rural areas, the urban movement had always been more institutionalized and was not known for road blockages, land invasions, and other "sharp" mobilizations (Avritzer 2007). However, that all changed when the Homeless (or "Roofless") Workers' Movement, or *Movimento dos Trabalhadores Sem Teto* (MTST) and similar groups took the public stage in 1997, startling Brazilians with highly visible campaigns for the right to dignified housing. The urban version of the Landless Worker's movement, or MST as described in chapter 2, the MTST is a squatters' movement that by definition relies on direct action. It is its unexpectedness that gives the MTST's disruptive collective action its power (Levy 2010).

Although the MTST is autonomous of its rural counterpart, the MST, like the MST it is a visible expression of outrage against land concentration and inequality, the two most highly contested issues in Brazilian politics. The two organizations share a broad vision based in socialist ideals and both are calling for more fundamental transformations, for structural change because they know that land reform is an issue on which elites will not budge and therefore the state will resist. In terms of tactics and goals, compared to most neighborhood movements, the MTST is radical. Both the MST and the MTST promote change from below. They are distinct from more conventional reformist groups in that although both challenge and seek dialogue with the state, neither the MST nor MTST seeks to participate in traditional politics. Although both groups once worked alongside the PT before it won the presidency, both the MTST and MST expected more from leftist PT governments, and both have been disappointed by them (White 2008). Still, it is important to emphasize that the MST is the most powerful oppositional group in Brazil, but it does not seek to overthrow the government. It knows that that would be suicidal (Carter 2010).

But the MST and MTST definitely take a confrontational approach and learn from each other. For example, the MTST shares the MST's symbols and language; both organizations use the color red predominantly in their flags to symbolize the blood in their veins and to indicate that they are willing to fight for the transformation of society, and both speak of equality, struggle, and peace through social justice. The MTST has adopted the MST's tactic of direct action, and its signature tactic is occupations. To show the government that it means business, it chooses to occupy strategically located, state-owned buildings. As proof of their resolve and to attract attention to their cause, the MTST has emulated the MST in shutting down highways temporarily and leading thousands on marches to the seats of political power. However, unlike its rural counterpart, the MTST's invasions are faster paced and don't last as long as the MST's occupations in the countryside. But for both organizations, occupations are the name of the game. The only difference is that in the cities, MST members, many of whom are women and most of whom are unemployed or underemployed, invade vacant or abandoned buildings and set up urban camps. Otherwise the camps—rural or urban—are much alike, centered on the practice of mutual self-help. For example, members run communal kitchens and gardens and provide other services such as child care (Levy 2010; Osava 2007b; White 2008).

The MTST and similar groups refusing eviction and fighting for decent housing in Brazil have used the rising economic hardship associated with economic slowdowns as an opportunity to mobilize low-income populations by underscoring the disconnect between the abundance of abandoned real estate and the lack of housing for the poor. Thanks to the MTST, even Brazil's poor, traditionally passive masses have gained an awareness of their rights as citizens. According to Levy (2010), the MTST's ability to produce such a turnabout in perception is hugely important. The shift marks a change in the long-internalized culture of oppression, the reverence for authority identified in chapter 2 that keeps the poor in check. The MST can claim similar success in raising a sense of political competence and efficacy among rural populations. Spurred by a recession that worsened already precarious and deteriorating housing conditions, in São Paulo alone, these groups surprised the government and other onlookers by pulling off more than eighty occupations between 1997 and 2005 (Levy 2010). As a result, in the 2000s the MTST grew rapidly in membership and influence. As of 2014, the MTST had a membership of fifty thousand families nationwide. Its occupations, such as when two thousand families squatted near a stadium just before the World Cup, put the issue of housing on the state's agenda. The MTST has even persuaded Dilma's government to grant more contracts to non-profits versus private contractors. But it has had mixed success in creating permanent housing projects (Barbara 2014; Osava 2007a).

Although this section's focus has been the MTST, it should be noted that particularly when it comes to urban policy, neither society—nor the state—is monolithic. Rather, there is great variation in Brazil between and within states and localities when it comes to receptivity or resistance. Some state and local governments have incorporated the recommendations of urban popular movements to improve housing conditions and the quality of life for low-income populations. Elsewhere, however, state and local authorities have refused to develop programs, or have set aside only very modest funding for low-income housing. They have refused to negotiate with the housing movement, and occupations have ended in evictions and violence as police have forced the closure of camps. In other words, who is in power matters. Changes in ruling alignments, as well as cleavages among elites, mean changing political opportunity structures—and these can make all the difference in the success or failure of negotiations (Levy 2010).

Similarly, society develops in concert with changing opportunity structures. The state can end up producing collective actors by facilitating or blocking the development of certain groups; if the government is attentive to urban popular movements it can often bring them in and integrate these groups into its policies. If it represses or ignores their demands and seeks to exclude such groups, movement leaders will be forced to pursue non-institutional means of getting their point across (Levy 2010).

But the Brazilian state doesn't seem to have learned this lesson. In 2013, grassroots-based advocates for housing once more found themselves in a fight with the government over its plans to forcibly evict and relocate entire neighborhoods in preparation for the 2014 World Cup and the 2016 Olympics. Perched on the hills overlooking the city, the favelas offer some of Rio's best views. In São Paulo and other major cities as well, the land under these illegal informal settlements, some of which have been recognized as UNESCO World Heritage sites and which generations have called home, is now considered prime real estate. This is hardly good news for residents, as hundreds of communities around the country are at risk. In urban (as in rural) areas the Rousseff government's embrace of giant projects and developmentalism, described in chapter 5, has taken hold. As part of the "development" of these areas, the state is evicting large numbers of the poor (many of whom are Afro-Brazilian, indigenous, and/or female). Often with very little or no warning, entire communities are razed to make room for infrastructure and private development projects. From the government's perspective, this is progress and plans are extremely ambitious. In 2012, the National Coordination of World Cup committees estimated that as many as 170,000 people in twelve cities across Brazil would be evicted to build stadiums and transit systems and the like in preparation for the two upcoming mega sporting events (Romero 2012a; Williamson and Hora 2012).[8]

But, as opposed to similar evictions in the 1960s and 1970s, this time residents weren't having it. For example, construction was temporarily delayed as twenty-five thousand workers at World Cup sites around the country threated to strike. The MTST and other groups united in a *Resistencia Urbana* movement protesting "the crimes of the World Cup" and called for a national referendum on whether the money spent to host the World Cup should instead be spent on housing and other needs ("Group Plans More Protests" 2012). Although the MST has characterized the government's actions as an act of war, President Rousseff initially responded as her predecessors had: by declaring that the relocations were for the residents' own good because they lived in areas where landslides were a risk. According to the state, "de-densification" would improve their quality of life. Instead of dealing with communities as a whole, it took what some characterize as a divide-and-conquer approach, singling out individuals for resettlement, offering compensation, and permitting no community-wide negotiations (Romero 2012a; Williamson and Hora 2012).[9]

This approach failed to work as the state had hoped, as residents made it harder for the government to move them. Some worked with state prosecutors

---

[8] The final number of people displaced is disputed, but common estimates run as high as 250,000 (Somin 2014).

[9] Critics of the plan pointed out that there was little evidence to support these claims; engineers disagreed about the risk factors and it was clear to residents that relocation would mean not only the loss of their investment in their homes, but the loss of the economic and social support systems offered by their communities (Williamson and Hora 2012).

Anti-government demonstrators protest police violence, government corruption, and poor public services in Brazil, 2013. *Source:* Reuters/Davi Pinheiro.

to file injunctions against their removal, but without much success. With the state resistant and legalistic routes blocked, citizens turned to more muscular, extrajudicial avenues. Protesters rioted, burned cars, and blocked major roads. Riot police responded to citizen resistance in towns and cities with the use of truncheons and tear gas, all of which has been recorded with cell phones and posted on social media. Worse, it should be noted that the state's unilateral, authoritarian response was a bad sign for democracy in Brazil. Meanwhile, protesters argued that all they were doing was claiming their citizenship. From the bottom-up, ordinary people were mobilizing, fighting the relocation as just the latest chapter in Brazil's larger story of exclusion ("Mass Evictions at Pinheirinho" 2012; Williamson and Hora 2012).

And this time the story went viral. In 2013 independent journalism known as "*Midia Ninja*" provided a counternarrative to show what the mainstream media, relying on the police version of events, hadn't been showing. For example, it was street-level citizen journalism that put forward the theory that police infiltrators were serving as provocateurs, setting off the Molotov cocktails that drew a violent police response during massive demonstrations. Often broadcasting live from cell phones, these guerrilla journalists were betting that ugly pictures would play a pivotal role in bringing just enough attention to this problem for a government to feel the pinch—and this time, it did (Watts 2013d).

Social media, especially Twitter and the progressive blogosphere, have proven invaluable in channeling energy. It has succeeded in bringing first-time protesters into the streets, helping the movement to evolve rapidly and mixing politics in a way that is fresh and new to re-create the democracy (Romero 2013c; Becker 2013). Eventually even some of Brazil's mainstream media deviated from its usual path, showing protests in a negative light, and picked up the story as both an economic and a social justice issue, using some of Midia Ninja's footage. Videos posted on YouTube showed violent police reactions, such as Indians being forcibly removed from their homes and a museum torn down. They told stories counter to the official narratives: that all removals were in accord with the law, and that the government had consulted the residents (Etim 2013; Dip 2012).

Analysts contend that the corporate-controlled traditional media's acknowledgment of new media's influence amounts to a turning point for Brazil (Watts 2013c). In a last-ditch effort not to become irrelevant, old media has joined the new in naming residents' resistance as acceptable behavior and reasonable demands, and directing sympathetic public attention not only to this desperate action by the poor but also the mistreatment by police, as well as corruption and cost overruns associated with the mega sporting events (Romero 2012a); "Mass Evictions at Pinheirinho" 2012; Levy 2010). The old media's turnaround was forced by the rise of the new, and it gave hope to all who believe that change is possible in Brazil. That remains to be seen, but it is clear that the media was able to shine the light so brightly that no one can escape the irony: these mega events were supposed to be Brazil's grand coming out party; instead, suddenly the government was attracting only the worst kind of attention. Two days before the opening game of the 2014 World Cup, the state, which had exhibited a mix of both receptivity and resistance, had made concessions to the MTST. It pledged to build new housing for the poor and limit the use of force by military police in return for calling off strikes and protests. Society's confrontational stance had worked; the MTST, which had threatened to further radicalize if the government failed to follow through, had at least for the time being won limited reforms (Rossi, de Moura, and Bedinelli 2014). In effect, this is an example of the state allowing itself to be led by society seeking to improve human security—the kind of behavior expected of a democracy.

Criminality and the Rule of Law: High Crime and Official Impunity

As mentioned earlier, the traditional definition of human security, with its focus on "freedom from want," has been broadened to include "freedom from fear," as the two are interwoven. Increasingly, the state's capacity to manage the totality of its territory is recognized as a component of it, along with other basic human needs, such as food, health care, and housing (O'Brien 2015). As in every country in the world, criminality exists in a variety of guises in Brazil. There, atrociously violent crime takes the headlines, but corruption is arguably the bigger problem. In Brazil the most common form corruption takes is the politics of favor, but this category of crime runs the gamut, and one can find it all in Brazil: from the traditional techniques of corruption—namely garden-variety fraud, influence peddling, pork, and kickbacks—to the illegal use of campaign funds, illicit markets, corporate fraud, and more. It is corruption that is systemic, institutionalized—and it is corruption that is eating away at the country, disrupting its development in a variety of ways. And such excesses have very real political, economic, and social consequences. Not only does corruption impede Brazil's economic growth and development, it erodes confidence in the democracy. In a recent poll, 81 percent of respondents shared that they are disgusted with a system they see as unresponsive (Rohter 2013).

This festering problem is sometimes blamed on Brazil's passive political culture, which places great value on avoiding confrontation and ends up accepting inequality. Protests usually draw low numbers. However, periodically the people have awakened. Every now and then the showcasing of greed goes too far and the Brazilians become so enraged that they have turned out into the streets in impressive numbers. In 1985 citizens came out, making cross-sectoral and cross-movement coalitions to demand the end of the dictatorship. The pattern was repeated in 1992, when millions turned out to demand the impeachment of the first directly elected president since the return to democracy, and since 2013—some twenty years later—to vent their dissatisfaction with the government, to call for a better and fairer society, and to make it clear that politics as usual "doesn't represent us" anymore (Hochstetler 1997; Becker 2013).

However, such outbursts have been the exception, not the norm in Brazil. Any country's political culture is based in its history—and colonialism and slavery provide the subtext for corruption and a disregard for human life, both of which are very old traditions. In Brazil then and now, there are few constraints on behavior, there are no checks on abuses of power, and some are simply above the law. Both corruption and violent crime are traditions in Brazil, dating back to colonialism, under which Brazil was treated like a milch cow, and slavery, based in the view that some lives are worth less than others. These two forms of criminality exist in a chicken-and-egg relationship with the lack of the rule of law. Sure, Brazilians recognize both violent crime and corruption as enormous problems. But many are forgiving—and even willing to join in—when it comes to corruption, sharing the view that because the rules don't work, the best thing to do is to work around them. One way of doing this is with the jeito or little fix, a bending of the rules or improvisation to get around an obstacle; this is a national institution of which many Brazilians are proud.

Thus, there is little respect for the rule of law because citizens view the judicial system as weak, biased, and ineffective, soft on criminals. Instead of reforming the legal system to make it more effective, many Brazilians have taken to simply bypassing it. For them, the lack of such meaningful restraints on behavior is both the cause of, and solution to, their problems. Corruption is so pervasive that many citizens have resigned themselves to it, thus accommodating it. There's an old saying that sums up the way many Brazilians view politicians: "He steals, but he gets things done." When it comes to combating violent crime, this acceptance of bending of the rules takes the form of tough, even extrajudicial tactics. Drug trafficking has become a real scourge, and many citizens are so fearful for their safety that they're willing to give security forces all the latitude they say they need "to get it done." Moreover, Brazilians have elected so many politicians with backgrounds in law enforcement and the military that they form the *bancada da bala*, "the bullet caucus," as of 2014 one of the most influential groups in Brazil's Congress. They are part of a nationwide, right-wing movement that calls for, among other things, increased gun ownership and shielding police from accountability for abuses. The only thing new about this is its growing influence. Although some say the rise of this movement marks an ideological shift in Brazil, many Brazilians have long supported vigilante actions, which are widely viewed as an effective and legitimate way to eliminate evil (Romero 2015a; Caldeira 2000).

Inequality before the law and impunity for those who have power helps to create what some analysts have termed "a culture of violence" that continues to thrive even in Brazil's democracy (Wells 2013). Brazil's homicide rate is unusually high for a democracy; according to the United Nations, it had more homicides than any other country in the world in 2012 (Romero 2015a).[10]

---

[10] Although on a per capita basis, the homicide rate is higher in Honduras and Venezuela (Romero 2015a).

Between 1980 and 2011, that rate has grown by 132 percent—since the return to democracy, over one million people have been murdered (Croix 2011; Waiselfisz 2013). Clearly, such numbers suggest that Brazil just isn't as cordial and peaceful as it has always prided itself on being.

But such exceptionalist claims were always questionable, and the return to democracy in the 1980s coincided not only with the growth of the drug trade and drug use in Brazil, but also with an economic crisis. Today a new generation of organized crime syndicates such as Red Command and First Capital Command (PCC) are run from the prisons and specialize not only in drug trafficking but also kidnapping and extortion.[11] Armed with heavy weapons, gang confrontations between these groups over turf and with elite police such as the Special Police Operation Battalion (BOPE, made famous in the 2007 film *Elite Squad*) can resemble urban guerrilla warfare ("Bringing the State Back" 2012; Misse and Vargas 2010).[12]

Fearful for their safety, most citizens support the democratic state's punitive response to violent crime. As a result, the penalties for drug trafficking have become more severe and Brazil's prisons are full beyond capacity. Capital punishment was abolished in Brazil in 1979 (except for treason in a time of war), but a 2008 *Datafolha* poll showed 47 percent support reinstating the death penalty, and extending it to include several crimes, including corruption ("Death Penalty Splits Views in Brazil" 2008). However, most analysts do not expect the country to do so; the death penalty exists in Brazil, but it is applied only extrajudicially.

Ironically, not only has violent crime increased as the country has democratized, so has violent crime conducted by state actors. According to former national security secretary Luiz Eduardo Soares, during the two decades of the dictatorship (1964–1985), about six thousand people were executed. However, during the first two decades of the democracy (1985–2005), police in Brazil killed about forty thousand people each year, many of their corpses showing signs of summary execution (cited in Amar 2009; Ramos and Lemgruber 2004).

---

[11] Gangs such as the PCC have used military-grade hardware (including shoulder-launched missiles to take down helicopters) and often these weapons are provided by police collaborators, acquired from the government's own arsenals ("Bringing the State Back" 2012).

[12] Former President Fernando Henrique Cardoso confirmed the fears of a great many Brazilians when he characterized Brazil's problem with violent crime as an urban guerrilla war. In 2006, after one gang actually brought São Paulo—Brazil's biggest city and commercial hub—to its knees on multiple occasions, then-President Lula offered to send the national forces into the streets to restore order (Phillips 2006).

In 2008, Brazilian police killed one person for every twenty-three arrested (in the United States the rate is one death per thirty-seven thousand arrests) (Wells 2013). Most damning, it is estimated that security forces in democratic Brazil killed more people in their urban operations than their counterparts in any war in Latin America since the nineteenth century, with the possible exception of the long-running war in Colombia (Amar 2009).

Operating under a conception of national security that dates back to the dictatorship, the Brazilian criminal justice system has tended to view most citizens with suspicion, as potential enemies to be controlled. This tendency is aggravated by the 1979 amnesty that granted impunity to the military and other government agents for the politically motivated crimes of the dictatorship (Barbassa 2012). Given this record of impunity it should come as no surprise that, according to Freedom House, Brazil's police are among the most violent in the world ("Brazil: Freedom in the World 2011"). Moreover, it is not unusual for murders to be written off as "resistance killings" that the police claim as self-defense ("Brazil: Freedom in the World 2012" 2012; "Brazil: Freedom in the World 2013" 2013).

To be clear, no one is saying that all Brazilian law enforcement officers are killers, but too many are treated as above the law. Most are poorly paid and poorly trained, and the lack of restraint on their behavior also opens them up to the lures of corruption. Anti-violence activists argue that simply giving the security forces more firepower and more latitude in their dealings with criminals intensifies already existing illegal networks, escalating the rate of violence while allowing corrupt police, often tied to politicians, to demand protection money and a cut of the drug trade (Hudson 2003; Arias 2006). Meanwhile, in the countryside, being above the law leaves undisturbed the practice of security forces working for ranchers as paid gunmen, who kill anyone who gets in their way (Ortiz 2013).

One example among many of their victims is Dorothy Stang, a seventy-three-year-old American-born nun, murdered in 2005 for her advocacy for the rights of the Amazon's poor. She worked with civil society groups in Brazil such as the *Conselho Indigenista Missionario* (the Indigenous Missionary Council, CIMI), a Catholic missionary organization known for promoting the rights of indigenous people and the poor since 1972. Sister Dorothy and others raised the alarm about the mistreatment of these groups and plunder of the forest by loggers, ranchers, and land speculators in rural areas. However, Stang and activists like her must contend with a relatively apathetic state and society, as the public seems largely unconcerned and democratic governments have displayed at most lukewarm interest in the matter. The state had refused to provide the nun with protection, despite the fact that her name was known to be on a death list. Trapped on a dirt road, Stang reportedly started reading the Bible aloud as hired thugs approached and shot her six times (Ellerbeck 2015; Ortiz 2013).

Environmental activism in rural areas is fraught with danger. In the cities, groups working on issues that are also challenging but less threatening to powerful interests have had more success. For example, Viva Rio is an innovative, grassroots-based anti-violence movement that was founded in response to the Candelária massacre of 1993, in which fifty street children were shot by vigilantes—some of them off-duty police officers—while sleeping on the steps of a cathedral in Rio de Janeiro. Eight of the children died. Outrage over this disregard for human life served as the catalyst for the group, which views extreme inequality and social exclusion as the major cause of violence in Brazil. Originally based in Rio, it grew rapidly, utilizing a mass protest model and promoting inventive engagement. Viva Rio is now a large, privately funded NGO with operations inside and outside Brazil. The group is a "network of networks" against urban violence (Hochstetler 1997). It makes creative use of conventional tactics, utilizing protest as pressure to get the government to do the right thing. The state has been receptive to this movement; it has led the state and worked synergistically with the government, developing hundreds of partnerships on community projects within the favelas across the country. Viva Rio has even partnered with the Brazilian state in Haiti, where Brazil has led the UN peacekeeping mission. It is a reformist movement that engages those most affected by the violence. Promoting inclusion, Viva Rio provides residents with credit, education, and jobs programs as well as programs specifically targeting at-risk youth and alcohol abuse (Hochstetler 1997; Logan 2003).

The state has proven more receptive on some issues related to the rule of law than others. Viva Rio was unable to press the state to allow for citizen evaluation of policing and criminal justice policy. However, citing the easy accessibility of illegal weapons and the high rate of gun deaths, these groups won the passage of a disarmament statute in 2003 (Hall 2014). This landmark legislation provided for some of the strictest gun laws in the region, banning the sale of guns to anyone under twenty-five, providing for background checks, and numerous other restrictions. Although all agree that the rate of gun violence in Brazil is still too high, it did drop by 8 percent the first year after the law went into effect (Barnes and Llana 2011). Viva Rio tried to build on this momentum and joined other NGOs in demanding a national referendum on banning gun sales to civilians in Brazil. But this time it wasn't only the state that resisted the initiative. With a "tough on crime" sentiment popular among Brazilians, Viva Rio faced—and faces—countervailing pressure within society. The vote in 2005 was rejected by 64 percent of voters, many of whom wanted to keep guns for their personal safety. After Brazil's first mass school shooting resulted in the deaths of twelve children in 2011, there was talk of reviving the referendum, but there were not enough lawmakers willing to take it forward ("Brazil Lawmakers to Propose Referendum" 2011).

Still, over the years Viva Rio has persevered, partnering with the state to coordinate gun buy-back programs and with networks to include anti-violence themes in popular TV programs ("Brazil: Ten Years of Viva Rio" 2003). The focus has turned to education; civil society and the media have collaborated to address myths about gun violence and fight crime by taking on Brazil's culture of machismo (Amar 2009; Richardson and Kirsten 2005). In "Choose gun free! It's your weapon or me," one of its most successful public education campaigns, women from all classes pressured the men in their lives to give up their guns in 2001. Celebrities joined in, suggesting that men attracted to guns were attempting to compensate for sexual inadequacy with the slogan "Good lovers don't need a gun." Issues of gun violence and gun control became part of the national conversation when integrated into the central story line of a popular soap opera (Wilkinson 2013). Timed to go along with this peak in interest, Viva Rio and other groups collaborated with the Rio de Janeiro state government and the military, setting records as they destroyed more than one hundred thousand guns in police custody ("Viva Rio: Farewell to Arms" 2003). In a similar disarmament effort, FIFA (the football governing body) and the Brazilian government have considered offering free or discounted World Cup tickets to those who turn their guns over to the authorities (Phillips 2011b).

In addition to promoting gun control, groups such as Viva Rio dig further to deal with violence in the streets as well as corrupt institutions. It is on these issues that it becomes clear that the state is not a monolith. With an emphasis on transparency and "civilian security" over "national security," anti-violence groups call for the creation of mechanisms for civilian oversight and monitoring of police abuses. To strengthen the rule of law, these groups push federal, state, and local governments to replace the "top-down," punitive approach with one based in dialogue and preventive efforts. They advocate a harm-reduction approach that emphasizes community service and treatment for drug users and addicts, not prison. Still, taking on the criminal justice system is a formidable task, since worldwide it is known as the most closed of bureaucracies, with police, judges, and prosecutors the least open to civil society engagement or scrutiny and interference in the conduct of their work (Macaulay 2005). As mentioned earlier, Brazilians have traditionally had a high degree of tolerance for violence committed by state actors. If it caught on, the idea that the police should be accountable and responsive to citizens would amount to a major cultural shift in Brazil (Macaulay 2005).

Perhaps it can be argued that this shift was necessitated when Brazil was named to host the 2014 World Cup and 2016 Olympics. Since the mid-2000s, Brazil has worked hard to overcome its reputation as "beautiful but violent"—to prove international concerns about security wrong ("Bringing the State Back" 2012). With the spotlight on Brazil, safety became a priority, and it became clear that giving the police a free hand wasn't helping. Recognizing this, federal, state, and local government shifted course and became more receptive to proposals from anti-violence groups. Local leaders, civil society, and the private sector collaborated to design a new, ambitious, and innovative approach.[13] The result was the creation of Police Pacification Units (UPPs) in what is called "the Olympic Belt," neighborhoods near major venues. UPPs employ a mix of tactics in a two-prong approach: retaking territory and establishing state control by "pacifying" more than twenty favelas with elite police squads conducting counterinsurgency-like armed raids *and then* creating, for the first time, permanent police stations in these areas (Sweig 2010; Hargis and He 2009; "Brazil Drugs Raids" 2012).[14]

When Brazil hosted international events in the past, police would make incursions into poor neighborhoods. But it was in and out; raids didn't solve the problems, nor were they followed with a consistent state presence. Any change was temporary. Now, the state is working with society to build trust and promote cooperation between the police and the public. The new approach places the emphasis on rehabilitation, not retribution, and community-oriented police work. The police confer with community liaisons to discuss local needs, get to know the community, and the two overcome mutual mistrust. Community policing units are a new, reformed cohort of officers who seek to build ties with the community and mediate disputes within it. Just as crucially,

---

[13] According to the World Bank, not much is known or discussed about the specifics of state-society interaction in the creation of UPPs or the inner workings of this alliance ("Bringing the State Back" 2012). This amounts to a curious lack of transparency about a relatively democratic approach.

[14] As of 2012, there were 28 UPPs in Rio de Janeiro alone, serving more than 100 communities and 400,000 people. The government planned to eventually expand the program to serve 750,000 citizens ("Bringing the State Back" 2012).

the occupation phase is followed up with a social UPP, or police pacification unit, which includes the provision of social services as well as the regularization of electricity and water and the establishment of programs for at-risk youth. This is all part of a more comprehensive plan that society has long pushed for: it seeks to reduce crime not by shutting shantytowns off but by integrating them into the city (Forero 2011). This time the state is seeking to establish something more permanent, to change the relationship between residents and law enforcement. Central to this strategy is an effort to gain the trust of communities, build respect, and change the image of the police and, ultimately, the state.

The social element of this strategy only became policy due to the prodding of society, and an unusual combination of actors, both left and right, from the government and grassroots and including intellectuals, business, and the mainstream media to varying degrees support the idea of community policing and the police pacification units. The Brazil program is considered a success and has inspired similar efforts in Mexico, Colombia, and Afghanistan (Isacson 2011). But the program has faced criticism. Some question whether it can be sustained while others doubt that there has been any change in police culture and larger patterns of impunity. In 2013, it was only after mass protests in several major cities that the well-publicized disappearance of a laborer resulted in police officers being charged with his torture and murder (Romero 2013f). That same year, shocking photos of police brutalizing unarmed, often female, protesters reinforced concerns about deeper problems, and led to renewed calls for the demilitarization of the police ("Brazil: Clashes in Rio Slum" 2013; Kinosian 2013).

Another criticism of the pacification approach is that it does little to reduce inequality and therefore fails to get at the root of the problem. Others question the much-touted success of the program, pointing to a "pacification of the statistics" (Isacson 2011, 39). Yes, the murder rate in large southeastern cities like São Paulo has declined—the homicide rate there dropped by 67 percent between 2000 and 2010—but the number of murders has since shot up throughout the north and northeast. Where security reforms are slow in coming, it has doubled or quadrupled ("Brazil Fights Crime" 2013). Thus, in what some term a "balloon effect," the UPP has only pushed the gangs, and the violence associated with them, into farther outlying areas (Wells 2013; "2011 Global Study on Homicide" 2011; Garcia-Navarro 2013b).[15] Once-sleepy towns are

---

[15] The situation is especially dangerous for young people: in the northeastern city of Maceió, for example, the homicide rate for those 14–25 years old is an astonishing 288 per 100,000 (the national average in Brazil is 21 per 100,000) (Wells 2013).

becoming hubs of criminal activity. At the very least it is clear that a UPP limited to Olympic venues is not the answer; it must be expanded across the country. But it is thanks to the efforts of civil society that the state no longer simply equates security with pacification. "The right to the city" is coming to be understood more broadly in Brazil as inclusion: as a right to dignified housing, recreational and cultural life—and public security ("Bringing the State Back" 2012; Osava 2007b).

Health Care and HIV-AIDS: Citizens Lead the State

Like many of the initiatives described in this book, Brazil's national health system, the *Sistema Único de Saúde* (Unified Health System, SUS) is another outgrowth of the pro-democracy movement of the 1970s and 1980s. A social health movement, the *Movimento para Reforma Sanitaria* (Movement for Sanitary Reform), started out as explicitly political, emerging as a response to the dictatorship's failure to provide basic health care. In it, a disparate group of Brazilian citizens called for a "health care revolution," confronted the government and demanded access to health for all—as a right and obligation of the state ("Flawed but Fair" 2008; Mendonca 2004; Foller 2010). In effect, through its oppositional protest against the dilapidated social welfare system and the government's lack of responsiveness regarding a whole host of issues, including the right to health care, the health reform movement sought to establish a public health system responsive and accountable to the citizenry. On another level, it sought to broaden Brazilians' understanding of democracy to promote equality, participation, and inclusion. It promoted basic rights for all, particularly the poor and rural populations who had historically been excluded, not only from political rights, but other human rights as well. But against one threat in particular, HIV-AIDS, the state has made real progress in incorporating principles of the country's unified health system (the SUS), including universalism, integration, decentralization, and social control, into an AIDS policy (Mendonca 2004). It is thanks to the efforts of civil society that Brazil is recognized worldwide as a role model for how to fight this disease.

The Movement for Sanitary Reform's greatest success is that its ideals are reflected in the promises of the 1988 constitution: the recognition of health as a fundamental human right and the requirement that the state provide free and universal coverage (Safreed-Harmon 2008). To the consternation of many, Brazil has not yet made good on most of those promises and the country's health-care system is often described as shameful. But the failure is due to capacity, not because this is a contested issue. Yes, since the return to democracy, Brazil's public health system made some progress toward the Movement for Sanitary Reform's early goals; the health-care system is decentralized and is the responsibility of states and municipalities, financed by the states and federal government. The movement for health reform has grown from inside the government, as many activists were brought in to design and implement it. The synergy of civil society and state in the national health system is perhaps best expressed by its reliance on community participation, as citizens share in a variety of health-care discussions, including how budgets are allocated, and pass on their recommendations to health councils whose job it is to remain responsive to their needs ("Flawed but Fair" 2008).

The complementarity of state-society interaction in Brazil has contributed to a system that provides free primary and curative care as well as medications for all its citizens. As a result, life expectancy has risen from sixty-seven in 1990 to seventy-four in 2013 ("Brazil's March towards Universal Coverage" 2010; "World Development Indicators" 2015). The morbidity rate from infectious diseases such as malaria is down, maternal and child health and nutrition has improved, and infant mortality has been cut significantly since the return to democracy—from fifty-one deaths per one thousand live births to twelve ("World Development Indicators" 2015). Many who had gone without now have access to quality care, but lack of funding is a problem and inequities remain with long waits, overcrowding, and outdated equipment, especially in rural areas. Citizen concerns about the coverage, quality, and efficiency of the SUS have led to calls for reform. There is still work to do, but the federal government increased its funding for health care to 9 percent of GDP in 2012 and is focusing on providing primary health care to vulnerable, traditionally underserved groups ("World Development Indicators" 2015). One of the greatest challenges for Brazil's health-care system today is that the country is caught in a double bind, one that reflects the gap between rich and poor: it must deal with the infectious diseases of poor countries as well the non-communicable, lifestyle health problems of richer and aging populations ("Flawed but Fair" 2008).

Still, people expected more, and, as evidenced by demonstrations in 2013, Brazilians were growing angry and impatient with the pace of health-care reforms. Perhaps the optimists among them can draw some solace from the fact that they've risen to such challenges before. HIV-AIDS once appeared to pose an insurmountable obstacle for Brazil's still-new health-care system.

In 1992, just a few years into the democracy, the country was staring into the abyss. That year the World Bank predicted that 1.2 million of their country-men would be infected with HIV by the turn of the century ("Straight Talk" 2003). That was the wake-up call the state needed: in 1992 the government negotiated a US$160 billion World Bank loan to develop and implement a comprehensive national AIDS program. But thanks to an innovative and en-ergetic partnership of state and society that has lasted over five presidencies and a progressive, comprehensive, and multifaceted national policy, the rate of HIV infection stabilized (Safreed-Harmon 2008). As of 2012 the number of people living with HIV-AIDS was approximately 490,000—well under half the predicted number—and the prevalence rate was just 0.3 percent ("HIV & AIDS in Brazil" 2012).

As a result, Brazil has received international acclaim for its pioneering efforts to fight HIV-AIDS, which many consider to be the most effective and inspiring in the world (Parker 2009). Virtually all analysts agree that the state would never have become so proactive without the prodding of civil society. While the anti-AIDS movement shares things in common with other social movements, it is unique in many ways. As with all these groups, the critical juncture at which the movement developed certainly affected its trajectory. As is the case with the other examples of state-society interaction we're discussing for Brazil, most trace the origins of the movement back to the 1970s and the ab-ertura, or the period of political opening in which Brazilian society mobilized in an unprecedented manner to face off with the dictatorship. By the early 1980s, the negotiations for a transition to democracy were well underway. But it is a remarkable coincidence that HIV-AIDS had just begun to appear in Brazil at this historical juncture, in 1982. This confluence of events likely shaped Brazil's unique response to the disease (Safreed-Harmon 2008).

At the start of this story, Brazil's experience with HIV is much like that of many other countries. As elsewhere, this mysterious new disease at first appeared in the larger cities such as São Paulo and Rio and was quickly iden-tified as "the gay disease" because it appeared to be striking only men having sex with men. As in other countries, the response of governments (military in Brazil until 1985 and civilian since) was devastatingly slow as growing numbers of people were suffering and dying from the disease. Because no one else was stepping up to do it, members of Brazil's gay community, travestis (transgender individuals), and sex workers (male and female) began networking to press for assistance with the problem. Together with church groups, women's groups, and academics, these activists called for solidarity and universal human rights to jolt the government out of its complacency.[16] Using creative protest as pressure tactics, it was society that forced the state to recognize HIV-AIDS as a national public health problem, not charity (Foller 2010). Society led the state, and it is due to society's efforts that the state offered reforms: Brazil established the National AIDS Program (NAP), the first governmental AIDS program in the Americas, in 1983 (Parker 2009).

Although the NAP was established in the early 1980s to focus on providing information about the disease to high-risk groups, activists were dismayed that the government continued to treat these populations as invisible. A decade in, activists knew that they had to force another policy shift, as the body count was climbing. During the 1980s and 1990s, many AIDS activists were rightly concerned that government neglect of the disease had something to do with society's marginalization of the populations widely believed to be at greatest risk of contracting it. Formed in 1989, *Grupo Pela VIDDA* (GPV, or Group for the Affirmation, Integration, and Dignity of People with AIDS) focused on the political dimensions of living with AIDS. It and other groups knew that to effectively fight the disease they would have to fight prejudice and discrimination—not only against people living with HIV-AIDS but also various sexual and gender minorities hit hardest by the epidemic. AIDS activists insisted that the program design include attention to the fact that higher levels of vulnerability are related not only to unsafe sexual practices but also to social determinants including race, class, and gender inequalities (Pimenta et al. 2010). At their prodding, the federal and state governments passed laws in the late 1980s forbidding discrimination in housing, education, the workplace, health care, and so forth, and courts struck down discriminatory laws such as those requiring mandatory HIV testing for job placement (Vianna, Carrara, and Lacerda 2008; Safreed-Harmon 2008).

These activists were emphatic that people living with AIDS should not be viewed or view themselves as victims and they should not be stigmatized—or self-stigmatize. Instead, they promote the social inclusion on marginalized groups, and for them to use their own voices. No longer invisible, those directly affected by the disease encouraged others to participate in the movement. This approach stimulated the development of more relevant and therefore effective

---

[16] Religious activists were hardly monolithic on this issue. Out of concern over the suffering caused by HIV, followers of Afro-Brazilian religious traditions and members of Catholic Ecclesiastic Base Communities—and some Catholic bishops—eventually allied with the state, focusing on treatment and care (Murray et al. 2011).

prevention policies, many of which were designed and implemented by members of the very groups they sought to target (e.g., sex workers and men who have sex with men, who are hired by the government as peer educators to disseminate information and distribute condoms) (Foller 2010; Vallance 2012; Pimenta et al. 2010).

Such an approach was necessary, since analysts agree that the earliest of the state's prevention campaigns were largely counterproductive; the message was dark and serious—one of the most famous depicted a human skull—and wound up mostly only scaring people without offering much practical information to the public. Gradually, society adapted its repertoire and the model shifted. Campaigns were tailored to target specific groups such as gay men, teenagers, and sex workers, and the program came to depend on the expertise and credibility of peer educators. First adopted in São Paulo in the 1990s, Brazil's prevention campaigns are famous for taking a frank and open harm-reduction approach, which does not expect people to radically alter their sexual practices (Vianna, Carrara, and Lacerda 2008; Foller 2010). Brazil's is clearly a sex-positive approach; it emphasizes safe sex—not abstinence—and its displays of sexuality (including homosexuality) in public service announcements are often no-holds-barred.[17] For example, to get its safe sex message to the right audience, the Ministry of Health has taken to posing as dates on hookup app Tinder with the message, "Looking for men and women for no-strings-attached sex, preferably no condoms?" ("Brazil Entices Tinder Users" 2015).

But Brazil's anti-AIDS program has drawn a wide audience not only with its racy ads. Rather, the country has been applauded internationally for its integrated approach, which combines preventive and curative services (Foller 2010). The architects of this program regard health care as a package, and its success is in large part due to their refusal to separate prevention, care, and treatment. For example, because treatment is available and accessible, more

---

[17] However, what is celebrated by some is regarded as shameful by others. Conservative groups, most notably many ecclesiastic leaders of the Catholic Church and evangelicals, amount to strong countervailing pressure on the state. They have lobbied hard to pressure the government to shift to a harm-avoidance approach that promotes abstinence or monogamy (Deomampo 2008; Foller 2010). Although the state has stuck with the harm-reduction approach, conservative members of Congress threatened to block other legislation unless President Rousseff suspended the distribution of "anti-homophobia kits," education packets that they condemned as promoting homosexuality. Dilma canceled the program (she said, for her own reasons), but either way, conservatives chalked it up as a "win" ("Brazil Sex Education Material" 2011).

people are tested, which helps not only in lowering morbidity and mortality rates, but also with preventing the spread of the disease (Safreed-Harmon 2008).

Moreover, civil society practiced conventional politics while consistently maintaining that the right to health includes the right to treatment with the best drugs available. After years of lawsuits by NGOs the state proved receptive; a landmark law was passed in 1996 that required the free distribution of anti-AIDS medicines (anti-retrovirals, or ARVs) through the public health system to all its people who need them (Safreed-Harmon 2008). Former president José Sarney championed the idea after learning of the efficacy of these still relatively new medicines at an international AIDS conference. Arguing that the 1988 constitution provided a legal mandate recognizing the right to health, and, despite concerns about the expense, the state accepted that it was its duty to make treatment available to Brazil's AIDS patients. Over twenty years later it is clear that the provision of ART has saved the country money by reducing mortality by 40 to 70 percent, morbidity rates by 60 to 80 percent, as well as hospitalizations by 85 percent (Nunn 2010; Nauta 2011).[18] It is thanks to the combined efforts of state and society that, despite a variety of challenges, Brazil contained the disease and prevented it from becoming a generalized epidemic (Beaubien 2012).

As mentioned earlier, a large part of the success the movement has enjoyed is said to be due to its efforts to be culturally specific, to understand the cultural construction of sexuality in Brazil. Although analysts characterize state-society relations in regard to HIV-AIDS as combining collaboration and conflict, state and society partnered to take a characteristically Brazilian approach that values conciliation over confrontation. Activists have not shied away from confronting those who stand in their way, but state and society have found a way to work in a complementary fashion. Over time the relationship between state and society has become more synergistic and the two more interdependent, as civil society has become increasingly involved in the planning, monitoring, and evaluation of anti-AIDS programs (Mendonca 2004). One could argue that a policy like this, based on flexibility and pragmatism, could only come about in a country like Brazil. The anti-AIDS movement has raised larger issues of sexual and gender politics, demanded profound changes in society, and broadened

---

[18] Brazil currently faces the challenge of how to cover the ever-escalating costs of the second- and third-line regimens that must currently be imported (Pimenta et al. 2010; Safreed-Harmon 2008). People are living longer due to these drugs; however, they will need to continue to take them for the rest of their lives. The result is priceless, but the cost of sustaining treatment is still difficult to bear (Safreed-Harmon 2008; Pimenta et al. 2010).

what it means to be a citizen—and to be a democracy. In this way, society had an enormous impact on the state's AIDS policy, and at times the executive, legislative, and judicial branches have proven themselves responsive to this call. While civil society's strong mobilization against HIV has spilled over to feed and contribute to citizen involvement more broadly, there is certainly more to be done in reforming class, race, and gender inequities (Foller 2010; Parker 2009). Disparities continue, as the poor cannot or do not access the support that they need, which includes medicines for other diseases (like tuberculosis) and social assistance (Nauta 2011; Carneiro 2012).

And so, as they say in Portuguese, "*a luta continua*" (the struggle continues). As it unfolds, Brazil's anti-AIDS movement, as well as its Rights to the City and anti-violence campaigns, is contributing to a transformation of Brazil's hierarchical, authoritarian political culture to one that is more participatory, inclusive, and transparent. Making good on the promise of human security is an ongoing process, and it is no easy road, but it moves forward because of a society that is eager to lead a state that is, at least on certain issues, ready and willing to be led (Foller 2010).

CHINA

In many ways China appears to be making good on the promise of human security, and on certain issues one could argue that it has allowed itself to be led. Even despite the significant slowdown that began in mid-2015, it has become almost cliché to reference China's growing economic might and so-called economic miracle. In just over fifty years, China progressed from being the country that people feared would not be able to feed itself (in the 1950s) to the world's second-largest economy, surpassing Japan's GDP in 2010. On one hand, China is characterized by the World Bank as an upper-middle-income country; yet on the other it has the second-largest number of poor people in the world, after India. In 2009, the Chinese GDP surpassed Great Britain—the goal set by Mao Zedong during the disastrous Great Leap Forward (it took fifty, rather than five, years). From 2003 to 2008, China stopped receiving aid from the World Food Program and overtook the World Bank as the biggest investor in Africa. The so-called China model of economics has promoted mercurial economic growth rates that reached the double digits throughout the 1990s. Nonetheless, the "miracle" has had cracks from the beginning, with an urban bias favoring big cities, environmental stress (especially water and air pollution), and vulnerability to external forces, as well as constant concern about economic overheating, especially inflation. The model especially started to show tension underneath the surface in 2012, when growth dipped below 9 percent, and continued through late 2015, as growth slowed to just over 7 percent, the lowest rate in twenty-five years.

Engaging in a gradual, piecemeal approach to economic reform, Chinese leaders have followed the maxim attributed to Deng Xiaoping, "crossing the river by groping the stones." Gradual though it may have been, China has crafted the "fastest sustained economic transition in world history—a transformation that has brought with it not only greater wealth and international influence but also growing regional inequalities, a flood of migration, and rampant popular protest" (Perry 2011, 135). The so-called "iron rice bowl" of lifetime employment in the public sector was shattered with the introduction of hard budget constraints on state-owned enterprises in the late 1990s. Economically speaking, in terms of the relationship between state and society, the vaguely characterized "economic reforms" since the early 1990s have created masses of seemingly permanent migrant workers, private entrepreneurs, and a growing class of self-employed, each of whose connection to the state is weaker than in any time since the establishment of the People's Republic in 1949.

We should never assume that China's path toward economic growth was a sure thing, especially as the politics behind it sat on shaky ground in the late 1980s, when many of the contradictions in its economic path started to come to light. You will remember the Tiananmen protests of 1989 that we discussed in chapter 2—many of the initial grievances of participants were related to inflation and economic corruption. After widespread demonstrations and a fierce political crackdown throughout the country in the spring of 1989, political and economic retrenchment was a very real possibility, as conservative leaders argued the sources of the "disturbance"—as the mass protests were officially labeled—were directly linked to reforms implemented throughout the mid-1980s. As then paramount leader Deng Xiaoping attempted to resurrect reform efforts in the early 1990s, launching the so-called "southern tour" through the young commercial city of Shenzhen in 1992, he avoided labels such as "capitalism" and even "socialism," declaring the acceptability of letting "some people get rich first." It was a deft—if not wholly transparent—move that helped free the post-Tiananmen leadership of their paralysis from the crises of 1989.

Deng famously exulted that "to get rich is glorious"—and many have. The frenetic capitalism of the 1990s was expressed in a variety of ways, from free-wheeling stock markets and luxury homes to popular literature, where society's preoccupation with money was the favored theme of the "new generation" of

Chinese writers who began publishing after Tiananmen.[19] These and other forums have become staging grounds for expressing dismay at the failed promises of leaders. But the income and development gap have only become worse, as China surpassed the "warning level" of a severe income gap in 2000. In 1981, the Gini coefficient was estimated to be .29, making China one of the most equal societies at the time; but by 2002 the gap had increased to .45 (Carrillo 2012; Whyte 2011). Perhaps most politically damaging, for Beijing, is the finding that CCP cadres are now the richest politicians in the world, with their net worth increasing by 15 percent in 2011 and 2012 (Frank 2012). While there are many ways to measure the income gap, one set of statistics puts it in plain view: according to the PRC Ministry of Finance, most of the country's population doesn't earn the minimum salary (US$545 monthly) to be subject to income taxes (Pierson 2011). While much is made of China's rising middle class, its future is perilous as the economy becomes increasingly divided into haves and have-nots. As Zhao and Lim (2010, 2) note, "In a generation's time China has gone from not having enough inequality to having excessive inequality."

China is now home to lists of "mega-rich," mostly property investors, and is the location for some of the world's fastest growth of conspicuous consumption. One Bloomberg report claims that Chinese millionaires will likely make up half of the list of "high-net-worth" people in Asia in coming years (Vallikappen 2011). China is becoming the go-to place for the luxury market, including one of the most visible symbols of ostentatious wealth: yachts. One yacht consultant noted that the nouveau riche in China seek "a name-brand watch, a Ferrari, an apartment" (Kolesnikov-Jessop 2011). As another sign of opulence that could not have been foreseen even a decade ago, China's Ferrari drivers are the youngest in the world: their average age is thirty-five, which is ten to fifteen years younger than those found in most markets (Burkitt 2012).

Even former premier Wen Jiabao, who attempted to make "harmonious development" and "develop the West"[20] the hallmarks of his administration, argued that the current system is "unbalanced, unstable, uncoordinated, and

---

[19] These authors, including Wang Shuo, Jia Pingwa, and Zhu Wen faced an entirely new business environment as writers as well, no longer facing the "iron rice bowl" of the state socialist literary bureaucracy, but rather facing market forces for their work, producing, in some viewpoints, a pandering to populist cravings for sex and drama rather than the intellectual approach advocated by prior leading authors.

[20] The western reaches of China tend to be more financially challenged, often exacerbated by the fact that most ethnic minorities in China tend to be concentrated in the lesser developed regions of western China.

unsustainable" (Feigenbaum 2011). Economists tell us that China is caught in a "transition trap," attempting to shift away from export-oriented growth to an economy based on domestic consumption and investment. It is a move that won't be easy, (as we observed in mid-2015 when it became clear that export numbers were declining) and it could significantly shift the impetus in the country more in the direction of society and social initiatives rather than the current model of state capitalism. It is likely to divide the country further, though, as those who have gained from the current model don't want to put their future at risk.

Migration: Registered Rights—or Not

One sign of economic disparities and vastly unequal economic opportunities is the choice by many to uproot and move away from their hometown, traditionally an extremely important aspect of Chinese identity. Rural residents are leaving the countryside in huge numbers—leading to the largest internal migration rates in the world—seeking temporary employment that they often hope will lead to longer-term opportunities in the cities. Fueled in part by this rural-urban exodus, Chinese cities continue to expand. As we have seen in other developing world countries, China is urbanizing at an astonishing pace; current government plans are to move 250 million rural residents into new towns and cities over the next twelve years (Johnson 2013).

Migration can present challenges and opportunities to fall through the cracks anywhere, but in China, the trials are made more difficult because of a deeply penetrating system of formal registration, essentially a permanent residence permit. Fearing a deluge of citizens storming the cities from the countryside, and needing to organize labor for a concerted industrialization drive, authorities established the household registration system, known as the *hukou* in 1958. This system was partially modeled after both Chinese imperial institutions requiring formal residency registration and the Soviet Union's "internal passport." With this record in the system of household registration, which has origins in the family registers of ancient China, come the social benefits of access to housing, education, unemployment insurance, and others. One's hukou registration status connects the bearer to a particular city, town, or village, with access to social services connected to that locality, labeling the citizen with either "agricultural" or "non-agricultural" status, and giving a "permanent" residence. Acting as an internal passport, hukou has been dubbed "China's No. 1 Document," significantly influencing life chances for the vast majority of the population, called by some a form of "economic apartheid" (Magistad 2013). The existence of this registration system challenges the freedom of mobility that is enshrined in the Chinese Constitution (Chan 2009). From the outset, the hukou institutionalized China's urban-rural household divide, providing different welfare and civic services to urban or rural citizens, creating a second class for the latter. Even in the 1950s, China's rural residents were expected to be more self-reliant than city dwellers and were provided fewer state services.

Still, as some observe, registration requirements have not kept people from moving, but rather they have reduced the quality of life for those on the go, creating significant inequalities in social status. The central government reports the official size of the migrant population within China at just over 252 million (Zheng 2013), with approximately 130 million migrant workers making up what is commonly referred to as China's "floating population," on the move from job to job, sending remittances to their home. Due largely to migrant laborers violating their hukou, Beijing's population has increased by 50 percent in ten years (Foley 2012). It is estimated that registration limitations prevents the approximately eight hundred million citizens who are labeled as "agricultural" from settling in cities and enjoying urban welfare and services, including education, unemployment insurance, and other benefits. Although limitations on movement are difficult to enforce, access to services are not. Essentially, citizens living beyond their registration allowances "are treated like illegal immigrants inside their own country" (Stout 2013). In Beijing, for example, people without local hukou are not allowed to buy apartments or to register cars unless they have paid personal income tax or paid into social security accounts in the city for five consecutive years (in China's largest city, Shanghai, it is seven). Non-hukou holders can't easily buy a house or car outside of their permanent residence. Migrant children are rarely able to enroll in the public schools in the city where their families work, forcing families to enroll in private, unauthorized schools that can lack legitimacy and, oftentimes more importantly, accountability. One Shanghai kindergarten designed specifically to meet the needs of the city's large migrant population simply locked its gates one morning, to the surprise of families who had paid tuition and lacked any other alternatives in the middle of the school year. In 2011, Beijing authorities shut down at least twenty schools for the children of migrant workers, stranding more than fourteen thousand children without a chance for an education where their parents work (Zylberman 2011). More recently, Shanghai has permitted migrant kids to attend school in the area where their parents are working—through the ninth grade—but this has been met with protest from urban dwellers who find

A family of migrant workers carry their belongings toward a bus stop from a migrant workers' village in Beijing during Lunar New Year, 2015. *Source:* Reuters/Kim Kyung-Hoon.

the schools already overcrowded and overburdened. The precarious access urban children have to schooling goes beyond a simple inconvenience, as most migrant children are forced to return to the locality where their parents are registered—often more than a day's train ride away, to sit for the grueling national college entrance exam that remains the largest, single most important determinant of upward mobility for Chinese youth.

The official resident status is quite difficult to change: an individual with a rural hukou identity will maintain this, even if she or he lives in an urban area, and children are connected to their parents' hukou no matter where they are born. And, for those who venture into life beyond their formal registration status, it seems there is neither belonging to one's newly adopted city nor returning to one's rural residence. One male migrant to Beijing, who had left his village in 1982 to spend over twenty years in the city, lamented the changes in the countryside that became nearly unrecognizable to him upon his return: "It feels as if the countryside has had its marrow sucked away."[21]

---

[21] Literally translated from "*Gusui bei chou le.*" This statement was from a forty-one-year-old man, who had been in Beijing for nearly twenty years (quoted in Yan 2008, 225).

The mass exodus from the countryside has also worsened the return of a scourge that the CCP had ceremoniously removed after the 1949 revolution—street children. Notoriously difficult to measure with much accuracy, estimates of the number of children eking out a life on the street range from the government's official tally of 150,000 to UNICEF's claim that there could be as many as 1.5 million children forced to fend for themselves in a country where child welfare and social work institutions are meager at best (Whiteman 2012; Xue 2009). Their plight was highlighted when five boys died in a garbage bin in southwestern Guizhou Province after their parents moved to an urban area in search of work. Four of the five children in this particularly heart-wrenching case were being cared for by an elderly blind grandmother who was barely making ends meet herself (Whiteman 2012). On the street or not, it is believed that there are approximately fifty-five million so-called "left behind children" who are being cared for grandparents in rural areas, who are often unable or uninterested to provide sufficient supervision when their parents leave for the cities.

The official street children statistics do not include the approximately sixteen million "floating children" in China who travel with their parents and are ineligible for services (Stout 2013). These challenges are directly attributable to the household registration system, since parents who leave their place of residence to seek employment elsewhere are unable to enroll their children in school or other services outside of their registration status, and most company housing that does exist for migrants explicitly forbids children residents.

In official and non-official circles alike, there has been significant debate about changing or removing household registration requirements altogether. The system has been reformed before—in large part due to popular non-compliance—when the state began to issue temporary residency permits in 1984. While it was a nod to the reality that agricultural hukou holders were leaving the countryside in droves and engaging almost exclusively in non-agricultural work, the concession merely created a new "temporary" urban class whose rights and privileges were precariously connected to their vulnerable labor status.

Many have been speaking out in favor of ending formal registration requirements, including domestic and international NGOs, activists, and journalists, and even some local governments who visualize increased tax monies emanating from the change. Some large cities, including Guangzhou and Foshan, have attempted to end all residency limitations, although these efforts are incomplete. Shanghai classifies migrants into two categories: Class A for the more educated and talented migrants who add to the most desired labor pool; and Class B for migrants who have lived and paid taxes to the municipality for at least seven years. However, for the (vast majority of) informal migrants who move from job to job in search of funding for remittances, they simply have no chance of achieving Shanghai residence (Magistad 2013).

In a daring move just before the beginning of the annual meeting of the national legislature, the National People's Congress, thirteen daily newspapers published a joint editorial calling for the government to end the hukou system ("China: NPC Should Scrap" 2010). Sensing the issue is less contested than in years past, some citizens are even turning to Chinese courts. Even though hiring discrimination based on registration is widespread, it is believed that the first lawsuit explicitly challenging this didn't take place until May 2013. A college graduate was turned down for a job with the Nanjing Municipal Bureau of Human Resources and Social Security, since his registration was in a city one hundred kilometers outside of Nanjing ("Graduate Makes Formal Complaint" 2013). Still, as we will see in so many issues throughout this book, the simple duality of state-society does not accurately reflect the situation on the ground, and urbanites exert countervailing pressures against this possible influx of new residents. Many Chinese city dwellers, who now are the majority of the population, fear chaos if cities—admittedly already overburdened in many ways—become home to large numbers of new citizens demanding access to social services.

Hukou reform efforts are driven by pragmatic concerns, such as the center's desire to increase urbanization and modernization, which planners believe will fuel domestic demand and promote economic growth, the mainstay of CCP legitimacy in recent decades. The goal is to move people beyond the informal, untaxable labor into regulated formal labor in order to continue the record of economic gains. Even with significant pressure from some contentious elements within society, it seems that the most likely path to change in rights for migrants, especially in terms of the abolishment of a formalized registration system that classifies citizens at birth, is likely to come from above, albeit slowly.

Central leaders have faced increasingly agitated and empowered citizens in land-rights battles in recent years, leading to significant clashes between representatives of the local state and individual citizens over land rights. In major urban areas, especially Beijing and Shanghai, citizens have been clashing with local leaders, often aligned with powerful land developers, who attempt to apply eminent domain to achieve compulsory state acquisition of land that—although technically not privately owned since all property in China is state owned—has been maintained by families for generations. Often in question are the traditional narrow alleys and lanes with courtyard houses, known in Mandarin as *hutong* (derived from the Mongolian term for "alley"). In the 1990s, it is estimated that approximately six hundred hutong were demolished each year, displacing approximately five hundred thousand residents in Beijing alone (Kaiman 2012). Some citizens hold out, playing a bargaining game akin to "demolition roulette" in the hopes of receiving more compensation from developers (Osnos 2011). Many who resist are thrown in jail, although there have been a few famed dwellers who live in their house surrounded by empty land after others have been demolished—the most famous being a so-called "nail house" in Chongqing that sat atop a ten-meter-high mound of earth.[22] The residents of this home eventually agreed to a higher compensation package and their home was razed hours after the deal was crafted. Others have followed suit, and the term "nail houses" or "nail individuals" has been applied to any individual who resists developers and local officials seeking to raze one's home; they apply visible, media-friendly stunts, and appeal to property laws and pressure in order to achieve their ends (Hess 2010). What Hess (2010) and others have observed in this style of protest is that it not only forges new ground in its methods—notably the media savviness of participants—but also the inclusion of a more diverse social group than we have routinely observed taking on government officials.

Other, less confrontational resistance has elicited state receptivity, as a major citizen heritage group in Beijing successfully blocked the construction of an underground shopping complex that would have razed ancient hutong near the famed Drum and Bell Tower (Foster 2010), part of the central axis of the capital city. One observer noted the possible significance of this achievement, stating that "it was local people, not foreigners who led this protest," highlighting an appreciation of history and heritage that may not always have been so strong (Foster 2010).

In the countryside, attempts at perceived land grabs by developers in cahoots with local government officials have been facing even more resistance from citizens, in the forms of outright rebellion. Uncompensated land grabs in China are not new, but their impact across the past thirty years has been severe, with one noted Chinese economist estimating that farmers whose land has been seized have lost a combined total of between US$3.1 and 5.4 trillion in land value since 1978 (Tatlow 2013). The non-profit Landesa reports that 43 percent of villages surveyed in seventeen provinces have experienced the

---

[22] The characterization derives from the image of stubborn "nails" on a plank of wood that refuse to be easily hammered down. See Hess 2010.

compulsory taking of land for non-agricultural purposes since the late 1990s ("Summary of 2011" 2012). Approximately four million rural people's land is taken by governments (often local) each year (Economy 2012; "Findings from Landesa's" 2012), and conflict over land rights has accounted for 65 percent of the charted mass conflicts in China in 2010, according to Chinese sources ("Findings from Landesa's" 2012).

There are likely a number of underlying factors influencing the increase in these state acquisitions, which are experiencing a steady increase since 2005 (Economy 2012), including a growing sense of disparity, land scarcity and the resulting rise in property values, increased awareness of resistance in other parts of China (fueled by information communication technologies), as well as changes in rural financing. It seems that many localities increasingly rely on the proceeds of land sales from the deep pockets of developers as means to pay for daily operations (Jacobs 2011b). Because of hukou, the challenge goes beyond losing access to one's livelihood: when rural residents are forced to vacate most of their land—oftentimes after local authorities consolidate plots or move farmers to urban areas from where they have to commute to their farmland—these new "urbanized farmers" are rarely able to gain the necessary urban residential registration to be able to draw on social services in their new community ("Summary of 2011" 2012).

Discontent about corrupt leaders and weak property rights in one fishing village in China's southern Guangdong Province—known as the "world's factory"—hit a boiling point for nearly three months in late 2011 after the village-owned pig farm was sold to developers. The sale followed demands by villagers for not only greater compensation for the land they were being forced to surrender, but also democratic elections of village CCP officials, one of whom had been in office since the early 1980s (Jacobs 2011b). There were two days of demonstrations before the police attempted to restore order, after which two local CCP leaders were fired. Villagers were then presented a significant concession when county officials agreed to negotiate with a group of village representative chosen by consensus. When one of the thirteen people selected died during the negotiations, demonstrations again ensued for weeks, until local officials agreed to halt questionable land sales and release the body of the deceased villager to his family. Elections for local leaders were held—utilizing a secret ballot—and protests in other localities employed the "Wukan model" of engagement ("Guangzhou Land Rally" 2012; Wines 2011b). Just a few years after the Wukan incident, though, it remains unclear whether or not policies initiated to stem illegal land grabs and other forms of corrupt real estate deals will be able to stem rampant local corruption in many villages. Migration, land rights, and residency remain very much in dispute across contemporary China.

Criminality and the Rule by Law: Low Crime and Official Impunity

Acknowledging significant challenges with the reliability of crime statistics, most recognize that China's crime rate is very low—even graffiti can be hard to find. Private gun ownership is illegal, and the notoriously tough justice system has certainly kept some forms of crime at bay. During the Maoist era, Chinese cities were among the safest in the world. With the "reform and opening" policies of the 1980s came increased mobility, even if it was illegal; unemployment; and a relative loosening of social controls, which contributed to an increase in crime rates even though official statistics suggest that many forms of crime are currently on the decline. Here we run into a problem often encountered in China. Data suggesting that China's murder rate is lower than Switzerland and Japan, and that robberies are down more than 40 percent since 2002, are extremely suspect, in large part because it is not clear precisely how such crimes are counted ("Murder Mysteries" 2013). There are also political motivations for local officials to massage crime statistics to show their commitment to solving crimes, not to mention a fast-acting justice system that includes capital punishment for white-collar crimes (Badkar 2013). If the rates are close to what is being reported—and Chinese scholars believe the murder rate is falling, even if less than official stats claim—China is flagrantly going against the often-observed trend equating high levels of income inequality with high murder rates ("Murder Mysteries" 2013). It is clear that China has far fewer crimes per capita than we observe in most developed states (Bayron 2009). Theft and robbery constitute the majority of crimes; car robberies in the late 2000s, for example, climbed 18 percent, in a country that until recently had few private cars (Bayron 2009). Strict gun control laws have prevented mass shootings, but recent years have seen an uptick in violent attacks using axes and knives, including in schools.

When criminal behaviors are officially acknowledged, blame is most squarely placed on two targets: migrant workers and "spiritual pollution" from foreign movies and television programs. But, increasingly, even official sources note the inherent connection between economic challenges and crime, a tie that is also revealed in Chinese opinion polling. Forty-eight percent of Chinese surveyed identified the gap between the rich and the poor as a very big problem in 2012, up from 41 percent in 2008 ("Growing Concerns in China" 2012).

Perhaps even more disconcerting is the survey in which more than 60 percent of respondents believed that many of the nouveau riche in China acquired their wealth through improper or illegal means (Wang 2010).

As we discussed in the above section on migration, China's system of formal residence registration often separates young children from their parents, putting them at risk for trafficking—both within China and beyond. There is very little research that has been conducted on kidnappings in China, but recent incidents are raising awareness of this challenge, including connections between child abductions and China's notorious population control policies, which, despite recent changes, continue to formally place limits on family size. Again, we see social networking playing a huge role, sometimes helping adults track down their birth family decades after they were abducted ("Volunteers Take Search" 2013). Avid cyber-citizens, often referred to as "netizens"—translated in Chinese as both "net-people" and "net-friend"—circulate satellite maps online, providing resources and connections that the seemingly impotent local police are either unwilling or unable to provide. Even though authorities have been slow to officially recognize the extent of the human trafficking challenge in the PRC, recent efforts to promote social stability have prompted citizens and leaders alike to embrace new means of tracking down missing children, who most commonly are boys under five (Branigan 2011).[23] Parents have employed popular forums within Sina (a Chinese-style Twitter) to track down their missing children—some kidnapped, others runaways. One father, thrilled after being reunited with his son, told official Chinese media, "It's a miracle, a miracle that could not be true without the help of netizens" (Branigan 2011). Many of the street children found in Chinese urban areas include "working children" who are begging, selling items, scavenging, and even prostituting themselves. They are often kidnapped from rural areas by highly organized trafficking gangs, and there are even cases of the purposeful crippling of healthy children so that they can earn more money begging ("Missing Children Spark Outcry" 2009).

Recent incidents point to a worrying connection between kidnappings and international adoption. In 2005, a major investigation within China found more than one hundred children who had been illegally abducted from their parents in China's southern Hunan Province and sold into adoption (Leland

---

[23] The dominance of boys over girls on the streets has been confirmed in other quantitative studies as well. See Fucai Cheng and Debbie Lam, "How Is Street Life? An Examination of the Subjective Wellbeing of Street Children in China," *International Social Work* 53: 3 (2010).

2011), and a similar enforcement effort in the summer of 2012 freed over 180 children abducted from fifteen provinces across China and led to the arrests of members from two famed child trafficking gangs ("Police Pledge to Fight" 2012). The US State Department estimates that approximately twenty thousand children are kidnapped in China each year, while the Chinese government reports fewer than ten thousand, although some estimates put the number as high as seventy thousand (Custer 2011; Custer 2013). Chinese sources acknowledge cracking eleven thousand trafficking rings involving minors since 2009 ("Volunteers Take Search" 2013). The topic is largely taboo in China— and often internationally as well—given the sensitive nature of the ramifications of such accusations, but the evidence is mounting that this problem is much worse than many imagine. Few examples of police corruption are more appalling than the police's role in covering up child trafficking—using their energies more to track parents who report kidnapped children than in searching for missing children.

As we observe elsewhere, police eager to supplement their meager salaries increasingly collude with some of the rich and powerful figures of China's underworld (Canaves 2009). Organized crime in China includes the usual gambling, drugs, prostitution, loan-sharking, counterfeiting, and, increasingly, human smuggling that we find elsewhere. In rapid succession, major Chinese gangs have moved from operating "traditional" businesses to the establishment of major corporations with far-flung industries that serve to shield their real activities. Hong Kong and Macau have well-known and documented gangs, and mainland China is facing a resurgence of gang activity, despite having been virtually wiped out after the 1949 Communist Revolution, at which time most gang leaders relocated to Hong Kong, Macau, and Taiwan as well as Chinatowns oversees. Criminal syndicates have taken on an array of identities, and often include regional and international ties; they are difficult to differentiate from legitimate civic associations and the police who are supposed to check them. Well-known gangs include the "hand choppers," brazen motorcycle thieves in Guangzhou who attack people from the street and employ a well-known trademark used by traditional Chinese gangs of severing a limb with a meat cleaver. A maternal crime gang in Hangzhou, known as the "Big Belly Gang," attempted to take advantage of social leniency toward pregnant women by sending in small groups of women to distract storekeepers while shoplifting and robbing customers; it operated for nearly a decade before being shut down (many members violated population planning policies in order to remain active in the gang). Another major street gang is the *Fuk*

Ching (short for *Fukian Chingnian* or "Young Fujianese"), which is connected with a civic group of Chinese Americans hailing from Fujian Province in the south. Many of these organizations trace their origins and international linkages to the establishment of organizations set up to help immigrants from China settle in their new surroundings, whether in Southeast Asia or beyond. Today, membership in a gang is considered criminal, although we find the same collusion and bribery in China that we find elsewhere. That being said, comparatively speaking, Chinese gangs tend to be less visible, with their members concentrating their behavior on the hidden black market rather than visible street fights with rivals or police. While highly publicized gang crackdowns by Chinese police may suggest a possibly changing trend, China does not appear to have a gang problem concomitant with its size and degree of social dislocation.

Triads, a term coined by British rulers in Hong Kong to highlight the triangular symbols used by many gangs in Hong Kong, are other long-standing criminal associations in China and abroad, with links throughout Taiwan, Singapore, and the United States, known for their deep connections and violent actions. While there is much lore associated with their origins, most accounts connect triads with patriotic groups who organized in the attempt to overthrow the Qing Dynasty (1644–1911). The core groups, approximately fourteen, command the most attention of police and are believed to have membership in the tens of thousands each, with far-reaching yet loosely structured subgroups that help conceal identities. It is believed that some triads and their networks were crucial in smuggling individuals included in the nationwide "most wanted" list after the government crackdown in 1989 (Jacobs and Buckley 2014; Lim 2014).

The police in China are, as state employees, beholden to the interests of the CCP over the interests of citizens, and they are famously corrupt, often inept, receiving very little respect from the population. It is also clear that officials are exempt from the same laws that they are attempting to enforce upon others—leading to a system of arbitrary "rule by law" rather than the blind application of legal principles to all. There are multiple types of forces, complicating lines of accountability and transparency and strengthening the security apparatus of the state. The main unit includes the Public Security Bureau (PSB), which serves as local police and internal investigative agents combined. PSB cars, often large black sedans, evoke fear in many for their ability to act with impunity. The local PSB oversee a separate force known as the People's Armed Police (PAP), a paramilitary force established nationwide in 1983 to quell domestic disturbances. They rose to prominence—and disdain—for their role cooperating with army forces to expel protesters from Tiananmen Square in 1989, and continue to focus their responsibilities on internal social control.

The most dreaded police are the *chengguan* (short for "Urban Management Law Enforcement Bureau") forces, established in 1997 to regulate mobile groups such as street vendors and workers at unlicensed construction sites. Some claim these chengguan—involved in the beating and maiming of many citizens—are a uniquely Chinese phenomenon as a "byproduct of the country's seismic economic changes over the past three decades" (Schiavenza 2013). With little oversight, these shady forces, who often operate in plainclothes and are little more than hired thugs, are called in to police those at the margins who already find themselves on vulnerable ground due to their residency status, as we discussed above. They are employed by local officials to carry out the unpopular tasks of police work, including collecting taxes and shutting down unauthorized businesses or public gatherings; they also have a penchant for violence and abuse of power, with very little accountability. As one observer notes, chengguan have become "synonymous for many Chinese citizens with physical violence, illegal detention, and theft" (Ford 2013).

And while we could find a renegade officer in likely any country in the world, when a government official was caught on tape stating, "If the police don't beat people, what's the point of keeping them?," it hit a chord with Chinese netizens. The post went instantly viral on popular social networking sites, with people stating, "The police are the government's thugs," and similar sentiments (Feng 2013). The official approach to crime is to employ high-profile crackdowns—akin to the political campaigns we discussed in chapter 2—including periodic campaigns against narcotics trafficking and kidnapping gangs, leading to mass trials and, often, publicly televised executions (Bayron 2009). In the effort to show a quick response, innocents are caught in the fray, and executions for usually non-capital offenses are held.

Individual citizens, aided by social media, are filling in for the seemingly inept, or disinterested, police forces, crafting "thief maps" to chart locations of individual run-ins, with cautious support from government agencies—producing a synergy of local interests. One online forum in Nanjing, the "anti-pickpocket alliance," organizes volunteer patrols to respond to crime, and netizens in Shanghai have produced a public transportation thief map, using Google maps or similar knockoffs (Ness 2007). These actions build on the smart mob–style of organizing that we have seen in China and elsewhere, which mobilize via forums and instant messaging services.

Beyond the lack of oversight and the relative impunity with which most police operate in China, the justice system is strangled by the existence of a brutal system of "reform through labor" (RTL) camps, as well as unofficial "black jails" that are completely under the radar of defense officials or families of those detained. RTL sites include prison factories and reeducation camps that are known to use prison labor to manufacture exports, and where prisoners can be held for up to four years without open trial. One cadre, writing in official sources, stated that in late 2012, more than sixty thousand people were going through RTL, down from over three hundred thousand in prior years (Bai and Yan 2013; Minter 2012). In recent years, a number of academics, lawyers, and activists have released public letters calling for the elimination of these shadier aspects of the Chinese justice system. One of the most high-profile cases—which prompted rare, open debate on central policy—involved the mother of an eleven-year-old girl who had been kidnapped and sold into prostitution by seven men. After her daughter was released and the perpetrators were caught, the mother was frustrated that only two of the seven men were sentenced to death. She petitioned the government, even sleeping in the courtroom for fifteen nights in protest when it became clear that her calls were not successful. For her "disturbance," the mother was sentenced to eighteen months of RTL, sparking an unprecedented wave of protest throughout Chinese social networking sites, racking up millions of posts and several newspaper editorials (Minter 2012). Perhaps most surprising was the microblog's post on the official account registered to the *People's Daily*—the flagship news agency of the Central Committee of the CCP—in support of the mother's cause (Minter 2012). The mother did win damages (approximately US$500) in her appeal against labor camp authorities, but the court rejected her demand for a written apology, as the local police chief stated he had already made a public oral apology (Zhai 2013). The protest as pressure worked, and we observe some receptivity, as the CCP Central Committee announced efforts to reform the RTL system in January 2013 after a series of high-profile abuses of the system came to light within Chinese social media (Bai and Yan 2013). However, it is feared that the possible eclipse of RTL will lead to an increase in detentions in the more difficult to trace black jails that can operate almost completely under the radar of outside observers; this questions the degree of progress that is actually being achieved (Lubman 2012).

Known as the world's leading executioner, China puts to death more of its citizens than any other country in the world. The precise number is held as a state secret, although most estimate that it is thousands annually. Capital offenses include corruption, embezzling, drug-related crimes, even wrongdoings that would be viewed as white-collar crimes elsewhere. The sentence is carried out efficiently, often via lethal injection or a single gunshot to the head, and it is not uncommon to have televised executions. In 2007, the Chinese Supreme People's Court regained the power to conduct a final review of all death penalty cases, power that had been delegated to the provincial high courts as part of the so-called "strike hard" campaign in 1983. The supreme court overturned many sentences, and China banned the death penalty for anyone over the age of seventy-five (Fisher 2011). In 2011, authorities removed thirteen economic crimes from the list of capital offenses, including tax fraud, tomb robbing, and the smuggling of cultural relics, even though the change barely impacted the total number of annual executions, believed to total more than the rest of the world combined (Hogg 2011).

Surprisingly to some, there is quite a bit of social support for capital punishment, with the widespread belief, both in official and unofficial circles, that capital punishment serves as an important deterrent to criminal behavior. A 2008 survey by the Max Planck Institute reported 60 percent of citizens support executions (Zi 2013), although this is a significant decline since the mid-1990s, when 95 percent expressed support for capital punishment (Zhang 2014). Part of it is because China lacks a system for life imprisonment without parole, but there is also a deeply held tradition roughly equivalent to the Western concept of "eye for an eye" in traditional Chinese literature. In an op-ed debate in *China Daily*, a Beijing-based criminal defense lawyer stated, "The existing system to combat corruption is very severe, and the death penalty is still one of the strongest deterrents to criminals" (Meng Lin 2010). Even as the public discourse on capital punishment becomes increasingly open, the result can be a double-edged sword, as forms of "mob justice" can prevail when observers believe the court's sentence to be too lenient (Rajagopalan 2011).

Some changes in executions, enacted in 2007, were influenced by pressure from prominent Chinese academics calling for reduction in use of the death penalty, even though relatively few Chinese intellectuals favor the complete abolishment of the death penalty (Rajagopalan 2011). Lawyers have also been increasingly vocal. Beijing lawyer Teng Biao founded China against the Death Penalty in 2010. It remains the first and only grassroots organization in China working to educate citizens about the alternatives to capital punishment within the country. Another lawyer (who, in her prior career, supervised executions), Kong Ning, has been actively employing Internet tools, private advocacy, and other individual acts to help raise awareness of the cruelty of the death penalty (Zhang 2014). Opposition to capital punishment in China is increasingly being framed in class lines, especially after Gu Kailai, the famed wife of disgraced former Chongqing party chief Bo Xilai, received a suspended death sentence for mental illness, when rural residents with fewer resources are routinely denied psychiatric assessments by the court (Zi 2013). Whether such appeals will be enough to sway supporters of executions—both within the state and society—remains to be seen.

The criminal justice system in China is plagued by a number of factors, including the arbitrary application of laws and procedures, overlapping jurisdictions, and authority networks that prevent accountability, as well as a growing sense of impunity for groups operating, if not in collusion with corrupt officials, at least with a blind eye toward their actions. When individual citizens or even some scattered civil society groups negotiate room to engage state players on some of the issues, the direction of change desired by outspoken groups cannot always be assumed to be in one direction or another, complicating the simplistic duality of state or society preferences.

Health Care and HIV-AIDS: State Tolerates Society

Providing quality health care to over one billion people has always been a challenge, especially given the significant disparities between rural and urban areas. From the 1930s through the 1950s, farmers were provided with basic medical training as "indigenous paramedics" so that they could act as the so-called "barefoot doctors" providing preventive, paramedical care, basic hygiene, and family planning care to rural residents, later becoming a key aspect of Maoist rural policy and becoming a national policy in 1968 (Zhang and Unschuld 2008). The barefoot doctor program, which was praised as a model for other developing countries by the World Health Organization (WHO), began to collapse in the 1980s, replaced by a more formally certified—but less readily abundant—corps of medical professionals in 1985. In many ways, the rural health-care system is still trying to recover from this loss, and urban areas face challenges as well, especially since doctors remain very poorly compensated, and bribery for even basic services can be common.

Many think that health care in China is wholly government owned and operated. In its first phase, it was a state-owned welfare system, lacking any real incentives for efficiency or effectiveness. This started to change in the mid-1980s, and proposals implemented throughout the 2000s began to introduce more market-oriented incentives for health-care provision. The system was always marked by stark contrasts, both in access and quality, between rural and urban areas, a difference exacerbated by the hukou system, discussed above. The perpetuation of this system continues the division between rural and urban areas, with survey data indicating that both urban and rural residents indicate health-care costs soaring beyond what they are able to afford. The system has produced enormous gaps in coverage: in the late 2000s, it was estimated that more than 90 percent of the rural population still lacked medical insurance of any sort (Gill, Morrison, and Lu 2007).

Throughout the 2000s, there have been major nationwide attempts to reform the health-care system, including the introduction of a shared financial responsibility for treatment between patient, employers, and the state. In 2003, after being abandoned for two decades, a rural cooperative medical scheme was reestablished. The *Dibao*, or "Minimum Livelihood Guarantee Scheme," provides for an 80 percent contribution from central government and lower levels, with 20 percent being provided for by the patient. Rolled out in 1999, it was initially aimed at the urban poor, especially those who had been laid off from the behemoth state-owned enterprises that used to be the backbone of the Chinese economy, and it constituted the first cash transfer program in the Chinese social welfare system. It is part of a system of programs, divided by region and employment, which includes the Urban Employee Basic Medical Insurance Program, the New Cooperative Rural Medical Scheme, the Urban Resident Basic Medical Insurance, and the urban and rural Medical Assistance System, comparable to the US Medicaid program (Boynton, Ma, and Schmalzbach 2012). The Dibao was expanded to rural areas in 2005, as a way to supplement the growing need for assistance. Major health-care reform was launched in 2009, including the investment of US$124 billion in state funds to increase coverage as well as meet the growing need for qualified, better-funded doctors who would be less susceptible to bribes (Boynton, Ma, and Schmalzbach 2012).

While providing basic care—especially in the countryside—was a major medical challenge throughout the 1970s and 1980s, the challenges were exacerbated by the spread of HIV-AIDS beginning in the late 1980s. The stigma surrounding HIV transmission and sexually transmitted diseases in general complicated both government efforts to combat the spread of the disease as well as public efforts throughout society to have the necessarily candid discussions in order to halt its spread. AIDS was originally viewed as a symbol of Western contamination in China and an ill effect of China's opening up to the outside world, then later viewed as a disease only impacting drug users. It is believed that the country's epidemic began in the early 1990s through needle sharing among heroin users. The crisis deepened after an epidemic of HIV cases in

Henan Province, one of China's most populous and impoverished provinces, connected to unsanitary blood transfusions and plasma donations. Many infected families contend the government still has been less than forthcoming about its role in the crisis and its cover-up, and current premier Li Keqiang served as governor of Henan shortly after the major period of infections. It is believed that between five hundred thousand and seven hundred thousand citizens of the province—mostly poor peasants—were unknowingly infected with the virus throughout the mid-late 1990s, almost exclusively through the sale of their own blood (Hayes 2005). Why the state cover-up? Blood selling was marketed to local officials as a means of financing rural health care at the time (Hayes 2005).

The outbreak and global spread of severe acute respiratory syndrome (SARS) in 2003 is credited with waking authorities to the threat of an AIDS epidemic, as well as the need to promote greater governmental transparency in dealing with health crises. At the end of 2003, the central government rolled out the "Four frees, one care" program to promote free anti-retroviral (ARV) drugs, free prevention of mother-to-child transmission, free voluntary counseling and testing, and free schooling for children orphaned by AIDS, as well as social welfare care to people living with HIV-AIDS. Although there certainly have been criticisms of the implementation of this program—especially by those infected in the Henan blood outbreak—the openness with which the government began to take on responsibility for assisting with HIV cases was a significant change. Central officials no longer shun discussion of HIV. Li Keqiang, even before he had formally been named premier, met with NGOs in events leading up to World AIDS Day in 2012, proposing tax breaks and procurement services for NGOs related to HIV (Li 2012).

Increasingly, patterns of HIV-AIDS infections in China are mirroring the experience in other countries, although China continues to have a relatively low infection rate at 0.1 percent, with approximately 750,000 confirmed cases ("AIDSinfo: China" 2012). A number of changes within society, including the return of China's commercial sex industry, changing norms on premarital and extramarital sex, risky behavior in the floating population of migrant workers, and others, are increasing the spread of the epidemic into the general population, transforming HIV from a disease transmitted largely through blood donations and drug use to sexual transmissions. It wasn't until 2007 that the major means of HIV transmission in China was sexual—prior to that it was primarily blood transfusions and intravenous drug use (McGivering 2007). In 2012, health authorities released data claiming that sexual transmission accounted for 85 percent of all new cases of HIV infections, with more than one-fifth involving men who have sex with men (Li 2012). Because of the continued stigma of homosexuality (discussed in chapter 4), the health needs of men who have sex with men, many of whom tend to publicly maintain heterosexual relations, is a growing challenge in China. Sexually speaking, China today is awash in change, yet with a traditional veneer, especially in rural areas. Despite a sexual revolution in China's large urban areas, even basic sex education is rudimentary—in the official curriculum, the word "sex" is hardly even mentioned (Speelman 2013). On the verge of puberty, Chinese youth remain woefully unaware of their bodies, and parents are skittish about sex education in schools. All of this complicates the provision of health care in general, but especially the response to sexually transmitted diseases.

The public's response to HIV-AIDS has combined daring individual activism with an increasingly welcome climate for civil society organizations. We observe a seemingly contradictory mix of permissible actions, including the creation of gay support groups in various localities, some even receiving government funds for education and advocacy, with the brutal persecution of individuals who seem to go too far testing state limits. Long-standing cultural norms continue to exert countervailing pressure: even the development of self-help groups is limited by the severe social stigma that limits the likelihood of coming out. The outspoken have suffered greatly, including Hu Jia, who served three and a half years in prison before he was released in 2011. He has long been on the watch list of local authorities for his activism during the protests of 1989, and was forcibly confined to his apartment for the three months prior to the twenty-fifth anniversary of the Tiananmen Square crackdown in 2014. Two other prominent AIDS activists, Gao Yaojie and Wan Yanhai—a former health official who was arrested in 2002 after publishing a government report on the Henan crisis (Branigan 2010)—both moved to the United States because of harassment by local police. Both expressed concerns of escaping persecution.

Another activist, the filmmaker Zhao Liang, produced a documentary film called *Together*, about discrimination against Chinese with HIV and AIDS, and the film was commissioned by the Chinese Ministry of Health (Wong 2011a). Zhao's film astutely avoids mentioning the government cover-up of HIV-AIDS, especially the Henan epidemic. But for attempting to craft a synergistic response to the crisis, he finds himself disdained across the spectrum: perceived by other film directors and prominent activists including Ai Weiwei as "going to the other side" (Wong 2011a) for agreeing to work within the system.

Some small civil society organizations have been able to (delicately) carve a role for action in response to HIV in China, walking a fine line to be careful not to get caught in criticism of state responses to the disease. The number of civil society groups specifically working on HIV-AIDS jumped from zero before 1988 to over four hundred in 2009, with just over one-third of those sampled being officially registered (Li et al. 2010). Observers contend that "some of the most active and vocal organizations in China today are HIV-related or were started by activists who began their careers in HIV-AIDS organizations" (Hood 2013, 148). The visible departures of activists Wan Yanhai and Gao Yaojie, however, signaled a cooler environment, reminding all of the fragility of their synergy with the state. Civil society groups will not replace the government, but will fill in where there are gaps—one group in Sichuan Province, the Chengdu Gay Community Care Organization, produced the first gay community bulletin in Chengdu that included HIV-prevention information, even though the organization still lacks formal registration (Gill, Morrison, and Lu 2007).

Clearly, HIV remains a sensitive area for public organizing. The vast majority of HIV-related groups are small organizations, with few full-time staff members, and are often linked to the regime-connected Red Cross or All China Women's Federation. Studies have shown that the government, especially local authorities, could be "exceptionally supportive" when they wish, helping groups with application materials, moving applications along quickly, and enabling and even facilitating formal registration (Shallcross and Kuo 2012). Various civil society groups, including grassroots organizations and some NGOs, work closely with government agencies to connect with key target groups, including needle drug users and commercial sex workers, since drug use and commercial sex work are illegal.

NGOs have been viewed as "instrumental" in bringing to trial landmark legal cases, including HIV transmission through blood selling and transfusion (Hood 2013, 149). Some have achieved surprising legal victories, winning compensation for HIV sufferers and setting precedents for claims related to other diseases, including hepatitis.[24] The continued criminalization of sex work (despite some changes, as we discuss in chapter 4) limits the growth of cohesive NGO actors working with sex workers to prevent spread of the disease. Unlike some other areas of state-society relations, we observe a growing presence of

[24] See Jiang Xueqing and Wang Shanshan, "Special Report: Hepatitis B Carriers Challenge Discrimination," *Global Times*, September 25, 2009.

international organizations including USAID and the Bill and Melinda Gates Foundation, which opened an office in China in 2007. These organizations have increased the availability of voluntary counseling and testing. In part because of international attention, Chinese groups are experiencing a much more positive environment for researching HIV-AIDS. One scholar speaks of graduate students who changed their research focus to HIV-AIDS in order to increase job prospects upon graduation, a phenomenon Beijing academic Li Dun calls "eating AIDS rice" (Hood 2013, 145).

Despite this record of growing receptivity, social actors employed in HIV-AIDS advocacy have also encountered some resistance by state officials. Throughout 2007, as the country prepared not only for the 2008 Olympic Games but also for the significant leadership conclave, authorities in Guangdong and Henan Provinces disrupted meetings and closed HIV-AIDS related organizations (Gill, Morrison, and Lu 2007). Individual activists—including some who were essentially employing conventional and legal means to promote the implementation of national laws—were harassed and detained ("Restrictions on AIDS Activists" 2005). Those repressed included some lobbying for assistance for AIDS orphans, as well as others seeking economic assistance publicly promised to HIV-positive persons, and yet others for reporting that ARV drugs distributed by the local health department were past their expiration dates. It seems their offense was that they were spreading information that was not favorable to the record of local officials. The control of information was deemed more important than the provision of health care.

ANALYSIS

When it comes to contentious politics in regard to human security, figure 3.1 distills our comparison and the discussion that follows. The three issues that are the focus of this chapter—migration, criminality, and health provision with a focus on HIV-AIDS—are not core, "dangerous" issues in either country. Groups and individuals have adopted an impressive repertoire of approaches—from polite to muscular, but all of them conventional—to press the state on these issues. Contentious politics in both countries could be characterized as tense regarding two of the issues—migration and criminality. What is interesting is that the states in both democratic Brazil and authoritarian China utilized similar responses to society: a mix of receptivity and resistance. Analysts can debate how to characterize this response, whether concessions or promises are only meant to demobilize society or offer the promise of reform. For these reasons we characterize the outcome in both countries in regard to migration

FIGURE 3.1   CONCEPTUAL FRAMEWORK FOR HUMAN SECURITY

Brazil		China
Migration		
Moderately Contested: Struggles over land in urban areas are not as highly contested as they are in rural, but are very tense and have sometimes become violent.	Issue	**Moderately Contested:** Pressure to decrease formal registration requirements acknowledged by state and social actors; fights over land rights are more contested.
Conventional: Seeking dialogue but threatens insurgent practices. Oppositional stance but not seeking to overthrow government.	Societal Approach	**Conventional:** Protest as pressure, some use of courts for attempted change. Countervailing pressure from urbanites.
Both: State uses violence against protesters but also negotiates with them.	State	**Both:** State focus on urbanization produces harder stance; yet desire for stability produces some receptivity for rights in city.
Indeterminate: State granted concessions, but root problems remain unaddressed.	Outcome	**Indeterminate:** Registration changes are being formally considered, but requirements remain.
Criminality		
Moderately Contested: Disagreement over how to combat crime and whether official impunity is the bigger issue.	Issue	**Moderately Contested:** Collusion between state and police makes criticism more of direct attack against CCP. Some synergy on corruption.
Conventional: Seeks to work with the state, but countervailing pressure from society fearful of crime.	Societal Approach	**Conventional:** Pressure exerted via social media and protest, as well as legal channels.
Both: State divided on what approach to take and cross-pressured for a "tough on crime" approach.	State	**Both:** Resistance to challenges of police as state; receptivity to fixing worst forms of abuse and to some changes in capital punishment.
Indeterminate: Some reforms but police impunity and state use of extrajudicial violence remain common.	Outcome	**Indeterminate:** Reform as propaganda to offset calls for change; situation worsening with creation of more hidden forms of repression.

FIGURE 3.1 CONCEPTUAL FRAMEWORK FOR HUMAN SECURITY *(continued)*

Brazil		China
HIV-AIDS		
Less Contested: All agree on need to address issue.	**Issue**	**Less Contested:** Acceptance and increasing education.
Conventional: Protest as pressure and working with government; synergy.	**Societal Approach**	**Conventional:** Organizing and awareness campaigns; limited confrontation; fragile synergy. Countervailing pressure connected to social norms.
Receptive: Society leads the state.	**State**	**Receptive:** State (belatedly) tolerates society; resistance to most vocal activists who implicate government.
Reform: Pioneers prevention efforts and guarantees treatment as a human right. Becomes a role model for the world.	**Outcome**	**Indeterminate:** Openness to accepting importance and source of challenges; repression when too organized.

and criminality as indeterminate. Even if the reforms prove real, they do not address the root of the problem(s). As figure 3.1 shows, our cases lined up as nearly identical on the issue of HIV-AIDS. There are differences between the cases, but they're mostly in timing and speed: HIV-AIDS has been a relatively less contested issue on which the state has exhibited receptivity. Brazil is far ahead of China in this regard, where a similar process has unfolded more slowly, but society led the state—or the state allowed itself to be led. Not only in both countries did state and society agree that some action was required to deal with the disease, society has worked with the state on HIV in both countries. In Brazil, society led the state on HIV-AIDS and the outcome (reform) has become widely recognized as one of the country's greatest accomplishments. But because of Beijing's suspicions about anti-AIDS activism, which slowed cooperation and progress on the disease, the outcome is best characterized as indeterminate. Most would probably agree that on this particular issue, regime type goes far in explaining the difference between the two cases.

But a consideration of the larger context is always recommended when conducting comparisons. Before going on to further compare and contrast Brazil and China on human security, it may prove useful to remember their histories and line up the two countries' political trajectories side by side. As you may recall from chapter 2, the Brazilian dictators, whose rule coincided with Mao's last years, prioritized economic growth to the detriment of development. But by the late 1970s, at about the same time that China was turning the ship around and was opening to capitalism, Brazil had begun its transition to democracy. By the 1990s and 2000s, as China became more capitalist, doing away with many social welfare programs without becoming more democratic, Brazil became more democratic and social welfarist. In effect, Brazil too had changed course—but in the opposite direction of China.

Despite some important similarities today, Brazil and China's histories diverge significantly in that one had a revolution and the other did not. Consequently, China has no "old money families," whereas Brazil has plenty of them. Both have their nouveaux riches and both have raised millions out of poverty, but, as mentioned earlier, both top the list of most unequal societies in the world. Although both were burgeoning economies in the 2000s, neither China nor Brazil is riding quite so high today. Their middle classes are growing, but there are cracks just beneath the surface. Both states are facing mounting protests regarding human security and their experience is counterpoised in other important ways as well. For Beijing, an emphasis on economic growth above all else has replaced an interest in human security and development. On the other hand, Brasilia has a progressive government that leads the world in taking the opposite approach. Its priority is development; it pioneered CCTs, and it has been using economic growth to finance it.

Although Brazil's PT-led governments have been criticized from the left for not going far enough to dig deeper and make more transformative, structural change, the Chinese government has been going in the opposite direction. As mentioned earlier, under Mao, China was poor, but it prioritized development. However, the iron rice bowl, Mao's effort to guarantee human security with a massive safety net, was smashed as the country opened up to capitalism. And the state has chosen not to create anything to replace it; China has only one CCT program to date. The communist government has clearly put economic growth over social development. Its sustained growth rates are epic, breaking world records, as are the numbers of Chinese who have been pulled out of the depths of poverty—in this regard they resemble Brazil. But the other side of this

---

[25] Although the CCP pursued it with the goal of promoting social stability, the growth-at-any-cost strategy has taken an environmental toll, as discussed in chapter 5. The strategy has backfired and so enraged the population that Beijing has recently begun trying more to balance the two, finally, out of political necessity.

is that the rich have gotten ever richer, so despite this accomplishment, the gap between rich and poor has actually widened.[25]

But it's not quite as simple as a matter of China moved to the right, Brazil moved to the left. In many ways, the otherwise progressive Brazilian state continues the tradition of previous, more right-leaning governments in its treatment of those considered "marginal." As we see in figure 3.1, it resembles the CCP's policy. Both countries face the pressures of rural-urban migration because neither has been willing to give people a reason to stay in the countryside and neither is willing to make the structural changes that would slow this urban migration. Whether it is China's "floating population" or Brazil's *favelados*, rural dwellers have come to the cities, desperate to find opportunity. In both countries the problems these populations face are very similar and compound each other. But the ways in which the Chinese and Brazilian states treat migrants comes down to a difference between acts of commission and acts of omission. China attempts to staunch the flow of migrants with its formal registration system, and Brazil, which doesn't actively seek to stop the migration, offers precious little for migrants and treats them as if they lack the rights of citizenry once they arrive. For example, in China, the children of migrants aren't allowed to attend school; Brazil has compulsory education, but it prepares the kids who attend its public schools for little other than a life of servitude. Either way, in democratic Brazil and authoritarian China, migrants are second-class citizens.

Over the years, both states have behaved similarly, using receptivity and resistance. They both declared the homes of so-called marginals illegal and evicted them. Significant numbers of citizens were forced out for "modernization" drives, especially so the state could host large-scale sporting events.[26] One telling difference between them is that whereas authoritarian China doesn't have to offer an explanation, the Brazilian democracy counsels residents that the evictions are for their own good. Because they are answerable to the population, the Brazilian state has made a greater effort at appearing even-handed. Under the gun with a World Cup deadline looming, the Brazilian state did make concessions and promised reform. But other times, when faced with mounting opposition from groups like the MTST, they too have resorted to strong-arm tactics that are reminiscent of the dictatorship—therefore rendering their policy

---

[26] It is estimated that from 2000 to 2008, 1.5 million people in Beijing were forced from their homes to modernize the capital in preparation for the Olympics (Reynolds 2008). At least 170,000 Brazilians have lost—or are at risk of losing—their homes on prime real estate to make way for the 2014 World Cup, 2016 Olympics, and gentrified neighborhoods (Watts 2013a).

different from the Chinese more in style than in kind. On the other hand, no group like the MTST dares to operate openly in China. However, people do find more subtle ways to get around the system, and sometimes less subtle ones, as citizens turn out in growing numbers to protest land grabs. The Chinese government has promised reforms. The irony is that despite the fact that both states have given every indication that they don't want the migrants—now sometimes second- and third-generation—there, both have relied on this cheapest of labor pools to build their high-rises, serve their food, and scrub their floors. In effect, both countries treat their own citizens in the way many others worldwide treat undocumented (foreign) workers.

Another aspect of human security discussed in this chapter is crime, which many might expect to be high in both China and Brazil, given the high levels of inequality in the two countries. While China's rate of crime has grown since its opening to capitalism, the most common crime is larceny. The rate of violent crime in China is still relatively low, whereas Brazil's homicide rate is much higher. It is often touted as the worst for any country not at war ("2011 Global Study" 2011; Wells 2013). Many of us might also bet that crime rates fall as countries become more democratic, more open, transparent, and accountable, but that is clearly not the case.

So it's a fact: democratic Brazil is a more violent place to live than authoritarian China. What explains this divergence? Well, it's not quite as simple as you might think. China's lower violent crime rate is likely due in no small part to a heavy police presence, the scarcity of guns, and deterrence: fear of the pain of punishment makes a lot of people think twice about getting into trouble. In China—for violent crime, if not corruption—punishment is swift and severe. The PRC government executes more people than any other country in the world and public support for it is strong, even if it is starting to decrease. In Catholic-majority Brazil nearly 50 percent of the population supports reinstating capital punishment ("Death Penalty Splits Views in Brazil" 2008). But even without its reinstatement, punishment in Brazil can be swift and severe (and arbitrary) as well—it's just extrajudicial. In both countries, whether it is police abuse or another form of corruption, accountability is the exception, not the rule ("Brazil Court Upholds" 2010). There are no organized groups currently taking on such issues in China. Concerning Brazil—although there has been more public outcry against police abuses in recent years—it needs to be pointed out that groups like Viva Rio, which leads this battle, are the exception. The Brazilian state exhibits some receptivity on the issue, with reforms that promote community policing and a better relationship between the police and the communities they serve. But impunity for state actors is largely the rule in both countries and that is unlikely to change anytime soon. In part this is because most Chinese and Brazilian citizens are fearful of crime and support a tough law-and-order approach for dealing with it.[27]

A related frustration is the rule of law, as both China and Brazil suffer from arbitrary, unaccountable, and ineffective criminal justice systems. Brazilian and Chinese citizens alike hold their courts and court officials in very low regard, as soft on criminals. Only 5 to 8 percent of murder cases in Brazil result in convictions (Wells 2013). On the other hand, China's criminal justice system isn't weak at all—but it's not strong, it's "hard." When it comes to violent crime, according to the Chinese government's statistics, 94.5 percent of those charged with murder are found guilty. Perhaps such a success rate is due to the government's use of torture to extract confessions ("Murder Rate among World's Lowest" 2013). Brazilian police are known for such tactics as well, only they use them extrajudicially, off the clock.

Both states have exhibited receptivity on HIV-AIDS, but Brazil's policy has resulted in reform, whereas China's policy is indeterminate. Both countries got a slow start in responding to AIDS, but Brazil began its turnaround in the early 1990s whereas China largely claimed it didn't have an AIDS problem until a blood donation scandal forced the issue nearly a decade later. As of 2011, both countries had low adult prevalence rates (Brazil's is 0.3 percent, China's is 0.1 percent), but Brazil's rate was once much higher and was brought down, thanks to its proactive policy, whereas China, whose rate was never as high, could have done a better job in dealing with the disease had it been more receptive to society and started sooner ("2012 Progress Reports" 2012).

Similarly, the Brazilian and Chinese states couldn't be more different in the treatment of groups still stigmatized by much of society, such as sex workers and men who have sex with men. As described earlier, in Brazil, despite the large number of conservative Catholics and evangelicals, the state has proven receptive to anti-AIDS activists. It is pretty clear that when it comes to AIDS, society led the state, the state allowed itself to be led, and Brazil took its first steps at becoming a world leader using a harm-reduction approach. Interestingly, in many ways the democratically elected government ended up years ahead of the population, willing to take a risk by being more progressive than

---

[27] Ronald E. Ahnen (2007) showed that Brazil has actually become more reactionary since the transition to democracy, as police abuses have increased and citizens elect politicians who compete to show who can be tougher on crime.

many Brazilians. Its frank, sex-positive public health campaigns promoting safer sex are a perfect example of this.

On the other hand, this is not the case with the Chinese state, which for a variety of reasons, including its absence of religious conservatives, one would think would have the latitude to lead society. In relatively puritanical China there is virtually no sex education; state and society shrink from discussions of sexuality. Although some of the most powerful civil society groups in China have their origins in AIDS work, the disease remains a sensitive area for public organizing. But it's because of the potential threat these groups pose more than "morality" that has Beijing ambivalent about working with homosexuals and prostitutes, the groups that led Brazil's battle against the disease. Still, although it has the latitude to break with popularly held stereotypes and take the lead in destigmatizing these populations, police routinely run sweeps and round up people suspected of falling into these categories (Kao 2013). Discrimination against people who are HIV positive is a problem in Brazil as well. There are signs that China is headed in Brazil's direction in terms of the state's receptivity to society on fighting HIV-AIDS, but at this point the two are different in speed and style as well as substance.

Again, much of the difference in regard to the states' handling of HIV-AIDS may come down to regime type (i.e., Beijing's paranoia about the potential power of civil society, even on less contested issues). However, as mentioned in regard to figure 3.1, there are many similarities in the two cases' approach to migration and criminality that call into question many assumptions in regard to regime type. Earlier we discussed their trajectories as mirror images of each other: China has been moving to the right just as Brazil moved to the left—with China putting growth before development and Brazil using growth to promote it. Both countries also have major problems with corruption and the rule of law, but citizens live in greater fear for their lives in Brazil than in China. We expect human rights to improve with democratization, but violent crime is worse—and has worsened—since Brazil's dictatorship ended. Correspondingly, we often assume communist regimes to be corrupt, but many would argue that corruption has worsened in China since it opened to capitalism. Unfortunately, corruption is just one of those problems that exists beyond regime type; it has remained endemic in Brazil—under dictatorship and democracy.

One final commonality to mention is that beyond their variations in experience and policy, both states are recognized as "superpowers"—China as the economic giant that is poised to challenge American economic power, and Brazil the human security superpower recognized for achievements promoting social welfare. Here we see that issue has more salience than regime type in explaining motivation and behavior: it is imperative that both states achieve strong economic growth because both have made big promises that remain to be fulfilled. Similarly, issue is more important than regime type in explaining society. Regardless of whether they find themselves living under a dictatorship or in a democracy, citizens in Brazil and China have higher expectations now, and if they aren't satisfied, they have shown that they will not be shy about pressuring the state to meet their demands. As a result, Chinese leaders pledge to promote social harmony and the so-called "Chinese dream." With promises of zero hunger, access to health care for all, and the eradication of poverty, Brazilian leaders promise that Brazil will finally achieve its potential. Authoritarian or democratic, leaders of states at opposite ends of "the messy middle" often do speak in ways that sound remarkably similar. For example, urged on by citizens, Brasilia and Beijing both promise ardently to clean house on corruption and endeavor to prove how tough they can be on crime. It is only on softer, less contested areas of policy where these states have indicated any significant level of receptivity, perhaps to distract attention away from less negotiable issues. Again, one thing is clear: if we rely too heavily on simple narratives about regime type to predict state-society relations and issue outcomes, we'll be surprised as often as not at the way things really are.

DISCUSSION QUESTIONS

1. As of 2015, both countries' economies were slowing. What ramifications do you think this will have on state-society relations in terms of human security?

2. When it comes to human security, it could be said that society in Brazil and China is reacting to exclusion, impunity, and lack of responsiveness. Are these problems in your own country? And are they attached to any particular issues of human security? Explain.

3. How did Brazil set out to become a human security superpower—and why hasn't China done the same? In what ways is Brazil found wanting in this regard and what explains this?

4. Much of the story of human security, in terms of "freedom from fear," is a story about the relations of citizens and police. Compare crime and the criminal justice systems in the two countries. Which is a more dangerous place to live? Why? What role does regime type play in this? What are the most prominent forms of activism in this regard and their aim(s)?

5. Why, in explaining state receptivity and resistance on human security issues, is it not simply a case of "China moved to the right / Brazil moved to the left"? When it comes to migration, crime, and health care, in what ways are the two states more alike than different? Ultimately, in what ways do both treat their citizens very similarly?

4

POLITICS OF SOCIAL DIVERSITY

Branca para se casar (A white woman to marry)
Mulata para fornicar (A mulata woman to fornicate)
Preta para cozinhar (A black woman to cook).

   —An adage in Brazil (Gilberto Freyre, *The Masters and the Slaves*)

This society is so full of inequalities. Family background, opportunities, rights, development . . . even sex is unequal.

—Tweet from Liumang Yan during her day providing free sexual services to migrant workers (Kenneth Tan, "Blogger-Activist Liumang Yan Turns Prostitute for a Day to Speak Up for Sex Workers")

INTRODUCTION

Every government struggles to accommodate contention over ethnicity, religion, and sex. In democratic and non-democratic societies alike, there is give-and-take between leaders and the led, albeit usually with degrees of difference accounting for levels of risk. Again, we argue that regime distinctions capture only part of this vital state-society dynamic. Both China and Brazil are richly pluralistic, with extremely diverse societies of multifaceted ethnic groups, spiritual traditions, and means of expression. Within both countries, we see behaviors that belie simplistic explanation. We also observe a dynamic similar to what we have identified in prior chapters: contentious politics play out differently depending on the issue. Whereas democratic Brazil and authoritarian China

149

have both shown themselves to be receptive on some claims against the state, the most highly contested matters are core issues, on which the state will not budge. Therefore, when it comes to identity, we observe some significant differences in receptivity and resistance between Brazil and China.

In this chapter, we examine some of the significant areas of individual and group expression in Brazil and China as a window on state-society relations. We observe both social activism and social stress. To capture some of the most significant trends within social politics in both countries, we examine ethnicity, religion, and sexuality in both states. Social actors are dynamic interpreters of a variety of messages: traditional mores, contemporary trends, and personal aspirations. Each of the topics we examine in this chapter shows how difficult it is to capture state-society dynamics in one sweep, and each also demonstrates that in both states, the boundary lines of authority and influence are consistently being redrawn by a variety of actors on both sides of the metaphorical state-society dividing line.

Transnational actors, movements, and organizations also play important parts in influencing the state—in as much as the state seeks to influence these actors. China remains sensitive to and resists the involvement of outside forces, and in the case of formal religious institutions, strictly forbids association with external organizations. Some of this comes from China's fairly recent history of semi-colonialism and control, yet much of it derives from the regime's defensive posture about the contagions of change, especially in light of the 2011 Arab Spring. So the changes that we observe in China (the decriminalization of homosexuality, for example) are rarely traced back to pressure from international organizations—the perception of external interference can doom any movement in China. Many of the changes that have occurred in Brazil can be attributed to the state's interest in cultivating the illusion of inclusion. This inclusivity is no small part of Brazil's national identity and self-image as a liberal, modern, progressive democracy (Pagano 2006). Analysts disagree over whether the social changes in Brazil over the last few decades are remarkable, or whether they are largely symbolic. At best these changes are only a start; because there is little if any institutional foundation for them, any progress that has been made could easily be turned back—although civil society in Brazil, now roused, would likely fight.

BRAZIL

When it comes to social issues regarding religion, race, and ethnicity (or, as they say in Brazil, "color"), as well as sexual orientation and gender relations,

Brazil's national identity is said to suffer from multiple personality disorder. One image has long been projected to the world and it coexists with an alternate reality. When it comes to bringing the former more into line with the latter—in other words, what needs to be done for Brazil to live up to its image—there is no consensus. Nor is there consensus on (as Htun puts it) "how ideas drive policy change" or how best to characterize the contentious politics in Brazil (Htun 2004, 60). There is near universal agreement that domestic and international civil society play at least some role in the evolution of state policy. Although some analysts argue that the state has mostly taken the lead in a shift of social policy, or was at least an equal partner in the trajectory of change that we have witnessed over the last few decades, the majority view contends that since the re-democratization that began in the mid-1980s, favorable conditions were created so that the state has largely acceded to a combination of domestic and international pressures (Htun 2004; Pagano 2006). The dominant view today is that on these controversial but less contested issues, the state has been led. Actually, when it comes to issues of color, gender, and sexual orientation, the greatest tension has been not between state and society but between progressive (often but not always secular) and conservative (usually but not always religious) groups. Thus, countervailing pressures within society have cross-pressured the state and slowed the pace of change. This effect is particularly pronounced in regard to issues of sexuality and reproductive rights, but in Brazil even color has become part of the "culture wars."

Layers of Identity: Color in Brazil

Brazil's evolution on "color" or race relations is the result of the push and pull of state and society. Although the matter is hardly settled, over the last two decades Brazil has made an about-face and experienced a paradigm shift when it comes to how the state constructs and how the nation understands race and race relations. Since at least the 1930s, Brazil had prided itself on being unique in the world when it came to race; for most of the twentieth century it basked in the glory of being known worldwide as a racial democracy. With approximately half the population today claiming some African descent (the actual figure is widely believe to be much higher in this country where racial intermarriage is the norm), Brazil has the largest African-descended population of any country in the world (except Nigeria). A point reiterated throughout this book is that Brazil is unique—or at least views itself as such. Certainly one major part of Brazil's self-identity is that it has never suffered from the divides that plague other multiracial societies such as the United States. Whereas the United States has largely adopted a racial dichotomy (that one is either black or white) and the racial divide in the United States has until recently been delineated by "the one drop rule"—anyone with one drop of "black blood" is considered black—Brazil's understanding of race is very different. For Brazilians, there has been no simple dichotomy and (until recently at least) most Brazilians haven't identified in terms of race. Rather, they speak of color, and instead of just two, it is said that Brazil's population is made up of more colors than a Crayola box. The official narrative and one expressed (until recently) by most of its citizens is that the country has many colors—some say over one hundred—but only one race and culture (Pagano 2006).

More slaves were brought to Brazil than any other country in the world (approximately four million), and Brazil was the last country in the Americas to outlaw slavery, in 1888. However, the official version of history (one that apparently nearly all Brazilians bought until recently) held that Brazil is different because its history is different. Some argued that the Portuguese (because they were once conquered by the Moors and had a long coexistence with them) were uniquely enlightened colonizers. Consequently, Brazilians have long argued that the form of slavery practiced there was more humane, more benevolent than elsewhere. Most famously, sociologist Gilberto Freyre (who came from a family of plantation owners) in 1933 put forward the view that it was the permissive attitude toward miscegenation, the mixing of the races throughout the country's history, that produced a unique, hybrid, mestiçagem population. This view became accepted as doctrine in Brazil, as Freyre and Brazil's opinion leaders celebrated this mixing as the essence of Brazilianism, arguing that it was the blending of European, African, and indigenous populations that gave Brazil its exceptional national character and made it a model for the world (Daniel 2006). The dominant paradigm cast Brazil as a racial paradise compared to the United States; Brazilians considered racism to be patently un-Brazilian. This part of Brazil's national identity granted Brazilians a feeling of moral superiority over countries riven by race divides, like the United States. It certainly did build in Brazilians a strong sense of unity. But it also had a deracializing effect; not only did it blur racial divides, the dogma of racial democracy forbade any discussion of them (Daniel 2006). The ideology of racial democracy diffused discontent and lulled Brazilians of all colors into believing that any inequities were a matter of class or individual initiative, not race.

Nonetheless, such arguments are hard to sustain when one examines a few statistics. According to Minority Rights Group International,

Evidence of the exclusion of the vast black minority is rampant. Nearly 80 per cent of Afro-Brazilians live below the nation's poverty line, compared to 40 per cent of white citizens. Afro-descendants in Brazil earn half of what white groups earn; life expectancy is 6.5 years lower for blacks than for whites; and one half of all Afro-Brazilians are illiterate—some two and a half times the number of whites who cannot read or write. Only 4 per-cent of Afro-Brazilians between the ages of 18 and 24 are in universities, compared to 12 per cent of whites. Three-quarters of all Afro-Brazilians have not completed secondary school, and 40 per cent of blacks have not completed elementary school. ("World Directory of Minorities" 2007, 6–7)

In the United Nations Development Program (UNDP) Human Development Index (HDI), a composite measure of well-being, Brazil ranks 69th. According to the report, if Brazil's HDI were calculated just for its black population, it would come in 101st, while a white Brazil would rank 46th ("World Directory of Minorities" 2007). As it became increasingly difficult to explain away the overall disparity in life chances between whites and Afro-descendants as simply due to class, not race, Brazil began a paradigm shift (Daniel 2006).

Although 2001 is often identified as the turning point, the origins of this paradigm shift can be traced much earlier, and is due to the political opportunity structure created by the confluence of three factors: domestic pressure; a receptive, democratizing state led by a president interested in the issue; and international pressure. There is no agreement on the precise mix that explains the resulting change in the official discourse and how the government came to adopt reforms aimed at promoting racial equality, namely affirmative action. Htun (2004, 60) describes the turnaround as "a dialectic between social mobilization and presidential initiative framed within unfolding international events." The way she sees it, the ideas were put forward by Afro-Brazilian activists, legitimized by transnational actors at international conferences, and made salient by then president Cardoso, who happened to be a sociologist specializing on race (Htun 2004).

Still, just bringing forward the ideas to spark the dialectic seemed an impossibility during much of the twentieth century because so many Brazilians, of all colors, had accepted the dogma of racial democracy. Racism exists in Brazil, but it is said to be veiled; it is a cordial, informal racism in which motives are hidden by code words and blatant racism is rare. It is commonly said, "If in the United States, racism is like a gun pointed between the eyes, in Brazil it is pointed at the back of your head."

Imagine how difficult it is to fight an enemy that most of the population says doesn't exist. Sure, informal racism certainly is real, but Brazil never had legal segregation. There was never a ban on interracial marriage; rather, it was—and is—quite common in Brazil. Although the standard of living for blacks there was even lower than it was for blacks in the United States in the mid-twentieth century, it has been harder to mobilize the population to rally against racism because there has never been any Brazilian Jim Crow, no Ku Klux Klan (Daniel 2006). Correspondingly, while Brazil has had some great black leaders, they have never had the stature of a Reverend Martin Luther King Jr. or Malcolm X. And Brazil has yet to create and sustain an organization with the power of the National Association for the Advancement of Colored People (NAACP) or a civil rights movement like the ones in the United States. In part this is because earlier in the twentieth century such groups were outlawed and censored. During the military dictatorship (1964–1985) those who questioned Brazil's racial democracy were considered threats to national security, and subversives faced torture and imprisonment (Daniel 2006).

However, during the political liberalization known as the abertura in 1978, Afro-Brazilian activists formed the *Movimento Negro Unificado* (MNU, or Unified Black Movement). Although it is said that Afro-Brazilians have a "thick" black cultural identity, they have a "thin" sense of themselves as a racial collectivity (Daniel 2006). The MNU has played a vanguard role in changing that. It put the issue of race on the agenda and, using the tactic of co-sponsorship, joined with black cultural organizations, women's groups, and others to enter the political arena. The largest black consciousness organization in the history of Brazil, the MNU had a main goal, among others, to challenge the ideology of racial democracy, expose hypocrisy, and develop alternative public policy (Pagano 2006; Covin 2006). Still, even since Brazil's return to democracy in 1985, those who raised discussions of race were themselves accused of racism, and groups like the MNU have had a hard time appealing to the majority of Afro-descended Brazilians, who, as a sign of how entrenched racism actually is, don't even necessarily identify as black.[1] Poor and poorly educated, most

---

[1] A central tenet of the ideology of racial democracy was the idea of social whitening, as expressed through the common saying in Brazil, "money whitens," and a belief in social mobility through "the mulatto escape hatch." Since the days of slavery, there had been a social differentiation of mixed race (then known as mulatto) people from blacks (and whites), with preferential status granted to mulattoes over blacks, including a significant degree of white social acceptance for those with the lightest-colored skin. The mulatto escape hatch therefore refers to the vertical mobility offered to those who whitened through miscegenation. Although

blacks consider the middle-class academics of the MNU to be elitist and out of touch with their real, day-to-day concerns. Consequently, the MNU has never been considered a mass-based movement. However, after decades of work, by the late 1990s, a more diverse, heterogeneous, race-based "issue network," or critical mass of engaged groups and individuals, had combined their energies to shift direction from consciousness-raising to a focused campaign making demands of the state —just as the state was becoming more receptive to such demands (Htun 2004; González 2010).

Although the democratic state was not totally unresponsive to these pressures prior to this time, it was not until the presidency of Fernando Henrique Cardoso (FHC) that there was a significant shift in policy and discourse. A sociologist who spent time in exile for his criticism of the dictatorship, Cardoso had long written about inequality. Interestingly, in an early address as president, FHC himself awkwardly claimed to be *mulatinho* ("slightly mulatto") and to have "a foot in the kitchen"—a reference that dates back to slavery. This made him the first president in Brazil's history to characterize himself this way— although it is highly unlikely that he was actually the country's first African-descended president. There is disagreement about whether FHC was the catalyst for the paradigm shift or simply another contributor to it (Pagano 2006). There are some who believe that the change in state policy was individually based and elite-led, not due to the pressures of the social movement. For example, Cardoso orchestrated the opening and became a champion for affirmative action. According to one human rights activist, "If FHC had not been president, the debate would not have started" (as cited in Htun 2004, 80). Others give the president less credit, saying that his enthusiasm for the issue was always limited and had fizzled out toward the end of his term (Pagano 2006).

---

such ideas were offered up as "proof" that Brazil wasn't racist, many characterize the promise instead as ethnocide: it purged Brazilian culture of African (and indigenous and other non-European) traits by assimilating them until they disappeared (Daniel 2006).

These ideas, predicated on the view that inequality was based in class, not race, preserved white privilege and effectively stifled any nascent racial identity. The effect was divide and rule, as the majority of the population (all colors) accepted such arguments. However, despite claims that none of Brazil's problems had to do with race, the very idea of social whitening and its tenets resulted in an internalized racism. For decades the black movement has worked to overturn such ideas. The MNU encouraged more Brazilians to identify as *preto* (black) rather than *pardo* (brown), not only to promote black pride but to unite Afro-descendants to better claim their rights in Brazil. Although only 7 percent of Brazilians self-classified as black in the 2010 census, it appears that this rethinking is catching on, at least in the media, government, and among academics, which are phasing out use of the term *pardo* (Phillips 2011a; Pagano 2006).

At the very least, there is agreement that a number of forces converged to produce this outcome. In 1995, after conducting an investigation of race relations in Brazil, a Special Rapporteur of the United Nations Human Rights Committee released a report that embarrassed the country in front of the whole world, seriously questioning Brazil's long-held claims of being a racial democracy (Pagano 2006).[2] Later that year, Afro-Brazilian activists marched to Brasilia to mark the 300th anniversary of the martyrdom of the African resistance leader Zumbi, in the biggest demonstration of its kind (Covin 2006). In response, the federal government—for the first time—created an office to initiate a discussion of remedies for racial inequality (Htun 2004).

But the moment of reckoning for Brazil—and the end of the myth of racial democracy—is widely believed to have come five years later, when a mirror was held up to Brazil and the country saw itself in a new light. In 2000, a government body, the Institute for Applied Economic Research (IPEA), released groundbreaking reports about the pervasiveness of racism and inequality in Brazil. What struck most Brazilians was that for the first time, this information wasn't coming from "black militants"—the source was a textbook example of conventional politics: prestigious white economists working for the government. As the press published these findings, illusions were shattered and it became increasingly impossible for the state—and most of the public—to remain in denial (Htun 2004).

International civil society, in the form of the 2001 World Conference on Racism in Durban, South Africa, also played a catalytic role in this paradigm shift because it built stronger networks between black organizations in Latin America, the United States, and South Africa. Most crucially, perhaps, Durban reminded the world of what is expected of democracies when it comes to race. It legitimized not only the debate on racism but also discussion of reparations. Inside Brazil, the Durban conference is most remarkable for the role it played in "waking up" the Brazilian media and stimulating public interest. Suddenly, the topics of racism, racial inequality, and affirmative action were being discussed as never before. Moreover, the strategic partnerships that coalesced as Durban mobilized civil society and strengthened the political will necessary

---

[2] Such a report was especially galling for many Brazilians because in the 1950s UNESCO visited Brazil to see what it could teach the world about avoiding racism. Although the study reported that blacks were disproportionately represented among the poorest in Brazil, it also found that Brazil was unique in that blacks who attained wealth and education were fully accepted by whites (Daniel 2006).

to push for new policies to combat discrimination. In the end, according to Htun (2004), civil society, presidential initiative, and international events arose independently but were mutually reinforcing. Each of the three variables shaped and was shaped by the other two. Collaboration between domestic and international civil society persuaded the state to take their claims seriously and changes in the political opportunity structure, most notably, the presence of an ally in the executive branch, certainly had a positive impact on the ability of domestic and international civil society to mobilize, thus setting the country on a trajectory for change (Htun 2004; Pagano 2006).

After 2001, the environment was ripe for change and the result was a significant shift in policy. It is important to point out that this adjustment did not occur simply because it was politically expedient. When the state finally abandoned the dogma of racial democracy, it wasn't because it felt threatened, and it didn't do so for material incentives or because it would win votes. Rather, according to Htun (2004), the reform occurred because the state was receptive and because it was no longer much of a contested issue, for two reasons: 1) because more people were finally convinced by the idea that Afro-Brazilian activists had been arguing for decades, that racism was pervasive and something that needed to be addressed; and 2) because Brazil was concerned about its image and the new democratic government wanted to prove its credentials to the world.

Society led the state, but the state claimed center stage, not only to proclaim how it has changed, but to show that it is a world leader in the fight against racial discrimination. The Lula and Dilma governments have built on the start provided by the Cardoso administration, leading a variety of efforts to address racial inequality. Most of these have centered on affirmative action programs, promoting the use of quota systems in university admissions and government hiring. Taking the arguments of groups like the MNU to heart, to varying degrees these executives have been the champions of programs of positive discrimination, which also include non-quota initiatives targeting black populations such as health programs and preparatory courses for the vestibular, all-important college entrance exam (Pagano 2006). As we will see again and again, for controversial causes, executive leadership is a necessity in Brazil. However, for the most part, the federal government has promoted affirmative action, but not imposed it (Htun 2005; Daflon 2011). There have been some remarkable gains; most public universities now have sizable black and brown populations. But implementation has been pursued "in the Brazilian way," allowing for a great deal of flexibility in how each institution enforces the policy.

As a result of this accommodating approach, affirmative action is practiced in a variety of ways and only in some government agencies and universities. Moreover, the legislative and judicial branches of government have largely proven less enthusiastic about such interventions. Some proposed measures have never been passed, while others have been tied up in the courts (Pagano 2006).[3] One could argue that the uneven implementation of the reform means that it amounts to a new version of *para inglês ver*—mostly for show.

Such a policy reflects countervailing pressures within society. In terms of private discourse, there are still plenty of Brazilians arguing about whether racial democracy is a myth. Public opinion polls suggest significant support for affirmative action, particularly among the young.[4] Although a 2008 survey found that a majority (64 percent of respondents) admit that color or race does affect one's life, there are many, on the left and right, who cling tenaciously to the ideal of racial democracy and insist that if racism exists in Brazil, it is nothing like the problem anywhere else ("Survey of the Ethno-Racial Characteristics" 2011; Chang 2007). According to a 2013 *Economist* article, a recent poll found that two-thirds of Brazilians supported affirmative action for university admissions ("Slavery's Legacy" 2013). But earlier polls report that one in six Brazilians strongly oppose racial preferences, and as one might expect, there has been some backlash against it. Whereas many on the left insist that the problem of inequality is more about class than race, the right rallies nationalist sentiments by condemning affirmative action as "un-Brazilian," an import not suitable for their country. Both groups worry that such policies will create racial conflict in a society where it did not exist (World Directory of Minorities 2007). Beyond their philosophical objections to affirmative action, these authors, who include some of the wealthiest and best-educated Brazilians, also point to practical problems in implementation, particularly in determining who is white and who is non-white. (Interestingly, affirmative action's supporters counter that the police certainly have no difficulty determining who is black.) But not

---

[3] Although Article 5 of the 1988 constitution declares racism to be a crime, in reality bringing forward a charge of discrimination is an exercise in futility. It is extremely unusual for anyone to be punished for the crime of racism because it is so difficult to prove it. Only the most egregious acts are outlawed, and even then the punishment is so severe that judges have been reluctant hand down guilty verdicts. For example, one study found that only 394 of 651 discrimination cases brought forward ever went to trial, and of those not one single case ended in a conviction ("World Directory of Minorities" 2007; Pagano 2006).

[4] According to a study by the Latin American Opinion Project, more than two-thirds of Brazilians view affirmative action favorably (Smith 2010).

even all advocates for racial equality support such measures, fearing that quota systems reinforce racism and ignore the roots of inequality. They argue that universalist—as opposed to race-based—programs like Bolsa Familia have had more of an impact on reducing inequality than affirmative action ever will (Daniel 2006).

Although the debate on affirmative action continues, there is near universal agreement that a paradigm shift on race has occurred in Brazil. The ideology of racial democracy has been dismantled, and even if it is largely discursive—and the glaring inequities remain intact—Brazilians have snapped out of denial and the change is significant, palpable. For decades in Brazil, it had been heretical to talk about race or even suggest that racism existed (Htun 2004). Now the conversation has begun and it is about national identity. And while advocates of racial equality still wait for more profound institutional changes, in Brazil private and publicly held conceptualizations of race do appear to be transforming (Reiter and Mitchell 2010; Htun 2004). That Brazil is finally looking critically at itself and recognizing that there might be a problem is huge, and that is thanks to contentious politics: the back and forth between state and society, or the interplay of citizen activism, executive leadership, and world events.

Sexual Politics and LGBT Rights

Let's cut to the chase: like most of the world, Brazil is a patriarchal, heterosexist society with highly restrictive ideas about traditional families and gender roles.[5] In Brazil, traditional gender ideologies are based around the concepts of *machismo* and *marianismo*. These powerful worldviews assign males and females to perform distinct gender roles and teach that the result is harmonious gender relations, as the roles are complementary. Men are believed by nature to be macho: powerful, fearless, dominant, and sexually aggressive. They are the breadwinners and heads of the family, and they have traditionally dominated the worlds of work and politics. Women, on the other hand, were traditionally taught to model themselves on the Virgin Mary, for whom *marianismo* is named; whenever possible they have been relegated to the home and their primary role is as mother. According to Neuhouser (1999), machismo and marianismo divide

---

[5] As is the case elsewhere, there has always been more variation in "the family" than traditionalists would have us believe. This is particularly true of Brazil, where diverse family forms are known to exist and the expression of gender roles has always been complicated by race and class (Adelman and de Azevedo 2012).

the world into male and female spheres and are like scripts that individuals must follow closely at the risk of social ostracism. Proof of this is that traditionally in Brazil, the worst thing a woman could do is abandon her children. Interestingly, working as a prostitute might be deemed acceptable if she is doing it to provide for her children. A "bad" man is a homosexual, whereas drunkenness and infidelity are tolerated. Historically acts of what was considered "gender deviance" were often punished harshly, and sexual stereotypes and double standards of sexual morality are built into the law and culture (Neuhouser 1998). For years, Brazil's laws on sexual harassment, rape and intimate partner violence reflected patriarchal norms—and arguably its strict prohibitions on abortion still do. But even as legal codes have changed to punish gender violence, implementation of them has proven difficult. The idea that females are sexual objects and the property of men is so normalized that sexual harassment, rape, and intimate partner violence is believed to be inevitable (Portela 2014).

These traditions in Brazil date back to colonialism and remain strong; however, this is also a country that has been experiencing rapid social change, particularly in regard to gender relations and family life, since the return to democracy in the 1980s.[6] Today, traditional gender ideologies are increasingly questioned, particularly by younger women; urbanization, industrialization, and economic growth have accelerated these trends (Neuhouser 1999). The result is yet another set of contradictions in Brazil, as tensions play out between contending civil societies that duke it out for influence over the state. This is the arena for contentious politics in regard to women's rights in Brazil: in one corner, the reigning heavyweight champion, the Catholic Church, has joined with evangelicals to fight against "a crisis of the family" and to maintain the status quo, or even turn back the clock.[7] In the opposite corner it faces the

---

[6] The Church upholds abstinence, heterosexuality, and a vehement opposition to abortion, but in reality, when it comes to these issues most Brazilians are relatively progressive and increasingly secular, although the majority of them remain silent on abortion—even those who have had one (Rosenberg 2011; Cardoso 2010).

[7] Evangelicalism is the fastest-growing religion in Brazil (it has grown from 4 percent of the population in 1960 to 15 percent in 2000). While Catholicism's influence is waning (it is still significant, claiming 70 percent of the population), evangelicals in particular have had great success in developing a media empire, and both conservative Catholics and Protestants have harnessed the political power of their congregations by sending more of their representatives to Congress, who have combined to form a formidable voting bloc. These near hegemonic forces argue that they are fighting a defensive war, defending the traditional family against all who seek to "rethink" it (Ogland and Verona 2011; Bevins 2012). The result is a struggle over a highly contested terrain, and all bets are on that it will continue for some time to come.

challenger: what has been described as perhaps the largest and most lively feminist movement in Latin America, which is seeking to, according to Adelman and de Azevedo, "redefine gender relations and to transform ways of thinking about men, women, sexuality, and family—just to name a few" (Adelman and de Azevedo 2012, 73).

Although organized forms of women's activism date back at least one hundred years in Brazil, much of the progress that has been achieved is attributable to the country's second-wave feminist movement of the 1970s, which joined with other civil actors in taking an oppositional stance to fight the authoritarian government, unseat it, and reestablish democracy. Since then, Brazilian feminists have taken a more conventional approach, using protest as pressure to broaden understandings of democracy by questioning ascribed gender roles and contesting women's juridical and social inferiority. Just as the MNU had challenged racial democracy as a myth, Brazilian feminists challenged as imaginary assumptions about the harmonious nature of male-female relations (Pitanguy 2002). They had a lot on their plate. The 1988 constitution declared, for the first time in Brazil's history, equality between husbands and wives, but prior to that time a woman "only had power to make decisions in which her husband was incapacitated, could not work without his permission and a pre-marital loss of virginity was a basis for marital annulment if the husband so desired" (Adelman and de Azevedo 2012, 67). Working with the system, the women's movement in Brazil lobbied hard to have these and similar laws overturned in the 1988 constitution. They largely succeeded; the state proved receptive and reforms were made. When it comes to women's rights, Brazil's constitution is considered one of the most expansive in the world.

As a result, a number of indicators suggest that when it comes to gender relations and gender inequality, Brazil is changing, albeit slowly. It is ranked 62 out of 136 countries in the 2013 Global Gender Gap report, which offers a snapshot of how women are doing. Brazil's ranking has improved over the last few years mostly because of strong showings for female health and education. However, Brazil is still ranked very low, particularly on wage equality, as women on average earn two-thirds of what men do. Brazilian women have been entering the paid workforce in larger numbers since the mid-twentieth century, more women are unionized than ever before, and more are entering formerly "male" professions, such as physician. But occupational segregation is still the norm and women are concentrated in the less valued jobs. Meanwhile, despite the fact that they are entering the workforce in ever-greater numbers, women (or for middle- and upper-class women, their maids) continue to be responsible for nearly all the housework ("The Global Gender Gap Report 2013" 2013; Simões and Matos 2008).

Of all the indicators, it is ironic, given that Brazil has a female president, that some of the country's worst scores are for female political participation. Although parties are supposed to reserve a minimum of 30 percent of their slots for females, the gender quota has not made much of a difference in breaking this glass ceiling. As of 2013, women composed only 9 percent of federal legislators ("The Global Gender Gap Report 2013" 2013; Simões and Matos 2008). Thus, as Simões and Matos (2008) conclude, there have been some improvements in women's status since the mid-1980s, but gender inequality persists, and is compounded for some women by simultaneous oppressions based on race and class.

Although feminists describe Brazil's reality as changing very slowly, it is much too fast for conservative religious groups, who chastise their counterparts for breaking taboos in discussing sexuality and who characterize feminists as promoting divorce and promiscuity, as pro-abortion and pro-homosexual. As these two social actors battle to the death over whether the traditional family will be protected or historic systems of power and inequality dismantled, the state finds itself caught in between, often working pragmatically with one side but unable to ignore the political clout of the other. The resulting clash is frustrating for all involved and has left Brazil with a policy that some have characterized as bordering on the schizophrenic (Adelman and de Azevedo 2012).

The struggle over abortion is a good example of the power of countervailing pressures within society and how society can lead the state—to maintain the status quo. As is the case with race relations, the state finds itself cross-pressured, this time by the clash of traditional and modern gender ideologies and understandings of human rights. Since 1940, abortion has been defined as a crime for which a pregnant woman or the person performing the abortion can spend up to three years in prison. Brazil currently has one of the most restrictive abortion laws in the world: it is only legal if the pregnant woman's life is at risk or if the pregnancy was caused by rape.[8] Even under these circumstances, time-consuming and difficult bureaucratic obstacles (e.g., until 2005, a police report was required for an abortion to be permitted in cases of rape) greatly impede women's access even to legal abortion (Simões and Matos 2008).

---

[8] In 2012 the law was expanded to allow abortion in cases of severe and fatal fetal impairment, such as anencephaly ("Brazil Lifts Ban" 2012).

Brazilian feminists and health-care advocates press the government for the decriminalization of abortion because abortion may be illegal, but it has hardly been abolished. Approximately one million illegal abortions occur each year in Brazil. Many of the women receiving them never recover from the physical and psychological wounds associated with self-induced or kitchen table abortions. It is estimated that every year hundreds of thousands of Brazilian women seek emergency treatment for these clandestine abortions, where they are often "punished" by health-care practitioners who suspect foul play and neglect them or refuse them painkillers (Garcia 2010; Vianna, Carrara, and Lacerda 2008). Untold numbers delay seeking medical care because of shame or fear of the legal consequences. Although no one knows the precise number, it is estimated that five thousand women die each year in Brazil from complications due to unsafe abortion (Garcia 2010). We do know that most of the women at risk are relatively poor and likely to be brown or black since middle-class and relatively affluent women (mostly white) can afford to pay for still illegal but safer abortions performed in private clinics (Guilhem and Azevedo 2007).

It was against this backdrop that groups like the Feminist Health Network have utilized conventional approaches to agitate for change. Much of the work of pro-choice groups prior to 2000 is described as "firefighting," with feminists lobbying Congress to maintain at least their limited, established rights to abortion. But they have also employed protest as pressure. For example, they have engaged the media with creative and artistic interventions and promoted a dialogue by bringing in opinion leaders, including supermodel Gisele Bündchen ("Model Gisele Slams Church" 2007). And over the years they have put forward many legislative proposals for decriminalization—all of which have been rejected by Congress. By 2002, feminist groups decided to take a different tactic: to work more directly to create conditions ripe for the legalization of abortion. They adopted the slogan, "Abortion: Women Decide, Society Respects the Decision, the State Ensures its Execution," and actively campaigned to help elect Lula, an executive they believed would lead on their cause (Soares and Sardenberg 2008, 57). In 2005, President Lula affirmed Brazil's international commitments regarding reproductive rights and appointed a commission to review the country's abortion legislation.[9] The result was a bill to decriminalize abortion until the third month of pregnancy.

---

[9] Such international commitments included the 1994 United Nations Conference on Population in Cairo and the 1995 Fourth World Beijing Conference on Women.

The response was a holy war, declared by the Catholic Church and supported by other religious conservatives, who view abortion as a moral issue and threat to the family, not as a privacy or health issue (Simões and Matos 2008). As mentioned earlier, the Catholic Church has long been a powerful institution in Brazil. The Brazilian state has been considered secular since the 1891 constitution, but throughout history it has been strongly influenced by the Church, especially on decisions concerning sexual and reproductive rights. More recently, conservative Catholics, led by the Brazilian Bishops' National Conference, have been joined by evangelicals in Congress to form a faith-based movement that has not only blocked all legislative reforms of the abortion law but even sought to make abortion completely illegal in all circumstances.[10] Abortion is a grave sin and a paramount concern for both religious groups—and such a bold move is a good indicator of the power of religious conservatives in Brazil. This bloc contends that the rights of the unborn must trump all others (Simões and Matos 2008).

One has to wonder if in taking on the abortion issue, Lula somehow overestimated his personal appeal to Brazilians or thought that Brazil's keen desire to attain international legitimacy would give him the power to step into the fracas unscathed. Whatever the case, he was clearly wrong. Maybe it was just bad luck: the proposal was put forward just as a major corruption scandal threatened the president's reelection in 2006, and just as the bishops were using every weapon in their arsenal—from parish pulpit to mass media—in a campaign to rally public opinion against him. Religious leaders there and throughout the country stoked nationalist passions, characterizing the pro-choice movement as pro-abortion zealots funded by the United States. During this period, Church leaders referred to the president as "Herod" (the king of Judea who ordered the killing of baby boys) and Rio parishes distributed plastic dolls to represent aborted fetuses, with full support of the bishop. Despite his multiple headaches, Lula managed to get reelected in 2006, but by the time of a 2007 meeting with Pope Benedict, Lula had recalibrated and was pledging that he would never seek the legalization of abortion (Mollman 2012).

Yet another turning point occurred in 2009, when the Church excommunicated a nine-year-old rape victim, her mother, and her doctors for her abortion.

---

[10] It should be noted that not all practicing Catholics form a monolithic block on this issue. The NGO Catholics for the Right to Choose has played an important role in raising awareness about the need to deal with the problem of unsafe, illegal abortions and its race- and class-based implications (Simões and Matos 2008).

Under Brazilian law, the termination of the pregnancy was legal on two counts: she was raped, and her life was at risk—the eighty-pound girl was pregnant with twins. For a moment it appeared that Lula had rallied: he condemned the bishops for excommunicating everyone involved—except the stepfather who had impregnated the girl (Kulczycki 2011; "Brazil: 9-Year-Old" 2009). However, in the end, Lula disappointed advocates for reproductive rights. With elections just months away, he bowed to conservative pressure and took an about-face, and, in order to boost his protégée's chances at the polls, his party dropped decriminalization from its human rights plan (Mollman 2012). However, this had become the topic that wouldn't go away. Abortion, which had never been a front-burner issue in past elections, became a flashpoint in the 2010 vote. Dilma nearly lost her first campaign for president over accusations that she flip-flopped on abortion and Internet rumors about her support for changes that would al-low terminations as late as the ninth month of pregnancy. In the end, analysts say that she pulled off the victory only by insisting that she personally opposes abortion and vowed not to legalize it (Downie 2010; "Abortion Becomes an Issue" 2010).[11] Thus, abortion offers a prime example of the political power of social actors and how society can lead the state—in this case, to maintain the status quo.[12]

When it comes to the rights of sex workers in Brazil, contentious politics is about state receptivity. As with the other social issues discussed here, society has led the state, which adopted reforms. In fact, this is an example of synergy; the state changed its repertoire and has moved from marginalizing prostitutes to partnering with them to better implement its HIV-AIDS policy. Here again Brazil is unique. It has the world's largest Catholic population at the same time that it celebrates its reputation as an "erotic democracy"—one of the world's most sexually liberal societies. Brazil is a major draw for sex tourism—in 2012 it was close to overtaking Thailand as the world's number one sex-tourist des-tination. The country's sexual vitality is central to its national identity, sym-bolized by Carnival and prized since at least the 1930s as a social, cultural, and

---

[11] All three of the leading candidates for president in 2014 tried to avoid the issue, but came out in favor of keeping the law as is (Carneiro 2014).

[12] Interestingly, the majority of the Brazilian public (65 percent, according to a 2007 *Datafolha* poll) favors maintaining the current abortion laws without reform (cited in Garcia 2010). However, it is estimated that 31 percent of pregnancies end in abortion and one out of five Brazilian women under age forty have had an abortion (Guilhem and Azevedo 2007; Garcia 2010).

economic resource (Amar 2009). However, as the following discussion will demonstrate, perhaps it is no more an erotic democracy than it is a racial one.

In Brazil, the commercial exploitation of prostitutes is illegal, but not prostitution per se, as long as the sex worker is eighteen or older (Pimenta et al. 2010). Until recently the result of this contradictory policy has been that sex workers lived in a legal limbo without any formal protections. Today, even though prostitution is legal, it is still a very dangerous profession. In fact, the first organized movement of sex workers formed in 1979 to protest police brutality, after police murdered three prostitutes (female and travesti, or transgender) in São Paulo. In those days, sex workers, including transgender and male prostitutes, who are particularly targeted for violence, were pariahs in Brazil. When they marched to call attention to the widespread police abuse, it was the first time that Brazilians heard prostitutes speaking up for themselves. Not only were they successful in their demand to have the precinct captain removed, this event marked a watershed for Brazil, as this previously excluded group joined civil society (Hinchberger 2005). By the late 1980s, using protest as pressure, Brazilian sex workers from all over the country formed the Brazilian Network of Prostitutes. They joined "whores' movements" in other countries to fight for labor rights, including social benefits such as government pensions, to reduce the vulnerabilities associated with sex work and to combat violence against prostitutes, and to eliminate the stigma attached to it (Crago 2008; "Human Trafficking, HIV/AIDS, and the Sex Sector" 2010).

But it was the government's concern over the spread of HIV-AIDS that brought the state into partnership with sex workers. In Brazil as elsewhere, early on in the epidemic the state stood by as certain groups (sex workers and homosexuals) were blamed for the disease. Meanwhile, as HIV-AIDS spread rapidly in Brazil, it became more of a priority for the state and eventually both groups were able to persuade the government to see the problem differently. The critical juncture came in the late 1980s and early 1990s, when a combination of pressures (domestic and international) forced a shift in attitudes and the public health officials changed their approach, signaling state receptivity to society's demands. Recognizing that gay men and sex workers were in a unique position as citizens to combat AIDS, the state recalibrated its policy and chose to work synergistically with these groups (Jeffrey 1997). By 2000, these groups had formed NGOs and were working in government and receiving federal funds to promote HIV prevention efforts. In effect, the state paid female and male prostitutes to work as peer educators, running workshops to teach other sex workers about condom use and AIDS prevention. The programs have worked well because they deal with the issue of access; more people are getting access to information and technology because peers are accepted in ways that officials are not (Hinchberger 2005).

Despite the effectiveness of such programs, in 2005 the Bush administration made continued US foreign aid to fight HIV-AIDS contingent on the Brazilian government's formal condemnation of prostitution and rejection of prostitutes' rights.[13] The Lula government chose instead to reject the $40 million in US funding rather than accept the anti-prostitution pledge and violate what it considered a matter of sovereignty. In other words, Brazil refused the United States' attempt to tell it what to do. For Brazil, it was also a matter of ethics and citizenship. This is another example of Brazil's exceptionalism: for standing up to the United States, Brazil stood out as an example to the world. It is one of the few countries that views sex workers as partners in public policy. Most countries treat them as part of the problem instead of the solution. The partnership between sex workers and the state on AIDS continued to evolve over several presidencies, as prostitutes served as advisers for policy and meanwhile continued their calls for prostitutes' rights (Pimenta et al. 2010).

Taking a different approach and calling themselves "*putas politicas*" (political whores), more prostitutes are pressing for their rights as citizens through the political process. Not only do they lobby politicians; Gabriela Silva Leite, a retired prostitute and sex workers' rights activist, ran for a congressional seat in 2010 with the slogan, "*uma puta deputada*" (which can be read to mean "congressional whore" or "a bitchin' awesome congresswoman") (Blanchette 2010). Clearly, some individuals have chosen to consider sex work as a profession and part of their identity. They've appropriated slurs once used against them and drawn power from them.

Other putas politicas presented a bill before Congress obliging clients to pay prostitutes directly and to legalize brothels and the commercial employment of prostitutes. Such moves would have afforded protections to sex workers that they currently do not enjoy, as the illegality associated with brothels means that prostitutes often wind up working in miserable conditions that they can't complain about since they can't have a formal working relationship with their employers. From the sex workers' perspective, yes, there has been progress. But until sex work is fully decriminalized there will be corruption, as police extort

---

[13] Under the Obama administration, the United States has continued to require all organizations that receive HIV-AIDS funding to take the anti-prostitution oath.

them or look the other way when employers mistreat them (Vallance 2012; Jeffrey 1997).

Just as is the case with its racial democracy, Brazil's self-image as an erotic democracy does not hold up against reality. Brazil is a paradox. On the one hand, Carnival is a celebration of shifting gender identities and the country is a mecca for gay travelers; in 2010 it was estimated that a quarter of all Rio's tourists were gay (Keating 2012). And Brazil has staked out its place as a world leader in the promotion of lesbian, gay, bisexual, and transgender (LGBT) rights at international forums. But Brazil is also infamous as one of the worst places in the world to be LGBT. Once more, the story is about how bigotry fosters activism, which fosters backlash, and how one group of non-state actors has joined with the state in opposition to another non-state actor whose power once rivaled the state.

Of course, that actor is the Catholic Church, and although it has never been as powerful in Brazil as it is in other Latin American countries, many—if not most—of Brazil's traditional conceptions of sex, the family, and morality are based in Church doctrines. Traditional Brazilian beliefs about homosexuality reflect Catholic teachings that it is unnatural, sick, sinful, and an abomination to God.[14] And evangelicals have indicated that they are ready to join conservative Catholics in throwing down the gauntlet against gays and lesbians ("Brazil Evangelical Christians" 2012).

As a result, homophobia and transphobia live on in Brazil, as the country has become infamous, even record-setting for violent attacks persecuting people for their real or perceived sexual orientation and/or gender identity. Homosexuality (except for in the armed forces) has been legal in Brazil since 1823. Here again there is a disconnect between the real and the legal Brazil: Brazil's rate of victimization of gays and lesbians is higher than in Europe or the United States. Brazil, the capital of Carnival, is said to have the world's highest rate of transphobic violence (Rosenberg 2011; "Brazil at a Crossroads" 2011). It is estimated that between 1980 and 2009 over 3,100 people were murdered in hate crimes across the country, specifically targeted for their sexual orientation or gender identity ("Brazil at a Crossroads" 2011). And the number of homophobic and transphobic hate crimes appears to be climbing. According

---

[14] Most Brazilians are well acquainted with this view but are more liberal than their religious leaders and considerably less homophobic. Still, many analysts warn us not to make too much of this; they would only describe the average Brazilian's view as tolerant—which is far less than accepting (Encarnación 2011).

Members of Sao Paulo's gay community protest the Catholic Church's views on homosexuality with posters that read "No more hypocrisy! Condoms and Health," and "Jesus loves gays," 2007. *Source:* Reuters/Luludi-Agencia Luz.

to the Gay Group of Bahia, transphobic and homophobic attacks resulted in 326 murders in 2014—nearly one every day in Brazil. This democracy, which aspires to be a leader of the world's marginalized people, may also be the world's deadliest place to be transgender (Bevins 2015; "Brazil at a Crossroads" 2011).

On the other hand, this is the same country that hosts the largest gay pride parade on the planet, with three million participants in 2013 ("São Paulo Gay March" 2014). Its gay rights movement also grew out of the *abertura* of the 1970s and 1980s, as LGBT activists put aside their specific concerns and joined in solidarity with other civil society groups using a confrontational, oppositional approach to push for the end of the dictatorship. For years LGBT persons lived in a climate of repression and in fear of the state, which claimed to represent Christian values and the traditional family. In the 1970s in Brazil, the authoritarian government threatened advocates for gay rights with charges of offending public morality, and police conducted raids to "clean up" the cities. In a variety of ways, citizens resisted this persecution; in what is known as the May Day March of 1980, in the largest political act by Brazilian LGBT groups up until that time, nearly a thousand people marched in São Paulo to protest police harassment (Green 1994). During the early years of the democracy, by the early

1990s, some groups (such as the Brazilian Association of Gays, Lesbians and Transvestites) had begun partnering with the state and working in government. As mentioned earlier, gradually the state became reliant on LGBT activists' technical expertise on HIV prevention. In return, these groups received funding from the state and the two built on the relationship, gradually expanding into other issue areas (de la Dehesa 2010).

In Brazil, as in much of the rest of the region, this movement is surging and considered one of the best-organized worldwide. LGBT groups have even (often provocatively) shown that they're willing to take on their adversaries. For example, one group caught the country's attention for distributing HIV prevention posters depicting scantily clad male models dressed as Catholic saints with the caption, "Not even a saint can save you. Use a condom" (Bevins 2011). In what has been described as "cross-pollination," gay groups fighting discrimination in Brazil have influenced and been influenced by their counterparts in Europe (especially Portugal) and the United States. For example, gay rights activists have used the Internet to create a "gay cyberspace" that provides a variety of services but is most notable as an alternative to mass media outlets, as a place where the LGBT populations represent their views and share information (Encarnación 2011).

In many ways, despite the fact that the 1988 constitution does not explicitly prohibit discrimination on the basis of sexual orientation—it does prohibit it on the basis of race and gender—LGBT activists have been more successful than feminists or Afro-Brazilian activists in achieving legislative and policy changes. When it comes to gay rights, there is said to be a true partnership between state and society, although that has not always been the case. Whereas Cardoso was the president serving as the catalyst for change when it came to race, President Lula is widely considered the patron of LGBT rights in Brazil, famously claiming that discrimination on the basis of sexuality is "perhaps the most perverse disease impregnated in the human head" (E. Friedman 2009, 429). Thanks to the Lula government's support, Brazil is one of the few places in the world where free gender reassignment surgery is considered a basic right for all citizens (Rosenberg 2011). Moreover, the federal government sponsors São Paulo's annual Gay Pride march (E. Friedman 2009). Perhaps the most celebrated triumph for supporters of gay rights to date is the recognition of equal marriage rights in 2013 (civil unions have been recognized since 2004). Most of the gains on this front have come through Brazil's judiciary, which argued that Brazil's constitution guarantees same-sex couples the same rights as their opposite-sex counterparts (Romero, 2013a; "Same-Sex Marriage: Global

Comparisons" 2013). As a result of this state-society partnership, Human Rights Watch has recognized Brazil's exemplary progress in the promotion of LGBT rights (Rosenberg 2011; Vianna, Carrara, and Lacerda 2008).

However, conservatives are challenging the court's decision, seeking to overturn what they see as the efforts of activist judges, whom they claim are violating Christians' religious freedoms by forcing them to recognize same-sex marriages. They are turning to Congress for support, which is increasingly dominated by evangelical Christians and has been less willing than the other two branches to view gay rights as human rights (E. Friedman 2009; Bevins 2015). Conservative groups and their allies in Congress seek to annul existing marriages and to reestablish marriage as the union of a man and a woman (Leal 2014). They are also making their voices heard on other issues regarding sexual orientation. In an effort to stop hate crimes, during the Lula administration PT and other progressive lawmakers have proposed a landmark anti-homophobia law that seeks to guarantee the rights of the LGBT population and turn homophobia into a crime—much as racism is treated as a crime in Brazil (Ortiz 2011). Religious conservatives, however, have lobbied hard against the bill. Because it criminalized public utterances against gays, they characterized it as a "gay gag" and argued that it promoted homosexuality and interfered with freedoms of religion and speech. After multiple revisions the bill was blocked and as of 2015 appears to be going nowhere, in part because executive support for it has diminished. Dilma, Lula's successor, was once outspoken in favoring the bill. However, to be reelected in 2014 and needing conservative votes and support in Congress, she (and her main rival) avoided the issue in the campaign. Weakened by a major corruption scandal in her second term, Dilma has not been nearly as willing as her mentor to take a lead on the issue. In this case it's not simply a matter of receptivity or resistance; for a variety of reasons, even in her first term the president chose to avoid the controversy, vetoing the "Kit Gay," an educational packet designed to promote tolerance among schoolchildren (Jebsen 2012).

Some are concerned this is a sign of the times in Brazil, that Brazil is becoming a less liberal nation as evangelicals, supported by international evangelical groups such as one led by American televangelist Pat Robertson, are ascendant. For example, a controversial preacher known for his homophobic and racist remarks was appointed president of the Commission for Human Rights and Minorities (Watts 2013b). Clearly, neither state nor society are monolithic on this issue.

Although Brazil was once considered a unique racial democracy, few continue to make such arguments today. It is a country with a female president serving her second term, but women are still widely treated as sexual objects. It is recognized throughout the world as a leading voice for the human rights of LGBT populations, but those concerned about equality know that there is still work to be done in Brazil. The country is changing in ways that many people never expected in their lifetimes—as is awareness of the issues raised in this chapter. But many fear that it is war now; the very success of these movements is creating a backlash. "Anxiety" over change is commonly argued to be behind the rising number of hate crimes against people who are still characterized as a threat to tradition (Bevins 2011; Jebsen 2012). Until the "real Brazil" comes into line with the "legal Brazil," the country will not live up to its reputation.

CHINA

Too often, observers of China discount the role of society. As one Western business adviser laments, "The huge misconception in the West is that China moves forward and changes because all-powerful officials at the top issue orders that everyone follows" (McGregor 2005, 194). Chinese society is more stratified—economically, socially, and politically—than ever. Despite visible and brutal crackdowns, "China lays claim to one of the oldest and most influential traditions of popular protest of any nation on earth" (Perry 2011, 136). As we will see in the following discussion, there is a combination of both receptivity and resistance by state actors to many social initiatives.

Since 2005, Chinese leaders have promoted the image of China's "harmonious society"—an aspirational statement that belies China's record of contention and challenge. Given the size of the country, and the well-known limits of the center's reach beyond Beijing, leaders face a legacy of promoting local flexibility while insisting on the rigid interpretation of central mandates. Elizabeth J. Perry (2011) introduces the concept of "pragmatic populism" to capture the CCP's ability to dispel ideological orthodoxy in favor of a managed social response, a heritage she traces to the Confucian principle of benevolent governance. She argues that the state's response to popular demands may actually strengthen the state and state legitimacy. Yet much is in contention. Some maintain that the types of protest and contention in China have significantly changed since the late 1980s, with a rise of blue-collar protests that involve far fewer students and intellectuals than prior waves. From the standpoint of state-society relations, one of the biggest differences in these protests is that they are directed toward the local state, rather than Beijing. In fact complainants often appeal to higher authorities for help, invoking the need for the enforcement of national laws (Walder 2011).

Layers of Identity: Religion and Ethnicity

In recent years, Chinese leaders have gone out of their way to extol the regime's official tolerance of the diversity within the Chinese population, highlighting China's fifty-six recognized ethnic groups (the majority Han constitute approximately 92 percent) and the constitutional promise of freedom of religion. At the same time, unrest in spiritual and ethnic identities found within Tibetan and Uighur communities challenges the official narrative of China as a cohesive multiethnic country. And, even though many Chinese view prejudice as a "foreign problem," racism and other forms of discrimination remain doggedly persistent (Canaves and Oster 2009). Prejudice against "foreign devils" is centuries' old, and discriminatory, racist slurs against Japanese and Koreans are uttered in public without reticence. Chinese have long harbored negative attitudes toward people with darker skin, a predilection that was often used to mask the class identity that was supposed to be non-existent; upper-class Chinese shield their skin from the sun and purchase beauty products to avoid the appearance of peasant farmers, who are tanned because of their labor. Color-based racism, deeply embedded in the imperial period, was again highlighted during the run-up to one of China's wildly popular reality shows, *Oriental Angel*, modeled after the *American Idol* series. Lou Jing—the daughter of a Chinese mother and African-American father, and a native of Shanghai who is fluent in Mandarin and has even mastered the extremely difficult art of Peking Opera—faced a barrage of online criticism after she failed to make the finals of the show. She had been nominated for the show by one of her instructors at the Shanghai Drama Academy, where she was studying broadcasting (Doran 2009). Despite widespread recognition of her musical talent, she was vilified for her skin color and mixed ancestry, labeled a "black chimpanzee" and a "zebra" whose mixed parentage was an ugly "mistake" (Callahan 2013, 100). The fierce response to her appearance also captured another truth about Chinese society: a lack of acceptance of interethnic unions.

Due largely to government censorship and the influence of official discourse, many Chinese fail to see negative attitudes toward China's ethnic minorities as being rooted in cultural homogeneity or underlying racism. Rather, they castigate "instigators" within ethnic minority communities as agitators against Chinese culture. Incidents of ethnic strife in China, including

Han-Uighur and Han-Tibetan violence in recent years, are viewed as isolated incidents often due to foreign influences. Such clashes are not understood as based in ethnic differences or prejudice. Rather, the Chinese understanding of racism is apparently very narrow; as one university student stated, "There is no racism in China because there are no black people."[15]

Within China, it can be quite difficult to separate nationality, race, ethnicity, and spirituality.[16] The term "*minzu,*" literally meaning "tribe people," includes an understanding of the interactions between race, ethnicity, lineage, and nationality (Makley 2010, 151). Adding the religious connection to many ethnic minority experiences has produced significant areas of contention.[17] Facing increased persecution for religious expression outside of prescribed channels, "more people see religion as a form of resistance rather than personal piety" (Demick 2011). Contention arises, at least in part, to challenge the official characterization of group identities. Within the PRC, five faiths are formally recognized: Buddhism, Daoism, Islam, Catholicism, and Protestantism. Except for the indigenous Daoist traditions, official scrutiny is rooted in the foreign nature of these traditions, and they garner attention for their role in territorial integrity and international relations as well. Religion and ethnicity coalesce to create a multilayered identity that coincides with geographical divisions—most Chinese ethnic and religious minorities live in the country's southwest and border regions, and two strategically significant provinces that are home to minorities (Tibetan Buddhists and Uighurs in Xinjiang) possess significant natural resources as well. Chinese universities—strained to enroll even a fractional percentage of eager applicants—employ affirmative action policies for minority applicants, boosting minority students' enrollment in higher education at an

---

[15] Statement from a Chengdu University student, quoted in the *Shanghai Star*, April 17, 2003 (as cited in Coleman 2009, 5).

[16] Bovingdon contends that the CCP use of the term "*minzu*" to refer to both the Chinese nation and its subgroups ended up (unintentionally) promoting space in which Uighur identity and nationalism could flourish—the same word is used for subnational and national groups. There is a rather lively debate within government circles over the official English translation of minzu, with some encouraging a move away from "nationalities" and toward "ethnicity" in order to avoid framing contentious Uighur and Tibetan issues as "national" rather than "ethnic" disputes. See Bovingdon 2010, 15–17.

[17] The religious resurgence in China has historical grounding and communal religious culture is extremely important. China has a rich history of lineage temples, local gods, Confucianism, and other significant belief systems that have provided identity, morality, and a sense of community, especially in rural areas. The Qing state (1644–1912) was itself the dominant religious institution of its time.

average yearly rate of 12 percent between 1978 (when most universities re-opened after the Cultural Revolution) and 2008 (Yang 2010).

In the eyes of Chinese leaders, faith and ethnicity are instrumental; they help the regime achieve various objectives, including modernity, stability, and at least the appearance of respect for diversity. Some have used the image of "faiths on display" to highlight the economic component of spiritual tourism, especially with the growth of leisure and the luxury market for upper-middle-class consumers (Oakes and Sutton 2010). Local and national ethnic theme parks are avenues, in elite eyes, to promote both heritage and profit, publicizing regime tolerance.[18] Religious and ethnic tourism appeals not only to curious foreigners but to the growing Chinese upper-middle-class as well (Friedman 2006).

Since the foundation of the PRC, Party leaders have been suspicious of the influence of religion in citizens' lives. Despite the constitutional guarantee of freedom of religious belief and activities (Article 36),[19] state leaders sanction and monitor approved (aboveground, or registered) churches, and CCP and government officials are officially forbidden from engaging in formal religious activities, although for some years now a "don't ask, don't tell" approach has been applied ("Render unto Caesar" 2012). In spite of these limitations, religious identity in China has flourished, especially in Muslim and Christian communities. The faithful worship in officially sanctioned mosques and churches, as well as so-called underground (or unregistered) house churches that attempt to operate beneath the radar of state monitors. The two dominant types of adherents, sometimes referred to as "registered" and "unregistered," are not mutually exclusive categories, making it difficult to gain an accurate count of members at any given time. Even with the possibility of double-counting, it is clear that we are talking big numbers: "there are already more Chinese at church on a Sunday than in the whole of Europe," and many believe there are far more Muslims than Christians (Gardam 2011). These trends seem likely to increase, even though "China could already be considered one of the world's major Christian *and* Muslim nations" (Goossaert and Palmer 2011, 388, emphasis in original).

---

[18] For an interesting analysis of the Chinese Ethnic Culture Park that is part of the "Olympic Green" in Beijing, as well as other ethnic parks that have arisen since the early 1990s, see Makley 2010, 127–156.

[19] This article of the 1982 constitution also notes that "no one may make use of religion to engage in activities that disrupt public order," and "Religious bodies and religious affairs are not subject to any foreign domination," a clear reference to the imperial history of some foreign religious institutions in China.

While Beijing is receptive to religious adherents, it also insists on the aptly titled "3 Separations": separation of religion from politics, education, and health care. Religious organizations submit to official governmental audits during which they must submit financial records, activities, and employee details.

Similar to many other issues in contemporary Chinese society, religious identity is not a "new" but rather "re-emerging" identity. Confucianism, Daoism, and Buddhism each have deep historical roots within China; Islam and Christianity, two major forces today, were later arrivals from abroad. Attention among leaders to the "religious question" (*zongjiao wenti*) has turned into a complicated game of mutual accommodation, with the CCP grudgingly recognizing that religious institutions may have the staying power to help the regime achieve some of its social priorities (Goossaert and Palmer 2011, 2). This interplay, which includes elements of both state receptivity and resistance, has produced a duality of religious expression, with traditions employing both official (approved) organization and "underground" or "unregistered" communities, distinctions that are rarely exclusive. At times, leaders have even promoted religious expression as a way to promote social harmony and stability, especially in the era of breakneck growth and consumerism, although this has significantly retracted since 2011.

State resistance to religious expression, and confrontational responses by social actors, are especially evident throughout Tibetan-inhabited areas. The majority of the 5.4 million Tibetans in China live within the Tibetan Autonomous Region, with large numbers also living in Sichuan, Qinghai, and Gansu Provinces. They face acute challenges grounded in fundamental questions of religious and political authority, which have been heightened by tensions between Han Chinese and Tibetans. There have also been similar challenges with Uighur identity. A potent sense of cultural dilution has been exacerbated by Han migration to Tibet and the construction of massive infrastructure projects, most notably the Qinghai-Tibet railway, linking Tibet to other parts of China.[20] State resistance to religious expression has targeted authority structures, culminating in Beijing's exertion of influence over the recognition of reincarnated lamas, or the chief teachers and spiritual leaders within Tibetan Buddhism. In 1995, two young boys were named as legitimate reincarnations of the Panchen

---

[20] Also known as the Qinghai-Xizang railway (Xizang is the Chinese translation of "Tibet"), this track, completed in 2006, was the first to connect Tibet by rail to any other province in the PRC. The line includes the world's highest track (5,072 meters above sea level at the Tanggula Pass), and over 500 kilometers of track rests on permafrost.

Lama, with the boy selected by the Tibetan search team whisked away into confinement, followed, months later, by Beijing's rival announcement and a secret installment ceremony.[21] The globally staged protests in the spring of 2008, timed to coincide with the Olympic torch relays for the Beijing Games, were followed by significant state resistance, most concretely in terms of living restrictions and hard bargains offered to monks. New social security measures, enacted after 2008, include stipends to monks as an old age benefit, benefits that are contingent upon meeting a state-regulated standard of patriotism that includes relinquishing the religious services monks used to perform for a fee. Non-monastic Tibetans have also been impacted; nomadic groups have been forcibly moved to resettlement towns and banned from grazing, with over one million relocated since 2007 (Parshley 2012). Individuals who resist the move to these reservations have been stripped of their personal documents and threatened ("Tibetan Nomads" 2014). As one of the most extreme types of protest as opposition, since 2007, we have observed a surge of immolations, which have included nuns and monks as young as seventeen years old. One observer fears that this could be a sign of the beginning of a "larger, accumulating outrage"[22] within the Tibetan Buddhist community.

Muslims in China also face harsh resistance from central state leaders, especially following major uprisings in Xinjiang, one of the Muslim-majority provinces in China's northwest. The region has experienced four significant uprisings since mid-2008.[23] Despite attempts to protect some religious traditions, including the Muslim exemption for traditional burial (the only exemption to cremation in the PRC), state resistance looms large. Laws in Xinjiang (known

---

[21] The tenth Panchen Lama died suddenly in early 1989, shortly after giving a speech critical of Chinese policies in Tibet. The Tibetan search team (which had traditionally included the Dalai Lama, and was rumored to have consulted with him) announced Gedhun Choekyi Nyima, from Nagchu in northwestern Tibet, as the eleventh reincarnation. However, the Beijing Religious Affairs Bureau drew the name of Gyaincain Norbu from the golden urn, installing him against opposition from both the domestic and overseas Tibetan communities.

[22] Steven Marshall, senior adviser for the Congressional Executive Committee on China, has more than two decades experience researching human rights violations in Tibet. Quoted in Parshley 2012.

[23] Bovingdon asserts that Uighur resistance is fundamentally based in Uighur nationalism, rather than in any Islamist threat as articulated by Beijing. He also reports that until July 2009, there were no major organized protests in Xinjiang since 1997, although he highlights a substantial amount of "everyday resistance" on the part of ordinary citizens. See Bovingdon (2010), especially chapter 3 ("Everyday Resistance") and chapter 4 ("Collective Action and Violence").

as Eastern Turkestan to many activists) prevent minors from participating in religious activities, and government employees and CCP members are routinely reminded that they are not to practice religion. Ramadan is especially monitored: students are escorted to meals to ensure they are not fasting during daylight, restaurants are threatened with fines if they close during the period of fasting, and universities lock down during the three-day Eid al-Fitr feast to make sure students do not celebrate with their families or other community members (Demick 2011). Beijing's resistant stance toward Muslims bleeds into terse interactions among ordinary people as well, leading to heightened ethnic tensions between majority Hans and ethnic minority groups. Within Xinjiang, the Han tend to be viewed as opportunistic outsiders. Hans derisively refer to Uighurs as *chantou* ("head wrapper"), with Uighurs calling Hans *bu akam* ("big brother") and *kapir* ("infidel") (Bovingdon 2010). However, foreign guests of China would hardly experience such restrictions or bias. During the 2010 Asian Games in Guangzhou, approximately 30 percent of the food served at the games was certified halal, and of the forty-five participating nations, more than half were predominantly Muslim (Hayoun 2012).

Christianity is one form of Chinese religious identity not connected to ethnicity. In the eyes of many, though, especially among central officials, Christianity is directly associated with China's weaknesses during its "Century of Shame," discussed in Chapter 2. As outside powers, including Britain, France, Russia, and Japan, worked to expand their trading rights and territorial access in the Middle Kingdom, religious conversion became a favored tool of many foreigners who lived and worked in China during this period. Unlike earlier periods of religious interaction (Matteo Ricci and the Jesuits in the 1500s were famed for their respect for Chinese civilization and adaptations of Confucian thinking into their work) (Peale 2005, 5–6), nineteenth-century missionary movements were less tolerant of local traditions and more actively evangelical. Anti-religious sentiment became a rallying cry later for communist revolutionaries and other nationalists who mobilized their followers to take back China and expel all foreign influence. Today, as an increasingly popular form of religious expression, including in many rural areas that have maintained a religious identity and community for decades, misgivings by Beijing are largely based in the foreign nature of Christianity, as well as the connection between some popular uprisings and Christian groups, most notably Rome's role facilitating the Solidarity uprisings in Poland. Part of the challenge posted by faiths beyond Beijing's borders is the appointment of authority figures: Beijing requires that local congregations severely limit their interaction with international leadership, which has presented the most visible challenge to Chinese Catholics. Beijing asserts its right to appoint bishops, producing an odd combination of communist leaders literally wearing religious hats, and Rome asserts its primacy over such personnel appointments. This investiture dispute of recent decades belies the fact that the vast majority of bishops have actually been recognized by both Rome and Beijing, although notable exceptions remain. Large numbers of organized congregations, especially the unofficial "house churches" in rural areas, continue to gather in defiance of central mandates to submit their names for registration and official leadership. Protestant communities have reported significant gains in numbers in recent years, viewed by many as a sign of the moral bankruptcy of official ideology. State resistance in the case of these communities appears grounded in the concern not of religious values or identity, but of the unofficial nature of their gatherings, outside of the auspices of the state's formal channels.

Chinese sensitivities to external influence, particularly when it relates to ethnic minorities and religious identities, were on display during the 2009 meetings of the World Conference on Racism, where Chinese delegates attempted, on several occasions, to remove the term "freedom of thought and conscience" from official conference documents, since they do not, in the eyes of the Beijing delegation, directly relate to the freedom of religion. Beijing projects the oft-challenged image of harmony, and exercises loud resistance to international challenges to its record on religious freedom.

Sexual Politics and LGBT Rights

In a society well-known for its "favored sons," a predilection for boys that significantly predates contemporary population planning policies, perhaps it is not surprising that gender issues fare prominently in Chinese state-society relations.[24] Influenced in part by the demographic marriage squeeze, and in part by the pervasiveness of traditional cultural values embedded in the nuclear family, the pressures to conform to social and state norms are severe. If one isn't married by the age of twenty-five, the gossip mill kicks in—even though this is far from uncommon, as there are an estimated forty million Chinese men who

---

[24] China is not unique in its imbalance and marriage squeeze; Taiwan, Hong Kong, Japan, and South Korea face difficulties as well, although not nearly on the same scale as China. China's sex ratio at birth is 118.08 boys per 100 girls, according to the 2010 census ("China: Country Summary" 2012, 5).

will likely be unable to find a Chinese wife. China is believed to have as many unmarried young men, viewed as "bare branches," as the entire population of young men in America ("Gendercide" 2010). With the growth of the Chinese middle class, women look for prospective husbands to provide at least an apartment, if not other measures of material comfort; as the popular saying demands, "no money, no honey." Despite decades of formal government policies aimed at promoting gender equality, many women continue to see men as providers. To agree to marry a man who doesn't own property is known as a "naked wedding." Unmarried women are also stigmatized as "leftover women," by both social and official governmental sources: a state-sponsored media campaign openly stigmatizes women who are too choosy selecting a partner, encouraging (especially urban) women to avoid delaying marriage—ideally tying the knot before age twenty-seven—lest they be forever lonely (Fincher 2014).

Nevertheless, to believe the official narrative, China is the hallmark of gender equality: the Communist Party has focused on women's issues since its beginning, and the first piece of legislation passed in the People's Republic was the Marriage Law of 1950, outlawing arranged unions and providing legal equality between men and women. The law was modeled after many of the practices of the communist base areas during the Chinese revolution in the 1930s and 1940s. Chinese leaders have long touted the oft-quoted line from Mao that "women hold up half the sky." However, the World Economic Forum ranks China sixty-ninth in making improvements to gender equality, behind Mexico and Senegal. China especially lags behind other countries in the forum's "health and survival" measurement, coming in at 133, the third-lowest ranking in the study. This study also highlights the persistent drag on women's wages compared to their male counterparts, even though the 2013 "Global Gender Gap Report" ranked China 32 out of 136 countries for labor force participation ("The Global Gender Gap Report 2013" 2013). Beijing's Renmin University estimates that Chinese women earn two-thirds that of men's salaries (Eimer 2011).

Feminism has an uneven history in contemporary China, in large part because early state and party leaders attempted to fold feminist concerns into the communist structure, relegating gender concerns second to class consciousness. But feminism has a long history in Chinese culture, including suffragettes during the 1911 Republican Revolution, shortly followed by women's rights activists who helped inspire the May Fourth Movement of 1919, which is widely viewed as the birth of mass politics in China. Since 1949, the inclusion of women's concerns in foundational documents, including both the PRC and CCP constitutions, has provided an abundance of formal rhetoric for the rights and interests of women. However, the promulgation of laws rarely means the acceptance of practices, as we saw with the "new era" introduced with the Marriage Law of 1950. Even though divorce was made legal in this legislation, separation— especially when initiated by the wife—was not socially acceptable because it violated lineage requirements. Women seeking a divorce from their husbands were criticized as bourgeois and individualistic, even "Western." While many in the West are familiar with the conservative images of the family as the foundation of stable society, this view is even stronger in Confucian societies. The institution of the family preserves traditional culture, yet this institution is facing great stress and change. In traditional China, the family included at least two—often three—generations living under one roof, with clearly defined roles and responsibilities for the wife (and for the elite, multiple wives). Household registration requirements and the widespread urban migration that we discussed in chapter 3 also add pressure to the mix. Increasingly, young children are being raised outside of the immediate family, often by grandparents far away, with visits from the parents mainly during the Lunar New Year celebrations once a year.

In response to many of these changes, Chinese feminists—often in opposition to the official mass organization, the conservative All China Women's Federation—are increasingly speaking out, even in the face of great risks. Feminist individuals may not be as linked together as we see in Brazil, the United States, or other countries, but individual activists committed to the rights of women remain dedicated to the cause, including filmmaker Ai Xiaoming and lawyer Guo Jianming, recipients of the 2010 Simone de Beauvoir Prize for Women's Freedom, among others. Only Guo was able to travel to Paris to receive the award; Ai, a professor of Chinese language and literature who has produced documentaries on gender violence, HIV-AIDS, and the aftermath of the Sichuan earthquake, has not been permitted to leave the PRC. Shortly after receiving the Beauvoir prize, Beijing University banned Guo's Centre for Women's Law and Legal Services, an NGO established to promote judicial reform as well as improve living conditions for Chinese women (Kristeva 2011).

Historically, Chinese feminists helped inspire one of the earliest mass movements in China, the May Fourth Movement of 1919, fought to end polygamy and arranged marriages, and lobbied to ensure that wives would keep their maiden names. Today's Chinese feminists protest against the lack of educational and career opportunities for Chinese women, criticize the seemingly ubiquitous dating game shows on television, and speak out against corruption. Increasingly, they are organizing against sexual abuse as well as trying to raise awareness of culturally taboo topics. The iconic play *The Vagina Monologues* has been performed by small groups since 2003 and continues to stir controversy and sometimes vitriolic responses, especially on social media (Jaffe 2013). Performances have not always been permitted to go forward, however, as local officials can pull the plug shortly before curtain, and some have forced organizers to change the provocative title of the show. As we have seen with other forms of activism in China, feminists tend to be active more as individuals, rather than as groups. The groups that do form watch leaders carefully for cues on permissible behavior. For example, shortly after Facebook COO Sheryl Sandberg was invited to speak in Beijing, "Lean In" circles (focused on analyzing her well-known book), organized in many major cities. Participants view this as a safe form of organizing—advocates imply that, since Sandberg had been invited by the PRC government to speak throughout the country, they are "not in violation of anything" by getting together to discuss implications of her book (Tatlow 2013). Ironically, the company that Sandberg directs remains off-limits to most Chinese Internet users.

Similar to religious identity, personal relationships are grounded in formal bureaucratic structures that defy acceptable expression. This is especially the case with marriage and childbirth: one change introduced by the 1950 Marriage Law is that unions must be registered with the local government, with permission from work units for those couples employed by the public sector. The social recognition and wedding ceremony can come much later, sometimes after pregnancy, which, due to the planned birth policy, requires permission as well. Even in the most personal of choices, government scrutiny and community monitoring are present. The reinterpretation of the country's marriage law by China's supreme court in mid-2011 is viewed as a huge step back for women, as residential property is no longer jointly owned and divided equally in the case of divorce. Since 2003, divorce no longer requires the permission of one's work unit, but, given the new interpretation of the country's marriage law, state mandates loom large in private decisions. Most estimates are that, on average, five thousand couples divorce each day in the PRC, and in the first half of 2011, the Ministry of Civil Affairs reported a 17.2 percent increase in divorces over the same time period in 2010 (Eimer 2011), with an upward trajectory as the clear multiyear trend (FlorCruz 2010). The change, viewed by many as a way to make divorce a much less attractive option for Chinese couples, now rewards property to the party that originally paid for it, rather than splitting it evenly. The changes turn husbands into landlords, exacerbating the already existing wealth gap between the sexes. Even prior to the 2011 changes, it was common that the husband received custody of any children. Many believe that the country's rampant mistress culture will only get worse as these laws take effect (Eimer 2011).

Another aspect of family identity and personal relationships is abortion. Contraception and family planning are openly discussed and formally promoted as medical and social tools to promote economic well-being for the greater good of the Chinese population. Even since changes in the population planning policy, the norm remains that most births are registered with a neighborhood committee, a quasi-governmental structure in most urban and some rural areas. Even though birth control is widely available, and often subsidized by either the local government or other employers, abortion is widespread, especially sex-selective abortion. Three factors influence this prevalence: an ancient preference for sons, a contemporary desire for smaller families, and advanced ultrasound and other technologies that identify the sex of the fetus early in its development ("Gendercide" 2010). Even though abortion and compulsory sterilization have never been openly endorsed by Beijing, it is widely known that they have been an element of the planned birth policy since at least 1980, when the Chinese population topped one billion (Pan 2005).

Most attribute China's rate of abortions to its planned birth policy, widely referred to as the "One Child" policy. Even with recent changes in national policy, the Chinese "baby bureaucracy" (Levin 2014) remains powerful: married couples are required to follow local guidelines for both the timing and number of births in their family; they must obtain the stamped approval of multiple officials, with the vast majority of Chinese couples limited to a single child.[25] Changes in this controversial policy—believed to have prevented as many as four hundred million births since its introduction in the late 1970s—were long debated, and implemented only in the first quarter of 2014. While there has been longstanding public pressure to decrease the heavy hand of local officials, especially those who famously averted all population limitations for their own kin, most believe that practical considerations, including the demographic imbalances and growing elderly population without children to care for them,[26]

---

[25] In 1978, Chinese leaders established as a national goal the desire to limit population growth by delaying marriages, requiring permission to have children, and limiting most urban couples to one child. From the onset, exceptions existed to this general goal of the one-child family, including for national minorities and for families in the countryside. Over the years, localities have established other exceptions, including permitting couples to bear two children without penalty if one of the parents is a sole child themselves—as long as the second child is born at least four years after the birth of the first child. Most families were permitted two children after changes adopted in late 2015.

[26] In 2012, Chinese state media reported that there were 40 million more men than women in the PRC, forecasting that by 2020, there could be 30 million eligible bachelors unable to find a Chinese wife (Levin 2014). Other research suggests the number could range as high as 40 million ("Gendercide" 2010).

motivated the final push by the National People's Congress Standing Committee to adopt such changes (Levin 2014).

Still, Chinese scholars note that increasingly, young women, including teenagers, make up the majority of abortion cases in cities such as Shanghai and Beijing, as changing cultural mores that include a rampant mistress culture, nearly non-existent sex education, and the availability of safe, relatively inexpensive abortions—complete with hospital marketing campaigns offering "the Model Abortion for a New Generation!"—collide (Yardley 2007). Despite changes in social attitudes, single motherhood in China remains extremely rare, and unmarried pregnant women rarely carry a pregnancy to conclusion in order to place the child up for adoption. As one medical clinic manager in a facility that treats students, mostly twenty-four-years-old or younger, stated, "The moral outrage over having a child before marriage in our society is much stronger than the shame associated with abortion" (Olesen 2011). The Guttmacher Institute reports that, after years of decline, the abortion incidence rate in China appears to have increased since 2003, which it attributes to an increase in premarital sex as well as substantial gaps in access to contraception, due to rapid urbanization and job mobility ("In Brief: Fact Sheet" 2012). The validity of abortion statistics is often doubted, and national statistics do not categorize marital status, but Chinese family planning officials insist that the abortion rate among married women is dropping because more than 80 percent of them use long-term contraception such as IUDs, or sterilization (Yardley 2007). In contrast, "Young people think if they are not married or are not having a regular relationship, then they can just have an abortion" (Yardley 2007). Contraception use among unmarried couples is extremely low—due to both ignorance of the technology and the social stigma associated with sex outside of marriage.

In any country it is difficult to assess true opinions on matters as private and personal as abortion; these difficulties are exacerbated in China, where family planning is considered a "pillar of the nation's economic development strategy" and adherence to population targets serves as one of the most important qualifications for local officials' promotions (Pan 2005). After his decade of fieldwork studying attitudes and medical ethics, Jingbao Nie attempts to debunk the perception of a cavalier attitude toward abortion among the general Chinese public. He found that there are controversies within Buddhism, Daoism, and Confucianism about conception, as well as groups that point to the impact of abortions on women's reproductive health and well-being. The few anti-abortion campaigners in China are often Buddhists or Christians, but their arguments are subdued because of the status of official policy toward population control (Olesen 2011). The "beginning of life" argument that tends to domi-nate Christian opposition to abortion is nonexistent in China. Given China's recent history of high infant mortality rates, the beginning of life was marked when they were named on the one-hundredth day of life, when it seemed more likely that they would survive (Olesen 2011). Feminist arguments centering on choice or women's control over their own body don't resonate either. As one Chinese psychologist put it, "When we argue that a woman owns the uterus, and it's her right to decide whether to deliver the baby or not, people won't buy it. If you are a woman, your personal choice is monitored and supervised by a lot of others, and they expect you to do what everyone else does" (French 2008).

Another aspect of China's changing attitudes toward sexuality can be found within the market for sexual services. Prostitution has a long history in China, dating back to the imperial period in which a man would have several concu-bines in addition to his wife and the industry flourished as official, taxable busi-ness. During the time of the Opium Wars, at the height of China's humiliation at the hands of outside governments, Shanghai was nicknamed the "Whore of the Orient" for its role in promoting vice, especially among elite Chinese and the significant expat community. Communist campaigns were largely successful at virtually wiping out prostitution, at least from public view, by the late 1950s. With China's opening to the outside world after 1978, prostitution found a place again throughout the country, and there was even a cadre close to Deng Xiaoping, named Cao Manzhi, who argued for the legalization of prostitution as a part of the natural progression of capitalism. His pleas were ignored, and, since the 1990s, "China's sex industry has gone from bust to boom" despite its illegal status (Zheng 2009, 3).[27] Human Rights Watch estimates that sex workers num-ber between four and ten million ("Country Summary: China" 2012). As one noted scholar of Chinese sexuality points out, "China has visibly conflicted at-titudes towards sex, officially condemning licentiousness while turning a blind eye to a hugely prevalent sex trade, where it is routine for businessmen to take clients to karaoke bars to 'relax' with girls."[28] Karaoke bars are considered the upscale variant of the sexual entertainment industry, just ahead of saunas. The ubiquitous KTV (karaoke television) bars boast raucous sing-alongs in main

---

[27] Prior to 1911, prostitution had never been condemned by statute in China—in fact, it was regulated and taxed as a formal business. Official attitudes started to shift in the late Song Dynasty (960–1279), with the advent of calls for public morality that dominated the neo-Confucian discourse of the period. See Cao and Stack 2010.

[28] Katrien Jacobs, as quoted in Foster 2011.

dining areas as well as private rooms. KTV venues are famously staffed by the so-called *sanpei xiaojie* (women who accompany men in three ways): serving alcohol, dancing/singing, and servicing the sexual desires of clients (Zheng 2009).

Sex work is becoming increasingly visible, serving a vital economic function and generating local revenue.[29] Liuming Yan, a well-known blogger and activist who wanted the plight of sex workers and migrant laborers to become better known worked as a "prostitute for a day" and offered her services free of charge to migrant workers, posting updates on Twitter-like sites (Tan 2012). There have been some limited attempts at organizing. In 2010, sex workers in Wuhan networked fourteen small non-profits to form a network providing medical exams, condoms, and even funeral services for women whose families no longer claim them. In Choi's field research, she found that most sex workers in southwestern China were migrant workers from rural areas, regularly sending remittances home to their family. She reports that nearly 80 percent were introduced to sex work by relatives, neighbors, or friends. Among the women she interviewed, economic factors lured them and kept them involved in sex work, and more than 95 percent of them maintained close family contacts with their family networks. She also found that police campaigns against prostitution seem to do little to curb the practice or to promote safe sex, but rather feed police coffers (Choi 2011).

Research has highlighted a significant shift in official attitudes toward sex workers in China, from that of "victims of social systems to victimizers who spread diseases," which has justified harsher police crackdowns and penalties (Choi 2011, 97). The official tactics have changed from targeting pimps to punishing sex workers, according to Choi, in large part because of the AIDS crisis, including an amendment to the Criminal Law that includes detention for anyone knowingly buying or selling sex while infected with syphilis, gonorrhea, other sexually transmitted diseases (Choi 2011). Prostitution crackdowns are framed as part of a larger state campaign to "bolster core socialist values and promote cultural and ethical progress" ("Prostitution Crackdown" 2014). Officials within the ministry coordinating radio, film, and television even recently announced that actors with a history of drug use or involvement in prostitution will be banned from film or TV roles, all connected to the ongoing "moral crackdown" against vice (Child 2014). However, state-run CCTV

---

[29] Zheng reports that karaoke bars pay 33 percent of their net income and an additional 20 percent operating tax to the Dalian city government, exceeding the 5 percent tax rate on other local businesses, all but guaranteeing their secure future (Zheng 2009).

(China Central Television) recently experienced a significant backlash after it ran an investigative report detailing prostitution in Dongguan, a southern city in Guangdong Province known for its sex trade. Citizens rallied to the defense of sex workers, chastising the callousness of the broadcast as undermining the livelihoods of ordinary people, and expressing anger that authorities were diverting attention away from more serious problems, especially official corruption (Makinen 2014). Human Rights Watch researcher Nicholas Bequelin highlighted the outrage triggered by the nationwide report, which he believes sparked the first serious and widespread discussion about the possibility of legalizing sex work in China (Boehler 2014).

Corruption in prostitution crackdowns became most evident in the well-publicized arrests of "virgin prostitutes" during the early 2000s. Seven young women were arrested and accused of prostitution, forced to "confess," only later to have their virginity medically confirmed. Their cases were picked up by national media, including CCTV, *Xinhua*, *People's Daily Online*, and *Beijing Youth Daily* among others, launching a nationwide debate on police malfeasance and the unlawful fining of alleged minor offenders (Jeffreys 2010). In one sign of progress—it's all relative—the central Ministry of Public Security has ordered police to stop parading prostitution suspects in public, attempting to bring an end to the time-honored "shame parades" of shackled prostitutes after public outrage on Chinese Internet sites expressed sympathy for the women involved, with posts such as "Why aren't corrupt officials dragged through the streets?" (Jacobs 2010).

Not surprisingly, data on public opinion toward prostitution in China is difficult to come by, and the highly publicized "virgin prostitutes" and response to the nationwide exposé reveal only a partial view. With Chinese netizens avidly embracing the Internet, and public outrage toward police corruption teeming, it is important to note, in the case of the shame parades, that the central state blinked. Even scholars who have used cross-national opinion polls, such as the World Values Surveys, point to complex layers of public attitudes toward prostitution. Despite sporadic outcries when prostitutes are victimized, it seems that public opinion remains against the legalization of prostitution.

Given the traditional emphasis on the nuclear family and gender roles, it is probably unsurprising that lesbians, gays, bisexuals, and transgendered Chinese face an uphill battle within the Chinese public. Despite official pronouncements to the contrary, homosexual identity has been expressed throughout China's rich past. In the sixteenth century, Italian Jesuit missionary Matteo Ricci even noted, with disapproval, Chinese society's inclusion of homosexuality, and scholars have long noted the homosocial world of Imperial China, including Beijing Opera, the imperial court (including gay emperors), and the many linkages between culture and commerce during China's Middle Kingdom period (Brook 1998; Hinsch 1990).[30] Lesbian characters fared prominently in Cao Xueqin's *The Dream of the Red Chamber*, one of the four great Chinese novels written in the middle of the eighteenth century, and China has a history of third-gender discussions or formal acceptance of variations of gender, including eunuchs (Levine 2013). In 1997, Beijing formally decriminalized homosexual identity, and in 2001 removed homosexuality from the list of mental illnesses under which gays were prosecuted under vague "hooliganism" statutes—punishable by up to seven years in prison. Still, same-sex relationships lack legal rights, including marriage and adoption, and gay men often take girlfriends because they are afraid to tell their families about their true identity (Chan 2004), since they risk extreme ostracism for "ending" the family line. This pressure is only made worse by the lack of siblings in most parts of China, due to population control policies. Also, many mental health providers seem to remain unaware that homosexuality has been declassified as a mental illness, curtailing the likelihood of adequate professional support for individuals seeking it ("Violence on the Basis" 2010).

Transgendered individuals in China contend with police harassment and employment discrimination, in addition to being cut off from their families in most cases. Gender reassignment surgery is prohibitive not only in terms of cost, but also red tape. The Ministry of Health released guidelines in 2009 that require individuals seeking gender reassignment to formally register with police in order to change their hukou registration, to consent to extensive therapy, not be married, and document that they have shared their wishes with their immediate family (Levine 2013). However, according to one mainland activist, Chinese society may be more accepting of transgender individuals—who engage in "regular" heterosexual relationships after reassignment—than those who are gay. China has known transgender celebrities, but none who are openly gay (Speelman 2013). The mainland's most famous transsexual, dancer Jin Xing, regularly draws huge crowds for both her dancing performances and her role as a guest judge on a popular TV talent show, but she continues to face

---

[30] In his groundbreaking book on homosexuality in Imperial China, Hinsch claims that the open acceptance of homosexual relations dates to the Bronze Age, crossing class divides from emperors to laborers, and included the open recognition of same-sex marriages for both men and women (Hinsch 1990).

Two lesbians pose for photographs in Beijing on Valentine's Day, a holiday some have used to campaign for acceptance of homosexuality, 2009. *Source:* Reuters/Jason Lee

scorn within the official media and on social networking sites. It seems the ministry guidelines codify the countervailing pressures of traditional society, which coincide closely with social morality campaigns perpetuated by the CCP. As one Chinese scholar put it, "Within mainstream society, you simply cannot come out. It would be the end of your career. Can you image a Communist Party member being openly gay? There is no way" (cited in Speelman 2013).

Especially in urban areas, LGBT groups attempt to host pride events within the public sphere, including same-sex marriage campaigns, lesbian salons, and pride festivals—although, depending on the mood of the leadership, such events risk disapproval or a late sleight of hand in which all activities are called off. Much of the political space afforded to LGBT associations by local governments has been in response to government attempts to mobilize citizens to fight the HIV-AIDS epidemic, using civil society groups to reach out to high-risk groups that government officials are unable or unwilling to engage—even though many leaders of gay and lesbian groups do not identify AIDS as a primary interest for their groups (Hildebrandt 2013). The emphasis on health issues within the LGBT community and its interaction with the government limits the discourse to biological terms, rather than civil rights issues (Speelman 2013). Lesbians have expressed much more difficulty organizing and finding acceptance than gay men, and most associations have been unable to formally register as an NGO, meaning they must rely on overseas sources of funding (Fincher 2014).

Public opinion toward same-sex relations—at least as expressed via digital repertoires on the Internet—may be shifting: Chinese netizens have shown international savvy, calling for a boycott against a famous film couple, Lü Liping and Sun Haiying, after they retweeted the anti-gay statements of a Chinese-American Baptist pastor in Rochester, New York. Lü and Sun reposted Pastor Feng Wei's lamentations against the increasing legal acceptance of gay marriage laws in the United States and called on all of their fans to do the same. Instead, they faced the ire of many of their fans, including the Parents, Families and Friends of Lesbians and Gays–China and Shanghai Pride, who lambasted the couple's intolerance and ignorance of China's history ("Gay Groups Urge" 2011). Government agencies and international NGOs provide funding for popular telephone hotlines. And one of China's premier universities, Fudan University in Shanghai, has offered a course on homosexuality since 2005, taught by noted sociologist Li Yinhe (Simon and Brooks 2009). Li, famous for her annual (since 1993) submissions to the Chinese legislature, the National People's Congress, proposing a same-sex marriage law, reports that 16 percent of Chinese male university students have had had a homosexual experience (Chan 2004). Despite having a legislative sponsor, supporters were unable to muster the thirty people necessary to place Li's proposed legislation on the agenda. A cross-dressing garbage collector who was featured on a TV news report in Qingdao ignited a national debate about sexual identity after the news anchor mocked Liu Peilin, who also goes by Da Xige (which translates as "Mr. Great Happiness"). After video of the news report was posted on *Weibo*, with derogatory statements, Liu was turned into an online celebrity, with widespread calls for care and tolerance (Lu 2012).

Homosexuality and transgenderism remain largely hidden identities within China. In public opinion polls, many express a nonchalant attitude toward homosexuality, but most also end up admitting that they have never actually met a gay or lesbian person. One study reported that nearly sixteen million women in China are married to gay men, due to the overwhelming pressure to conform and especially to avoid dishonoring or letting down one's parents (Shan 2012); another contends that 80 percent of gay men married women due to social pressure (Simon and Brooks 2009). The pressures to conform to "traditional" heterosexual relations are exacerbated by local policies that, in many urban areas, prevent unmarried individuals from being able to purchase real estate—leading some gay men to marry lesbian women in weddings of convenience or "functional marriages" to maintain face (Fincher 2014, 183). Clearly, homosexual identity in China is less taboo than it has been in the past, with gay bars, websites, and organizations emerging, sometimes even in public view. Yet in a culture where the public expression of intimacy remains rare for all couples, sexual and gender minorities, and the activists who support their cause remain cautious.

ANALYSIS

As figure 4.1 and the section to follow indicate, when it comes to social diversity in Brazil and China, the picture is more complex. It is in China that we identify a rarity: a highly contested core issue and civil societies that adopt confrontational approaches that directly challenge the state. Matters of religious and ethnic diversity in China are unique among all the other issues that we consider in this chapter, not only because Tibetan and Uigher calls for self-determination are viewed as existential threats to the PRC, but also because this is the only example of contentious politics in this chapter in which violent repression is the outcome. There's nothing like this in regard to diversity in Brazil. Racial inequality is a major problem, but state and society have largely come out of denial in regard to its once-upon-a-time "racial democracy" to recognize it as such.

A more in-depth examination of social identity in both of these large, diverse countries presents us with both some startling similarities as well as differences. On one hand, both countries are multiethnic, even if the embrace of this richness is much more welcomed in one (Brazil) than the other (China). Both states espouse official narratives describing their societies as cohesive and multiethnic, and both face challenges trying to live up to that standard. The Brazilian state during the dictatorship (1964–1985) was a lot like the Chinese government of today, censoring those who would claim otherwise. Brazil's generals were never as harsh or as heavy handed as the CCP, but the effect was perhaps just as damaging. Both states can be accused of promoting cultural dilution: the mass migration of Han to Tibet and Xinjiang is as much ethnocide as is Brazil's social whitening and the mulatto escape hatch. It is said that the myth of racial democracy is dead (or dying) in Brazil, but even since the return to democracy, Brazilians who suggested that racism might exist faced social pressure and were accused of being "un-Brazilian." The various ethnicities in China are highly aware of their distinct identities—which go beyond the neatly defined boundaries crafted by the CCP in the 1950s—and are often also based on their association with particular regions, languages, and sometimes spiritual traditions. So far, the discourse on race in China has been uncivil at best. At one end of the spectrum, it denies that Chinese society could even face a problem with racism; at the other end, it spews ugly slurs. In Brazil, it is only recently that a slight majority of Brazilians claim to be African-descended, and most of them identify as *pardo* or mixed race. There is a discussion about race in Brazil, but it is less clear that attitudes are truly changing because of it.

FIGURE 4.1 CONCEPTUAL FRAMEWORK FOR SOCIAL DIVERSITY

Brazil		China
Color/Religion and Ethnicity		
Less Contested: Most recognize that the "racial democracy" was a myth—and recognition of the fact is good for Brazil's image.	Issue	**Highly Contested:** Attempts to speak out that vary from officially presented narratives on religion and ethnicity are perceived as direct challenges to the central state.
Conventional: Protest as pressure to raise awareness and demand remedies. Society led the state.	Societal Approach	**Confrontational:** Repertoires range from illicit gatherings and association to self-immolation.
Receptive: Allies in the executive branch, starting with President Cardoso.	State	**Resistance:** State requires approved registration, despite widespread defiance.
Reform: "Positive Discrimination," but uneven implementation.	Outcome	**Repression:** Official rules limiting expression and organization.
Abortion		
Moderately Contested: It is highly contested within society but untouchable for the state because of the power of Catholics and evangelicals— and because it is a core issue for these powerful groups.	Issue	**Less Contested:** Abortion itself is a non-issue for most (population planning and abuse of it is more contested).
Conventional: Attempts to decriminalize by using the political process. Holy war of countervailing pressure.	Societal Approach	**Conventional:** Those who do speak out tread careful line due to central policy of population planning.
Resistant: Politicians know better than to touch the issue … Lula tried and got burned.	State	**Receptive:** Closeness of majority social view with state policy makes issue less inflammatory.

continues

FIGURE 4.1   CONCEPTUAL FRAMEWORK FOR SOCIAL DIVERSITY   *(continued)*

Brazil		China
Repression: See above. Abortion rights groups are stonewalled.	**Outcome**	**Indeterminate:** Policy reform based as much in state preferences as social pressure.
Sex Work		
Less Contested: Most recognize that the constitution guarantees rights — even for marginalized groups.	**Issue**	**Moderately Contested:** Illegality of status invites pressure to conform, despite boom.
Conventional: Uses the political process, protest as pressure, working with state.	**Societal Approach**	**Conventional:** Mostly legal means; limited attempts at organizing. Backlash when state seems to target ordinary people, yet countervailing pressures from traditional culture.
Receptive: Recognizes sexual vitality as part of Brazil's identity. Synergistic partnership to fight HIV-AIDS.	**State**	**Resistant:** Central to state campaigns to promote socialist morality.
Reform: Legalized sex work, but not completely decriminalized and still dangerous.	**Outcome**	**Indeterminate:** Collusion with police invites corruption. Sex work remains illegal, despite increased debate.
LGBT Rights		
Less Contested: As far as the state is concerned, at least. Highly contested within society.	**Issue**	**Moderately Contested:** Largely hidden identity; contested within society, although shifting.
Conventional: Protest as pressure and working synergistically with state against HIV-AIDS, etc. Goes head to head with religious groups.	**Societal Approach**	**Conventional:** Countervailing pressures from traditional society; synergistic work with state against HIV-AIDS.
Receptive: Divided government: President Lula led the way, but conservatives in Congress lobby hard against gains.	**State**	**Resistant:** Concerns about power of organized groups and challenges to social stability trump other concerns, with exception of HIV-AIDS.
Reform: Exemplary progress in recognizing rights, but homophobia and transphobia persist. The "real Brazil" hasn't caught up with the "legal Brazil."	**Outcome**	**Indeterminate:** No longer illegal identity, although awareness and acceptance remain low and repression remains an option.

Lining up Brazil, the largest Catholic country in the world, next to officially atheist China makes for an interesting juxtaposition. In terms of religious identity, both countries are experiencing a shift of sorts, but we have two different stories. They are similar in that most Chinese and Brazilians do not actively mix religion and politics. Although in Brazil, religious teachings are deeply engrained and coexist with secular leanings with contradictory and unpredictable effects. Most Brazilians consider themselves to be religious, although fewer attend services. Brazilians pride themselves on their receptivity to other religions; Protestantism, especially evangelicalism, has experienced rapid growth in Brazil in the last few decades, and Afro-Brazilian religions such as Candomblé have long coexisted (and sometimes blended) with Catholicism and other religions. Most Chinese are not religious, but many Chinese citizens conjoin religious experiences and traditions, sometimes adopting religious association as a remedy to the daily grind. For these individuals, perhaps religion is more a form of resistance than an expression of personal piety. Chinese are associating with both registered and unregistered congregations in record numbers—it's just that the chord can be yanked away by the regime (or by local officials) at any time—and the CCP continues to prohibit cadres and their families from joining unsanctioned spiritual organizations. On the other hand, even though their policies in regard to sexuality have sometimes challenged conservative Christians, Brazilian presidents have been the ones having to walk a fine line. Lula and Dilma have accommodated this wing of civil society on more than one occasion.

Elites in both Brazil and China recognize that when religion and politics mix, the result can be potent. In China, the state seeks to monitor and control religious organizations; in Brazil religious organizations seek to monitor and control the state. In Brazil, power relations between state and society are inverted—and this is precisely what the CCP is trying to avoid. In China people can be persecuted for religious identity beyond approved channels. This would be unthinkable in Brazil—it's the Church and evangelicals who crack down on the government, by threatening to swing elections. Lula's about-face on abortion is an example of their power. As figure 4.1 shows, abortion is a highly contested issue in Brazil—but not between state and society. There is a holy war going on, but the battle lines are drawn between different groups within society. As a result, abortion is a "dangerous" issue unlike any other that we discuss, in either country. Those who support the status quo in Brazil have so much clout that abortion—along with the most highly contested of all issues in Brazil, land reform—is too highly charged for the state to touch, the third rail of politics. And so the state doesn't touch it; rather, it "represses" pro-choice activists by stonewalling them.

Our two cases are fascinating to compare on abortion. As we discussed, Brazil has some of the most restrictive laws in the world whereas in China, abortion is available on demand and there is little stigma associated with it. In Brazil, where it is illegal with very few exceptions, women and girls who resort to clandestine abortions are highly stigmatized, and many times those suffering from botched abortions tend to be mistreated by medical professionals. But abortion is common in both countries. China is notorious for having one of the highest rates of abortion (if not the highest rate), while even in Brazil it is estimated that more than one million abortions are performed each year (Wyler 2013).

As is usually the case, both national and international factors combine to explain the differences. Once again, we see the Catholic Church, both domestically and internationally, as a major player in Brazil's cultural politics, with a candidate's rumored stance on abortion nearly costing her the election. In China, we see much less debate about the morality of abortion, even if brave campaigners take great risk to publicize officials' abuse of family planning policies. Married couples forced by the state to terminate pregnancies get more play in the international media, but increasingly singles are turning to multiple abortions to avoid the stigma of unwed pregnancy. In contrast to Brazil, where the state allows debate on abortion—but the Church forbids it—inside China there is little public interest in debating the procedure (the topic of abortion in China is much more controversial outside the country) (Nie 2005). Part of the reason it's a non-issue inside China is due to widespread cultural acceptance, in part due to years of family-planning campaigns and slogans. But state coercion also plays a significant part in explaining the relative lack of discussion of the issue, as individuals in China know full well.

Although the status quo is very different in the two countries, both states face significant resistance to changing the status quo when it comes to reproductive rights—and for the most part Brazilian and Chinese publics want it that way. In Brazil, the easing of abortion restrictions is blocked by social norms and the influence of the Vatican. In China, challenges to family planning (of which abortion seems an integral part) run into the forces of social norms and the acceptance of state mandates, even if there is widespread resistance to abuses of it. In Brazil, feminist networks work to decriminalize abortion by drawing attention to the high maternal mortality rates associated with it, but the public is largely complacent. Public opinion polls show that most Brazilians are satisfied with the abortion laws the way they are. In China, individual activists fight not against abortion, per se, but abusive leaders who engage in selective policy implementation (this form of corruption is something that people care about, since violations of the policy can run as high as US$40,000–50,000 per unauthorized birth) (Denyer 2013). In both countries, crusaders for reproductive freedom face considerable odds: Brazilians are up against the Vatican; Chinese face the full force of the state.

On the other hand, as our framework shows, in neither country is sex work or LGBT rights highly contested. In Brazil, the state agreed to be led and the outcome has been clearly reformist, even synergistic. In China, where these are largely hidden identities, society has adopted conventional approaches to promote the rights of sex workers and LGBT rights. However, although it has indicated some willingness to cooperate with these groups on HIV-AIDS, the Chinese state's response to these groups has largely been resistant, and the outcome is indeterminate. When it comes to sex, except for the fact that the sex business in both China and Brazil is booming—and that most sex workers in both countries start out as young migrants to the cities, driven by poverty—it appears that the two countries couldn't be any more different. Although not all Brazilians (including the state) are exactly comfortable with the title, Brazil struts its stuff as the erotic capital of the world. It is a leading—if not *the* leading—destination for sex tourism, and prostitution is a booming, legal business.

Meanwhile, prostitution is illegal in China, and sex workers are more highly stigmatized than ever, although some are taking brave steps to independently organize when possible. In China, whereas they were once viewed as victims exploited by pimps, now prostitutes—rather than the procurers or clients—are the targets of crackdowns. Interestingly, on this issue it is China that behaves like a country with a strong religious lobby; sex workers are blamed by the government for the spread of sexually transmitted diseases and they are increasingly at the mercy of police, who extort or arrest them. In predominantly Catholic Brazil, it was once a very similar story. Prostitutes were, and still are, to some degree, stigmatized, but their relationship with the state has changed dramatically. In the 1990s, as prostitutes pressed for their rights, the Brazilian state recognized that these workers could help it meet one of its priorities: reducing the incidence of HIV-AIDS. Since then it has—in a very Brazilian way—adopted a policy of mutual accommodation. Today it is the exploitation of sex workers (through pimping and brothels) that is illegal, not sex work (and sex workers have played a pivotal role in preventing the spread of the disease).

In contrast, Chinese sex workers have not yet organized to push back or to change their relationship with the state in the way that Brazilian sex workers have. In China they have been limited to social networks, especially hometown connections formed among migrants from the same village. Small NGOs have formed, but they operate with an ever-watchful eye on the police, who hold the keys to sanction or punish members. Such behavior is hardly what most would expect in atheist China—and Christian Brazil.

When it comes to LGBT rights, Brazil is known for its openness whereas China is known for its legal restrictions. Brazil hosts the largest gay pride parade in the world; conversely, LGBT activists in China operate with the nearly constant possibility that their permits can always be revoked. The one similarity both countries share is that both governments, true to their pragmatic forms, have sought the cooperation of LGBT NGOs on HIV-AIDS.

Still, beneath the surface we see that the picture within Brazil is much more challenging. Gays and lesbians have the right to marry and adopt in Brazil, but a backlash of sorts can be identified as homophobic traditions hang on tenaciously: someone is killed every thirty-six hours in Brazil for being homosexual or transgender (Pearlman 2012). Yes, the state has been identified by Amnesty International for its exemplary progress in recognizing the rights of sexual and gender minorities. Yes, Brazil's LGBT NGOs are some of the best organized in the world, and in many ways they've had more policy successes than the feminist or Afro-Brazilian movements. But Brazilian civil society is activist on both sides of the issue. The most formidable adversary that LGBT rights advocates—and, many would argue, women's rights advocates—face is the Catholic Church and evangelicalism (E. Friedman 2009). This is a good example of how civil society can be heterogeneous and work at cross purposes. Here it is the state that is caught in between.

It could be argued that China is now going through many of the changes Brazil experienced since the 1970s, but without the backlash. Sure, homosexuality is stigmatized (it was considered a mental disorder until recently), and people have been arrested for their sexual orientation. They're still sometimes harassed by police and relatively few homosexuals live openly, but one huge contrast between Brazil and China when it comes to the treatment of their LGBT populations is the difference in the power of religion. Most Chinese are secular and accepting, and Confucian traditions encourage marriage and childbearing but do not prohibit homosexuality or characterize it as a sin. Religion simply isn't part of the sexual discourse in China. As opposed to Brazil, there's no power akin to the bishops instructing Chinese that homosexuality is an abomination. Similarly, the state's stance has been described as cautious and low-key; it doesn't take much of a position on sexual orientation one way or the other. Perhaps it is just not publicized, but human rights advocates contend that homophobic violence is actually rare in China, and the violence that we are aware of comes mostly from within the family itself ("Violence on the Basis" 2010).

For all of their differences, to some degree in both countries change is ultimately dependent on executive leadership. The downfall of this is that such change is fragile—and less effective in challenging long-standing cultural norms. In Brazil, analysts disagree over whether the reforms of the last decade are more symbolic than substantive, and even those who characterize them as substantive worry that they aren't underpinned by the institutional supports needed to sustain them. For example, in terms of race, given the not insignificant resistance to affirmative action in Brazil, some of it led by well-connected citizens most likely to make their voices heard, such policies are built on a fragile foundation and may not be sustained, let alone carried forward. Remember, much of Brazil's shift on LGBT and sex workers' rights has come in large part because the state came to view both groups as partners in the fight against HIV-AIDS—one that is important not only for the lives that it has saved but also for the international acclaim—and soft power—it accrued for Brazil. According to Htun (2004), under Cardoso's leadership the state changed course on race not because of material incentives or to win votes (after two terms, he was restricted from seeking reelection), but because he wanted to show that it was the right thing to do—and that, as a new democracy, Brazil was doing the right thing. Lula and Dilma have continued these reforms, but experts agree that if future governments don't give the same relevance, or seek to sustain these policies or institutionalize them, they will fall apart (Htun 2004). When the executive retires or if executive interest flags, any progress is at risk—and the "legal Brazil" indeed comes closer to reflecting the "real Brazil."

In the last twenty years, China has experienced a rapid increase in public discourse and engagement. Some of this alteration has been facilitated by a receptive state (it allows participation in congregations that have been officially vetted), and some of it has been carved out by risk-taking members of society (for example, sex workers). What the discussion of China in this chapter reveals are the limits of state control, or state resistance to society. Although the state is doing everything it can to control it, due to the proliferation of the Internet and social networking, Chinese citizens have a better chance of being able to weigh the words and policies of their leaders against evidence and challenges beyond their borders. For example, Chen Guangcheng's dramatic escape from house arrest and asylum was paraded around the world through Internet 2.0 sites, demonstrating the force that such communication channels may have in China's future.[31] Changes in social policy in China have been both symbolic (remember, Mao said "women hold up half the sky") and genuine (the decriminalization of homosexuality), but they have been gradual and incomplete.

What is clear is that although regime type may have something to do with policy, the picture is rarely as simple as that. For obvious reasons, policy change in an authoritarian state is less fragile than in a popular democracy— alternations in Chinese administrations rarely bring significant shifts in policy direction. We find it intriguing, though, that even strong authoritarian governments, which should be freer than democracies are to make unpopular or controversial changes, often choose to avoid antagonizing citizens. Conversely, on certain issues democratic states take the lead on policies that aren't popular with most citizens.

We return to our finding that issue may trump regime. In this chapter, we have seen how dictatorships and democracies have struggled to accommodate contention over ethnicity, religion, and sex, and there has been give-and-take between leaders and the led, with different levels of risk depending on the issue. For example, interpretations of ethnic unity that are alternative to the official policy are highly salient and contested in China, and Beijing regards them as a direct challenge, an existential threat. Clearly, issues of social identity are not nearly as highly contested in Brazil, as they do not directly threaten vested interests. In the end, despite the different ways in which they regard issues of identity, the two do share one attribute: in both China and Brazil there is still quite a discrepancy between the legal and the real, between the laws on the books and the facts on the ground when it comes to the differences that define us . . . and we see the ramifications of this in people's lives on a daily basis.

---

[31] Chen Guangcheng is a well-known activist who has focused on official abuse of power, especially with regards to China's population planning policies. Blind since a young age, Chen taught himself the law and developed a reputation for petitioning authorities and representing clients against local officials. In 2012, he escaped house arrest and dramatically fled nearly three hundred miles to the US Embassy in Beijing, leaving first for medical treatment, and then later (along with his family) for the United States.

DISCUSSION QUESTIONS

1. Both Brazil and China project images that belie reality. Consider a few examples presented in this chapter. Why does such a gap between day-to-day reality and the official narrative exist? Do you think this is a common characteristic of governments, or is this something specific to Brazil and China? Why?

2. Sexual identity and behavior are viewed as among the most personal, private, and important characteristics of individuals. Brazil is more than promiscuity and Carnival; it is also a state grounded in traditional Catholic identity emphasizing sexual abstinence and is strongly anti-abortion—but it has some of the highest abortion rates in the world. China is more than sexual repression and abortion; it is also a state in which sexual identity is being more openly explored than at any other time in its modern history. What do you believe explains the divergences of approaches within and between these two countries?

3. Within this chapter, there were many references to the slowness of change within Brazil and China. Why do you believe this is the case? Is this rate of change being fostered mostly by the state or is it a gradual approach adopted by social actors? In which areas of social identity would you believe the fastest pace of change can be observed? What about the times in which society is actually the leading voice in maintaining the status quo?

4. In this discussion of social identities in both states, we have observed mixed records of state receptivity to demands from groups. If regime type doesn't capture the bulk of the explanation, what in your view does? What motivates change—and, conversely, continuity—on these contested issues?

5. Both Brazil and China are known to have diverse societies. In what ways have both governments responded to diversity? When do governments view diversity as a strength, and when do they frame it as a weakness? How would you explain the differences?

5

ENVIRONMENTAL POLITICS

> If you don't leave, you're going to end up with ants in your mouth.
>
> —A common death threat in the Amazon (Larry Rohter, "Brazil's Lofty Promises After Nun's Killing Prove Hollow")

> China's economic miracle will end soon because the environment can no longer keep pace.
>
> —Pan Yue, vice-minister, Chinese Ministry of Environmental Protection (Christina Larson, "The Green Leap Forward")

INTRODUCTION

As we have argued before, the distance between Brazil and China is not as great as it may seem. With regard to pollution, deforestation, and the challenges of providing sustainable sources of energy, there is a push and pull between state and society in Brazil and China as they struggle to find the right balance between two needs: promoting economic growth and protecting the environment. Here's where we make the strongest argument that our cases are theory-infirming. In fact it is in these issues that contentious politics operate in ways that are most challenging to conventional understandings of regime type. In this chapter, we highlight both governments' ongoing responses to the continued challenges of environmental sustainability. Several factors, such as resource pressures and state capacity, can explain why the state is receptive on some issues and resistant on others. Countervailing pressures play a role as well. Once again, we recognize that civil society is rarely monolithic. Rather, particularly when it comes to questions of economic growth and environmental sustainability, civil society is composed of competing constituencies employing a variety of tactics.

BRAZIL

It may be hard for non-Brazilians to imagine it, but Brazil is more than the Amazon. Most Brazilians have never been there, and therefore if there are environmental concerns at the forefront of their minds, they are more likely about urban pollution than the faraway deforestation outsiders talk so much about. Still, for a variety of reasons, the Amazon captures the imaginations of Brazilians, too. Because it is home to the Amazon, however, the nation of Brazil considers itself environmentally exceptionalist. As far as much of the world is concerned, this immense and diverse region—it spans eight countries and occupies one-twentieth of the earth's surface, including three-fifths of Brazil—has for decades been the theater of war for environmental politics in Brazil.[1] However, battles over resource use and sustainability are played out elsewhere in Brazil as well. As the following sections will reveal, contentious politics regarding the environment in Brazil unfolds very differently, depending on the issue.

Pollution: Oil, Water, and the Valley of Death

Brazil faces a variety of ecological challenges, including recurrent drought in the northeast and floods in the south. But it is the awareness of environmental degradation, often only brought up to speed by dramatic, unfolding events (like deadly mud slides and fires) that have led the state to become more receptive and—at least temporarily—shift away from a developmentalist policy that prioritizes resource extraction and economic growth at any cost. Air pollution serves as an example of the possibility of how a startling event can amount to a critical juncture, resulting in the collaboration of state and non-state actors and reform. Interestingly, although international environmental NGOs get a lot of attention for their efforts in Brazil, it has been the Amazon that is their

---

[1] Brazil is an enormous country, only slightly smaller than the United States. Although Brazil is favored with extensive river systems and the Amazon basin comprises 60 percent of the territory, the country has a diverse topography, including five major climatic regions, each with a distinct ecosystem ("World Factbook" 2014).

issue, not pollution. Still, pollution is a significant issue for Brazilians, affecting more of their everyday lives in a way that deforestation in faraway places does not. For example, as Brazil was democratizing in the 1970s, rapid industrialization had left São Paulo one of the most polluted cities in the world. Cubatão, a town on its outskirts, came to be known as "the Valley of Death" in 1978 after laborers died there from workplace contamination. It is estimated that at its peak, industries in this steel and petrochemical industrial center were releasing a thousand tons of pollutants a day into the air. Mercury levels were twenty-five times the recommended maximum in the waters outside the city, and damage to vegetation from factory emissions was visible (Hochstetler and Keck 2007).

The relatively small Brazilian environmentalist community called for the factories to be closed. At first there was some countervailing pressure in the form of blue-collar resistance to environmentalists' demands. Factory workers were concerned about anything that might threaten their jobs. Unacceptably high infant and child mortality rates among the poor were nothing new, but when the stories of sick and deformed babies (in particular, an unusually high rate of anencephaly) became too common to ignore, it had a galvanizing effect on Brazilians of all classes.[2] Urban pollution became an environmental justice issue. The problem of environmental quality was suddenly recognized as connected to problems of poverty and inequality. Grassroots actors, allied with local opposition politicians and churches, took a conventional approach and held neighborhood meetings to use protest as pressure. Once the press got onto the story, the publicity induced enough political will in the state government to recalibrate and form an investigative commission.[3] Society led the state and, in the end, the state proved receptive. Public pressure forced the shutdown of a factory and the state ordered a cleanup in 1982. Thereafter Cubatão went from notoriety to an example of how change is possible. Cubatão resulted in

[2] Anencephaly is a serious, congenital birth defect in which the baby is born without parts of the brain and skull. Most survive delivery, but almost all babies born with it die within days after birth ("Birth Defects" 2014).
[3] With the return to democracy, the 1988 constitution did create the Ministério Público (MP), independent public prosecutors at the state and federal levels with the discretionary power to defend the environment and other collective interests. Known in Brazil as "the fourth branch of government," these lawyers have represented civil society's claims against the government on multiple occasions and for multiple causes. In addition to pursuing cases against individuals and companies as well as state and local agencies, MPs can sue public bodies that do not obey the law, which is especially useful with environmental law. For example, the MP has successfully prosecuted hundreds of cases on behalf of citizens harmed by pollution (de Oliveira 2003; Scholz 2005).

an innovative combination of reforms: positive incentives for industry as well as the threat of punishment.

In years since, a Brazilian NGO, the Environmental Justice Network, has carried on these anti-pollution efforts from more densely organized areas of the country to less organized areas (Hochstetler and Keck 2007). In a 2010 poll, 95 percent of Brazilians agreed that pollution is a very big or moderately big problem and characterized public accountability on the environment as weak. But since the 1980s, because civil society forced the issue, extreme episodes of air pollution have mostly disappeared ("Brazilians Upbeat about Their Country" 2010; Ferreira and Tavolaro 2008).

There have been similar efforts against water pollution, which has improved but remains a serious problem. Today many poor rural and urban people lack access to piped water, and whereas the problem is mainly water scarcity in the northeast, it is pollution in the southeast. One group, the Movement in Defense of Life, became known in the 1980s for its dramatic, attention-getting tactics when it repeatedly dumped cargoes of dead fish on the doorsteps of public agencies, legislative assemblies, and municipal councils that had shirked their responsibilities to deal with the problem of water pollution. But it wasn't until 1990, when the taps of *Paulista* elites poured foul-smelling water, due to high concentrations of algae, that citizens put sufficient pressure on the government to do something about it (Evans 2002).[4]

More recently, despite increased spending on sanitation and some improvement to show for it, the water quality in Brazil's larger cities has ranged from poor to very poor. In addition to untreated waste water (60 percent of the country's sewer water is discharged without first being treated) and the massive release of toxic agrochemicals into waterways, state governments are struggling to clean up the masses of garbage and other pollution that fouls Brazil's lakes and oceans in time for the 2016 Olympic competitions. Rio state in particular has been embarrassed into the cleanup, as it will be a major site for Olympic water events—and the ocean is sometimes unfit for swimming. As a result, the governor is leading one of the biggest environment programs to clean up Guanabara Bay in the country's history. While the state is promising a total transformation, residents hope that these efforts will be sustained after the games wind down (Frayssinet 2011; "Rights Activists Share Alternative Nobel" 2010; Croix 2012b).

---

[4] Paulista is a common term for residents of São Paulo.

Another long-term project for Brazil is how to manage its oil resources. When the country struck it rich in 2007 with the biggest oil discovery in the world in decades (it could be one of the world's top five oil producers by 2020), many chalked it up to just one more piece of evidence that God is a Brazilian (Romero 2011; "God's Gift to Brazil?" 2009). In order to appreciate the significance of this find for environmental politics, some backstory is necessary. Brazil has been a relatively minor producer of oil since the mid-twentieth century. However, Brazil has experienced major oil spills over the years. In 2000, a refinery pipeline near Rio de Janeiro burst, spilling 1.3 million liters of oil into its famous Guanabara Bay. According to de Oliveira (2003, 115), "This accident, in one of Rio de Janeiro's postcard locations, raised public outcry, especially from the media, NGOs, and environmental regulators in all levels of government." Citizen protests received massive media coverage, which only grew after two other major spills and several accidents (including the sinking of a deepwater rig off Rio's coast) occurred (de Oliveira 2003). At least temporarily, the developmentalists were on the defense for prioritizing production above all else.

But the uproar did not lead to a fundamental rethinking of priorities, as the particularly challenging and risky deepwater drilling for oil has continued apace. However, analysts characterize the accidents in 2000 and 2001 as serving as a catalyst for reforms. It can be argued that since these disasters the culture has changed; Brazilian public opinion and the media are now more sensitive to oil-related accidents and serve as important watchdogs. The state has proven receptive to citizen pressure. After the accidents, an emergency response plan was formulated, and the state invested in nine environmental protection centers. Environmental laws have been strengthened, and the risk of the state-owned oil company (Petrobrás) or others being legally charged for flagrant misconduct has actually grown.[5] Since the accidents, Petrobrás has even proactively implemented upgrades to remediate problems caused by past spills and to prevent future ones. But it's still a dirty business; Petrobrás had sixty-six oil leaks in 2011 alone (Romero 2012b; de Oliveira 2003).

---

[5] Civil and criminal charges have been filed against the companies and their employees (seventeen of whom were barred from leaving the country pending an investigation). Brazil's largest oil workers' union has filed a lawsuit seeking to cancel Chevron's and TransOcean's rights to operate in the country and is seeking unspecified financial damages to compensate the Brazilian people for the damage caused by the companies' "predatory and unsound environmentally unsound" actions (Romero 2012b; "Chevron Oil Spill" 2012).

206 | CONTENTIOUS POLITICS IN BRAZIL AND CHINA

So, it's not all happily ever after for the environmentalists, since here too there is a difference between the real and the legal Brazil, and policy is not always effectively implemented. Sure, there have been some clear improvements due to civil society's ability to make use of the political opportunity structure or openings created by these disasters for catalyzing public pressure (de Oliveira 2003; Carvalho 2006). For example, Chevron and drilling firm TransOcean, which you may remember from the BP Gulf of Mexico disaster, wasn't prepared to deal with the accident when one of its wells leaked three thousand barrels of oil off the coast of Rio in 2011. Officials accuse Chevron of lying about the extent of the spill and maintain that the stiff penalties they're seeking against the company are meant to show others that they must adopt effective procedures for preventing and cleaning up spills (Romero 2012b). Interestingly, it is the Brazilian public that has lost interest in the topic. Citizens do appear to be concerned about the methods the companies are using to clean up the spill, but otherwise there has not been much debate about the dangers associated with offshore drilling ("Brazil to Fine Chevron" 2011). In fact, most of society's engagement so far in regard to the pre-salt wells, which are found in deep-sea areas and hard to access, has been not over environmental damage but over how to divide the revenues. Once more, developmentalism trumps environmentalism.

Deforestation: Trees vs. People / Trees Plus People

Developmentalism certainly trumped environmentalism for the dictatorships of the 1960s, which favored large-scale, state-led colonization of the Amazon. The military governments built dams and highways as monuments to Brazil's modernity and progress. Through Operation Amazonia, the state offered tax incentives and loans to "colonize" and bring commercial investment to the region. Waves of migrants arrived in the 1960s and 1970s; more than one hundred thousand were lured over a five-year period by the government's promise that those who farmed "unproductive land" could keep it (Perruci 1999). Since the 1980s, the profitability of ranches, logging, mining, and large-scale farming has produced the economic growth that Brazil has needed for export expansion, to earn the hard currency to pay off its creditors and devote to social welfare, while devastating the forests. Some international actors, such as financial institutions like the International Monetary Fund, promoted policies that directly and indirectly contributed to deforestation by encouraging economic growth above all else (Hochstetler and Keck 2007).

As a result of such policies it is estimated that by 2005 one-fifth of the Amazon had been razed (Kingstone 2005). Since then, the extraordinary export boom associated with growing European and Asian demand for commodities has meant that forest conversion has expanded into other ecosystems of Brazil, such as the *cerrado* (savannah), which is also vital for biodiversity and now is actually being more rapidly denuded than the forests (Mackey and Zeller 2008). Although timber extraction, ranching, and the cultivation of cash crops in high demand (such as soy beans) are the major contributors to deforestation, many politicians—left and right—have allied with these interests, arguing that if the state's choice is trees versus people, people must come first. As a result, progressives wind up turning on each other, despite the fact that the poor rarely benefit from this kind of economic growth.

Although environmentalism in Brazil predates the pro-democracy movement of the 1970s, it certainly coalesced during this period. Environmentalists played a large part in that movement to throw out the dictatorship. Since the return to democracy the size and number of environmentalist groups has grown faster than any other kind of protest group. In 2005, there were estimated to be more than 2,500 environmental NGOs in Brazil (Alonso and Maciel 2010). This heterogeneous movement runs across the ideological spectrum from conservative environmentalists (or eco-capitalists) to radical socialists (or red greens). Although the vast majority of the country's environmentalists would locate themselves on the left of the political spectrum, environmentalism in Brazil is hardly monolithic. If anything, it can best be understood as a big tent that includes large and small groups as well as some who use conventional, and others confrontational, approaches. These NGOs run the gamut from being research-oriented to liberation theology and church-based; there are some that collaborate with and are dependent on funding from international NGOs and many more that are autonomous of them (Scholz 2005).[6]

Brazil's NGOs working on the environment include citizens of all classes, colors, and ethnicities. Most notably, many of them are led by Brazil Indians. These environmentalists, who make the most of the perception of native

---

[6] It is estimated that in the early 1990s more than 80 percent of the funding received by Brazilian NGOs working on the environment was from foreign sources. Hochstetler and Keck (2007) contend that the amount of money these groups receive from international sources has grown since then, particularly because there is not much of a Brazilian tradition of philanthropy. However, they maintain that most of this money goes to a relative few groups. Three-quarters of Brazilian NGOs addressing environmental issues receive no international funds.

peoples as stewards of the earth, often work alongside an indigenist movement that demands Indians' full rights as citizens and special rights as minorities, including claims to traditional lands and the exclusive use of its resources.[7] Although their interests are not always identical, advocates for the environment and indigenous rights worked together for a return to democracy, and they have often continued to work toward other common goals ever since.

As mentioned earlier, there are divisions between and within these groups, including substantive debates over tactics: whether to press for radical changes in institutions and structures or more gradual ones that are less likely to alienate. There are still some conservationists who want to protect the forests from all development (the "trees" folks); however, in Brazil these dark greens are increasingly a minority, as more environmentalists have come to support "natural capitalism" (versus extractive capitalism) or an economy based on preserving the forests (they're the "trees plus people" folks). Advocates of this new model of growth are all about promoting ecotourism, establishing ecofriendly cooperatives to develop medicinal and other products from forest plants, replanting and restoring forests, and using land that has already been cleared more productively. They join many Catholic and other church-based organizations that have long melded environmental and social concerns. It can be a messy partnership, but under this approach, peasants and indigenous peoples are the protagonists, saving themselves, instead of being saved—in bottom-up, pro-poor, and pro-forest initiatives to promote small, sustainable development and environmental justice (Friedman 2009b; Guijt 2010).

For all their variation, most of these groups are conventional in approach and are staunch advocates of non-violence. However, it is important to recognize that not all Brazilians who are politically engaged on the issue of the environment are green—and not all greens are non-violent.[8] Those who prioritize economic interests are engaged in this most highly contested of all issues as well. There are people on both sides who say that they are willing to die for their cause and who have warned that "blood will flow" unless their demands are met (Rohter 2005a).[9]

---

[7] There are over 232 different indigenous ethnic groups in Brazil, and the indigenist movement has been weakened by divides from within, as some groups have been accused of selling out and not always serving as the good stewards of the land many assumed they would be.

[8] For those who subscribe to this view, conservation is a social issue—and it can be profitable. For them the choice doesn't have to be between the irrevocable devastation of the forests and not using them at all. And the question should be as much about "how do we save the Amazonians?" as it is "how do we save the Amazon?"(Bruschi 2010).

[9] Environmentalists and indigenous groups demand that the government suspend logging licenses; loggers and their allies demand that the licenses be restored (Rohter 2005a).

Certainly one divergence within the environmentalist movement is over whether to engage in traditional politics or to reject parties, elections, and lobbying in favor of direct action. McCormick points out that different fields of protest are available to different sets of actors. In general, local activists tend to work more extra-institutionally while transnational organizers are more likely to work cooperatively, directly with the state or corporations (McCormick 2011). Although groups on both sides use this tactic, developmentalists are more likely to have the resources to successfully nurture relationships with politicians and lobby the state. Environmentalists who once campaigned enthusiastically for the PT have in recent years cooled on the party, which was never monolithic in its support for the environment. Perhaps the most famous of these is Marina da Silva, a former minister of the environment under Lula (and no relation) who left the PT and challenged Dilma for the presidency in the 2010 and 2014 elections, each time winning nearly 20 percent of the vote (Watts 2014a; Winter and Boadle 2014). No doubt, the PT is the greenest of the larger parties in Brazil, but some *petistas*[10] have always maintained that environmental concerns are frivolous whenever they interfere with the fight against poverty. It is understandable that many environmentalists would largely turn away from traditional party politics.

As a result, most environmental NGOs work as pressure groups. They are more likely to adopt direct action, as the environmental issues that get the most press are framed in adversarial ways, as public confrontations (Hochstetler and Keck 2007). It is not uncommon for these activists to seek to block something that they oppose, to overtly defy laws or "invade" an area and squat on land to get the attention of the state. Some examples of this include dam-affected people occupying the offices of the public utility or indigenous people occupying roadsides to protest the eviction from their ancestral lands ("Brazil Indigenous Guarani Leader" 2011). Interestingly, when it comes to direct action, it isn't the protesters but the media that play the crucial role. How the media portray the protesters—as criminals or as heroes, legitimizing or ignoring them—has enormous ramifications for these groups' ability to exercise influence. It may be surprising, but according to da Silva and Rothman, even since the return to democracy, journalists in Brazil are inclined to criminalize social movements. Activists contend that this characterization, along with the media's ability to divert attention with entertainment and shopping,

[10] Petistas are supporters of the PT.

amounts to a counterrevolution of sorts. Consequently, environmental NGOs are adding to their repertoire and increasingly turning to the Internet and alternative media to give their version of events to the public (da Silva and Rothman 2011).

But those in the movement know that they ignore the old media at their peril. Because the cameras love it, Brazil Indians have regularly relied on extralegal measures and used their "exotic" image as a weapon. They have dressed in war paint and carried bows and arrows to attract attention to the invasion and loss of their lands and cultures due to dam construction, illegal logging, fishing, and gold mining. However, loggers and their allies use direct action as well; they have blocked major highways, bringing commerce to a halt to prevent the establishment of Indian reservations. Some have gone even further, seeking to force negotiations by threatening to pollute waterways with chemicals.[11] Such tactics have at times proven effective; for example, the Lula government bowed to acts of civil disobedience and reversed its policy on several occasions (Rohter 2005a).

In addition to working the media, competing coalitions inside Brazil have focused much of their energy on the use of legal tools, to a degree unusual for other countries. This may come in the form of using legal strategies to block what they see as harmful proposals (such as the construction of a dam), or bringing forward environmental cases, or lobbying for new legislation. The 1988 constitution promises environmental protections that have yet to be enacted. However, under this constitution, much of environmental policy is left to the state and local governments. Governors often have more power than the president and responsibilities are dispersed among a wide array of government actors who are often at odds with each other. Therefore, fighting for new legislation to protect the environment is only one battle—enforcement is another—in the larger war. Brazilians know the problem well. They even have a phrase for it: *"a lei não pegou"* ("the law did not hold"). Getting the law to hold, especially getting it to apply to powerful elites who expect special treatment, is an enormous, expensive, and lengthy challenge. Corrupt notary publics and judges refuse to intervene to stop fraudulent land schemes involving forged land titles—and sometimes even participate in

---

[11] Under certain circumstances, taking one's life can be considered a "weapon of the weak," a less recognized form of protest. The suicide rate for indigenous peoples in Brazil was at epidemic levels in 2013 and six times higher than the national average, according to the Brazilian Ministry of Health (Lyons 2015).

them (Rohter 2005b). Moreover, in the vastness of the Amazon, even if the government has the political will and is interested in exercising authority, it isn't necessarily capable of doing so, as enforcement agencies are grossly underfunded and understaffed. In 2009, for example, three hundred environmental inspectors were responsible for the Amazon, an area the size of Europe (Hochstetler and Keck 2007; Phillips 2009).[12]

Particularly in Brazil's frontier, insomuch as the state exists, it is weak, co-opted by local bosses or warlords—now joined by criminal networks—who run large swathes of the territories as their personal fiefdoms. In this vacuum there has been a great deal of money to be made; land grabbing and clandestine resource exploitation by private economic interests has been the norm. It is estimated that only 2 percent of deforestation is authorized and 90 percent of it is illegal encroachment due to dubious land claims (Watts 2005; Bruschi 2010). Land disputes often end in violence and impunity is the norm. In regard to the key issue of land ownership, especially for indigenous people, the state has always played a contradictory role, slowly creating reserves and granting land titles while facilitating their doom by building highways through or near these lands. The conditions for indigenous people in Brazil were bad under the dictatorship, but they have actually worsened under the democracy, as lawlessness has grown and thugs hired by farmers act with impunity (Lyons 2015).

Although intimidation and repression are tools used by economic elites to stave off change, it has sometimes backfired. International outcry over the murders of Amazonian rubber tapper Chico Mendes in 1988 and American-born nun Dorothy Stang in 2005 embarrassed the state and prodded it to at least make the appearance of taking action. For example, after Mendes's assassination made the front page of the *New York Times*, internal and external pressures coincided with the establishment of IBAMA (the Brazilian Institute of Environment and Renewable Natural Resources), an umbrella organization created to coordinate the work of government environmental agencies. After Stang's murder, the government—which had ignored the multiple threats preceding her death—did make a concerted effort to show that it was capable of holding accountable the men who shot the seventy-four-year-old nun three times at point-blank range (Rohter 2005b; Keck 1995). According to Hochstetler and Keck, each

---

[12] IBAMA is Brazil's national environmental agency. It reports to the Ministry of the Environment and has a number of responsibilities, including enforcing environmental laws and evaluating environmental impact assessments. IBAMA plays the key role of issuing licenses for major projects such as dam building (McCormick 2007).

of these assassinations should be seen as contingent events that proved—at least temporarily—a game changer. They created martyrs, opening a window of opportunity for activists by focusing attention on the problem, capitalizing on public pressure and embarrassing the state into action (Hochstetler and Keck 2007).

As we have seen so far, the story of receptivity and resistance in Brazil has been about how dramatic events provide the openings or moments of pivotal importance for—usually progressive—change. However, it doesn't always necessarily work that way. Massive power blackouts and energy shortages that led to rationing throughout much of Brazil in 2001 provided the perfect opening for developmentalists to revamp and bring back to life an energy project that it had long had in mind.[13] Hydrological resources are extremely important to Brazil; it already has the third-largest hydroelectric capacity in the world (with more than 1,400 dams, including the one of the world's largest, Itaipu, which is a binational project with Paraguay) ("Classification by Installed Capacity" 2014). Hydropower produces over 80 percent of the country's energy and it has potential for even greater growth (Barrionuevo 2011a). The timing for pitching a massive new project couldn't have been better, as this was just as the public was willing to make sacrifices to ensure against more blackouts. A consequence of Brazil's tremendous economic growth in recent years has been a growing consumer class, as millions enter the lower-middle-class eager to acquire the material goods so long out of their reach (Brazil is the fifth-largest market for cars worldwide) (Ituassu 2011).

To keep the lights on and to power the boom that it hoped to continue, in 2007 the Lula government set off on a large-scale infrastructure development program that included building dozens of hydroelectric dams in the Amazon over the next ten years. The biggest (it would be the world's third-largest) and most controversial of these massive energy generation projects, Belo Monte, is actually a dam complex being built in eastern Amazonia. With construction costs estimated at US$13 billion, this mega-dam is the responsibility of the consortium Norte Energia, which is mostly owned by the utility company Eletrobrás. It, like Petrobrás, is a state-owned company that is partially privatized (Barrionuevo 2011a; Rapoza 2014).[14] Also like Petrobrás, Eletrobrás has access to resources and decision-making power—and is well insulated from

---

[13] Plans for the dam were revived in the late 1990s, but not pitched to the public until after the 2001 blackouts (da Silva and Rothman 2011).

[14] Since the electric sector was privatized in 1995, private corporations have become major investors in these dams (McCormick 2007).

public pressure (Carvalho 2006). According to it and the dam's proponents, Belo Monte promised to be capable of producing 11,200 megawatts of electricity, is an imperative to meet Brazil's demand for power, which is estimated to grow by 56 percent by 2021. Most of the electricity from Belo Monte will go—nearly two thousand miles away—to Rio de Janeiro and São Paulo (Barrionuevo 2011b; Diamond and Poirier 2010).

The dam is expected to begin producing energy sometime in 2015. However, so far the plans have generated more heat than light. Brazilian grassroots-based groups worked with international environmental NGOs in the late 1980s to successfully mobilize against an earlier version of what they now characterize as a "monster dam" (Rapoza 2014). They were able to dry up the funding for the project by persuading the World Bank—already under pressure for its poor track record on the environment—to cancel the loan and walk away from the project. But as the bell rang twenty years later for the second round of this fight, the state came out swinging (Carvalho 2006).

To help ensure that their plans would come to fruition this time, the designers resurrected and redesigned the project in a way that means less land would be flooded. But critics warn that either way, its construction will mean "game over" for the Amazon. Opponents of the dam have conducted their own scientific assessments to show that because of variations in the water volume of the Xingu River, Belo Monte will never operate above one-third of its capacity and would be unable to produce enough electricity to meet future demands—making it likely to be only the first, with more (perhaps one hundred more) dams to follow (Scholz 2005; Diamond and Poirier 2010). They point out that such changes to the flow of the Xingu River, a center of biodiversity and home to twenty-five thousand indigenous people, would likely result in unacceptable environmental and social costs. Some areas will be left in permanent drought, while floods over 120,000 acres of land will necessitate the relocation of twenty thousand to fifty thousand indigenous and other riverine peoples (Barrionuevo 2011a; Diamond and Poirier 2010). Those who do not leave will see their ways of life and livelihoods devastated by the loss of fisheries and by the fact that typically other commercial extractive industries such as ranching and logging follow the construction of roads built for dam construction (Hirsch 2009). In addition, such projects draw more migrants looking for work. These spin-off effects only further exacerbate land conflicts and exacerbate social ills such as drug use, violence, and sex trafficking (Carvalho 2006; Scholz 2005).

The anti-dam movement, which dates back to the late 1970s, brings together an alliance of groups, including domestic, international, landless,

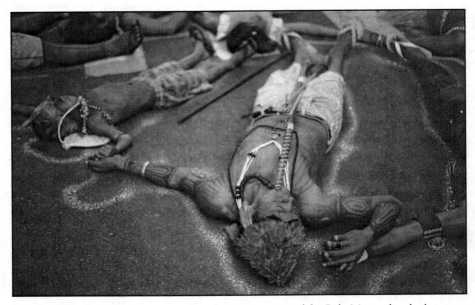

Munduruku Indians demonstrate against the construction of the Belo Monte dam by lying on the street to symbolize the dead, 2013. *Source:* Reuters/Lunae Parracho.

indigenous, church, and environmental varieties. It was also once closely tied to the governing PT. The Movement of People Affected by Dams (*Movimento dos Atingidos por Barragens*, MAB) is the largest national-level organization of its kind in Brazil, and it often partners with indigenous rights organizations like CIMI (the Indigenous Missionary Council) (McCormick 2011; Carvalho 2006). Groups indigenous to the Xingu River basin resorted to invading the construction site, but a judge ordered them to leave or risk fines of almost US$300 per person a day, an enormous amount of money for most of the hundreds of occupiers. They have spoken out forcefully against the project, vowing "we will not be silent. We will shout out loud, and we will do it now" (Barrionuevo 2011c).

They have argued that such tactics are necessary because the government isn't listening to them. Despite a constitutional requirement that the government consult indigenous people about the use of resources on their land, it continues a long tradition of treating the Indians "like nothing" ("Brazil, After a Long Battle" 2011). At least seventy residents promised to die before they would allow this assault on their homes; they told their warriors to prepare for battle. The uproar over Belo Monte was certainly a NIMBY, or "not in my backyard," protest; those for whom it is too late, the *atingados* (or dam-affected people), have turned out to support indigenous and riverine populations before it is too late for them, too. However, despite their best efforts to exercise power, this time the state proved resistant to their demands and the anti-dam movement failed to hold off construction (Diamond and Poirier 2010; Barrionuevo 2011c).

The movement and its supporters gave it their all, rallying international pressures on the state. Director James Cameron likened the fight over Belo Monte to the one depicted in his film *Avatar*, and also released a video that framed Belo Monte as a planetary concern (Rapoza 2011). An online petition was sent to President Rousseff with more than one million signatures, calling on the government to stop what was being called a "monster dam"; Brazilian celebrities made an anti-dam video that went viral, with millions of hits in just a few days ("Brazil, After a Long Battle" 2011; Rapoza 2011). In addition, Brazilian Catholic bishops, some of whom have received death threats, traveled to Rome to meet with Pope Benedict to mobilize global support against the dam (Allen 2010). In a world known for compassion fatigue, the anti-dam activists were able to wield power over long distances and therefore sustain the fight in a battle that has dragged out over decades.

However, one has to ask oneself whether bringing international civil society into the fight against Belo Monte ultimately proved counterproductive. Swayed by nationalistic sentiments, when it comes to the environment, even some progressive Brazilians resented what they saw as international interference in their domestic affairs. For example, when the Inter-American Human Rights Court called on the government to comply with its legal obligations to consult with indigenous groups and suspend construction of the dam, President Rousseff was applauded for striking back, suspending Brazil's 2012 participation in the court ("Almost 19 Million Urban Brazilians" 2012). On the other hand, environmentalists have begun to effectively deploy the nationalist weapon against the developmentalists as well, winning support by depicting their battle as one against rapacious—mostly foreign and increasingly Chinese—commercial interests that seek to exploit Brazil and take the profits back home (Rohter 2007a).

Although the environmentalists haven't given up, there are important differences between round one and round two of this fight. One of the most notable differences is that this time the state has proven resistant. It has the money to go ahead with the dam (funded almost entirely by taxpayers) and the state appears resolved to stick to the plan, no matter what the opposition (Diamond and Poirier 2010). President Rousseff, a former minister of energy under Lula, inherited the project and has proven unwilling to relent, "accusing opponents of living in a 'fantasy' realm if they thought Brazil could improve living standards with renewable energy alone" (Romero 2012c). This is a policy issue on which the PT-led state—which had once been allies with environmentalists—has been willing to stand its ground and confront the opposition. In a sign that positions have hardened, members of Congress characterized the MAB as a dangerous force that could foment uprisings and threaten national security; given this climate, it wouldn't be a shock to see anti-dam activists characterized as terrorists (da Silva and Rothman 2011). Such language raises concerns about the state's historic tendency to deal harshly with those who won't be accommodated—one way or another.

Meanwhile, both the Lula and Dilma governments have made efforts to demonstrate why their positions are reasonable and why the dam is necessary for Brazil to achieve its destiny. They contend that as a source of hydropower, Belo Monte is a model of green, clean energy, producing large amounts of electricity while emitting relatively little in terms of greenhouse emissions (Carvalho 2006; Romero 2012c). Moreover, they claim that they are sensitive to indigenous rights, have made every effort to offset any environmental harm, and are paying hundreds of millions of dollars to resettle families displaced by the dam. However, some officials have demonstrated their insensitivity, assuming that their own way of life is superior, by stating that the relocations will lift Indians from "precarious, subhuman conditions" (Barrionuevo 2010).

What is interesting is that many Brazilians watching far from the battlefield see nothing wrong with such statements. As we've seen with oil, when push comes to shove most Brazilians put economic development ahead of the environment. In the end, it is only a matter of time before Belo Monte becomes reality—the democratic process has slowed but will not halt the dams. This is a classic example of how states can simultaneously exhibit receptivity and resistance to society's influences. The result is what some would call a pragmatic, and characteristically Brazilian, accommodation: improvising ways to negotiate better project design, oversight mechanisms, and other safeguards to produce at least some environmental protection (Carvalho 2006). In assessing government response to the push and pull of society's efforts, it needs to be kept in mind that the line between state and society is blurred, in that it is not uncommon for activists to become civil servants nor is it uncommon for civil servants to support the agendas of activists.

Meanwhile, activists continue the fight on other battlefields. In recent years a controversy has been brewing over amendments to the Forest Code, a nearly fifty-year-old law that protects the forests. Environmentalists tried to hold off the changes, which they characterize as a step backward for Brazil.

Again the issue became extremely polarized; critics claimed it would "legalize the illegal" ("Brazil Eases Rules" 2011). The original Forest Code was never widely enforced; less than 1 percent of fines levied for violating it were ever paid, but what is worse, according to environmentalists, is that passage of the bill would mean the loss of as much as 190 million acres of forest ("Protecting Brazil's Forests" 2011).

There is no doubt that Dilma felt the pressures from all sides. During her campaign for president, she had promised to prevent changes in the law that would allow more deforestation or grant an amnesty to those who had already deforested (Adario 2011). A powerful agricultural bloc in her alliance (known as the *"ruralistas"*) argued that the overhaul was necessary to sustain Brazil's economic boom and feed its population. This bloc, which includes members of the Brazilian Communist Party advocating for small farmers as well as conservatives representing industrial agriculture, pushed hard for the change. It was opposed by Brazilian scientists, entertainers, and even some corporate leaders, and joined by international environmental NGOs and millions who made it into a social media phenomenon, urging her to keep her promise to veto the bill in a Twitter-based #vetaDilma movement (Recuero 2012).

It appeared to be a hugely successful campaign. According to a *Datafolha* poll, 79 percent of Brazilians supported a presidential veto of the Forest Code revision (Butler 2011). Plus, in terms of political opportunity structure, the timing of this decision couldn't be worse for the president, coming just prior to the United Nations Conference on Sustainable Development (Rio +20), which she hosted in June 2012. The spotlight was on her. However, in a classic example of the Brazilian tendency toward conciliation that serves conservative interests, the president sought to improvise a solution. With her party only holding 15 percent of the seats in Congress, she could not push through stronger environmental protections, even if she wanted to. Dilma did veto what environmentalists considered the worst parts of the legislation but allowed a more lenient version of the Forest Code to go through (Romero 2012d; Purdom and Nokes 2014).[15] As is the case with so many other issues in which the PT has left its old allies out in the cold, analysts will disagree about how to characterize the PT's policy on the environment. Do Belo Monte and the Forest Code prove that the PT as state has sold out, and moved away from the principles it stood

---

[15] The new law provides amnesties to those who illegally deforested areas prior to 2008 and reduces the amount of forest that landowners in the Amazon are by law are required to maintain on their lands from 80 to 50 percent (Purdom and Nokes 2014).

for when PT was society? Or, does Belo Monte adhere to the PT's consistent interest in using growth to promote development—and is the Forest Code just an example of the best the PT could do, given political realities?

CHINA

China has a richly diverse natural climate that includes multiple biospheres and habitats, from subarctic to tropical. Despite its size, 3.7 million square miles, roughly the size of the United States, less than 15 percent of the land is arable, presenting a dramatic resource squeeze. The northern regions of China are famous for drought, while the southern reaches have been plagued by floods. Historically, ecological challenges have included deforestation, widespread since classical times (Elvin 2004), and water, including attempts to tame devastating floods and to reroute rivers toward population centers. More recently, air pollution has come into the spotlight, especially as entire cities become blanketed in dangerous smog, forcing airports, schools, and factories to shut down.

The central government has been of multiple minds on environmental challenges, setting the stage for contradictory and even conflicting policies. In the early decades of the People's Republic, Mao Zedong viewed natural resources purely in instrumental terms, calling on the Chinese people to "conquer nature" and harness resources for the good of the Chinese nation. At times, these attempts were carried out to ridiculous—and harmful—extremes, including a 1958 campaign that rallied peasants to bang on pots and pans relentlessly to eliminate sparrows, which Mao erroneously believed were eating seeds and grain needed by the growing Chinese population.[16]

China may no longer be characterized by the wild swings of Maoist campaigns, but the speed with which it has embraced market forces, consumerism, and urbanization[17] have taken a significant toll on its natural resources. Labels

---

[16] The "Four Pest" campaign resulted in an enormous increase in the number of locusts, which devastated crops and exacerbated the famine brought on by the Great Leap Forward campaign (1958–1961). Estimates of the death toll due to the famine range widely, from 18 to 45 million people. See Dikötter 2010b.

[17] It is difficult to overstate the pace of China's urbanization. By 2025, many forecast that China will have at least eight megacities, each with a population of more than 10 million, and a projected 350 million people will move from rural areas into cities over the next twenty years (Larson 2011a). It is estimated that China's fastest-growing urban area, the western megacity of Chongqing, adds 1 million new residents each year. For the first time in recorded history, according to the 2010 census, urban residents (51.3 percent) outnumber rural dwellers in China ("China Becomes More Urban" 2012).

to capture China's environmental reality abound. The PRC has been characterized as an "environmental superpower" (Stalley 2009, 567) as well as an "environmental basket case" (Dalmia 2010) that some say is unfairly viewed as an "eco-villain" (Bleisch 2009). Evidence can be found to support each characterization.

The sources of environmental and energy challenges in China are clear: a laser-like focus on economic growth, energy demands fueled largely by coal,[18] and consumerism, as individuals embrace conveniences and products (including a burgeoning luxury market) that were, less than a generation ago, far out of their reach. As incomes have increased, so has the desire for consumer comforts, driving the need for energy higher. Even though China is a major crude oil producer, ranking fifth just behind Iran, it has been a net oil importer since 1993. There is also little doubt as to the role of the government in managing these resources—according to the 1982 constitution, China's land, rivers, forests, and mineral resources are all state owned. Environmental concerns slowly crept up the leadership ladder throughout the 1990s, taking on a new level of importance with the introduction of the twelfth Five Year Plan (2011–2015), which included the first Chinese blueprint to contain green indicators that hold local government officials accountable for sustainable targets, including new carbon emissions goals. The plan also contains a pledge to have 15 percent of the country's total energy come from non-fossil fuels by 2020—from 8.3 percent in 2009 to approximately 11 percent by 2015 (Apco Worldwide 2010).

Ordinary citizens recognize that "China is choking on its own success" (Liang 2010, 73), and they are finding innovative spaces to express their dismay. To a degree that we have not seen in other issue areas, the state is receptive to input and action on the part of some citizens, even as organized movements. Part of this is because Beijing has, since the early 2000s, recognized the environmental imperative and, especially, the impact of environmental degradation on the financial bottom line. The other part of it is the degree of publicly expressed anger and organized contention that pollution has prompted, in cities and especially in rural areas ("China's Urban Population" 2012; Luft 2013; Ramzy 2007).

---

[18] Even as the PRC attempts to reduce the share of coal as a percentage of its overall energy picture (with the short-term goal to reduce coal to less than 65 percent of energy production), coal provides nearly 70 percent of energy needs. Because of growing energy demands, China continues to increase coal output and absolute volume (Russell 2014). It is also beginning to address transportation issues from coal-generating regions, but currently nearly one-half of all rail traffic in China is dedicated to coal transport (Luft 2013).

Pollution: "Smogapolypse" Plus Water Shortages

China is notorious for its air pollution—it is not only competitive distance runners who try to avoid the hazy days of China's urban centers. Some of the earliest evidence of citizen awareness of environmental issues was related to air quality diminished by unfiltered factory output and China's breakneck economic expansion. For over half a century, Chinese businesses and citizens have plundered natural resources in the name of achieving growth, fostering what some have called a "Black GDP"—growth at all costs (Liang 2010, 73). And it is no secret that the Chinese government faces a long-term challenge in trying to meet the country's increasing demands for energy while, at the same time, reducing the stunning levels of water and air pollution throughout the country.

As we have seen in other issues, the challenge is as much one of scale as it is of speed: total energy use in China increased by 70 percent between the late 1990s and 2005, with coal consumption alone increasing by 75 percent ("Cost of Pollution" 2007). More and more, scientists are examining and publicizing environmental impacts on health. Infertility in China rose from 3 percent in the 1990s to 12.5 percent in 2010, and many argue that pollution plays a part in the infertility faced by an estimated forty million people (Yan and Blum 2013). Shortly after the WHO formally labeled outdoor pollution as a human carcinogen in 2013, news broke that an eight-year-old girl in eastern China was diagnosed with lung cancer linked to pollution (rather than genetics), becoming the youngest such patient in China, and likely the world (Brink 2013). Experts place the blame on the small particulate matter (PM), specifically PM 2.5,[19] produced by industrial activity and home-heating systems that rely on coal.

The appearance of seemingly apocalyptic smog since 2012 served as a clarion call for crisis —in large part because the smog was not limited to the industrial centers of Shanghai and Beijing, but forced flight diversions and closures as far west as Xinjiang. Even state-sponsored news saw commentators refer to the "Smogageddon" and the "Smogapolypse," launching off-color comments (that were the springboard for angry responses across Chinese social networking sites) about how the smog would unify the Chinese people, even protecting

---

[19] Particles that are 2.5 microns or less in width are known to penetrate the lung's bronchial tubes and cause respiratory distress, even in otherwise healthy individuals. PM 2.5 has become a standard measure of the amount of fine particulate matter in the atmosphere that may trigger health concerns.

Participants in a protest against a battery factory on the outskirts of Shanghai, May 2013. A series of protests influenced local officials' decision to limit production at the factory to decrease pollution. *Source:* Reuters/Aly Song.

them from enemy attack because the smog would limit the effectiveness of missiles and surveillance systems (Luft 2013). Because of the concentration of small particulates in the air, visibility was reduced to less than fifty meters, and midday scenes appeared nearly as dark as night. In some municipalities, officials ordered all non-essential government vehicles off the road, in a desperate attempt to tame pollution and rein in unrest. Environmental protests that employ a variety of repertoires are now recognized by CCP officials as the main cause of social unrest (replacing land disputes), with between thirty thousand and fifty thousand "mass incidents" related to pollution every year ("Chinese Anger over Pollution" 2013).

Still, as galvanizing and physically observable as China's air pollution woes are, many contend that water pollution is actually a bigger issue. The sources of contamination are easier to pinpoint, and Chinese environmental activists, and ordinary citizens angered by perceived cancer clusters, vocally protest the appallingly poor quality of the country's waterways. In a 2009 opinion poll conducted in fifteen countries, 67 percent of Chinese respondents cited water pollution as the country's most important environmental concern, more serious than air pollution and climate change (Ivanova 2009). Water challenges exist in part because of nature, and in part because of government initiatives to reroute nature. Globally, the average per capita water availability measure is 7,100 cubic meters, while in China it is 2,100 cubic meters, with significant regional variation (454 cubic meters in the north) (Larson 2014). The problem is so acute that the World Bank estimates that China's shortage of clean water could create thirty million "environmental refugees" by 2022 (Larson 2007).

Beijing only began to regulate water demand and supply relationships in the late 1980s, applying market-based techniques to a reality that was already stressed with overuse, even though some local governments, facing groundwater depletion, proposed licensing agreements in the late 1970s (Li, Beresford, and Song 2011). The relatively stable water supply has been drained by demand, with industrial needs nearly tripling between 1980 and 2007, along with a steady increase in household use as well (Li, Beresford, and Song 2011). Beijing's leaders have attempted massive infrastructure projects, at great human, environmental, and financial costs, to tame mighty rivers, redirect the flow of water, and generate renewable energy from water. The most famous is the Three Gorges Dam, along the mighty Yangtze River, the third-longest in the world.[20] After 1.3 million people were relocated, leaders announced the need to move an additional twenty thousand immediately, and an additional one hundred thousand by 2017, because they are at risk of "constant landslides" due to the dam ("China to Move 20,000" 2012).

Because of its scale, environmental impact, and degree of dislocation, the Three Gorges Dam project served, in many ways, as a catalyst for environmental organizing to follow. Part of this was because of the unprecedented defiance expressed by state lawmakers to this project: nearly one-third of delegates to the National People's Congress abstained or voted against the project in 1992, which continues to rank as the most vocal opposition to a government proposal in the national legislature. Risk-taking journalists, including Dai Qing, worked to expose both the ecological hazards and corrupt handling of relocation funds

---

[20] The Three Gorges Dam, the largest hydroelectric dam in the world, is five times larger than the Hoover Dam (completed in 1936), and it is believed to generate twenty times more power than the Hoover. It was completed in 2006, reaching its maximum depth in 2010. Although the Three Gorges Dam ranks highest in terms of generating capacity, it currently ranks behind Brazil and Paraguay's Itaipu Dam with regard to the annual amount of electricity generated.

associated with this grand project in the late 1980s.[21] In part because of the timing of this advocacy, much early environmental advocacy was tentative and cautious, due to the tense domestic climate that existed in China in the post-Tiananmen period. Then, in the early 2000s, the central government began to embrace the concept of sustainable development, even if the implementation of such targets faced significant obstacles. As Beijing prepared to host what it billed as the world's "greenest Olympics" in 2008, followed by the 2010 Shanghai World Expo, there was a sense among many in Beijing that they didn't want to lose face in the international community because of pollution problems. However, many of the so-called "blue sky days" were achieved by enforcing makeshift measures, such as temporarily moving or shutting down factories and removing more than 1.5 million cars from the road during the Games (non-Beijing residents were not allowed to drive). Data was being gathered and posted publicly, and many households started purchasing PM 2.5 measuring tools for their own use—the pollution cat was now clearly out of the bag.

Pollution-fighting activists began to garner more attention—not only from governmental cadres, but from ordinary citizens as well. One of the most prominent examples is the "China Water Pollution Map." This online database was created by China's most prominent environmentalist, Ma Jun, a former journalist at the *South China Morning Post* who was named by *Time* magazine in 2006 as one of the "100 people who shape our world" and who was also awarded the 2012 Goldman Environmental Prize.[22] The map posts information about water quality around the country, juxtaposing maps with locations of factories and water sources, with copies of the regulations by which factories can be evaluated, including government documents. From his non-profit Institute of Public and Environmental Affairs, Ma and his associates assemble public but difficult-to-find pollution data, exposing violators of national standards, which

---

[21] Dai Qing, a journalist activist who gained worldwide prominence for her opposition to the Three Gorges project throughout the 1980s, is often given credit for being among the first Chinese journalists to cover unorthodox views on Chinese social and political issues. For her advocacy she served a year in a maximum-security prison. Though forbidden from publishing in China, she continues to be based in Beijing and is recognized as a leading voice in China's emerging environmental discourse.

[22] The Goldman Environmental Prize is an annual award honoring grassroots activism. Each year, recipients from each of the six inhabited continents are named. The award committee is known to honor the personal risk of individuals engaging in environmental activity within their country. Ma Jun is the second recipient from China; Yu Xiaogang received the 2006 Goldman Environmental Prize for his anti-dam activism.

range from state-owned enterprises to private industry. Volunteers compile regulations and pollution statistics, serving as clearinghouses of information to mobilize citizens, lending clout to environmental officials trying to enforce the law (Larson 2007). Ma organized a coalition of Chinese NGOs known as the "Green Alliance" and has worked to hold major multinationals—including Walmart, Coca-Cola, and Apple—accountable for the environmental practices of their suppliers. His style has been characterized as more Paul Newman than Ralph Nader (Larson 2012), as he works to find the balance between advocacy, activism, and negotiation, and he has encouraged environmental groups to target major brands and international organizations due to their volume and relative sensitivity to the glare of international attention.

Part of why Ma Jun's environmental advocacy and Water Map work is that these efforts are done in collaboration with local and central governments—a level of working with government that we observe in relatively few cases in today's China. He has served as a consultant with the Ministry of Environmental Protection, and his map shines the spotlight on businesses reported by the government as polluters, showing once again that state-society relations need not always be adversarial, even in a non-democratic state. It helps to have powerful, well-placed advocates in the central government, and Pan Yue, currently one of the vice-ministers in the Ministry of Environmental Protection, fits the bill nicely. Rare among his pro-growth-at-all-costs government cadres, Pan is known to shut down industrial projects—many backed by his colleagues—for their practices, especially when they fail to file required environmental impact statements (Roberts 2005). Pan, a fearless advocate for environmental protection who has been rumored to be in line to serve as China's minister of environmental protection, was one of the leaders behind efforts in the mid-2000s to use a "Green GDP" to measure GDP losses because of environmental abuse. In 2006, a Green GDP figure was announced for 2004, calculating a 3 percent loss overall to the Chinese national economy (Liu 2008). This estimate, an admittedly conservative figure that focused nearly exclusively on air and water pollution, and which recommended significant growth reductions within many Chinese provinces, was viewed as too politically risky and damaging to Chinese growth to continue. Perhaps even more destabilizing were Pan's calls to connect local officials' advancement to green credentials. Due to bureaucratic foot-dragging and the widespread calculus that the country simply could not afford such pressures—as well as loud countervailing opposition from local governments—the release of Green GDP data was put on hold until the 2010 results were released in 2013.

Environmentally focused NGOs play a fundamentally important role in providing information to the public and, increasingly, to governmental bureaucracies willing to listen. The recognized connections between poverty, fiscal well-being, and environmental sustainability have convinced many within the Chinese leadership to be relatively open to limited feedback and information exchange with environmentalists, including organized environmental groups. Environmental organizing, including in the form of NGOs, is one of the safest and most common issue areas for citizen action in China—albeit within limits. Some NGO action opposes government interest, yet much of it is more informational than conflict laden. Environmental protests —often populated by individuals who have never before engaged in any direct action—have become nearly commonplace, with their participants numbering sometimes well over ten thousand. For the past decade, we can confidently speak of the emergence of environmental watchdogs, including environmental NGOs and journalists, who often work in tandem with both government officials and the emerging clean technology sector (Chan 2004; Yang 2005). Their impact—and future role in mediating China's many environmental challenges—is varied.

In the mid-1990s, the "Friends of Nature" helped lead the way for environmental NGOs within urban China (Yang 2005). This organization is often referred to as China's first true environmental group, rooted in the Daoist love of nature, sustained by a powerful patron, and with strong connections in the Chinese press.[23] Another advocacy organization focused on the legal rights of citizens, the Center for Legal Assistance to Pollution Victims, was launched in 1998. This group provides free legal assistance and volunteer attorneys to individuals and groups who want to assert to their legal claims of damage caused by pollution. It is staffed by professors and graduate students from many of China's top universities (including Peking, Qinghua, and Renmin Universities), geared toward assisting citizens in waging pollution cases in Chinese courts. In partnership with the US-based Natural Resources Defense Council since 2006, they host judges' workshops, provide litigation training, and promote public education to strengthen legal channels for environmental advocacy (Wang 2006). In its first ten years, it received ten thousand calls and pursued one hundred cases,

---

[23] The "Friends of Nature" was founded by Professor Liang Congjie (1932—2010) in 1994. Liang's grandfather was philosopher and reformer Liang Qichao (1873—1929) who was exiled to Japan after the Hundred Days' Reform in 1898, which attempted to transform China into a constitutional monarchy.

some with as many as 1,700 plaintiffs—and received a favorable settlement in nearly half of them (Ramzy 2007).

Not surprisingly, good connections in the government are important for fostering effective advocacy by NGOs. This often involves inviting government employees or retirees to work, either formally or as advisers with the NGOs, while maintaining their government appointment (Lu 2009). Such organizations fighting the problem of water pollution also commonly rely on contacts in the government for water pollution data. The group Green Han River, for example, has recruited the heads of government water-quality monitoring stations as its volunteers, which enables it to receive water quality data free of charge (Lu 2009, 73).

China is the largest dam-building country in the world, having built over twenty-two thousand dams since the 1950s, or roughly half of the world's total dams (C. Lewis 2013). Citizens have long been galvanized in efforts to prevent the destruction of their homelands, their crops, and their livelihood. In 2006, environmental NGOs, assisted by an aggressive media campaign within one of China's most respected newspapers, objected to multiple sets of dams throughout Yunnan Province in China's southwest, home to a wide array of ethnic minorities. They met both success and failure. Construction of a series of thirteen dams along the Nu (literally "angry") River was delayed from 2004 to 2011 after intense lobbying from groups within the province, in which fifty thousand people, mostly ethnic minorities, would be displaced. Dam opponents had a powerful patron in former prime minister Wen, a geological engineer, as well as international concern, highlighted by objections from the governments of Myanmar and Thailand, for whom the Nu River (also known as the Salween) provides water downstream. The Nu was China's last great waterway without a large-scale dam. Wen's high-profile opposition, though, was later eroded by intense lobbying from China's powerful industries, which successfully convinced central leaders that hydropower was a significant source of low-carbon electricity, and in 2013—shortly before Wen's retirement—the government announced plans to revive the original plan to build a series of dams in its upper reaches (Jacobs 2013a). Plans will require the relocation of tens of thousands of ethnic minorities in northwestern Yunnan Province.

Successful opposition was poised against construction of a major dam along the Jinsha River, in the Tiger Leaping Gorge, known as one of the deepest river canyons in the world (and close to Lijiang city, part of which has been designated as a UNESCO World Heritage site since 1997). This project would have displaced one hundred thousand residents, mostly farmers from the Naxi, reliant upon grain cultivation and tourism for their living. Their case was successfully made by Liu Jianqiang, a former senior investigative reporter at *Southern Weekend* (viewed as China's most influential investigative newspaper),[24] who composed a scathing exposé on the dams. He was able to document the illegality of the dam construction since it lacked the required approval from the central government, specifically the National Development and Reform Commission (formerly the State Planning Commission). Liu's essay caught the eye of then prime minister Wen, who suspended the project. However, Liu's role in this victory came with a price.

Journalists within both the local and national press have been increasingly aggressive covering environmental issues and mobilizing groups to go after polluters. The reception of environmental journalism straddles state receptivity and resistance. Investigative reporter Liu Jianqiang serves as one powerful example. Liu had switched from reporting on corruption to environmental issues because he believed he could "change something" (Levitt 2012). Yet he was framed an "enemy of the state" and lost his position at *Southern Weekend* for his critical reporting and advocacy. After the *Wall Street Journal* published a profile of him, Liu's editors were afraid they would get punished, so they severed ties with their branded employee. Recognizing the limits in seeking the government to do more, Liu, who currently serves as the Beijing-based co-editor of Chinadialogue,[25] has focused his efforts on informing the public about the truths of China's environmental record, believing that this will empower citizens to want to do more.

It is difficult to speak of a singular environmental movement within China. Despite the presence of key players—including groups discussed in this chapter—collaboration across groups tends to be ad hoc and short-term—large-scale organizing is politically dangerous, especially given the restrictive climate since

---

[24] The Southern Weekend (*Nanfang Zhoumo*) is a weekly newspaper based in Guangzhou. It is one of the most circulated newspapers in the PRC and is home to many famously outspoken journalists. Even though it is similar to other formal newspapers in China and it is owned by the provincial government, it is known for encouraging investigative journalism and testing the limits of free speech. For example, members of its staff went on strike in January 2013 to protest censorship orders from Beijing in the New Year's Day message, and the striking employees received an outpouring of support from ordinary citizens who stood outside of the gates of the newspaper offices.

[25] Chinadialogue is an independent non-profit organization based in London and Beijing that maintains a fully bilingual web 2.0 platform to discuss environmental issues in China and beyond. Since its foundation in 2006, it has received numerous international awards for its advocacy and engagement.

the commencement of the Xi Jinping administration in 2012. However, citizen engagement in environmental issues has most definitely increased, and the call for "public participation" in impact studies prior to the beginning of major projects was introduced in the mid-2000s. Ma Jun has stated that the Chinese public is demanding "transparency and even participation" in projects that affect the environment and public health ("Chinese Anger Over Pollution" 2013). A number of high-profile cases lend credence to the development of a burgeoning, but bureaucratically limited, environmental movement within China. Because of widespread outcry over dangerous air quality levels—and nearly a year after the vice-minister for environmental protection criticized monitoring at the US embassy as a violation of international conventions and Chinese law—the Ministry of Environmental Protection now includes measurement of PM 2.5. Chinese leaders continue to play the "developing nation exception," setting targets that are still two to three times the recommended exposure limit set by the WHO. In 2008, the Measures on Open Environmental Information came into force, requiring environmental protection bureaus to disclose information, including lists of known polluters, responses to citizens' complaints, and regional environmental quality records. These measures permit public applications for disclosure and could serve as a major tool for accountability.[26]

Major industrial projects are often targets of large-scale demonstrations. Protests forced changes in the plan to produce paraxylene—a key component of polyester—at a chemical plant in Ningbo, a major city in the northeast, as well as Dalian, a young city known for clean skies and affluent residents. Tens of thousands of people protested a proposed waste-water pipeline from a Japanese paper factory in Qidong, Jiangsu Province. Nearly a thousand people stormed government offices, even forcing the mayor to strip off his shirt and put on a T-shirt with an anti-pollution slogan. The anti-government action came with a price, though, as sixteen people were sentenced to up to one and a half years in prison for their actions, even though thirteen were given reprieves because of their confession and repentance ("China Sentences 16" 2013).

China's famed Tai Lake is still another example of how one man engaged in great risk to publicize pollution in the Chinese media. For decades, Wu Lihong, a resident along the banks of the Tai, kept track of factories on its shores,

---

[26] In 2007, the State Council issued China's Regulations on Open Government Information as an effort to help promote transparency and accountability. The Ministry of Environmental Protection, formerly known as the State Environmental Protection Agency, became the first government ministry to respond with its own measures.

documenting untreated waste by mailing samples to inspectors and television stations (Kahn 2007). He faced the wrath not of Beijing, but of factory bosses and local leaders in the city of Zhoutie: he and his wife both lost their jobs, he served time in jail, and his family was placed under local surveillance. As Tai Lake gained more and more attention—it is China's third-largest freshwater body—he exposed the charade of draining and dredging canals close to chemical factories before central level leaders stopped by for photo ops (Kahn 20007; Wan 2010). Foreign and Chinese media eventually picked up on his story, and he was transformed into a national hero, named by the Chinese national legislature as one of China's top ten environmental activists in 2005 (Wan 2010). His wife implored him to tame his advocacy, but, enraged when the local officials he had been fighting against succeeded in having Zhoutie named a National Model City for Environmental Protection, Wu was interrogated, physically assaulted, and imprisoned; he alleged that he was tortured in retribution for his activism (Wan 2010). Shortly after his arrest, Tai Lake was again in national headlines for its pond scum of blue-green algae, undrinkable water, and depleted fish harvests.

Beijing has faced boisterous calls for stronger anti-pollution measures from ethnic minorities; ecological strain has especially hit regions populated by the geographically and socially isolated aboriginal peoples of China, living mostly in the south. Similar to some of the issues that we identified in our discussion of ethnicity and race in chapter 4, the definition of minorities and nationalities in China is controlled by the government, and not necessarily reflective of the self-identification of group members, including a number of so-called "undistinguished nationalities," that include small numbers of Sherpas, Mang, and Khmu, as well as the indigenous Deang and Dai ("World Directory of Minorities" 2009). Ethnic minorities throughout southwestern China have had mixed levels of success challenging the grand energy plans of hydropower—industry representatives are often in cahoots with provincial leadership. Already settled in fragile ecosystems, many minority groups, especially along the Qinghai Plateau in northwestern China, are caught in a "vicious cycle" of climate change and embedded poverty, affecting more than thirty indigenous groups in one small region alone ("World Directory of Minorities" 2009).

Tibetan activists have also prominently resisted the exploitation of natural resources. Areas of contention include the completion of the Qinghai-Tibet railway as well as dam construction that has submerged temples and monasteries and displaced thousands. However, the challenges of climate change, which Chinese scientists openly recognize is behind the record glacial melting in the

Himalayas, are adding another element of contention to the Tibetan-Beijing mix.[27] As the source of most of Asia's major rivers, including the Indus, Yangtze, Mekong, and Brahmaputra, the Tibetan Plateau is a potential hot spot for both domestic and international criticism. With rumored central plans to divert water from the Tibetan Plateau to the water-scarce regions of northern China, as an extension of the controversial South-North Water Transfer Project, the potential for compounding resistance by multiple groups is among Beijing's worst fears. Energy politics combine with ethnic disputes in China's southwest, including many of the formal "autonomous regions," due to the rich deposits of natural gas and oil. Beijing has imposed significant limits on organizing by indigenous groups in China. The term "indigenous" is actually rejected by Beijing as too fracturing and unreflective of the unity of the Chinese people; Beijing insists on "minority nationalities" instead. The possibility of coinciding cleavages is too risky for Beijing to entertain.

Deforestation: Cracks in "The Green Great Wall"

The quality of soils and land cover, and efforts to protect them, presents another mixed record within China. On one hand, Beijing is viewed by the United Nations as a "superstar" for many of its forestry efforts, including increasing forest cover from approximately 8 percent in 1949 to over 20 percent in 2008 (Xu 2011). Although some question the long-term sustainability of the policies crafted to get there, the PRC has achieved a record unmatched by many other countries. At the same time, China is the lead importer, consumer, and exporter of lumber, yet its own forests provide less than 40 percent of its domestic needs (Laurence 2012)—demand that is only increasing with the emergence of China's middle class.

The largest national reforestation initiative, nicknamed the "Green Great Wall of China," has been operable since 1978. Although it is not slated for completion until 2050, this project, formerly known as the Three-North Shelterbelt Forest Program, has already produced the largest artificial (human-made) forest in the world, stretching five hundred thousand square kilometers. It combines civic duty (since the early 1980s, every citizen above the age of eleven is required to plant three saplings a year) with cash incentives for farmers to plant trees and shrubs in arid regions and governmental cadres dedicated to

---

[27] Climate change is discussed in further depth in chapter 6.

reforesting China's northern regions, stretching from Xinjiang Province in the far west to Heilongjiang Province in the east. Because of the embrace of this policy, more trees are planted in China than in the rest of the world combined (Watts 2009). Efforts are reminiscent of mass campaigns of a bygone era yet, because of common awareness of environmental degradation, are largely embraced by the populace.

Depending on whom you talk to, the Green Great Wall is seen as either the largest ecological restoration project ever attempted or a fairy tale, as portrayed by some ecologists at the Chinese Academy of Social Sciences (Luoma 2012). Much of the controversy surrounds the planting of non-native species and the possibility that new saplings will drain already strained water resources. Many fear that these efforts may again be an example of too little, too late. The legendary Gobi Desert in north-central China has expanded so much that some cities have opened "sand parks" where people ride camels and sleighs down dunes. The challenges have created a questionable export—dust—that has traveled from China to South Korea, Japan, and even the west coast of North America.

If clean air advocates in China try to promote "blue sky days" free of smog, those working to combat the windstorms brought on by the sandstorms that accompany desertification are trying to limit the number of "yellow sky days." More than one-fourth of China's total land is covered by desert or suffering from severe water depletion. China's desertification problem is widely believed to be caused by climate change, made worse by China's breakneck urbanization, demand for wood, and rising consumer taste for meat, which requires grazing land for livestock. China's Gobi Desert is expanding by four thousand square miles a year, with sand dunes visible less than fifty miles from Beijing. One official has stated that, at current rates, it will take three hundred years to "turn back" the deserts impinging upon China, especially the western reaches that border the Gobi Desert (Patience 2011). The challenge is anything but recent: in the fourth century BCE, the philosopher Mencius wrote about desertification and its human causes, including overgrazing and tree cutting. The modern challenge continues to feed an age-old rumor, mostly speculation in the Hong Kong media, that the capital may need to be relocated south to Nanjing.

Similar to the water challenges we discussed above, desertification is producing environmental refugees: farmers forced to abandon their land because it is stripped of its ability to produce agricultural products. Many of those most directly impacted by the loss of fertile agricultural lands are ethnic minorities, concentrated in the western reaches of the PRC. Ethnic Mongolians in China's northeast, traditional nomadic farmers who are said to be born on horses, have been forced to relocate from grasslands to urban areas due to grazing restrictions connected with anti-desertification efforts. Entire villages within Inner Mongolia have been relocated by the central government in order to build green barriers to the desert, and many are concerned that anti-desertification efforts only hasten the cultural assimilation programs that have already led to ethnic Mongolians being outnumbered five to one by Han who have moved to the province (Mulvenney 2007).

On the other hand, other forms of contention are severely punished. Liu Futang, a former forestry official in China's southern Hainan Island, was silenced for publicizing the environmental plight of his home, which lost one fourth of its woodlands in one decade to golf courses and hotels as local officials promote Hainan as the "Hawaii of the East" (Hancock 2013; Richburg 2012). Part of the irony of his fate is that just six months prior to his arrest, he had received a journalism and environmental press award for his exposé of illegal logging in Hainan, being praised as a brave "citizen journalist" (Watts 2012b). After he attracted too many followers on his *Sina Weibo* microblog, Liu was arrested and charged with running an illegal business printing environmental books without a license—even though officials acknowledged in court that he did not profit from the eighteen thousand books that he gave away (Branigan 2012). In poor health, Liu was released on the condition that he does not speak to the media, a limitation that faces activists of many stripes in the PRC.

When tensions between development and the environment overlap with ethnic divides, the volatile mix quickly puts authorities on guard, even though central and local government efforts to increase GDP by promoting the region as an energy center are much of the source of the problem. One such incident took place in Inner Mongolia in mid-2011. This is China's third-largest province, which has become its largest coal-producing region, as well as a source of rare-earth metals that are increasingly in global demand due to the proliferation of smartphones. Land privatization since the late 1970s has transformed the grasslands that sustained a formerly nomadic culture into increasingly barren, overgrazed lands that are surrounded by mining outposts. After a Han Chinese coal truck driver ran over and killed a young Mongolian herder who was part of a protest attempting to stop a convoy from driving over fenced prairies, the region burst into the biggest waves of demonstrations to face the province in over twenty years (Watts 2011). As signs of authorities' concern, a Western journalist attempting to cover the unrest was awoken at 4:30 A.M. in his hotel room and interrogated by plainclothes police (Watts 2011), and the mine driver accused of murder was sentenced to death weeks after the incident ("Death Sentence" 2011). Whether or not Beijing becomes swallowed by desert, it seems the international praise it has received for some government efforts pale in light of the treatment of those working to spread awareness of the challenges that lie ahead.

ANALYSIS

In its summation of contentious politics regarding the environment, figure 5.1 tells two very different stories about Brazil and China. As we will see in the comparison that follows, on pollution, what is remarkable is how closely their stories run parallel: in both cases pollution is a less contested issue on which society's approach is conventional, the state has proven receptive, and the outcome is reform. On deforestation, however, the two cases play against type; both countries play roles fundamentally different than most would expect. Here's where democratic Brazil shows how repressive it can be—through acts of omission or commission. At its heart, deforestation is linked to the most contested of all Brazil's issues: who controls land and resources. And this makes it a perfect storm of contentious politics, destined to result in repression: this is a core issue on which the state is highly resistant, with elements within society willing to adopt a confrontational approach, even oppositional approach. By comparison, deforestation is moderately contested in China. On this issue, the surprise is that the dictatorship proves mostly receptive to society using mostly conventional campaigns. However, as is the case in regard to HIV-AIDS and other issues, the state's suspicions about society keep it from following through: the outcome is indeterminate, complicated by an unfortunate coincidence: deforestation is mostly centered in regions where sovereignty is contested.

So, this chapter has shown that when it comes to all things environmental, Brazil and China are both heroes and villains. Both are major emitters, but when measured on a per capita basis, neither is ranked as a worst offender for carbon dioxide emissions.[28] China is a villain in that it enjoys the dubious

---

[28] In 2010 Brazil's per capita emissions rate was 124th in the world, well below the global average. Brazil is unique in that although it is a major emitter of carbon dioxide, the vast majority of its emissions are caused by land use. The country has one of the cleanest energy systems in the world because it relies on an energy mix of renewables, but its emissions are rising ("Brazil Fossil-Fuel CO2 Emissions" 2011; Watts 2014b).

FIGURE 5.1 CONCEPTUAL FRAMEWORK FOR ENVIRONMENTAL POLITICS

Brazil		China
Pollution		
Less Contested: Dramatic events create consensus on need for action.	Issue	**Less Contested:** Problem has become too large to ignore, both politically and economically.
Conventional: Protest as pressure works to embarrass state, but countervailing pressure by those who prioritize economic growth.	Societal Approach	**Conventional:** Protest as pressure and working with government. Synergy.
Receptive: But not exactly taking the initiative. Society leads the state.	State	**Receptive:** Evidence of collaboration after being resistant for decades. Resistance to more confrontational challenges.
Reform: Change is possible, but there's still a difference between the "real" and "legal" Brazil.	Outcome	**Reform:** Permissive approach to environmental NGOs, even though not all officials or levels of state are on board.
Deforestation		
Highly Contested: A core issue involving land reform and control over resources.	Issue	**Moderately Contested:** Conflation of the issue with ethnic identity and development.
Hybrid: Divides within movement. Most conventional but some oppositional and not all espouse non-violence. Strong countervailing pressure by economic interests.	Societal Approach	**Conventional:** Mostly conventional. Some confrontation against relocation.
Resistant: Economic interests trump environmentalism, although on occasion the state will attempt to appear accommodating.	State	**Both:** Receptive until advocacy receives too much support; centrality of issues for ethnic minorities makes state uneasy.
Repression: The state has made some concessions (which it lacks the capacity to enforce). The most dangerous type of activism in Brazil.	Outcome	**Indeterminate:** Large scale projects that won Beijing praise may cause more problems; coinciding tension with ethnic identity invites repression.

distinction of being the world's worst polluter, but it is the world's largest in-vestor in alternative energy.[29] Similarly, Brazil is the fourth-largest emitter of greenhouse gases, largely thanks to its burning of forests. And until 2008, it held the record as the country with the highest rates of deforestation—that year Indonesia took the title as Brazil began a period of declining deforestation that lasted until 2012. But Brazil is also home to the world's longest river and largest remaining rainforest, and few countries can beat Brazil for reliance on clean energies ("Brazil's Amazon Deforestation" 2011; Watts 2014b).

But there's no getting around the fact that both of these big countries have big environmental problems. For decades the governments of both countries regarded green interests suspiciously, largely refusing to discuss issues like de-forestation in international forums and putting economic growth, or develop-mentalism, ahead of all else. Their governments today have shifted somewhat, recognizing that a growth-at-any-cost approach has actually imperiled their economies and put at risk their abilities to maximize their potential. Beijing and Brasilia have both been badly shaken by costly natural disasters attributed to climate change. Out of fear that these droughts, floods, and fires were only a taste of what is to come, both states have taken an about-face and adopted fairly ambitious programs aimed at reducing their carbon footprints.

For all the talk about not caring what the world thinks of it, the Chinese state invested in what may be called "prestige environmentalism" (Dalmia 2010)—showy ecofriendly projects, such as the diversion of tens of billions of gallons of water to Beijing for the Olympic Games, as part of "Beijing's extreme environmental makeover," (Dalmia 2010) that both divert funds from other areas of need and fade away quickly. The "Green Wall" tree-planting project is another example of attention-getting Band-Aids that, in the end, are unlikely to secure much lasting effect.

Brazil is going through much the same thing with spring cleaning for its Olympics, but in assessing receptivity and response to society's pressures, one must remember that in terms of administrative and enforcement functions, the Brazilian state is relatively weak. Many of its failures are due to an inability to implement policy. Setting aside matters of capacity, one also must consider the factor of political will. The state is capable of rising to a challenge, as is evi-denced by its determination to build Belo Monte. It was buoyed by the support

---

[29] According to General Electric CEO Jeffrey Immelt, foreign companies interested in solar energy development are all watching China, where investments in renewable energy are on a scale that's "vastly superior to the U.S." (Martin and Goossens 2011).

of those who seek to put the economy ahead of the environment and faced down a formidable challenge from environmentalists.

In fact, populations in both Brazil and China have shown an increasing level of awareness and assertiveness in issues connected to the environment. Although greens can be found in any demographic, urban, higher-income, highly educated Chinese citizens are most likely to support large-scale ecological undertakings (Cao, Chen, and Liu 2009), but there are also elites, as well as those from other classes, who object to any intervention that might impede economic growth—especially since growth has been the measure of success for so long. Similarly, in Brazil, both environmentalism and developmentalism cut across class and ideological divides.[30] Brazilians' mixed messages to pollsters demonstrate a fundamental ambivalence about priorities. According to a 2010 Pew poll, eight in ten said that the environment should be a priority, even if it meant slower growth and the loss of jobs. Interestingly, the same proportion of Chinese agreed, and more Chinese than Brazilians were willing to put their money where their mouth is, to pay more to cope with climate change ("Brazilians Upbeat" 2010).

What's really important to understand is that once again, we see that in China, pressure is exerted mostly by individuals—in the case of environmental activism, often by journalists—whereas in Brazil, we see organized movements.[31] Part of this can be explained by pragmatism; we see individual, not group, pressure on the environment because organized groups are much less likely to be tolerated in China. This is also in part due to longevity: Brazilians began paying close attention to environmental concerns in the 1970s. This is much earlier than the Chinese, who began to develop a keener consciousness of ecological issues in the 1990s, which not-so-accidentally coincided with the rise of the Internet. For the most part, NGOs working on the environment are nascent organs in China; it is estimated that they average between five and ten members (Levitt 2012). Conversely, although not all those who turn out to protest will necessarily be considered members of a particular NGO, hundreds of Brazilians have turned out against building dams in 2011, and thousands of

---

[30] When the question is posed as "trees versus people," even many leftists view environmentalism as a luxury and put fighting poverty ahead of it (Keck 1995).

[31] There are numerous investigative journalists dedicated to the environment, including Dai Qing, as well as journalist activists including Liu Jianqiang, Hu Jia, Ma Jun, Liu Futang, and others. There certainly are Brazilian journalists trying to keep the spotlight on the environment, but most of them are bloggers and their audience is mostly international. McCormick (2011) contends that the lack of Brazilian reporters with green sympathies is a reflection of traditional media's domination by corporate owners.

farmers demonstrated in favor of the revised Forest Code (Daly 2011; "Brazil Farmers Mass in Protest" 2011).

In both Brazil and China we find a mixed bag of receptivity and resistance to citizen initiatives. Largely for economic reasons, green concerns have been one area of the greatest receptivity on the part of the Chinese state toward citizen initiatives. There is little doubt that Beijing's receptivity to green activism is motivated by its eye on the bottom line. Although there are probably more environmental NGOs than any other kind of single-issue NGO in Brazil, the dynamic is very different. If we define "acceptable areas" as issues that are relatively safe to protest, then it's amazing that environmental NGOs are so active in Brazil. As Chico Mendes, Dorothy Stang, and perhaps thousands more could attest, environmental politics is a relatively dangerous site for protest— although those posing the danger are mostly other non-state actors. The state's worst crimes are, mostly, acts of omission rather than acts of commission.[32]

We were certainly surprised to find that environmental activism can be riskier in democratic Brazil than it is in authoritarian China. Vested business interests in Brazil—due to their political and repressive power—often go unchallenged in Brazil, while that is not the case in China. Why has China not yet had a Dorothy Stang? Perhaps it is because in Brazil such martyrs are created by the clash of contending civil societies, while the state stands on the sidelines. In China, the developmentalists are part of the state and more effectively reined in by it. In Brazil, it often appears that the state is working for the developmentalists. Certainly, environmental activists in China have been arrested. Individuals have had their recording equipment smashed, and factory owners have sent thugs to beat activists up for challenging their supply chain. But, as regime leaders recognize the need to rein in environmental damages, and because they realize their low capacity to solve these problems wholly within the state sector, environmental contention in China has been, to date, relatively safer than other issue areas.

As has been the case historically in both countries, local power brokers— state or local government or bosses—largely call the shots. To some degree, the central governments of both countries have problems implementing policy, especially farther out in the countryside. In Brazil, the state is weak as a mediator

---

[32] According to Global Witness (2014), Brazil ranked as the world's most dangerous place for environmental activists: 448 environmental activists were killed between 2002 and 2013. Brazil came in as the second most dangerous country for journalists in 2012. However, it should be noted that Brazilian journalists writing about corruption and organized crime are killed in even larger numbers than those writing on the environment ("Brazil: Journalist Escapes Assassination Attempt" 2012).

between interest groups. Brazil needs state building if it is to attain its goals (Perruci 1999). However, even in China, widely considered a strong state, we see implementation difficulties that bring up the old adage, "the sky is high and the emperor is far away" (in Brazil you may remember it as "the law did not hold"). Despite common assumptions to the contrary, central leaders in Beijing and Brasilia often lack the ability to compel regional and local officials to follow their lead. In China, provincial governments depend on tax revenue from local industries—shutting down polluters runs against their interests (Larson 2007).

Perhaps because they are learning from a variety of fiascos associated with it, both China and Brazil are modifying the "get rich first, clean up later" model. In one example of receptivity, Shenyang's environmental protection bureau chief established an environmental blog and a citizen complaint line for air and noise pollution. In Shenyang this meant designing a green makeover that "made economic sense" (Larson 2011b). In Brazil, anyone can file a complaint against an alleged violation with a phone call to the Environmental Protection Agency or the Ministério Público (public prosecutor), created to pursue such cases on behalf of citizens. The system must have some legitimacy because it is common for community members to report problems. Better yet, Brazilians know that if the media picks up the story, these complaints can exert a good deal of pressure on the government, as EPA managers can be prosecuted for failing to do their jobs (da Motta 2003). Similarly, the Chinese state has also been praised for "steady progress" on environmental transparency after visible campaigns forced the hands of major actors, including Apple and the Beijing municipal government, to release pollution-related information—real-time data on the most toxic form of air pollution—to the public (Watts 2012a).[33] The conversation is more open, and the data more transparent, than it was a few years ago when Chinese government officials insisted that foreign embassies stop releasing data that was challenging the government's reports on air quality (the US embassy again releases hourly air-quality readings). Similarly, the Brazilian government is seeking to make an example of foreign oil companies that have made a mess along their coasts. The successes all those years back at Cubatão helped to provide the foundation for regulation of urban pollution, which, though still imperfect, is improved because of citizen activism. In this light, NGOs, despite their limitations, are achieving one of their most important functions: public education, even to the point of forcing corporate—and sometimes government—responsiveness.

---

[33] Apple revealed its supply chain and its methods for disposing of hazardous waste (Watts 2012a).

Citizens in both countries have attempted to force state responsiveness with demonstrations against dams. Often the outcome is surprising, as most of us would expect the opposite behaviors of authoritarian and democratic states. The Brazilian state is more receptive to dissent than the Chinese, but it went ahead with plans to build the Belo Monte dam, despite fervent opposition ("Brazil Grants Building Permit" 2011). Interestingly, in the face of similar domestic and international resistance, in 2007 Chinese leaders backed down on plans for a number of major dams, including thirteen along the Nu River. It was a different story with the Three Gorges Dam, where citizen resistance proved futile. Still, many of the leading voices from within civil society in China were drawn to the cause precisely because of the resistance they encountered, and the growing sense of urgency that their voices needed to heard—no matter the cost. Resistance to projects modeled after Three Gorges, including on the Lancang (Upper Mekong) and Nu (Salween) Rivers, continues. As we have seen, Chinese environmental activists, despite real risks to their livelihood and well-being, are increasingly inclined to challenge China's stature as the most dammed country in the world. Similarly, many of the latest generation of protesters against the Belo Monte dam grew up fighting—and winning—against earlier versions of it.

Interestingly, just as China appears to be recognizing the folly of its ways (in promoting growth at any cost), Brazil seems headed in the opposite direction. Whatever the policy, the challenge in both countries is implementation. Brazil's swings back and forth on environmental policy depend on any number of factors, including the outcome of the next elections. While Chinese leaders don't have to worry about the next election cycle, they can sign on to carbon caps, but must find a way to convert their edicts into reality (Larson 2007).

Once again, we have two stories that are much more alike than you'd expect—but they're still very different stories, nonetheless. As an authoritarian state, Beijing has a degree of latitude on environmental matters that Brazil doesn't. This power can be used both to propel and stifle discussion—if Beijing's leaders decide that environmental problems are top priority, the state can move with speed not found in democratic states. The Chinese state has shown itself capable of moving swiftly to reduce pollution and invest in renewable energy, with little of the policy paralysis found in other countries. Of course, the opposite is true at times as well: the CCP can just as swiftly shut down dissent, especially if environmental activists start to point to the CCP as part of the environmental problem. In Brazil it's a mixed bag. While the Brazilian state has at times proven responsive to environmentalists' demands in creating new laws, as often as not "the law did not hold." Worse, the state has committed crimes of omission, allowing repression of environmental activists to protect core interests of elites.

What explains these divergent outcomes? Once again, we see that states, democratic or not, protect what elites define to be their core interests. This helps us understand how some forms of environmental activism can be so dangerous in democratic Brazil, but tolerated—and sometimes even encouraged—in authoritarian China. It is difficult to view the back and forth engagement described in this chapter as clearly state vs. society or the other way around because a variety of factors affect the state's repertoire, including the alliances between activists and government agencies. An important lesson for contentious politics in general is that there are divides within the state as well as society; both serve as countervailing pressures on the state. Citizen activists select from a varied repertoire of responses and actions just as the state does. In the issues discussed here, at times policy implementation is complicated by the ill effects of uncoordinated bureaucracies, weak implementation, and mixed messages—from actors on all sides. Everyone knows that democracy is slow and messy, but who would have thought that it would be more dangerous to be an environmental activist in democratic Brazil than authoritarian China? We contend that issue may outrank regime: at least when it comes to the environment, those who rely on assumptions about regime type will have a hard time explaining the range of contentious politics in our two cases.

DISCUSSION QUESTIONS

1. It is in this issue area that we observe some of the most surprising findings with regard to contention and political regime. Why? How would you explain some of the contradictions within this chapter (e.g., Brazil's reputation as a green energy superpower but with limitations on some forms of environmental activism; China's notorious status as the world's worst polluter coexisting with central commitments to sustainable energy exploration)?

2. The media play central—and sometimes surprising—roles publicizing environmental issues and responses in both of these countries. Why do you think this is the case? How much of this has to do with environmental politics in Brazil and China, and how much of it has to do with the nature of environmental contention?

3. Environmental issues really seem to point out the complex nature of contentious politics, especially the absence of clear-cut solutions that are deemed acceptable by all sides of the issue. How did competing priorities, especially economic growth, nationalism, health, job security, et cetera, come into play? In your view, what were some of the most important cases

presented in this chapter? Were you surprised at the outcome(s) within any of the specific issue areas? Why or why not?

4. The conceptual framework for this set of issues is quite diverse: parallel on some, divergent (even against type) on others; we observe repression, receptivity, and reform in response to citizen mobilization. Why do you think this is the case?

5. Citizens (as individuals and within groups) have demonstrated significant understanding of environmental problems in Brazil and China, and have indeed taken great risk to publicize these challenges. How would you assess the level of risk assumed by environmental activists in Brazil and China?

LEADERSHIP FROM BRASILIA AND BEIJING

Since the world is so messed up, people think that Brazil is the savior. We used to be the problem. Now we are the solution.

— An unnamed member of the board of Teixeira da Costa, a Brazilian corporation (Bill Hinchberger, "Carnaval Is Over")

Well-fed foreigners have nothing better to do but point fingers at China. But China does not export revolution, we do not export poverty and hunger, and we do not interfere in the affairs of others. So what is there to complain about?

— Xi Jinping (Brue Gilley, "Meet the New Mao")

INTRODUCTION

Does the way a state interacts with society at home have anything to teach us about the role it will play on the world stage? We believe many of the theories from comparative politics that we have discussed throughout this book also work to describe politics between states. Whether the focus is domestic or international, contentious politics is affected by the political environment and the actors involved, as well as their performances (or ways to engage) and their repertoires. The previous chapters have outlined contentious politics on the domestic front. Do states engage in similar patterns of receptivity and resistance to international pressures, norms, and proposals in an increasingly multipolar and contested international arena? Scholars have long debated the sources of international relations, with many key players in the field, including Putnam, Evans, Katzenstein, and others, challenging the realist assumption that all states behave in essentially the same ways (Kapstein 1995; Evans, Jacobson, and Putnam 1993; Putnam 1988; Katzenstein 1976). Scholars emphasizing the domestic sources of international policies highlight domestic constraints on negotiation and bargaining. Putnam (1988) famously put it in terms of a two-level game, in which state leaders are positioned between two "tables" as they negotiate at the international level: one domestic and one international. In this view, leaders must calculate a delicate balance between what other states will accept (the international table) along with limitations they face at home (the domestic table), either in terms of formal ratification of treaties or the impact of this policy change on their domestic sphere. A decade before Putnam's influential research, Katzenstein (1976) argued that foreign economic policy can only be fully understood with careful analysis of domestic factors. For him, economic policy is significantly impacted by whether politicians operated in a mostly state-centered policy network (in his example, France) or a primarily society-centered network (as he observed in the United States).

In this chapter, we examine the types of influence Brazil and China are exerting as fast-emerging players, building on our understanding of state-society relations in both states. We contend that many of the concepts from the comparative literature we have employed throughout this book can be applied to political encounters in the international system: with rising powers playing the role of society, seeking to engage and influence established powers playing the role of state. As "monster states" due to their size (in terms of land mass, population, and economies), Brazil and China are both significant regional and transnational powers—with aspirations to match. If current trends continue, they will likely become only more important as the years progress (Hakim 2002).[1] This is because Brasilia and Beijing are speaking for themselves and plan to play a more prominent role in addressing many of the significant policy challenges of the early twenty-first century. As we will see in this chapter, both present themselves as counterhegemonic, and to some degree, they are both agents of change.

---

[1] Brazil's economy isn't in the same weight class as China's and it has experienced a slowdown since 2010, but as one energy analyst put it, "Even if it's not as attractive as it was four or so years ago, Brazil is still in better shape than plenty of other countries" (as cited in Johnson 2014, 5).

As agents of change, they are not only fast emerging *players*—they are fast emerging *powers*. Power (often associated with military or economic might) is commonly defined as the ability to affect others to achieve a desired outcome, and soft power (or social, cultural, political, and economic attractiveness) is one way to accomplish it. Much of their success will depend on their use of power, including soft power, which is about getting others to want what you want and obtaining preferred outcomes through attraction as opposed to varied forms of coercion (Nye 2013; Fijalkowski 2011). To do this, Brazil and China are asserting their presence, attempting to promote their "global brands" and launching charm offensives—regionally and globally—to win over supporters and inspire others with their new ways of doing things. Part of Brazil's cachet is that it is a young country, just five hundred years old. Brazil confidently offers itself up as an example of "tropicalist exceptionalism," an extraordinary country with vast potential (Amar 2009; Amorim 2010). On the other hand, China's main sources of attraction are the ancient foundations of its culture and the story of "China's rise" (or, more accurately, its "reemergence")—not to mention an economic success that is seemingly the envy of the world.

China, as the superpower on deck, and Brazil, the audacious up-and-comer, both consider themselves exceptional, unique. But as in so many other ways, the two countries often turn out to differ more in style than in content when it comes to foreign policy. They may belong at opposite ends of the democratization spectrum, but Brazil and China are both developed and developing, strong and weak. Both have social contracts at home, deals that they need to keep with their citizens to maintain stability. Both Beijing's and Brasília's ability to make good on these understandings is very much tied to their performance in the global economy—and much of that is predicated on their ability to promote and project their interests worldwide. As we will see, one way that they're both doing this is by posing as counterhegemonic, challenging the status quo but in very different ways, each playing to its strength. Brazil sells itself as a model for globalization with a social conscience, whereas China is trying to prove itself as a model for globalization . . . period. Keeping in mind how contentious politics at home shapes policy, we analyze the ways in which these countries are taking on the world and conclude by considering what kinds of powers Brazil and China are likely to become as the century unfolds.

BRAZIL

Like the soccer superstar Neymar, Brazil's foreign policy under Lula could be said to be "brash, bold, and brave" (Borden 2012). It is less so under his protégée,

Dilma, who is less personally suited for the role and is distracted by a variety of problems at home (Zanini 2014). Under PT governments, Brazil's foreign policy has been aimed squarely at changing the balance of power and attaining its dream of being an internationally respected power. To do this, Brazil has drawn from its successes at home and amplified them on the world stage. With its progressive social policies Brazil has developed an effective brand; it appears to be the image of an "activist state," a desirable model at home that inspires people abroad (Biehl 2004). Compared to many traditional powers, upwardly mobile Brazil is cool, ahead of the times. It has been unusually adept at understanding that the world has changed, and even at anticipating some of these changes (Amorim 2010).

Brazil is often characterized as practicing an imaginative diplomacy that includes a mix of non-interference with a high degree of "non-indifference" (Amorim 2010; Ekstrom and Alles 2012). Irreverent and audacious, as we will see, Brazil has demonstrated again and again that it is a consequential global player that isn't going to necessarily behave in the ways the traditional powers like the United States would like—and Brazilians love it. In a 2010 poll, 78 percent of those surveyed supported the way their foreign policy is conducted, and 77 percent believe that Brazil already is or will eventually become a superpower ("Brazilians Upbeat about Their Country" 2010). With Lula as the lead—and Dilma as a somewhat less inspired understudy stepping in to play the part—the role it is playing on the global stage suits Brazil—and Brazilians. Although foreign policy isn't a central concern of most citizens, Brazilians enjoy the acclaim and like their government's feistiness in defending their national interests.

Thanks to pressure from society and state-society collaboration, Brazil has some of the world's most progressive and admired policies. In promoting South-South solidarity and forging new coalitions to overturn unfair systems of privilege, Brazil is playing the long strategic game (Hochstetler 2003). But, as we have seen in our study of civil society in Brazil, the role of anti-system actor requires risks and takes a great deal of fortitude. But Brazilians, whether state or society, believe that like any great soccer player, it will all be about "finding the right mix of fast and slow, of possibility and caution" to get the outcome it wants—which in this case is mostly recognition (Borden 2012). Meanwhile, Brazil will have to find a balance between opportunities abroad and constraints at home (Sweig 2010). As we will see in this chapter, in its rush to center stage, Brazil has proven remarkably steady on its feet. But sometimes it has stumbled, and when this has happened, Brazil's detractors (mostly traditional powers) have been quick to ask if the upstart is ready to join the majors.

But if anyone can recover from this, it's Brazil. What makes the nation extraordinary, Brazilians (and many non-Brazilians alike) will tell you, is its potential, its charisma, its creative style of problem solving, and preference for conciliation over conflict—all of this a product of its history. This is partly possible because it faces no immediate foreign threats. Regionally and on the world stage Brazil combines this approach with an ambitious, expansive agenda. As we will see in the sections that follow, Brazil, long laughed off as "the country of the future," has global ambitions and an abiding belief in itself. Combining classic with unconventional strategies, it is determined to play the game of international politics. Sure, sometimes its efforts aren't appreciated; Israel referred to it as a dwarf for its involvement in the Gaza conflict. And it is a less alluring role model, now that its economy is tanking (Zanini 2014). But on the other hand, by staking out a position as a human security superpower, it has already found creative and graceful ways to pull off what are sometimes stunning sequences. The only question that remains is whether Brazil can leverage this acclaim into a very real form of power.

The Regional Arena: Is Brazil Too Big for the Room?

In the Americas, Brazil's rise has been associated with rising tensions. Its policy of "non-indifference" has roused anxiety with concerns that it may start behaving as a new imperial power in the region. Bold, continent-sized Brazil is aware of this problem. It tries to play down the fact that it is the region's dominant power. Seeking to diversify its trade partners but fearful of antagonizing its ten smaller neighbors, it has promoted multilateralism, encouraging greater regional cooperation through the extension of organizations such as Mercosul and the Union of South American Nations (UNASUL).[2] Brazil serves as an engine of economic growth in the region; since 2000 the country has led a monumental effort aimed at expanding regional ties through UNASUL and promoting

---

[2] Mercosul (Mercosur in Spanish) is known as "the Common Market of the South." A subregional bloc, it started out as a customs union and has expanded to promote free trade as well as political cooperation. Mercosul is composed of five full members (Brazil, Argentina, Paraguay, Uruguay, and Venezuela) as well as associate members Chile, Bolivia, Colombia, Ecuador, and Peru. UNASUL (USAN in Spanish) is an intergovernmental body integrating two customs unions (Mercosul and the Andean Community of Nations, CAN). With twelve South American members UNASUL promotes economic, political, cultural, and social integration and seeks joint solutions to problems the members share, such as health, drug control, and defense (Pothuraju 2012).

the closer integration of twelve Latin American economies. South American integration is a priority for Brazil and its efforts have paid off: between 2000 and 2009, Brazil's trade with the Andean Community grew by 253 percent—yes, 253 percent—and with Mercosul countries it has grown by a respectable 86 percent (Sweig 2010; Friedman-Rudovsky 2012).

Although Brazil sees it as a win-win with mutual economic benefit for everyone involved, expanding Brazilian investment and trade is welcomed with ambivalence in the region. Some are more skeptical than others. Argentina always has its eye on its rival, but for many of Brazil's smaller neighbors such projects are needed, as they have increased the accessibility and productivity of a variety of economic endeavors. Countries such as Paraguay are more likely to see that it is not just Brazil that has reaped rewards. But for economies large and small, increased interdependence has also inflamed concerns about power asymmetries. For example, Brazil planned and financed the construction of a network of "mega" infrastructural projects that would power up, span, and connect the continent (Friedman-Rudovsky 2012). But with so much energy and financial muscle behind it, Brazil is sensitive to accusations of being a regional hegemon. Anticipating a backlash, it has funded projects to promote balanced development and tried not to appear too eager to lead.[3] However, many of its neighbors remain immune to Brazil's charms; they accuse it of having outsize ambitions and being more about growing its own, already-giant economy than promoting regional development. As environmental activist César Gamboa put it, "Brazil doesn't want to be considered the region's new imperialist power, but that's what they act like" (cited in Friedman-Rudovsky 2012).

This kind of reputation is the last thing Brazil wants, and it's very sensitive to the accusation of being like the United States. Brazil contends that it is all about balancing the United States, which it views as a favor to everyone else—in the region and the world. In terms of the US-Brazilian relationship, although the two are a lot alike in many ways and share a number of mutual interests, they have never been as close as they could be. It looked as if that might change in 2008. Most Brazilians were ecstatic over Obama's election; they welcomed his embrace of multilateralism and message of bridging differences, which mirrored their own worldview (Mance 2008).

---

[3] Examples of Brazil's efforts to promote "balanced development" include funding the construction of housing for the poor in Paraguay and electric lines in Paraguay, Uruguay, and Argentina (Amorim 2010).

Yet hopes that the relationship would improve were soon disappointed. The United States and Brazil have a lot of historical baggage and mistrust; they just don't "get" each other. From Brazil's perspective, the United States continues to treat it like "just another poor country in the US' backyard" (Winter 2013). Many Brazilians continue to harbor suspicions of the United States, remembering it from the Cold War as an ally of the dictatorship and an obstacle to democracy. Moreover, they resent that the United States and their closer neighbors have been slow to acknowledge Brazil's rise as a consequential player, a regional and global leader. The United States has its issues with Brazil as well; whether the United States likes it or not, Brazil has adopted, and will continue to adopt, an assertive and independent foreign policy that is at times at odds with the United States. On multiple occasions Brazil has shown itself willing to confront the United States when it hasn't treated other countries as equals. For example, after the news broke that the United States had been intercepting her own personal communications as well as those of many other Brazilians, President Rousseff was indignant, first demanding a full explanation from the Obama administration and then retaliating, making the rare decision to cancel a state visit to the United States (Barbara 2013b; Romero 2013e).

Her strong response played well at home and abroad, burnishing Brazil's image as no pushover for the United States. Since then President Rousseff has gone on to lead on a United Nations resolution characterizing the US illegal surveillance and intercept of communications as a violation of human rights. Among other things, she is also proposing the development of a multilateral framework for the governance and use of the Internet ("Brazil and Germany to Propose UN Resolution" 2013; "Brazil Summons Canadian Envoy" 2013). While some in the United States might characterize it as petulance, Brazil's stand has won it points with all those ready for the rule makers to start playing by the rules (Winter 2013).

In the big picture, however, this exchange should be characterized as more of a tiff than a breakup. Brazil is unusual in that it is one of the few countries in the non-Western world that can call the United States out and still maintain a cordial relationship with the United States. As Sweig (2010, 183) puts it, "Brazil is neither fundamentally anti-American nor pro-American." Brazil and the United States continue to cooperate in a variety of areas; for example, trade and investment between the two countries has grown dramatically in recent years, but China has surpassed the United States as Brazil's number one trading partner. Trade is also one of the chief sources of contention between the United States and Brazilian governments, which see the world differently and often seem to vex each other. Brazil considers itself to be a major country with the right to have a say in how the world is managed. The United States apparently disagrees. As we will see in the sections that follow, Brazil is becoming more influential; increasingly it poses a counterweight to US influence, and this fact sets the two up for a series of low-intensity competitions (O'Neill 2010; Sweig 2010; Hakim 2002; "Views of US Continue" 2011).

The rest of the region, which doesn't want to be led by Brazil or the United States, must be amused by the wrestling matches between these two regional powerhouses. Sure, Brazil has global ambitions, but it is chagrined at being compared to the United States. What kind of relationship does Brazil want with its neighbors? It is very much in Brazil's interest to promote regional unity, prosperity, and stability. A stronger and more relevant South America reflects well on Brazil, and helps to better position it for negotiations with other countries farther afield. And whether its neighbors like it or not, Brazil is a new center of power in the region and a bridge to the rest of the world. Its regional foreign policy is really just a smaller-scale version of its act on the world stage, which is all about bringing in a new voice and taking on more responsibilities (Amorim 2010; "Global Brazil and U.S.-Brazil Relations" 2011). The only significant difference is the way in which this act is received. As we will see, Brazil has had better luck when it has taken its show on the road.

The Transnational Arena: Diplomacy as "The Beautiful Game"

As a nod to its economic chops, in 2013 a Brazilian was selected to head the World Trade Organization (WTO). For having the grace to take on rich countries without alienating them, Brazil is celebrated and admired as a leader of the South; for disavowing nuclear weapons, it's a model of nuclear non-proliferation. When it comes to diplomacy, Brazilians are widely regarded as naturals. There is no doubt that with its far-reaching foreign policy agenda, Brazil views itself as not just a regional but a global player. Known for its adroit dodging and dynamic, creative, and even flamboyant style, it seeks to lead by example and forge new coalitions on a wide range of issues at the global level. Based on successes fostering human security at home, the country is certain that it has contributions to make in promoting peace and prosperity; its domestic policy is the model for its foreign policy. Brazil basks in the limelight and has accrued soft power in international relations thanks to policies that the state adopted after being prodded by, and working synergistically with, domestic civil society. Society led the state. As we will see, with its own style of play—said to be reflective of its national characteristics—and policy of non-indifference, Brazil is working aggressively to reshape global institutions. In doing so, it is firming up its credentials as a leader on human security. Brazil is making its mark as a new kind of superpower, promoting cooperation worldwide. In fact, it is so active in multilateral organizations that its presence has been described as "near ubiquitous" (Sweig 2010; Ekstrom and Alles 2012; Borden 2014).

Although some accuse Brazil of having an outsize ego and exaggerated self-image, Brazil views itself as simply rising to its potential. It certainly threatens some in the Group of 8 (G8) because it is a non-traditional power and counterhegemonic leader, willing to stand up to the powers that be. With its South-South agenda, Brazil makes itself heard as the voice of less developed countries (LDCs) on a variety of pressing issues—issues on which the traditional powers have failed to lead. Brazil argues that it is high time for a new approach and that Brazil's participation should be welcomed for the country's productive contributions to resolving intractable problems (Cárdenas 2013).

With its blend of capitalism and social democracy, Brazil has branded itself as a new global player on the world stage. As Sweig (2010) put it, "Brazil can be the Mac to the United States' PC—with an ethos and international agenda to match." But in taking on the United States and other traditional powers, Brazil isn't looking to join "the Axis of Evil." It isn't seeking to overturn these institutions; rather it (rather assertively) seeks to adapt them to better serve Brazilian interests and more accurately reflect the multipolar world ("Global Brazil and U.S.-Brazil Relations" 2011).

The BRIC states (Brazil, Russia, India, and China) perhaps best symbolize the potential for collaboration among emerging, non-traditional powers. Among other things, these countries are known for seeking to reform the international system. Brazil has tirelessly worked for restructuring the IMF and World Bank to include emerging countries, make the organizations more representative, and therefore give the two organizations more legitimacy (for better or worse, this reformist approach mirrors the one long favored at home; it alters the system, but ultimately maintains it). So far, Brazil hasn't been able to persuade the status quo powers of the benefits of working synergistically with those on the outside. Because Brazil has had more success in putting together strong coalitions such as the Group of 77 (or G77, as a counterpart to the developed-country country club, the G8), it is mistaken for being radical. At these and other forums, Brazil has played a leading role calling for a reciprocal multilateralism in which rich countries are expected to also play by the rules. It has also called for allowing LDCs more equitable access to markets.

For example, at the WTO, Brazil burnished its leadership credentials when it challenged US subsidies of cotton and won the right to impose retaliatory tariffs on the United States ("Global Brazil and U.S.-Brazil Relations" 2011). For taking such stands Brazil is touted as an upstart—winning it great acclaim among LDCs but received with less warmth by developed countries, or DCs. But true to its accommodating nature, Brazil is really just seeking to take its place at the table, not upend it.

Brazil's foreign policy is a product not only of its history and traditions, but of state-society relations. Despite the fact that it still has work to do, Brazil is known as a model for how to develop with a social conscience, largely due to its successes in ameliorating inequality, poverty, and hunger—which the state led, but is largely due to the collaboration of state and society. As described in chapter 3, Brazil pioneered CCT programs, such as Bolsa Familia, that have been replicated around the world (including some DCs). It has also become an exporter of successful social welfare programs like Fome Zero (Zero Hunger). In addition, as the world's fourth-largest exporter of food, and with its vast potential for increasing food production, Brazil is well placed to lead in ensuring international food security. It participates in a variety of programs, especially in Africa, that share technological innovations adapted to tropical conditions and to create global food stores (Sweig 2010; Romero 2012e).

Thanks to prodding by civil society, Brazil has played a pivotal role in the global campaign against HIV-AIDS. Its home-grown approach to the disease is one of its most remarkable achievements, winning it accolades worldwide and confirming its image as a human security superpower.[4] As we saw in chapter 3, Brazil has been a pioneer when it comes to HIV-AIDS, combining a unique, counterhegemonic approach to prevention, care, and treatment. Long before the Joint United Nations Programme on HIV and AIDS (UNAIDS) advocated it, Brazil guaranteed free and universal access to AIDS treatment (Vianna, Carrara, and Lacerda 2008; Foller 2010). Since the discovery of anti-retroviral therapies, access to these essential medicines had been a problem, as their cost had always been prohibitive. In the 1990s, presented with the looming threat this disease posed for the country, the newly democratic government listened

---

[4] In 1990 the estimated prevalence rate of HIV in adults in Brazil was 1 percent (comparable to South Africa). Experts had predicted that the numbers of Brazilians who were HIV positive would grow exponentially, and that Brazil would follow South Africa's path—the country with the highest number of people living with the disease in the world. However, by 2012 the rate in Brazil had been cut in half (Ozug 2010; "2012 Progress Reports" 2012).

to activists at home and chose to take the problem head on. As it worked out its integrated, strategic approach to the disease within Brazil, it shared it with the world. Brazil eventually became an activist state, working in solidarity with global civil society against yet another behemoth—the big pharmaceutical corporations (New 2012; Nauta 2011). Sure, Brazil needed to protest patent laws on AIDS drugs in order to drive down their cost—or its guarantee of treatment would have bankrupted the country. But it clearly led on this issue and championed making these medicines affordable and accessible for the whole world, not just Brazil. It is due to Brazil's groundbreaking efforts that there has been a massive increase in access to medicines; nearly ten million people in developing countries have access to anti-retrovirals ("Around 10 Million" 2013). In this, Brazil has led by example, demonstrating that universal care can actually lower costs and reduce the transmission of HIV. In many ways, thanks to its policy on HIV-AIDS, Brazil has become known as "a soft power superpower."

The country has also adopted a counterhegemonic stance and been a trailblazer in efforts to prevent the disease. Rejecting what it describes as a "puritanical" harm avoidance approach in favor of harms reduction, it argues that its prevention plan is realistic and pragmatic: it emphasizes frank discussions of sexuality and promotes safer sex over abstinence or monogamy (Ozug 2010; Amar 2009). Recognizing the importance of inclusion and how its policy at home has been informed by the participation of often-marginalized groups, including needle drug users, it has led calls upon UN member states to recognize sexual rights and to fight discrimination against those who are HIV positive (Foller 2010). For example, Brazil has supported global campaigns advocating for the rights of sex workers, and since 2005 has given up more than $40 million in US aid because it refused to comply with a US requirement that it formally condemn prostitution (Amar 2009). To many people around the world, Brazil proved its credentials as a world leader when it stood up to the United States on this issue, characterizing such a requirement as North American hypocrisy and a violation of Brazilian sovereignty (Amar 2009; Vianna, Carrara, and Lacerda 2008). Moreover, when it comes to HIV-AIDS, Brazil has been recognized globally as an activist state with an imaginative, best-practice strategy that integrates prevention, care, and treatment (Nauta 2011). Brazil is proud of this accomplishment: it took a developing country to show the world how to deal with this devastating disease (Pimenta el al. 2010; Safreed-Harmon 2008).

Brazil has remained congenial while asserting its independence and charting its own course. It has remained friendly with all while making it clear that it is unwilling to play by anyone else's rules (Kupchan 2012). For example, at the

UN it votes with the United States less than 25 percent of the time, and it frequently abstains on votes to express its frustration with unfair or unsystematic treatment of issues. For Brazil, an abstention is not a "no" vote or an abdication of responsibility. Rather, Brazil sees it as an opportunity to improve the process by decrying double standards and the like ("Global Brazil and U.S.-Brazil Relations" 2011).

Brazil's independence on global security issues is put on display in its attempt to serve as a bridge to states on the margin, such as Venezuela, Cuba, and Iran (Sweig 2010). Preferring quiet diplomacy, Brazil has traditionally been known for a policy of non-interference: a respect for sovereignty and rejection of interference in the domestic affairs of other countries. With its status as a human security leader, Lula's Brazil surprised and disappointed many when it failed to speak up about egregious human rights violations in Iran, Burma, or Venezuela. His government responded that it is committed to the promotion of human rights at home and abroad but prefers a quiet, behind-the-scenes dialogue and leading by example. President Rousseff has been more willing to speak out on human rights violations, but the Brazilian approach to the world's pariah states is to reject double standards and to promote inclusiveness rather than isolation. For example, despite pressure from the United States, it has long maintained a relationship with Cuba and gone further, even urging the United States to lift the embargo ("Global Brazil and U.S.-Brazil Relations" 2011; Amorim 2010).

Brazil believes that it has a positive contribution to make and that with the right diplomacy, countries can be persuaded to work with—rather than against—the international community. For example, in an ambitious move in 2010, Brazilian and Turkish diplomats played breakout roles at the UN. They took the initiative to become interlocutors between Iran and the West, and came very close to finding a solution that some argue could have defused the crisis over Iran's nuclear program. However, the United States and other permanent members of the UN Security Council (UNSC) dismissed the initiative as naïve and refused to back the deal, preferring instead a round of sanctions prior to negotiations. This came as a blow to Brazil, which was embarrassed to be treated as an amateur, unwelcomed presence and portrayed as irresponsible, reckless, and cozy with Iranian president Mahmoud Ahmadinejad. Brazil argued that it had the credentials—and moral authority—to lead on this effort as one of the few countries to walk away from developing its own nuclear program (Sweig 2010; "Global Brazil and U.S.-Brazil Relations" 2011). Regardless, the Brazilian attempt to broker an Iranian deal says a lot about Brazil and how it

254 | CONTENTIOUS POLITICS IN BRAZIL AND CHINA

operates. It believes itself to be a pivotal state with the right to participate in matters of global security, such as the Israeli-Palestinian conflict. However, it must constantly face down the United States and other traditional powers that view this upstart as out of its depth.

As one might expect, Brazil bristles against such treatment and struggles with the fact that it is not treated as an equal by developed countries. Brazil is a founding member of the United Nations, and the Brazilian diplomatic corps has long been world-renowned for its professionalism. At the UN, the WTO, IMF, et cetera, it calls for democratizing reforms that will improve and strengthen these bodies. It is one of several countries that argues that the UNSC must expand the number of permanent members to reflect the current distribution of power. They argue that the Permanent Five (the United States, Russia, China, Britain, and France, the P-5) is a post–World War II anachronism, and that expanding the body's representation would increase its legitimacy and effectiveness (Amorim 2010; "Global Brazil and U.S.-Brazil Relations" 2011). The world's problems require a new, inclusive, and more democratic approach; Brazil contends that it has already demonstrated its leadership in a variety of areas. It could be characterized as having "semi-permanent" status; it has served as a non-permanent member of the UNSC longer than any other country except Japan (Stuenkel 2010).

Having proven itself to be a responsible stakeholder, Brazil argues that it deserves to join as a permanent member.[5] For Brazil, permanent membership in this most prestigious of all world bodies is important. Because it is not a military power, the only way for it to project its power abroad is through multilateral organizations (Stuenkel 2010). However, none of the P-5 members of the UNSC have shown any particular interest in expanding the club, and the United States has not endorsed Brazil for permanent membership, which further complicates the two countries' already somewhat problematic relationship. Although they agree that the South needs representation in the body, many developing countries—including almost all of its neighbors—oppose extending permanent membership to Brazil, despite its promise to represent the disenfranchised.

---

[5] Although it is extremely cautious about interventionist policies, Brazil has supported them where it feels that it can help to mediate crises. It has been an active participant in over twenty peacekeeping missions, including Haiti, Liberia, Côte d'Ivoire, and East Timor ("Global Brazil and U.S.-Brazil Relations" 2011).

Case in Point: Climate Change

When it comes to climate change and the issues associated with it, Brazil's foreign policy can be said to be a reflection of contentious politics at home. Because Brazil's environmental policy has varied over the years, alternating back and forth between prioritizing "gold" versus "green," putting money ahead of the environment, its foreign policy in regard to the environment has often appeared contradictory. Since the return to democracy, this policy has reflected the state's attempt to balance conflicting interests and countervailing pressures. During the dictatorship and the democratic transition (the Sarney presidency of 1985–1990), the state's response to pressure on the environment from outside Brazil was largely to resist it, and to characterize internal environmental actors as beholden to an international conspiracy. On this issue, Brazil actually took the offensive, bringing this fight to the international arena. In 1972 at the United Nations Conference on the Human Environment in Stockholm, the Brazilian government defiantly defended the right of less developed countries to use their natural resources as they saw fit, arguing that rich countries' concerns were hypocritical and that development should not be sacrificed for the environment (de Oliveira 2003).

Over the years, due to the pressure from environmentalists and advocates for the rights of indigenous peoples (domestic and international), Brazil's policy has been inconsistent, as various governments sought to balance nationalist, economic interests versus transnational, environmental ones (Serva 2011). During dictatorship and democracy, Brazil's leaders have tended to put economic development first. But over the years pivotal events that caught the attention of international media (such as the 1988 murder of activist Chico Mendes) have made them sensitive to the public relations nightmare associated with the environment, particularly the destruction of the Amazon. At these junctures, the pendulum would swing back, and governments pledged to do better on the environment. But as often as not, these changes were temporary and merely cosmetic.

As Brazil's democratic governments have come under increasing internal and external pressure to protect the Amazon and do their part to limit climate change, they have equivocated, at times seeking to impress the world with their leadership on the environment (for example, by hosting the 1992 Earth Summit)—and then presiding over, or at least not interfering with, its destruction. For example, at that conference President Fernando Collor de Mello signed an international agreement to protect biodiversity, but the destruction of Brazil's rainforest raged on through the 1990s (Perruci 1999). Although environmentalists had campaigned for Lula and were shocked to hear it, in 2003 President Lula famously declared that "the Amazon is not untouchable" and proceeded with a road-building project that opened up more of the forest to exploitation. Deforestation peaked in 2003 and 2004, as nearly eleven thousand square miles of forest was cleared (Kepp 2004).

Through it all, Brazil has been—and continues to be—very defensive about deforestation and its policy in the Amazon. For years (and not only during the dictatorship), Brazilian governments refused to discuss deforestation at international conferences, downplaying the problems associated with climate change and treating it as somebody else's problem. That posture changed briefly, as we will see later, mostly during the Lula administration. But no matter who is the country's president, because it holds more than half of the Amazon, Brazil has also had an outsize role in discussions regarding the environment and climate change. And it is important to recognize that the Amazon is a red line for Brazil—and ultimately, a nationalist, core issue. Many Brazilians are extremely touchy about international attempts to interfere with the country's management of natural resources (Perruci 1999). Generations have feared that foreigners covet the Amazon and that the international community's interest in deforestation and the rights of indigenous peoples are just pretexts for pillaging and colonizing it, keeping Brazil uncompetitive and underdeveloped (Perruci 1999; Barrionuevo 2008).[6] When outsiders disparage Brazil's fitness to regulate affairs in own territory and environmentalists make reference to the Amazon as "the earth's lungs"—and mention the idea of creating a supranational authority for the Amazon with sanctioning power over Brazil—it pushes all the country's buttons. Brazil considers such talk a threat to its sovereignty and is quick to remind outsiders that the Amazon is Brazil's—not the world's—patrimony (Hochstetler and Keck 2007, 115).

Such a stance has been adopted by every government since the return to democracy, including the PT-led state, which has disappointed environmentalists for prioritizing economic growth—and poverty reduction—over environmental concerns. However, in response to an unprecedented, devastating Amazonian drought, followed by wildfires in 2005, the Lula administration

---

[6] It's not just nationalist extremists who feel this way; concern about foreign interference in the Amazon is mainstream in Brazil, held by people on the right and left. In a 2007 national poll, 83 percent of those surveyed in the Brazilian military and 73 percent of civilians said they believe that the Amazon is at risk of foreign military occupation (cited by "Defesanet" 2011).

made an about-face on climate change. Due to the drought's impact on the economy and human health, it recalibrated its policy and declared a "state of public calamity."[7] By this point it was hard for the state to ignore the possibility of the drought's link to climate change as scientists generally agreed that the drought was due to the rise in water temperatures in the Atlantic Ocean. The first hurricane on record to form in the southern Atlantic hit the coast of Brazil in 2004, displacing thousands (Rohter 2007b).

The timing of these events is important: it was after these crises that we began to see another state turnaround on the environment. The government's fear was that the disasters of 2005 could be a precursor to many more catastrophic events to come—and not in the distant future (Rohter 2005c). In 2009, scientists predicted that climate change would increase rainfall in the Amazon and result in flooding there, whereas the south would be hit by an increased incidence of drought that would not only devastate its agricultural productivity, but also undermine its major sources of energy: hydropower and biofuels (Butler 2009). This is a serious forecast for a country already heavily dependent on these sources of energy. At least for a time, as far as the government was concerned, a reevaluation of policy was necessary. Polls those years showed that 85 percent of Brazilians considered climate change to be a very serious problem (95 percent considered it serious) ("Brazilians Upbeat about Their Country" 2010). Before, the concern was that preservation might interfere with Brazil's rise as an economic superpower; suddenly the worry was that "growth at any cost" might come at a price that could deprive Brazil of its dream.

It is no coincidence that after these dramatic events we also began to see efforts to stabilize the agricultural frontier and subsequent declines in deforestation, down by 30 percent in 2005 after the peak of 2003 and 2004. It is also since then that the state began to establish more conservation areas on public lands (state or federal parks) and demarcate more indigenous reserves (where logging is banned)("Protecting Brazil's Forests" 2011). The Lula government made the most of the world's interest in the Amazon, entering into a Reducing Emissions from Deforestation and Forest Degradation plan, in which DCs pay Brazil not to cut down its forests. In addition, similar to the CCT scheme Bolsa Familia is *Bolsa Floresta*. Also a system of cash transfers, in Bolsa Floresta the state pays citizens to use the forest sustainably, compensating them for "environmental services" in what is called "avoided deforestation" (Butler 2009; Rohter 2007b).

---

[7] There was another enormous drought (followed by fires) in 2010, and a record flood in 2009.

As a result of these reforms, between 2004 and 2012 Brazil reduced its rates of deforestation by 83 percent, and the state promised to go even further, with an ambitious plan to cut deforestation by 80 percent more by 2020. During this period Brazil pulled off what many thought was impossible: it achieved both high economic growth rates and falling greenhouse emissions. For a while (at least) these initiatives won Brazil some international acclaim; it had transformed itself into an international leader on the environment (Tollefson 2013; Rowlatt 2012).

Of course, for Brazil, progress on reducing deforestation translates into lower greenhouse gas emissions. At the 2009 climate talks in Copenhagen, Brazil—at the time the world's seventh-largest emitter of greenhouse gases—pledged to reduce its carbon dioxide emissions by 36 percent by 2020 (Wish 2010). Brazil was celebrated for proposing reductions that were larger than those of many DCs. The policy shift produced results: by early 2014 Brazil was acclaimed as the world leader in greenhouse gas reductions (Walker 2014). As we will see, it will not hold the title for long, but Brazil has been proud of its record and boasted of being ahead of its target to reduce CO_2 emissions (L. Friedman 2010; Black 2011; Trennepohl 2010).[8] It has been able to accomplish this because, among major economies, Brazil's is one of the least carbon intensive in the world; it has bragging rights that more than 40 percent of its energy needs are fulfilled by renewable energy sources (particularly hydropower) (Sweig 2010).

This impressive turnaround provided Brazil with the credibility and the cachet it needed to become a player in global talks on the environment. Up until this time the Brazilian state had been sensitive about being treated as a rogue actor that is careless about deforestation. The success against deforestation allowed Brazil to regroup, to stand out once more as exceptional, as a model—at least for a little while—of what it is to be exceptionally green, and to go from being a greenhouse villain to an emerging green leader (Hochstetler and Keck 2007). For years Brazilian governments have taken the position that rich and poor countries have "differentiated responsibilities" when it came to climate change.[9] It still holds to this position and is staking out an independent

---

[8] Since the amendments to the Forest Code in 2012, the rate of deforestation has increased significantly in Brazil (by 28 percent between 2012 and 2013) (Purdom and Nokes 2014).

[9] The argument for differentiated responsibilities goes like this: rich countries should not expect poorer countries to sacrifice their development to deal with climate change. Rather, developed countries were the biggest contributors to the problem and therefore are the most responsible for it.

stance in other ways as well. Since 2009, Brazil has become an "environmental donor," providing aid to help LDCs reduce emissions and cope with climate change. In sum, by sharing its own experiences with developmental challenges and showing how it is possible to promote the use of renewable energy and do its part against climate change while working to eliminate hunger, Brazil has become a role model for much of the developing world (Hochstetler 2012).

Such an approach is characteristic of Brazil and rooted in contentious politics at home. The moves that Brazil made on the environment did not go nearly as far as domestic environmentalists would have liked—and many would say that the state exaggerated its accomplishments in regard to the environment, that its green conversion was always a distortion of the reality on the ground. But at least in the global arena, the state was able to rebrand itself as green. This, along with its other accomplishments regarding human security, was just part of a larger strategy to assume the role of emerging soft power superpower and leader of developing countries. In this capacity, Brazil has won acclaim for calling out the United States and other rich countries for not doing enough to control their own emissions and for not making good on their commitments to help poor countries cope with the consequences of climate change. Meanwhile, Brazil demands to be taken seriously by DCs, until recently demonstrating that it would do its part to fight climate change—but without compromising its rise as an economic superpower (L. Friedman 2010; Butler 2009). Had Brazil been able to sustain its economic growth rates, it would have had a better shot at sustaining its green policies. But such policies, which would be difficult to maintain under the most favorable circumstances, are almost impossible to prioritize now, especially as Brazil moves toward becoming a major oil producer.[10]

If, during the Lula years, environmentalists celebrated victory, they did so too soon. Politics are still polarized on this issue and the pendulum may have already swung the other way. Since 2010, as Brazil's economy shifted into a slowdown, economic interests appear to have trumped environmental concerns. Rising rates of deforestation since 2012 have undone much of the progress made in previous years. Whether by choice or necessity, Dilma, who narrowly won reelection in 2014, has made alliances with the pro-growth, agribusiness ruralistas. She has appointed a new agriculture minister nicknamed "the Chainsaw Queen" and a new science and technology minister who is an

---

[10] In an example of how the state believed that it could have it both ways, the Lula government pledged that a portion of the proceeds from oil exploitation would be used to pay for the National Policy on Climate Change (Trennepohl 2010).

outspoken climate change skeptic (Watts 2014b). By late 2014 it was clear that Brazil was in the worst of all situations: its economy was in recession and it was emitting more gasses (Porter 2014). The state is clearly placing its priorities on growth over the environment.

But in taking this position, it's not Dilma who is breaking with convention—it was Lula. As we saw in chapter 5, regardless of who is running the country, the Brazilian state has generally proven more resistant than receptive to society on the issue of the environment. Under Lula, Brazil's leadership on the use of renewable energy and its slowing of the rate of deforestation has—for as long as it lasted—rehabilitated its green credentials on the world stage and provided Brazil with a newfound credibility and the legitimacy to lead as an active participant in international discussions on climate change.[11] In these talks, Brazil argued—and continues to argue—that it is uniquely placed to lead. As both a developed and developing country, Brazil is in a unique position. It is able to represent the South and serve as a bridge between DCs and LDCs, favoring an accommodation that promotes conservation without denying developing countries the right to develop. In fact, more than anything else, Brazil seeks to become a developed country ("Global Brazil and U.S.-Brazil Relations" 2011; Watts 2014b). Although progress in climate talks has been slow, Brazil has staked out a position with its demand for accountability and respect from DCs, and for its efforts it has earned a great deal of admiration in the developing world.

Types of Power: Soft over Hard

Much of the international admiration Brazil receives is for policies shaped by contentious politics at home. Not only is Brazil becoming known as a human security superpower, it is an emerging soft power superpower. Some argue that

---

[11] Brazil preaches by setting an example when it comes to nuclear non-proliferation. For years it had pursued a nuclear program in an arms race with Argentina, but in the early 1990s Brazil renounced its program and later became a signatory to the Nuclear Non-Proliferation Treaty (NPT). For years, Brazil claimed that it was committed to nuclear security and the total elimination of nuclear weapons and (in showing that it can be in a country's interests to abide by the rules) argued that it should be recognized as a legitimate participant in discussions of international nuclear policy ("Global Brazil and U.S.-Brazil Relations" 2011; Sweig 2010). Perhaps out of frustration at the slow pace of disarmament talks and finding that prestige alone is not enough, recently Brazil has shifted to a more assertive posture on nukes. Although it is not actively pursuing a weapon, Brazil has refused to adopt the Additional Protocol to the NPT and is exploring a nuclear submarine capability (Stalcup 2012).

soft power is a mere complement to hard power, a tool that can only yield results when backed up by coercive potential and the willingness to use it (Wergin 2014). By now it should be clear that what is exceptional about Brazil isn't that it aspires to be a superpower; rather, it is that it thinks it can do this without much in the way of hard power—at least in the sense of military strength. But what it lacks in military power, it more than makes up for with economic clout and soft power. Under President Lula, Brazil celebrated its "magic moment," when it outperformed most developed countries and became recognized as an emerging economy (Sharma 2011). In 2012 Brazil replaced Britain temporarily as the world's sixth-largest economy, and in the first decade of the twenty-first century, Brazil's stock market outperformed almost all others (Gómez 2012). It won economic clout for its financial responsibility; Brazil went from being a debtor to a creditor nation. It was able to control inflation, a perennial problem for the country, and it drew record shares of foreign investment. In part due to the demand from China and rising prices for its commodities (agriculture and mining), Brazil managed to maintain enviable growth rates (though not as high as China's) throughout the Great Recession. For a while, as discussed in chapter 3, Brazil proved its dynamism, managing what many others have not: it prioritized not only growth but also development. Once the most unequal country in the world, Brazil reduced inequality by spending on social welfare programs. Inequality is still a huge problem, but the percentage of the population living in absolute poverty was cut dramatically; most people's living standards improved and record numbers of Brazilians entered the middle class.

However, these gains are tenuous. By 2015 Brazil's economic growth rates had dipped to near zero from their peak around 2010. Brazilians have come out into the streets to register their displeasure at this turn of events, but analysts were predicting the economy to hit rock bottom before making a slow recovery ("Brazil's Coming Recession" 2015). Brazil's economy is diverse; it has significant industrial and service sectors but is best known as an agricultural behemoth. It is a world leader in the production of soybeans, corn, sugar cane, cotton, orange juice, et cetera (de Onis 2008). Rounding out its portfolio, it is also an energy giant—and not only in terms of renewables such as hydropower and biofuels, thanks to the discovery of major oil fields since 2007. There have been a number of setbacks in getting the oil flowing; a massive corruption scandal involving Petrobrás, the state-owned company leading the effort, has turned off investors. But with potentially billions of barrels of oil just off the coast, the country looks to become one of the world's major oil exporters within the next several years (Forero 2014).

So, it is easy to see how, when it comes to power, Brazil is the whole package—almost. Brazil is modernizing its defenses, but it is by no means a conventional military power. And it's not seeking to compete in that category. It walked away from a nuclear capability—although some argue that as long as it doesn't have the bomb it will never be considered a first-order world power. It spends only 1.6 percent of its GDP on defense—much less than the United States or China. It has no enemies; its last war was against Paraguay in 1864 (Phillips 2012). The only external threat to Brazil involves vague fears of foreign encroachment of the Amazon. Brazil seeks to be a new kind of global presence, one that truly reflects its history and culture. But of course Brazil's choice not to compete when it comes to hard power actually augments its stronger suit: soft power.

Most significantly, then, Brazil is different from so many other up-and-comers because it isn't seeking to rise to global stature by playing the hard power game. And it is doing quite well so far: Brazil isn't just a global actor; it's much more than that, it's a global brand (Sweig 2010). What makes Brazil unique is that it isn't banking on military (coercion) or economic power (payment) to win influence. Sure, its recent and potential economic success makes all the rest possible, but what Brazil is leading with is attraction: a model that inspires others and gets them to want what Brazil wants (Nye 1990; "Views of US Continue" 2011).

Brazil thus wins with soft power, with the image that it projects abroad. How does it do at branding and marketing itself? Brazilians are known (among other things) for the appeal of their ideas, their sociability, and their optimism about the future. But (like its harder counterpart) soft power is also about relationships (Fijalkowski 2011). As you may recall, according to a 2011 Latinobarómetro poll, when citizens from Latin American countries were asked which country was the friendliest, Brazil was ranked number one. When respondents were asked what country they would most like theirs to be like, Brazil ranked ahead of every other country in the world except the United States and Spain ("Latinobarómetro Report 2011" 2011).

Much of what makes Brazil attractive is produced not by the state but by society, members of NGOs and community organizations that pushed for the progressive policies with which the state is credited. Brazil's soft power is also produced by artists, athletes, style setters: all those who contribute to Brazil's image, associated with *Carnaval*, *fútbol*, and *caipirinhas* (Nye 2013). According to Fijalkowski (2011), the resources of soft power are a country's "innate cultural and ideological attractiveness," its values and foreign policies. Countries can accumulate and accrue soft power from the production of favorable outcomes (Fijalkowski 2011, 224). It is Brazil's soft power, including its calls for a more equitable international system and its willingness to challenge traditional powers without alienating them, that is an important source of attraction. Qualities such cordiality and accommodation, a preference for conciliation over conflict, have helped to dissipate any jealousy. The resulting soft power has translated into diplomatic power, especially in regard to South-South relations. Although to a lesser extent under Dilma, Brazil has been on a globe-hopping, glad-handing mission. President Lula spent so much time traveling the world that he actually was criticized for it back home. But through the establishment of personal relationships, Brazil has won friends and influence by reaching out to help more vulnerable countries, particularly in Africa, with issues that are high on the recipient countries' agendas.

Often said to have more people of African descent of any country outside of Africa (over 350 years, nearly four million Africans were brought to Brazil as slaves), Brazil has sought to diversify its strategic partnerships and prioritizes relations with the region (Gates 2011; Stuenkel 2010). Today Brazil refers to its historic debt to Africa and is giving back to the continent. It is increasing the amount of aid it provides and sharing its know-how in fighting HIV-AIDS and poverty as well as its expertise on tropical agriculture to promote food self-sufficiency (Romero 2012e; "WFP Centre of Excellence" 2013). Sure, like other countries there, it is seeking resources and markets: trade between Brazil and the continent has grown exponentially since 2001. Although its presence in the region doesn't compare to China's, Brazil's companies are looking for opportunities in Africa, and their investments thus far are said to have paid off politically and economically. But unlike China, Brazil doesn't need to import large amounts of oil and food. Make no mistake: Brazil's actions are not purely altruistic. Like everyone else, Brazil is pursuing its interests. It's just that it is using a smart power strategy; the particular mix (the proportions of hard to soft power) is different (de Onis 2008; Stolte 2012). As it shares its social development policies, it is making—not buying—friends at the UN and other international forums.

No doubt, Brazil's image is the envy of many, but it rests on shaky ground. Occasionally events at home turn this image on its head, revealing the paradoxes that continue to exist within the country. Two rapes in Rio de Janeiro in 2013 (and the way the government handled them) exposed how far Brazil still has to go to be all that it presents itself as being.[12] According to the NGO

---

[12] During the first in what would become a wave of public rapes, some of them videotaped, the police refused to investigate. Some Brazilians accuse the state of being mostly concerned about how it looks to the world, of burying the story for fear that it would scare away tourists. It was only later, after an American student was raped and beaten, that the government took action (Romero 2013b).

Freedom House, there has been no significant improvement in Brazil's civil or political rights since 2005—and there is room for improvement ("Freedom in the World Country Ratings" 2015; Altman 2014). If Brazil is continuing its long tradition of valuing some lives more than others, the country can't help but lose soft power—and its credibility as a human security superpower (Romero 2013b). Even that title has been called into question by demonstrations over why the state would spend billions on soccer stadiums when the hospitals are falling apart.

Does all of this mean that Brazil is a fake? Or, like any state, is it simply improvising—sometimes with more success than others? Analysts disagree over whether Brazil really is exceptional, or if it's all just a carefully crafted, but not always maintainable, illusion. Perhaps the best answer is that it's a little of both. Either way, failures such as the ones described above cast doubt on the depth of the change that has actually occurred in Brazil. But if all else fails, and concern about its international reputation prods it to make improvements at home, then maybe all that glitters is gold.

CHINA

In the much-vaunted (yet increasingly debatable) "Asian Century," China's top priority is not as much becoming a great country as it is being recognized for returning to the power that it once was. In a relatively short period of time, China's international calling card has transformed from revolutionary model (or nemesis, depending on your point of view) to isolated ideologue, then, thanks to ping-pong diplomacy with the United States in the 1970s, the comeback country that was welcomed with warm arms. The honeymoon of sorts came to a crashing end after the world witnessed—on relatively novel 24/7 news channels that had arisen only years before—the use of domestic military force against civilians in 1989, images that in some ways seem to grow stronger and taken on more meaning as China's relative power increases. China's reemergence since 2008 has been met with simultaneous awe and concern, especially regionally, where not only are there scores to settle, but territories over which to scuffle.

Within the PRC, government and citizens alike celebrate China's revival. This comeback is tinged with attitude: China deserves more regard as a grand civilization that was denied it by unequal treaties and unjust behavior by Western powers. In a recent Pew survey, 56 percent of Chinese believe their country should receive more respect around the world than it currently does ("America's Global Image" 2013). In the eyes of many, Beijing needs to stand up firmly to hostile international forces—often led by the United States—that want to keep China down. Citizens feast on a steady diet of governmentally crafted historical memory, including textbooks and broadly pitched educational campaigns that highlight China's national humiliation, which have been designed to craft a national identity that, similar to such notions in every country around the world, is part truth and part myth, both aspirational and real (Z. Wang 2012).

The Chinese see themselves as exceptional and unique. The Middle Kingdom complex of bygone centuries is alive and well, and ready to be displayed. For a while, it was captured in the discourse on "Chinese characteristics," the catch phrase used for China's (seemingly) unique approach to legality, economics, and more. The longevity and continuity of the Chinese civilization, couched in the Confucian virtues of harmony and benevolence, help leaders frame Chinese intentions as peace-loving and non-threatening. Even if Imperial China was not as dominant as the Middle Kingdom persona suggests, the legacies of this era and perceived Chinese dominance definitely color regional rivalries today. Since the presidency of Xi Jinping, popular expressions of Chinese exceptionalism have taken on musings of the "Chinese dream," which revolves around the necessary steps every Chinese individual must take in order to bring about the great rejuvenation of the Chinese nation. This narrative has inspired school speaking contests and even a national talent show seeking the "Voice of the Chinese Dream" ("Xi Jinping and the Chinese Dream" 2013). Each of these perspectives has the potential to influence China's sense of its role and power in coming years.

The Regional Arena: Crowded by History and Resources

There's no doubt that China's reemergence has put its neighbors on edge. Ties throughout Asia have long been complicated by ideological tensions rooted in China's revolutionary legacies, disputed territorial claims, as well as the regional rush for access to natural resources. China's peasant-based communist revolution gave rise to significant defensiveness in the face of Beijing's attempts to export revolutionary fervor. Across Asia, neighbors greet China's reemergence with fearful caution—especially because of the military buildup that has accompanied China's "peaceful development." Most estimates are that China's military budget is beyond US$130 billion, making it the second-highest military budget in the world. World War II–era tensions are always only slightly under the surface in a region experiencing significant rebirth and increased reintegration, with Beijing attempting to serve at the helm.

The big problem in the neighborhood is the animosity between Japan and China—hostilities that are not limited only to top-level officials. Within China, 90 percent of the public holds an unfavorable opinion of Japan, falling 17 points since 2006 ("America's Global Image" 2013). One rather surprising aspect of the terse relations between the two is that, despite widespread animosity, economic interdependence has increased greatly between the two states, including over US$300 billion in bilateral trade, as well as tens of thousands of citizens from both countries living, working, and studying in the other. Nevertheless, ill will results from a combination of historical animosity and changing narratives over Japan's ability to defend itself vis-à-vis potential Chinese aggression, including potentially significant revisions of the post-World War II constitution that specifically renounces war, also known as the MacArthur Constitution for the outsize role that the United States played in both crafting and enabling it. As increasingly nationalist leaders within Japan provide voice to the growing sentiment to renounce Article 9,[13] simmering tensions between the two states risk boiling over in a variety of contexts. The historical treatment of Japan's 1937 invasion of China, including the Nanjing massacre—in which it is believed that at least three hundred thousand Chinese civilians were brutally killed—is as tense today as if the events had just happened yesterday. The status of an estimated forty thousand Chinese forced laborers sent to Japan during World War II, visits by high level leaders to the disputed Yasukuni Shrine, and territorial disputes over islands, concomitant fishing rights, and energy resources, all round out a relationship that combines historical tension with economic interdependence. Visits to the Shinto shrine at Yasukuni, which dates back to the Meiji Restoration (1868), are particularly controversial. Over one thousand convicted war criminals are included among the more than two million individuals enshrined there. Each time a high-ranking Japanese leader pays a visit to Yasukuni—which has been happening with greater frequency in recent years—tensions within the region, especially in China and Korea, boil.

---

[13] Article 9 of the National Constitution of Japan (1947) codifies the state's formal embrace of pacifism. It prohibits the Japanese state from maintaining war potential and outlaws war as a means to settle international disputes. It does not, however, exclude the development and maintenance of self-defense forces. Long thought untouchable, in recent years there has been significant momentum among top Japanese politicians to revise Article 9, although it is not clear that elite support for this change is backed up by a majority of the Japanese population.

China's military footprint looms large, especially in its backyard. The status of the PLA as the largest military force in the world (approximately 2.3 million members) is more than a simple statistic in this crowded region. Recent developments in China's naval capabilities have significant regional ramifications. In 2012, China commissioned its first aircraft carrier (actually a discard from Ukraine that had been initially launched by the Soviet Union more than a quarter century ago) and, in 2014, confirmed rumors of its construction of a second (but first indigenous) carrier. Response throughout the region was fairly swift, as the Indians launched their first domestic carrier, the *Vikrant* (likely five years away from actual duty), and the Japanese announced the refitting of a former destroyer, the *Izumo*, shortly thereafter. Even as China's projections are perceived as expressions of threatening might throughout the region—and countries work to shore up alliances with the United States as insurance—some interpret Beijing's timing and actions as vacillating between highlighting its historical status as an underdog and its new posture as a military superpower (Cooper 2014).

Complicating its actions—and lending credence to the military superpower side of the equation—Beijing is assisting with significant port construction in Myanmar, Sri Lanka, Pakistan, and Bangladesh. This contributes to concerns about China's potential "string of pearls" encircling the Indian Ocean, fueling disquiet—especially within India—that the ports may serve as future naval bases for China's expanding naval forces.[14] Naval power has long been a major harbinger of strength throughout Asia, and current maritime conflicts in both the East China and South China Seas highlight this reality. Xi Jinping has been on a "re-branding" initiative related to these developments since late 2013, framing efforts as a "maritime silk road" focused on infrastructure and economic development, as well as support for anti-piracy campaigns (Tiezzi 2014). Few doubt the strategic gains that accompany such investment, despite the spin.

Again, we return to historical challenges. The dispute over the Diaoyu Islands, known in Japan as the Senkaku dates back at least to the first Sino-Japanese War of 1895, while the troubled regions of the South China Sea have

---

[14] The "string of pearls" concept was introduced in a 2005 report, "Energy Futures in Asia" by defense contractor Booz Allen Hamilton, and highlighted the construction and support of commercial port developments with possible future military implications from the Middle East to southern China. PRC officials long denied the concept, even though, by 2013, they admitted to a larger strategy of economic advancement and protection of sea lanes with the "maritime silk road" discussions in 2013 and 2014 (Zhou 2014).

been referred to as "dangerous ground," both in terms of natural barriers as well as geopolitical spats, since the early eighteenth century (Himmelman 2013). A perfect storm of conflicting historical claims, multiple claimants, and of course natural resources collide to make these largely uninhabited islands in both the East China and South China Seas extremely significant. In the South China Sea, considered to include some of the most important shipping lanes in the world, the discovery of oil in 1968 significantly upped the ante for territorial claims that carry with them the guarantees of exclusive economic zones; since then it has been determined that the region includes one of the largest reserve beds of oil and natural gas in the world. China's approach mimics some of the imperial-era mandates of biding time while building strength, and recent years have seen a significant increase in China's assertiveness in the region, including unilateral fishing bans and Beijing's harassment of vessels. Of course, Beijing is not alone—Japanese nationalists have constructed lighthouses on uninhabitable islands in the East China Sea to assert their claims. Beijing's tactic has been a "cabbage strategy," placing layer after layer of its presence (usually in the form of seemingly innocuous fishing junks) around disputed islands, effectively building impenetrable barriers to keep the other claimants at bay.

In what is likely to be a sign of things to come, collisions between Chinese and Vietnamese boats in mid-2014, after Chinese state-sponsored drilling rigs moved into waters near the Paracel Islands in the northern South China Sea, significantly heightened tensions. Footage of Chinese vessels ramming into Vietnamese fishing ships ignited a firestorm of anti-Chinese protests across Vietnam, and Beijing visibly evacuated personnel from the country. The stakes keep getting ratcheted up, as China has constructed small buildings, including a hospital, a library, an airport, and even a small school, on one of the islands ("China to Build School" 2014). These clashes were reminiscent of the late 1980s, when the Chinese and Vietnamese navies went head to head over the Spratley Islands, north of the Paracels, and several Vietnamese ships were destroyed. As Vietnam and other countries plea for international negotiation (the Philippines has threatened to take China to a UN tribunal under the auspices of the UN Convention on the Law of the Sea), Beijing insists on behind-the-scenes bilateral negotiations, in which it believes it has the stronger hand, to attempt to resolve disputes that date back centuries.

Precipitated in large part by the 1997–1998 Asian financial crisis, a new economic regionalism, noteworthy for the near exclusion of the United States, is developing. Especially financially, countries within the region are increasingly looking inward, and Beijing has become an enthusiastic promoter of Asia as an economic unit. For example, since 2010, China has been the largest trading partner of the Association of Southeast Asian Nations, ASEAN. China joins Japan and South Korea in the forum known as ASEAN +3, to help coordinate cooperation and dialogue regionally. China sits at the center of the supply and production chains, especially in Southeast Asia, with some framing the Chinese economy as the "decisive integrative force" (Feigenbaum 2011, 29) in the region. Nevertheless, tensions highlighted above, especially maritime disputes, continue to risk derailing larger frameworks, and the asymmetrical nature of China's increasing dominance is a consistent concern. Despite increased economic integration, it is clear that strategic trust is absent from the region, and Beijing's actions hardly assuage these concerns.

China has adopted a strong regional diplomatic role as well—from the leading voice in the Shanghai Cooperation Organization (SCO) as a security alliance to challenge the North Atlantic Treaty Organization (NATO) and unite regional allies concerned about the growing threat of Islamic terrorism, as well as its role with North Korea. The SCO (which originated as the "Shanghai 5" in 1996) formed to combat the "3 evils of terrorism, separatism and extremism" (Roney 2013), and is now adopting economic, energy, and cultural emphases, sponsoring joint military exercises and even entertaining the possibility of a free trade area. Some have framed the organization as "China's NATO," which has expanded its reach beyond immediate Central Asia (the original five members all bordered the PRC), through the admission of Pakistan, India, and Iran as observer states in 2005. To date, though, multilateral cooperation remains elusive, especially because of competition and lack of trust among member states; indeed it seems to be more about Beijing showing off its charm than achieving real results. Beijing's outsize presence is increasingly raising concerns of dependence, made worse by the lack of transparency. China is also not doing much to promote its soft power credo as it touts an organization whose members are known for their consistent human rights abuses, with Kyrgyzstan garnering the best Freedom House ranking among members.

Without a doubt, because it poses as an alternative to the hegemonic tendencies of the United States, one of China's most significant roles has been and will likely continue to be its leadership (since 2002) of the six-party talks on North Korea. Especially since the hugely unpopular Iraq War, China has framed itself as a good rebound for those rejected (or significantly influenced) by the West. It's come a long way since opening the doors to the outside world in the 1970s, vacillating from the world's curiosity during the televised ping-pong diplomacy of 1971, to one of the most reviled governments after 1989, to economic miracle worker in the 1990s, and then the Olympic shock and awe of 2008. Similar to Brazil, China has the potential to fill an important diplomatic niche because it straddles the weak/strong and developing/developed categories. While no one turns to the Chinese as natural diplomats—they are often viewed as cunning strategists—the fact that Beijing is the only country to at least have a chance at having the ear of the North Korean leadership has won it some diplomatic accolades, even if it appears less and less certain that even Beijing is able to influence the Hermit Kingdom. Nevertheless, on most issues before the United Nations, there appears to be a significant disconnect between China's perceived weight and its strategy. The PRC talked about becoming a "responsible stakeholder" in the early 2000s, but it hasn't stepped up to the plate so far. In many ways, given its reluctance to lead on so many issues, Beijing's strategy appears "more suited to a poor country than a great power" (Fullilove 2010).

Even as the convener of tense negotiations, China has been slow to the table and has taken great risks allying with its notoriously unreliable partner in Pyongyang. China has long attempted to serve as the leading spokesperson for negotiation and regional cooperation, but it seems even its most earnest diplomats are starting to wear thin, especially with the unpredictable—even by North Korean standards—administration of Kim Jong-un. Yet especially after Kim ordered the very public ouster and political execution of his uncle, Beijing has indicated increasing concern and even some reluctance toward dealing with the antics of the leadership in Pyongyang. Beijing, long vexed by the potential influx of North Korean refugees into its own northeast should there be a significantly destabilizing event in the North, seems to be losing patience with the North's bellicose rhetoric and attempts to use nuclear tests to force diplomats to the table. If Beijing is losing sway with its unpredictable pariah partner, it bodes poorly not only for Beijing's diplomatic cache, but more importantly, for a long-term solution to the division of the Korean peninsula.

Regionally, China faces complications and uncertainties. Beijing leaders often point out that the United States was "gifted" with the boundaries of the Atlantic and Pacific Oceans, presenting a lack of overbearing border tension that China has never enjoyed. China is tied with Russia for having the largest number of border states, with fourteen. In some ways it is tough to clearly label Beijing's strongest regional ally: Russia? Pakistan? Burma? In this climate,

Beijing's desire is to promote stable surroundings that will serve as a springboard toward its interests, regionally and beyond. In recent years, we note an uptick in multilateral organizations in the region—Beijing has helped form two major bodies for negotiating, the SCO and the six-party talks on North Korea, exercising considerable say in how these negotiations will proceed. By emphasizing its responsible regional role and identity as the central power within Asia, China is turning to regional institutions, especially the SCO, ASEAN, and its affiliated bodies, to begin to squeeze US influence out of its backyard. As Beijing's interests become more strategically and assertively defined, especially as energy concerns continue to plague development plans, the omnipresent tensions on its borders are likely to consume more and more of its diplomats' energies.

The Transnational Arena: Reluctant Reemergence

In terms of global reach, it has become a cliché to highlight China's rise. At times, Beijing welcomes this image and the attention that accompanies it, while at other times it attempts to deemphasize the perception of its power both to soften concerns about the "China threat" as well as to mitigate regional tensions. Consistently, though, Beijing emphasizes the dangers of hegemonic dominance by a single power, and attempts to remind everyone that it eschews hegemonic status for itself. Rather, Chinese leaders emphasize, even since the mid-1980s when China's aspirations were much more dream than reality, the need for a multipolar world in which no single power dominates. Gradually, successive leaders have adopted the attitude that China's increased engagement with global multilateral institutions will help solidify its image as a great power while lessening the sense of threat by providing reassurances that Beijing can be a responsible leader in global affairs. No longer behaving as the outsider on the playground, Beijing's diplomatic leaders have been working to engage the international system to help the PRC achieve its economic goals and to contribute to a multipolar world, especially since the turn of the century. Increasingly, we observe more of a proactive, rather than defensive, shift, as leaders work to increase political leverage and move beyond economic interests. As we will discuss, however, there remain clear areas that Beijing defines as out of bounds.

Transnationally, Beijing's priorities align around multiple goals: to continue to provide favorable economic treatment to the developing world, of which it often sees itself as both member and promoter; to support moral (and regime-type) relativism and non-interference; and to advance the United Nations as the ultimate guarantor of peace and security. So, in many ways, China's transnational emphasis has been to bring more players, itself foremost among them, to the international bargaining table—the democratization of international relations, if you will. Part of this has been in response to perceived weaknesses within the leading states, especially the United States, and the recognition that global problems need more globally inclusive answers. With its newfound transnational prominence, Beijing occupies a more comfortable role in the Group of 20 (G20), which counts developing countries and non-democracies among its members, and it is a far cry from being invited to sit on the sidelines at the G8 meetings of the industrialized countries. As a newcomer at these global economic forums and a rather reluctant leader—despite the bravado about establishing a post-dollar economic order in the wake of the 2008 financial crisis—China's role to date has been ordinary rather than outstanding. Photo opportunities with world financial leaders have been a gain; pressure on Beijing to rein in shadow banking and take greater economic risks that may endanger social stability have been perceived as a net loss. Still, the difficulties encountered by the more inclusive G20, including omnipresent debate about its utility, indicate both the lack of consensus between emerging and developed powers as well as the difficulties including more voices at the table, a seat that Beijing will insist it deserves. The G20, viewed as impotent by many, at least permits China to dampen the unwelcome talk about the emergence of a G2 (Washington, DC, and Beijing), highlighting China's preference for multiple seats of importance.

China's role as a member (and convener) of the BRIC (and BRICS) states is central to its vision of developing multilateral networks in a global fashion. This approach was formally enshrined as one of the four pillars of Chinese multilateral diplomacy, as highlighted since the 18th CCP Congress in November 2012, when Xi Jinping and Li Keqiang rose to the helm of CCP leadership ("Full Text of Hu Jintao's Report" 2012). Since that time, Xi has promoted a new emphasis on China's ties with BRICS states (especially Russia and South Africa) as a way of promoting a new vision of collective power against the more traditional developed countries. In some ways, China's BRICS advocacy is a recognition by Beijing that it can't challenge the system alone (Sun 2013). Nonetheless, it also provides a forum—global rather than regional in reach—in which Beijing can brandish both its emerging market and developing country credentials, especially by advancing the initiative to create a development bank that will provide assistance for infrastructure projects throughout Africa.

Rhetorically, the United Nations occupies an important position within Beijing's vision of global politics, perceiving it as the grand equalizer that enshrines one of Beijing's most important foreign policy goals—state sovereignty—within its founding documents. But even though it is recognized as one of the founding states of the United Nations,[15] holds a P-5 veto, and has long championed the UN as an important tool for counterhegemonic approaches, China is known as a "supporter but not a leader in the United Nations" (Womack 2010, 17). Once again we observe insistence for inclusion yet reticence toward responsibility. Pragmatism is part of the story; concern for losing control over what Beijing determines to be its own domestic matters is the other significant variable. Beijing views the UN as the best platform for multilateral response to challenges, especially because UN action is nearly always conservative in scope, particularly on the use of force. In their eyes, the UN is a tool for constraining progressive unilateralism—especially by the United States. Beijing thus attempts to serve as an outspoken supporter of safeguarding the authority of the UN, especially when this translates into maintaining the primacy of state sovereignty.

The seemingly constant discussions on UN reform have provided both opportunity and challenge to Beijing: China mildly supports UNSC expansion in general membership—especially if this includes greater representation by developing states. It is conversely harshly critical of adding any new permanent—especially veto-holding—members, a position that Brazil and other emerging powers decry. China and the United States have rejected Brazil's bid for a permanent seat in the UNSC. China's chief justification for rejection was that the proposal included Japan and India; Brazil felt snubbed that the United States supported India for the seat but not Brazil.

Related to Beijing's emphasis on moral relativism and each state having control over its own affairs is China's oft-voiced opposition to the universalizing ideal of liberalism. A litany of leaders, up to and including Xi Jinping, consistently state that China does not interfere in the affairs of others—every country should be able to pattern its politics and society after its own unique historical, cultural, political, and economic circumstances. To interfere would be to impose, something that, at least overtly, Beijing works to avoid. As part

[15] As one of the founding members of the United Nations in 1945, "China" was represented by the Nationalist Government of Chiang Kaishek, against whom the CCP fought a fierce civil war. After Taiwan's expulsion from the United Nations in October of 1971, the so-called "China seat" in the United Nations became occupied by the government of Mao Zedong on the mainland, or the People's Republic of China. Thus, even though China is widely recognized as a founding state of the United Nations, two significantly different governments, controlling different geographic entities, represented the face of China during these two periods.

of China's "no strings attached" approach to international relations, it shuns becoming involved in the domestic political crises of states. An inventory of recent high-profile non-interference actions by Beijing include Syria (two UNSC vetoes against a military response), as well as similar vetoes that ended up killing sanctions against Burma and Zimbabwe. In a statement of non-judgmental assistance, Beijing also provided financial and material support for Sudan, even during the fiercest discussions about the government's role perpetuating crimes against citizens in Darfur. As we discuss in the next section of the chapter, some of these associations do significant harm to China's soft power strategy of trying to attract others to its ideals, especially when China's motives become viewed as primarily self-serving rather than non-interfering.

Beijing is even more defensive about the potential for external involvement in its own issues, especially in matters that can be connected to sovereignty and territorial integrity. This includes China's western provinces with minority populations, most notably Tibet and Xinjiang, as well as the status of Taiwan—viewed by CCP officials as the so-called "renegade province" since the Nationalist Party established its government in exile on the island province during the Chinese Civil War in the 1940s. In the eyes of Beijing's leaders, these issues, often paraded as "core interests" of the PRC, are domestic matters for the Chinese government only, falling clearly, solidly, and perpetually beyond the purview of international organizations. Chinese leaders are prickly about any consideration of the rights of groups (especially the Tibetans and Uighurs, as well as other ethnic minority populations) separate from those of all Chinese citizens, and especially sensitive to suggestions that individuals have the right to lobby international organizations against their own governments. In a sleight of hand, Beijing supports international agreements, including the UN Declaration on the Rights of Indigenous Peoples, and then turns around and claims that it bears no responsibility under these agreements, since there are "no indigenous people" within the borders of the PRC ("Statement by Mr. Liang Heng" 2013). Because Tibetans have been so successful getting their cause out worldwide—it helps to have the attention of so many Hollywood supporters—Beijing has been particularly vitriolic in its response to any attention the Dalai Lama receives. As Beijing would have him characterized, he is viewed as the ultimate "splittist" for attempting to divide the Chinese motherland. Beijing spares few options in responding to perceived support for Tibetan independence. In one particularly unusual encounter, the Chinese and French governments issued a public joint statement reiterating France's lack of support for Tibetan independence in any form and its regard of Tibet as an inseparable part of China, as well as confirmation of the importance of the principle of non-interference in each other's affairs. This rare statement followed Beijing's cancelation of a bilateral meeting between Presidents Nicholas Sarkozy and Hu Jintao over an ill-timed—and much-publicized—formal meeting between Sarkozy and the Dalai Lama (LaFraniere and Cowell 2009).

Diplomatic pressure related to Taiwan is also strenuously resisted, going well beyond the diplomatic non-starter of discussion related to Taiwan's membership in the United Nations. China has special diplomatic censure set aside especially for states, especially Nicaragua, that support Taiwan's attempts to join the UN, either through the back door, specialized agencies, or formally, which would require the support of the UNSC, in which Beijing wields a veto. As we see in other "sensitive" issues for Beijing, its approach is to isolate advocates of views that challenge its own rendering of the situation.

As tensions heat up in the disputed waters of the East China and South China Seas, discussed above, Beijing backpedals on its commitment to multilateral inclusion and insists on its historically defined sense of territory. Provocatively, it even included East China Sea disputes within its "core interests" in 2013, what the editorial board of the *New York Times* referred to as "the issues considered important enough to go to war over" ("China's Evolving 'Core Interests'" 2013). For maritime disputes, Beijing clearly favors bilateral negotiations—in which it enjoys a solid upper hand, especially militarily. Chinese leaders have staunchly resisted efforts by transnational institutions, including The Hague as well as the International Tribunal for the Law of the Sea in Hamburg, to have jurisdiction over territorial claims, including the case lodged by the Philippines over competing claims in the South China Sea. Beijing is likely to simply ignore the rulings by both bodies. It's a selective application, however, as China accused Vietnam of violating its territorial integrity in the South China Sea by preparing a formal position paper, sending it to UN secretary-general Ban Ki-Moon and requesting that he circulate it to all 193 member states in the General Assembly—at the same time that it rejects UN arbitration over the matter ("China Takes Dispute with Vietnam to UN" 2014). China surely isn't the first state to attempt to have it both ways, but for a state that trumpets sovereignty and non-interference as loudly as Beijing does, the request seemed particularly bold.

Rather than embracing a bipolar world in which China would balance the United States, it aspires for a multipolar world in which power is not concentrated. This may seem counterintuitive until we remember that, for Beijing, domestic stability is much more important than foreign policy. Occupying one of two seats of power would place unwelcome responsibility in Beijing's hands—and, until Beijing gets more rights, including stronger voting rights in bodies such as the IMF and World Bank, it believes the responsibilities should be less as well (Sun 2013). As such, Chinese leaders have focused their aspirations not only on bringing more players to the table, but also on brandishing their credentials as a responsible world power, albeit "powerful" in novel ways. For most of China's transnational policy priorities, it seems that pragmatism trumps principle.

Case in Point: Climate Change

We have charted more than a fair amount of regime receptivity to environmental concerns raised by citizens, including organized citizen movements. When environmental concerns are raised outside of China's borders, the response from Beijing is quite a different story. Sensitive to outside involvement in domestic matters, China's leaders have a more defensive posture toward monitoring, awareness, and influence by actors, including domestic civil society. The buzzword for environmental responsibility has become "stakeholder," and to the extent that its interpretation includes responsibility and oversight by others, Beijing has been reluctant to embrace this title. Still, given its dubious distinction as the world's leading emitter of greenhouse gases, in addition to its seemingly insatiable appetite for natural resources to fuel its red-hot economy, some analysts propose the acronym of the G2 (China and the United States), noting that no meaningful climate deal will be implemented without the support of these two giants (Rothkopf 2009).

Beijing's stance was not always one of resistance. China was a high-profile signatory to Agenda 21, promulgated at the UN Earth Summit Rio (1992), drafting its own "China Agenda 21" and enthusiastically embracing the characterization as a developing country during the drafting of the Kyoto Protocols in 1997. However, as China joined the WTO (2001), surpassed the United States as the largest emitter of carbon dioxide emissions (2007), and overtook Japan as the world's second-largest economy (2010), this label fit less and less comfortably, at least in the eyes of some, most notably the United States. In fact, a large part of the United States' persistent rejection of the Kyoto Protocols had been the exclusion of China, arguing that such an exemption afforded Beijing a significant competitive advantage. In the post-Kyoto world, Chinese leaders have tried to balance their desired positioning as being "poor enough" to receive exemptions from binding climate change targets, while at the same time "rich enough" to be viewed as a leader in global talks. Since the Bali Conference in 2007, when the United States and China rejected binding emissions caps, Chinese leaders have worked to highlight the per capita emission rate (ranked ninety-second in the world), rather than gross emission rates (ranked first in the world) (Liang 2010). Beijing has long opposed binding commitments to emission reductions, despite pressure from the United States and others for the "large developing countries" (including China, India, and Brazil) to assume commitments immediately. Such efforts are often viewed in conspiratorial terms, as a way that the developed world—especially the United States—is trying to limit China's emergence.

As the public rifts during the 2009 Copenhagen negotiations revealed, China and the United States—and, increasingly, Europe—have fundamental disagreements surrounding the foundation for any post-Kyoto global pact related to climate change. The dilemma is in how to acknowledge the past, in which the bulk of emissions came from the West, while taking responsibility for the current situation, during which China is the world's largest emitter, a trend that is likely to continue for some time.

Chinese leaders use evidence from the Green Great Wall to respond to accusations of their irresponsible behavior on climate change. In this sense, reforestation efforts have become the strategic priority for Beijing in addressing climate change. However, the World Bank has urged a focus on quality instead of quantity, highlighting the criticisms—many expressed by Chinese ecologists as well—that the sheer volume of trees planted may be less important than their sustainability over time. Beijing is not afraid to toss its weight, or at least its words, around, highlighting both at home and abroad its leadership in key energy sectors (notably wind) and orchestrating fancy demonstrations of its commitment to all things green. Efforts have been so consuming that some analysts liken Beijing's environmental programs to prior mass campaigns, referring to Beijing's newfound fondness of all things environmental as the country's "Green Leap Forward" (Larson 2007, 2011a). Such efforts have the potential for deep impacts. Consider, for example, that half of the world's new buildings each year are erected in China (Larson 2011a), that China uses 60 percent of the world's scaffolding, and that the number of buildings in the country is expected to almost double by 2020 ("Tackling Building Energy Waste" 2007). Still, China's bark is oftentimes much worse than the bite.

The world witnessed Beijing's newfound assertiveness at Copenhagen, when Chinese state negotiators made it clear that they were not going to accept severe limits on their emissions—the British environment minister at the time even accused the PRC of hijacking the summit (Milliband 2009). However, when push comes to shove, we see the degree to which China wants to be recognized as a responsible member of the international community. To the degree that political leaders see they can gain more than they lose, we can expect compliance and an embrace of global norms. Indeed, some institutions have already been put in place to lure China's engaged participation, including the carbon trading exchange in Beijing, established by the United Nations in early 2007. As the first exchange established in the developing world, the World Bank estimates China has much to gain from this multibillion-dollar market (Chan, Lee, and Chan 2008).

The consistent theme in China's push for leadership in international negotiations on global climate change is its support of the "common but differentiated responsibility" principle adapted at recent meetings. In this sense, China is able to capitalize on its long-standing goal to frame an alternative to developed-world hegemony on steps forward. For example, prior to the opening of the Cancun meetings in November 2010, Chinese leaders eagerly hosted the Tianjin Climate Change Conference to help set the stage for the implementation talks in Cancun months later. It also hosted the preparatory meetings of the G77, African Group, and small-island developing states, asserting its willingness to lead these voices into the international talks. The G77 connection provides China "international legitimacy to receive all the special treatment granted to the developing countries in climate change" negotiations (Liang 2010, 78). Beijing is increasingly trying to play a "bridge" role between rich and poor countries, attempting to ameliorate the concerns of developed countries that the developing states would not face binding targets, while assuaging the concerns of the LDCs that they were being asked to do more than their fair share (Harvey 2011).

In China's twelfth Five Year Plan, announced in March 2011, leaders pledged to abide by China's international commitments to decrease carbon intensity 40 to 45 percent by 2020, with specific targets announced for provinces, and wealthier municipalities and provinces in the eastern part of the country facing more ambitious goals than the other regions ("China's Politics and Actions" 2011). Beijing also announced an increase in resource taxes on oil, gas, and coal ("China's Politics and Actions" 2011). Liang (2010, 70) contends that China's changing position on global climate change negotiations are "largely domestic-driven," recognizing the adverse impacts of the last three decades of double-digit economic growth. So, as much as China appealed to the world during its big Olympic moment in 2008, it seems once again the primary audience it is most concerned about is its own (smoggy) backyard. The executive secretary of the UN Framework Convention on Climate Change acknowledged as much when she stated, in praise of Beijing's leading role in making policy changes to mitigate global climate change, "They're not doing this because they want to save the planet. They're doing it because it's in their national interest" (Yoon 2014).

Types of Power: Soft with Hard

China is being rolled out as a superpower—perhaps before it is warranted, and definitely in advance of its own leaders' acceptance of the mantle. By many estimates, despite a recent slowdown in China's growth, China is likely to become a leading economic superpower by 2030—many say much sooner. The China Development Bank, one of China's state-owned banks, is already the world's largest lender, and Beijing has been actively seeking an influential role in global financial institutions for years, including discussions about possibly ousting the dollar as the global currency and even taking the lead on debt-reduction efforts in order to assist achievement of the Millennium Development Goals by the world's LDCs (Toh 2013). Beijing has gained quite a bit of luster for its own record of domestic poverty reduction, lifting over three hundred million people out of poverty since the late 1970s. Double-digit growth rates and significant state investment have led to China's catapulting economic record. But power means so much more. While Beijing aspires to supplant the "hard" measures of its strength, vitality, and influence with "softer" measures to include attractiveness and allure, the intangibles of China's powerful reemergence seem to rest on much shakier ground.

How "attracted" to China and the Chinese way of doing things are other countries? The push has been on for years: China has invested significant financial resources across Africa for decades and was an investor in African human capital—offering thousands of scholarships each year to study in the PRC. Since the 1950s, there have been an estimated twelve thousand African students studying in China with support of the Chinese government in 2012 (Allison 2013). China is now the African continent's largest trading partner (Toh 2013). However, the infusion of hard cash has produced mixed results: stadiums built by the Chinese have been collapsing, promises of job creation have not been fulfilled, complaints against mainland companies are on the rise, domestic markets are being flooded with knock-offs, and some Africans view the Chinese as new colonizers. In rich irony, Beijing has become frustrated by the turnover of African leaders—due to democratic elections—that make its traditional patronage structure less efficient (Toh 2013).

Another aspect of soft power and attractiveness can be found in cultural contributions. People around the world are much more in tune with Chinese culture and the contributions of Chinese artists, both historical and contemporary variants, than they were even twenty years ago. The 2008 Olympics delivered a massive soft power initiative around the world, which was successful in many ways. Although, there was a bit of embarrassment all around when it was revealed that the jaw-dropping coordination of synchronized fireworks all across Beijing, set to appear as "footprints" making their way across the former Imperial capital, were digitally created for the live TV broadcast in order to master the effect. Moreover, accusations that China was "faking their way to a perfect Olympics" did not win them much praise (Kent 2008). Hence, while people around the world see China becoming the world's leading power, most in their lifetimes, they are not equating this with more positive ratings for the PRC. Indeed, more people are likely to consider the United States a partner to their country than to see China in that light ("America's Global Image" 2013).

For all of the efforts that Beijing has put into its soft power initiatives, its work is derailed by many of its actions at home, including widely publicized crackdowns on dissidents, journalists, and petitioners who challenge policies. Their soft power credentials take a hit each time Beijing denies visas for journalists in perceived retribution for covering human rights abuses or for individuals writing for media outlets that dare to publish evidence of the wealth amassed by high-level leaders, as the *New York Times* did in 2012 (or *Bloomberg News*, which withheld publication of an investigative report on the hidden financial ties of senior Chinese leaders) (Jacobs 2013b). And, in stark contrast with China's attempts to promote an image of multilateral engagement and its challenge of hegemonic politics, it is perceived as a unilateral actor pursuing its own interests—in twenty-six of thirty-eight states, more than half of those surveyed say China considers their interests not too much or not at all ("America's Global Image" 2013). This is thanks in large part to Beijing's successful soft power efforts to market Chinese language and culture abroad through its government-financed Confucius Institutes. China's cultural attractiveness sells—more students around the world are studying the Chinese language; foreign exchange programs for students and educators at all levels swamp China every spring and summer; and Chinese artists are seriously breaking into the global scene, with major sales at Sotheby's, Christie's, and other major art houses (Errera 2014).

China's ideological vision, on the other hand, is a much tougher sell. Not surprisingly, few around the world believe the Chinese government respects the personal freedoms of its people ("America's Global Image" 2013). Beijing's soft power weaknesses risk being further exposed at home as well, as it seems the children of more and more CCP leaders find their way to prestigious colleges and universities around the world, living lives of luxury that contradict the austere image that CCP cadres attempt to project at home.

China continues to shuffle the sides of its dual identity as a developing country and great power, creating a source of strain internally and externally. It can't continue much longer to seek developing world exemptions at the same time it demands established power credentials at the table. For all of the emphasis its leaders want to place on soft power initiatives, at the end of the day, Beijing sits where it does because of the traditional, hard power conceptions of what makes states great: military might, economic reach, and the ability to cow others, including its own citizens, into submission. As the so-called "Fifth Generation" of CCP leaders continue to manage China's internal contradictions and project the twenty-first-century face of China on the world screen, it remains quite obvious that domestic matters—both positively and negatively—will continue to influence the direction Beijing charts, regionally and globally. It has also been sobering to many Beijing elite that China's reemergence has arrived at a time of significant international upheaval, replete with foreign policy challenges—many not of their own making. Somewhat ironically, China engages the world more now than at any other time in its modern history, but has fewer friends; the PRC has become richer, but less respected (Sun 2013).[16] Chinese leaders are accustomed to dealing with contradictions, but some of the recent foreign policy challenges—globally and regionally—may place more on their plate than they had expected.

ANALYSIS

When it comes to their foreign policies and international relations, are democratic Brazil and authoritarian China more alike that we would expect? Or should Brazil even be considered in the same category as China? Is it punching

---

[16] Depending on whom you ask, it is also more feared than respected. China's neighbors express trepidation at the country's growing military might—especially in light of maritime disputes with Japan, South Korea, Vietnam, and the Philippines, among others. The Japanese give China the worst ratings—only 5 percent surveyed express positive views toward the PRC ("America's Global Image" 2013).

above its weight, not a contender for superpower status—and for these reasons is in no way comparable to China? Predictions that China will be the world's next superpower are hardly new. China's claim to the title rests on economic and military power. Never a military power, Brazil appeared well on its way to becoming an economic power, at least until recently. It may still rise to prominence, but is likely to gain stature only through a more unconventional route. What the two countries have in common is that each is working to set itself apart from the rest and both are actively seeking to acquire soft power. So, how are Brazil and China making themselves global brands and what are their sources of attraction? According to Fijalkowski (2011), it could be the appeal of their ideas, their innate or naturally attractive cultural and ideological values, norms, or rules. Alternatively, it could be their willingness to stake out positions unpopular with the West.

Or it could be the relationships Brazil and China have constructed with a range of actors, including the West. As one of the world's oldest civilizations, China peddles its culture to increase its attractiveness to others. But on its political values (its ability to live up to them at home and abroad) and its foreign policies (and their association with moral authority), it's a harder sell—although some states certainly appreciate China's refusal to condemn them for their human rights records. Brazil, coming down from a recent economic boom that enabled it to pay for the programs that made it a human security superpower, is banking on its strong suit: soft power. On two of Fijalkowski's three variables (culture and foreign policy) Brazil gets high marks. It stands out as an example of humane authority, especially compared to the United States and China. But it is Brazil's ability to live up to its political values at home that remains an open question, especially when one considers persistent problems such as structural inequality.

Whether democratic or not, what happens at home sets the parameters for what any state can do on the world stage. Perhaps the biggest difference between the two countries is that both China's and Brazil's foreign policies are based in domestic politics, albeit in very different ways. Brazil is a committed democracy and much of Brazil's power is drawn from its successes at home, which are largely due to the state's receptivity to society. Progress on poverty, hunger, and HIV-AIDS has reflected well on Brazil internationally. Moreover, Brazil leads with charm and by example whereas China leads with attitude. From China's perspective, it's about time the world paid attention to the Middle Kingdom again. Its behavior over the years suggests that when push comes to shove, authoritarian China doesn't care to give much thought to its image abroad—its crackdown against protesters, televised around the world in the spring of 1989, provides a case study in a big country's disregard of global sentiment.

Another difference between the two countries is that while Brazil is extroverted and focused on its image worldwide, China is traditionally much more insular; even since Mao's death and its opening to the world, it is much more introverted and its focus is domestic. Domestic politics definitely trump international diplomacy in China. Beijing's continued self-identification as a developing country, and its domestic preoccupation with internal challenge—notably its development and social stability—take precedence over many of the other leadership opportunities before it. However, while China's lack of concern for international image may have been true for much of the 1990s and early 2000s, there are growing indicators that China is caring more about its image abroad. It appears that, to a limited extent, anyway, China now realizes what Brazil knew long ago: a successful performance on the global stage plays well with the folks back home and doesn't hurt the bottom line either.

This brings us to another important difference between the two: how they are positioned in the international system. China, widely recognized as the "inevitable superpower," doesn't really relish the job (Subramanian 2011). It is perhaps better characterized as a "fragile superpower" whose projection of strength and power is contingent upon the maintenance of domestic stability (Shirk 2007). It wants all the status and benefits of established power without the costs. It is thus a much more reluctant global leader than Brazil, which is eager to rise to the occasion—but perhaps not ready for prime time. The character Brazil prefers to play on the world stage is the non-threatening charmer willing to stand up to the big guys. It isn't going to rise to global prominence in a classic fashion; rather, its vehicle has been counterhegemonic: playing to the South by offering an appealing alternative. But already there are indications that Brazil too is becoming more of a developed than a developing country.

Although they appear to be playing very different games, Brazil and China are like minded on foreign affairs in a number of unexpected ways. Both have histories of independent foreign policies. Both are willing to stand up to traditional powers in that both talk a good counterhegemonic and revisionist game. But they don't want to usurp the status quo so much as they want it to work better for them. With dual identities as developing and developed countries, both share a common goal: broad reform of an international system that permits fast-growing economies to have more power in the decision-making processes of international organizations. These rising powers are determined to get a fairer shake in the international system and to put their mark on it. As rapidly emerging—counterhegemonic though not revolutionary powers—neither Brazil nor China seeks to subvert or replace the existing order; rather, they are providing alternatives within it. Neither one wants to overturn the existing system; both just want a better deal from the current one. For example, Brazil has received a lot of attention for its calls to democratize the international system ("Brazilian Discontent Ahead" 2014). But if the United Nations and other international institutions were to practice what they preach and become democratic, and Brazil becomes a member of the club, will it too become a status quo power? Is it really seeking to democratize international institutions or does it just want to expand the oligarchy so that it can join it (Stuenkel 2010)? Perhaps, as its critics note, the changes Brazil seeks in the global system are actually as limited as the ones it—and China—seeks at home: nice on the surface but amounting to just enough of an alteration to avoid real change.

One change that both Brazil and China would prefer is a multipolar world where there are multiple autonomous power centers and no single country can force its preferences on the rest. This may seem surprising, at least in China's case, but the lack of enthusiasm for a bipolar world is closely connected to Beijing's shunning of the responsibility that comes with such global leadership. At least in terms of "old politics," China is not a contender to become the main rival to the United States. Regionally, Beijing wants to balance the United States, but globally, whether it is recognition of its lack of capacity or not, the desire to assume the burden of hegemony just isn't there.

The two are alike in their independence and distance from the United States. When Brazil stood up to the United States and forfeited tens of millions of dollars in foreign assistance rather than bow to US demands, Brazil did what a lot of other countries would have loved to do: it declared such interference a violation of sovereignty and protested that the United States should not impose its very different understanding of human rights on other countries (Vianna, Carrara, and Lacerda 2008).

In their foreign policies, both are outspoken advocates of self-determination. Both are independent in their diplomacy, unwilling to toe the West's line on a wide range of issues, and more than willing to call it out for not playing by its own rules. A good example of such an issue is climate change. Until recently, both countries shut down criticism of their environmental policies and both still relish the opportunity to remind DCs of their differentiated responsibilities. But there seems to be a perceptible shift on climate change by both countries in recent years. They are each taking leadership roles; Brazil has called out

DCs for their failure to do much themselves about the problem, let alone keep their promises to LDCs about helping them cope with its effects. China has been slower to embrace global leadership on this issue, fearing an outpouring of domestic activism on environmental issues. But with its development of alternative energy technologies, Beijing has recognized that there is an opportunity to gain face internationally and support domestic economic growth at the same time.

Both countries are alike in that they are trusted less by their neighbors than the rest of the world. In much of its neighborhood China's rebirth is feared, predicated on historical animosity, military size, and distrust of its true ambitions. Brazil is hardly a feared military. But, like China, its economic power and potential can be off-putting. Both countries are greeted with a variety of emotions throughout their regions, ranging from deep ambivalence to alarm and doubt about their intentions and honesty. China faces some large regional rivals (Japan and India—and, depending on how you cut it, the United States), whereas Brazil doesn't have regional rivals anymore. For years it was Argentina, but today the closest thing that Brazil has to a rival is the United States—and, from the American perspective, Brazil is really more an offset than a rival (O'Neill 2010).

Both states have also often exhibited a counterhegemonic approach to states on the margins (e.g., North Korea, Sudan, Iran). On this matter Brazil holds true to its traditional policy of non-interference and respect for sovereignty. It argues for maintaining a dialogue and argues that excluding and isolating those countries does no one any good. China shares this position. China remains sensitive to concerns of national sovereignty, highlighting non-intervention as the policy choice, especially in the post-9/11 world, when contingent sovereignty seemed to become much more prominent. Brazil shares these concerns and has been outspoken in its criticism of massive US surveillance programs as a violation of not only privacy, but sovereignty. In general, the two oppose sanctions, the threat of military force, and other forms of intervention as heavy handed and ineffective. They agree that multilateral responses are superior to less inclusive exercises of power. And while it is possible to couch many of Beijing's objectives as self-serving, its policy of non-intervention has won it some respect.

For its part, Brazil opposes the coercive diplomacy often advocated by traditional powers. Rather, Brasilia credits its culture with a more imaginative approach that promotes the peaceful resolution of disputes and a flexible, soft diplomacy. In its assertion that there is another way, Brazil presents an alternative that much of the world finds appealing. But China's passivity evaporates and Brazil's soft diplomacy hardens over what each considers their core interests. They are both extremely protective of the principles of non-intervention and sovereignty when it comes closer to home and are touchy about international interference in what they consider their core interests (Taiwan, Tibet, and the Amazon). "Territorial integrity" is a red line issue for both of them. The charm offensive is definitely off when it comes to these topics, but at least they play by the Golden Rule: they refuse to meddle in the domestic affairs of other countries and they expect to be treated in the same way.

But because they refuse to meddle in the affairs of others doesn't mean that they don't try to project power and exert influence. In what is known as the Brasilia Consensus, which emphasizes development alongside growth, and the Beijing Consensus, combining political authoritarianism with state-supported growth, the two countries challenge the orthodoxy of the Washington Consensus, which emphasizes growth above all else—yet they challenge in very different ways. Beijing shows how the state, while shutting out society politically, can maintain significant latitude to manage the economy, resulting in record-breaking and sustained economic growth. Brasilia, on the other hand, shows that benefits can be reaped from a greater social inclusion and synergy of state and society. Both have the credentials to argue for South-South cooperation, since both, by their own rules rather than the West's, have lifted hundreds of millions of people out of poverty.

Taking all of this into account, what can we expect from these two countries, and what will we probably hear much more about in the coming years? We already see two very different countries that share some surprising similarities. Sure, the political opportunity structures may change, but regardless of the differences in regime type, culture, and style, Brazil and China are likely to continue to be rapidly emerging and counterhegemonic, though not revolutionary powers. Both are basking in the attention they believe is long overdue. Largely shaped by state-society relations at home, both will continue to make their own mark on the world. What we have is a virtuous—or, depending on the circumstances, vicious—circle. The push and pull of state and society at home shapes these countries' foreign policies and international relations, which in turn has important ramifications for domestic politics. The status that Brazil and China receive for gaining prominence on the world stage—their ability to engage traditional powers on equal terms—plays back at home as well.

On a variety of issues, we can expect both to continue to make a big show of challenging Western orthodoxies—all the while becoming part of the global establishment. Brazil's charm is that it presents itself as a partner that wants to bring the South on board with it; it's not the West's adversary, but it demands that the West do better. It would never go the way of Venezuela under Chavez or Zimbabwe under Mugabe; it might sometimes scold the West, but they would always make up. Brazil would only veer toward becoming an oppositional force when denied a role, and this is a mistake that the West should avoid making, since on so many different issues Brazil is increasingly a pivotal power, a go-to player. As it has shown on HIV-AIDS, trade, and hunger, Brazil is a shaper of outcomes, not a follower. Brazil may be accused of having outsize ambitions, but Brazil "matters"; its actions and decisions affect the world's economy and environment. Sure, it is hardly an inevitable superpower and no one would characterize it as an old-school superpower at all. But in a multipolar world, as a new kind of player, it is on the short list of countries that will most shape the twenty-first century ("Global Brazil and U.S.-Brazil Relations" 2011).

Surprisingly, it is the behemoth China that analysts contend is a "partial power" (Shambaugh 2013). Lacking the clout of the United States, shaky in its soft power and riddled by domestic debates over international identity and direction, Beijing may long remain a follower rather than a leader. For example, in response to the Syria crisis of 2013, China was decidedly reactive and passive, seemingly comfortable taking a backseat to Russia's attempts to broker a resolution to the chemical weapons crisis. Time and time again—from environmental negotiations, to Ukraine, and even disaster relief—we see the world looking to China as a pivotal go-to player, but it is responding as a reluctant leader. This may be surprising to some: some of this hesitance may be out of principle (non-interference), but another significant part of it is simple lack of capacity.

In the end, we contend the ways that Brazil and China will behave are likely to be shaped by how they're received. In the near future, at least, in the international system they will play the role of society to the traditional powers' state. Applying the state-society lens helps us visualize how actors view themselves, face challenges, and accommodate contending interests. As we've seen inside these countries, state-society relations are in very large part determined by how highly contested the issue is and how the state chooses to receive society. If it's with resistance, chances are that society will continue to operate as oppositional—though not necessarily opposing—forces. If it's with receptivity, the relationship could go one of two ways: 1) society will be co-opted (and the oligarchy expanded, with little changed); or 2) state and society (in this case, traditional and emerging powers) will work together for solutions to the problems that challenge us all. Ultimately, the lesson is this: for those wanting to forecast how these fast-emerging powers will behave on the global stage, consider their motivation and issue salience. But also watch how the traditional powers choose to engage them—and remember that for every action there's a reaction.

DISCUSSION QUESTIONS

1. Regionally and transnationally, both Brazil and China are seeking attention and actively courting soft power. How would you explain these similarities?

2. Brasilia and Beijing approach transnational diplomacy from very different angles, with Brazil framing their involvement as the "beautiful game," in which they are eager to engage, and China plodding along with reluctance. Why? Do you believe these approaches are likely to change in the future? Why or why not?

3. What do you make of the images of Brazil as "extroverted" and more concerned with its global image, and China as "introverted," focused on its own domestic politics? Are you convinced this may be a helpful way to understand some aspects of each state's operation? In your view, what is the impact of these differences on policy priorities and engagement with regional and transnational actors?

4. How useful do you find the conceptual distinction between hard and soft power? How are Brazil and China employing a mix of these resources in contrasting ways? How effective do you believe each state's claim to power is now, and will be in the future?

5. Brasilia is admired; Beijing is admonished. To what extent are these claims true? What do these simplifications miss?

7

CONCLUSIONS

BEYOND REGIME

> Brazil's Cup is not a choreographed performance of or-
> der and progress (the slogan on Brazil's flag). Instead it is
> a noisy clash of goals and demands, fans and protesters,
> hopes and anxieties. This is what a Cup in a democracy
> should look like.
>
> —Jerry Dávila, "World Cup Protests Signal
> Democratic Progress in Brazil"

> The foreigners who say that today's China is totalitarian are
> not paying attention. There are too many people, doing too
> many inventive things, across too great a stretch of territory
> to be under direct governmental supervision and control.
>
> —James Fallows, *China Airborne*

We started out this book with two claims that challenge what is widely regarded
as conventional wisdom. The first is that when it comes to contentious politics
(or non-routine political encounters between state and society) the distance between democracies and non-democracies (or countries at opposite ends of "the
messy middle") is not as great as some would wish or suppose; contentious politics is complex and not necessarily shaped by degrees of democracy in the ways
most would expect. Authoritarian regimes can have fuller and more changeable
repertoires than is commonly recognized. Rather than always resisting citizens'

claims, sometimes even they behave in ways that can be described as receptive to civil society. On the other hand, even states that most would characterize as democratic have shown that they are capable of behaving in ways unbecoming to their status, resorting to repression to protect what they consider dangerous, core, or "red line" issues. In this sense, the performance of actors—state and society alike—present some theory-infirming (Lijphart 1971) insights about the messiness of regime type and contention.

Related to this first claim is a secondary one: regardless of regime type, state-society relations back home also shape states' behavior in the global arena. To understand international relations, one must "do" comparative politics. Looking forward, our examination of contentious politics in two most-different cases tells us—in regard to foreign or domestic policy—that there is nothing inevitable about the paths that Brazil and China have taken to date, nor is there anything certain about their roles in the future. However, keeping in mind that few trajectories are ever straight-line, by placing their past and current trajectories next to each other, much is revealed.

With this maneuver, we can make some tentative projections. It's easy to predict that as consequential global actors, both Brazil and China will want to project power and exert influence. But comparisons provided in the preceding chapters indicate that China is more introverted, and likely to remain focused on changing domestic dynamics that, in varying degrees, threaten to limit its rise. It has opened, and is expected to continue opening, to the world in order to better serve those interests. On the other hand, Brazil is clearly an extrovert, and its domestic dynamics (when the state has chosen to partner with society) have contributed to the successes that are behind the country's rise. Despite the soft power push, China's strengths derive from more traditional notions of power, not only economic but military. As it demonstrated through its handling of its own citizens in the protests associated with the 2014 World Cup, the Brazilian state is capable of brute force, too. But set against China, Brazil compares favorably for its use of "soft power"; its (usual) open-mindedness, tolerance, and preference for the peaceful resolution of disputes measures up well against many countries (Cardoso 2012).

Leading by example and in a new way, Brazil's real power is as a role model for much of the world. As Amorim (2010, 239) puts it, "Our voice is heard with greater attention not because we scream louder, but because we are more respected." But that's largely because of the state's receptivity to society on a variety of relatively less contested issues. That synergy at home has made Brazil the life of the party on the global stage and everyone is interested to see what it will do next. Although the end of the economic boom in 2010 has proven deflating, these are heady times for Brazil on the world stage. Expectations for the country are still high. As mentioned in chapter 6, much of Brazil's soft power exists because it has been able to put the success of Bolsa Familia and its anti-AIDS program on display. But all of this is due to the alliance of state and society, which created the policies, and impressive economic growth in the 2000s, which paid for them. Brazil enjoyed the international recognition it received for its accomplishments, but as we have seen, domestic events can further boost that carefully constructed image or tear it down as a fake and flimsy façade. What happens to the programs at home and its image abroad now that Brazil's boom has been followed by a bust? The riots associated with the 2014 World Cup (including the largest, when hundreds of thousands of Brazilians in three hundred cities went out into the streets all over the country to protest the state's misplaced priorities) may serve as a harbinger of what is to come (Barnes 2014). In these protests, which jolted outsiders' views of Brazil as the land of samba, one placard read, "Sorry for disturbing . . . We are changing the country" (Becker 2013). This claim surely struck some as overly optimistic. However, this phrase, which reflects society's political energy for changing things at home, ironically parallels the state's efforts to shake things up on the world stage.

China, more certain of its right to take the stage, seems uncertain of its next move. From its perspective, its neighbors keep turning to big brother United States for assistance; its African partners welcome funding but question tactics; and, thanks to global social networking campaigns, it has much less control over its international (and to a lesser extent domestic) image than it ever had. Back in 1989, CNN broadcasted images of "tank man" all over the world; today, individual netizens post pictures and videos of confrontations in real time, even on sites that are formally blocked within the PRC. China's reputation as enemy of the Internet—with significant support of Western media corporations—does not exactly win friends around the world. Even its business savvy takes a hit when consumer safety is in question, affecting everything from dog food to toothpaste. With the announcement of various reforms aimed at promoting transparency and the rule of law, the Chinese state appears to have come to the realization that receptivity to society—or at least the appearance of it—can work for non-democracies, too.

DISSOLVING DICHOTOMIES

Nice on the surface but amounting to just enough of an alteration to avoid real change is a pattern we find in both countries. But, in case we haven't said it enough, for all their similarities, there are some crucial differences between Brazil and China. The Brazilian state is a consolidated democracy and the Chinese consolidated authoritarian. Our point is that dichotomies based on regime type can be overly simplistic; in charting state-society relations in the two countries, it isn't always that authoritarian China is resistant and democratic Brazil is receptive to social pressures. During the protests of 2013, the Rousseff government displayed receptivity and resistance. It took pains to show that it was willing to listen to society but also unleashed shocking police brutality on peaceful demonstrators. Sure, Beijing has done more than its share (and worse), but in recent years, we have also seen a growing number of examples in which the Chinese state has appeared surprisingly solicitous of society's demands. The partnering of state and society isn't something that only happens in countries with relatively democratic governments. As a means of building legitimacy, it occurs in authoritarian China more often than one might expect—especially on less contested issues and when the state can rely on the expertise of organized groups to craft better policy (e.g., pollution and HIV-AIDS). For the most part, though, group organizing is much riskier in China than individual action, and as we have seen, the state has the authority to pull the plug with very few limitations.

As we would expect of a democracy, partnerships between state and society are much more common in Brazil where, on more than one occasion, society has led the state and prominent individuals who lead civil society organizations have gone on to work synergistically with the state. This point raises some of the intriguing differences in how citizens have sought to engage the state. For a country that never had a revolution, Brazil has some impressively muscular civil society groups—though none of any size that seek to overthrow the state. On the other hand, many groups in China (home to one of the few authentic social revolutions of the twentieth century) have felt compelled to go with a lighter touch, and seek to work with government—or through it—rather than in opposition, perhaps for obvious reasons.

Our study also confirms what many would expect: it is only on softer areas of policy, the less contested issues, where these states have indicated any significant level of receptivity. The major difference between China and Brazil is how far such receptivity goes and what explains it—whether the state's response is based in self-interest, exhaustion, or any number of other possibilities. Thus, regardless of their differences, both states (to varying degrees) have indicated some willingness to appear receptive on some issues. Increasingly even China recognizes the power in this approach and shares with Brazil the desire to reap positive PR from their willingness to engage society. Whenever they believe that the benefits of receptivity outweigh the costs, leaders in both countries will (with varying degrees of success) use it to offset demands for more significant change. On the less contested issues, they will also exhibit receptivity to construct an image of benevolence aimed at foreign and domestic audiences. In this, Brazil and China are more alike than different—and again, one thing is clear: those who rely on regime type to explain state-society relations would have missed this nuance.

We are simply providing more evidence for an argument that others have made: states even at opposite ends of "the messy middle" separating democracies from dictatorships can be more like-minded in interests and values than most would assume.[1] One of the many things that all states have in common is that, like authoritarian China and democratic Brazil, they have core interests on which they will not yield. But the sources of the core issues are fundamentally different—and it goes beyond regime. In Brazil, it is non-state actors that decide what is a core issue; in China, it is the state. In Brazil, the core, most highly contested of all issues is land (control over resources), and economic elites call the shots. And this isn't associated with regime type; land was a core issue long before Brazil's transition to democracy and Brazilian governments of all stripes—democratic or not—have in one way or another been beholden to elite interests. The difference is whether they used receptivity (reforms in other areas) along with resistance to offset calls for land reform. Because China suffers from contested sovereignty, claims regarding ethnicity and religious identity pose an existential threat. They ultimately place CCP rule, and, by association, the current borders of the Chinese state, in jeopardy. All countries have their dangerous issues; it is a matter of whether it is directed by the state (China) or by non-state actors using the state (Brazil).

To be fair, it must be recognized that Brazil has made some important reforms. Sure, if the PT stuck to its once-radical platform, it would have pushed for bigger change. The PT in power is surely different than the PT was when it was society; it is more reformist than revolutionary, but the PT's anti-poverty programs have improved the lives of millions of people, raising their incomes.

---

[1] For example, see Wolfgang Merkel, "Embedded and Defective Democracies," *Democratization* 11 no. 5 (December 2004); Guillermo O'Donnell, "Illusions About Consolidation," *Journal of Democracy* 7 no. 2 (1996): 34–51; and Stephen Levitsky and Lucan A. Way, *Competitive Authoritarianism: Hybrid Regimes After the Cold War* (New York: Cambridge University Press, 2010).

In the end, the PT's move toward the center and receptivity to reform may only work to offset larger, structural changes (like land reform), but it is not mere window dressing. The PT has long claimed to be different; its opponents to the right accuse it of implementing class warfare and call for Rousseff's impeachment, but are PT governments much unlike their predecessors? Perhaps one could argue that Lula, Rousseff, and the rest are merely being pragmatic. Although PT leaders don't necessarily represent or ally with the elites, PT governments recognize the political and economic forces arrayed against change and know (like much of Chinese society) that in the face of political realities (and overwhelming odds), the best way to achieve their goals is by taking small steps but cleaving to orthodox economic policies. Sure, the PT can be criticized from the left for not trying to change everything at once (or much of anything). Some point to its alliance with agribusiness and say that the PT has been co-opted and is now corrupt, just like all the rest. Perhaps what the PT (and the democracy) is doing is just a continuation of the Brazilian tradition of para inglês ver, appearing to be accommodating but making just enough change to keep everything as it is.

We will have to leave the debate of whether change in Brazil is non-existent or just very slow to others. But it is clear that Brazil's ability to build the fairer, more democratic world order it claims to advocate will begin with whether it can maintain and build on its achievements at home ("Global Brazil and U.S.-Brazil Relations" 2011). Without the model at home to inspire, Brazil's power is evanescent, soon to pass out of sight. Even for those who admired it, China's model of authoritarian capitalism is starting to lose its gloss. This is especially true for civil society activists around the world. China's increasing power and presence has not led to more positive ratings for the PRC, with only 50 percent of individuals surveyed worldwide by the Pew Global Attitudes Project expressing a favorable opinion of China, compared to the 63 percent who expressed such views of the United States ("America's Global Image" 2013). Each year it faces an increasing number of protests to its rule—as documented in official media sources—on everything from pollution to corruption to illegal land grabs, and many other issues in between. Despite expectations that elites manage the game in authoritarian China, social actors (often as individuals) employ a vast repertoire of behaviors, ranging from the conventional to confrontational. State actors often recognize they need to heed the score, even when the outcome, for the time being at least, is indeterminate.

In many ways this story is about the persistence and breakdown of systems. But for all their differences (and they are significant), the states (which are really just the public face of a larger system) share at least one remarkable similarity: a venality that eats away at a base held together by patronage and corruption. This weakness has its origins in the transitions of the 1970s and 1980s that were ultimately orchestrated by elites. In both countries today, political and social forces beyond the state have undue influence. In Brazil several analysts have pointed out that because elites negotiated the transition to maintain their leverage, the democracy suffers from a "birth defect" (Hunter 1997; Hagopian 2011; Merkel 2004). We can debate whether the state represents those interests or is captive to them, but even the PT-led government serves them. In China these elites are the Communist Party, determined to hold on to political power, even at great cost. Protesting water pollution or calling for greater support for HIV patients is permissible. Calls for the liberation of Tibetans, Uighurs, or other challenges to national unity cross the line and are dealt with severely. Surrounded by instant communication and the proliferation of multiple messages, the monitoring, censoring, and censuring of social media reflects the regime's sensitivity toward managing the message.

Even though it is celebrated as a democracy and its achievements against poverty, hunger, and HIV-AIDS, in Brazil inequality is deeply embedded and the red line is land reform and control of resources. In both countries the state represents those interests and it will do whatever is necessary to maintain the status quo. Both have indicated that they can be pliable on interests that are less important to them—in order to protect the interests they hold dearest. In China it translates this way: in order to hold on to political power, the state has allowed citizens more economic freedoms. It has also indicated some willingness to yield on other issues, in large part to put off demands for more transformative change. In Brazil, in order to maintain their economic interests, elites have allowed citizens more political freedoms.[2] But when it comes to their core interests, the state (representing elites in China and Brazil) has made it abundantly clear it will not engage on what it considers an existential threat.

Both states will use a combination of receptivity and resistance to hold off bigger change. For example, both systems have bought time by raising millions

---

[2] In 2002, on his fourth attempt, Lula, long viewed by elites as a threat due to his calls for a redistribution of wealth, including land reform, won the presidency. Once in power Lula (and his successor, Dilma Rousseff, also of the PT) largely dropped the issue of land reform and have chosen instead to pursue more reformist measures to alleviate poverty and narrow the massive gap between rich and poor. Analysts disagree about whether the PT's scaling down of its goals is based in pragmatism, as once in power, it recognized what it was up against, or whether it was a matter of the party itself changing and, once in power, joining the elites.

out of poverty. Ultimately, though, they need strong and sustained levels of economic growth to maintain these systems. As different as they are, due to this commonality, both systems suffer from a rot from within: corruption is at the root of both. The threat in Brazil is not democratic regression or resurgent authoritarianism but democratic decay (Diamond 2014). The democracy is consolidated, but without this more substantive change in many ways the democracy is "para ingles ver," superficial. Without a deepening of the democracy, it will remain unsatisfying, a shell of what it could be.

In China, elites recognize the dangers that rampant corruption poses to their continued hold on power and, in fact, to the continuation of the CCP's monopoly on power. The revolution is a distant memory, and the promises made in the post-Tiananmen period (to forgo politics in order to enjoy the fruits of economic growth) are starting to show wear and tear. While Chinese citizens can accept coexistence with millionaires –even billionaires—who benefited from the growth surges of the 1990s (especially real estate), they have a harder time stomaching the lavish lifestyles of the family members of CCP officials. Yet Xi Jinping's much vaunted anti-corruption campaign—widely viewed as targeting political enemies more so than truly investigating malfeasance—risks being revealed for sheer political maneuvering, despite the resurrection of Mao-era "mass line" slogans and other attempts to win over loyalty for the Party. The revolution is distant, and society has transformed with significant expectations: economically, socially, and even, to a lesser extent, politically. Much of the resurgent authoritarianism that we are witnessing in Xi's China stems from the fear that the CCP risks losing its management of these complex dynamics.

A consideration of these countries' histories and political trajectories could lead one to conclude that it is perhaps the authoritarian system that may "give" before the democracy. Because it promises more possibilities for change, democracy generally tends to stave off calls for more radical adjustments. Even Brazilians who have benefited from reforms are impatient with the pace of change, but a reading of history tells us that change, if it ever comes to Brazil, is likely to happen very slowly.[3] On the other hand, in post-revolutionary China, the ability to enrich oneself amounts to the social contract between state and

---

[3] Brazil is hardly the only troubled shell of a democracy. Other countries, such as South Africa, have orchestrated transitions to democracy in which elites appeared to give up political power but their economic interests remained untouched. Those that have not seen a democratic deepening or any redistribution of wealth fall into the same category. These countries have some of the highest rates of income and wealth inequality in the world

society—it's all the communist system offered—and it is what holds the country together. If the state can't hold up its end of the deal, then all bets are off, and the state knows it—this as true of democratic Brazil as it is authoritarian China. These are the similarities we have sought to underscore.

At the beginning of this book, we promised readers a theory-infirming payoff, and this is it: although regime type certainly matters, in the end, it turns out that issue trumps regime. It is the topic under contention that has the most explanatory power for predicting the likelihood of state receptivity or resistance. The lesson is that we all need to be much more cautious about painting state-society relations in broad strokes, both across regimes and even within them. This study has shown that elites in democratic Brazil are not always receptive to civil society, just as their counterparts in authoritarian China are not always resistant. The Chinese state does not on every occasion shut down participatory channels from citizens, and sometimes the Brazilian state does. Clearly, some issues are more negotiable than others. Dictatorships and democracies alike are more inclined to appear receptive on issues that are relatively peripheral to their interests. Democratic or not, states share concerns about legitimacy. This is just one reason why authoritarian states don't always behave in the ways we have come to expect. Nor do the citizens seeking to engage the state necessarily fit the familiar molds: society also has a more complete repertoire than is commonly assumed and behaves in a sometimes startling variety of manners. Those living in democracies are often, but not always, in the government's face. Conversely, those living under dictatorships aren't always either cowed by them or seeking to overthrow them. It isn't useful to try to peg society by type any more than it is regime.

These arguments aren't entirely new. Scholars have long recognized variation across authoritarian regimes. Everyone knows that states can be differently democratic. However, our point is that state receptivity or resistance isn't determined so much by regime type as it is by issue salience. We contend that when it comes down to core issues, countries existing at opposite ends of "the messy middle," democracies and non-democracies, can—and do—behave in strikingly similar ways. For all states there are certain, structural issues that are non-negotiable; this is true of authoritarian regimes (i.e., for Chinese elites it is anything associated with political reform). But democracies draw their red lines as well (in Brazil that issue is land reform). Meanwhile, they're both willing to work with society on what they deem to be relatively peripheral issues in order to shore up protections for these core interests. Therefore, in contentious politics it's more about issue than regime. It is only by going beyond regime—and being willing to consider the complexity of contentious politics in two countries that most would never match for comparison—that all is revealed. Despite their differences, state (and society) at opposite ends of "the messy middle" can be more alike than many would suppose—or wish.

POSTSCRIPT

We opened this book with the call—for scholars and students alike—to move beyond conventional frameworks for comparative analysis and to take the risk of finding both similarities and differences between two countries that many would never place side by side. We encouraged this undertaking because we thought that a close examination of state-society relations in these two particular fast-emerging countries would prove illuminating. We hope by now that you agree, at least in part, that this process was more than a sleight of hand. We've been forthright in admitting at times the comparisons made us cringe, but we believe this is a worthy—indeed necessary—exercise in order to rethink some common assumptions of both democratic and non-democratic states.

Every day you hear it: the world is changing. Simple caricatures of countries—"powerful" and "not so powerful," "strong" and "weak"—are beyond misleading . . . they are irresponsible. We know that democratic states are more likely to "get it right" when it comes to responsiveness to their citizens, and we have ample evidence that recalcitrant non-democratic holdouts abuse their power and ignore the will of their citizens. But we hope that we've been able to show that there's much more to the story than this. A more nuanced appreciation of the inner workings of contentious politics—the pushing, pulling, dragging, and even tailing between the powerful and the ostensibly less powerful—helps all of us understand politics in countries around the world in a more complete way. The individuals and groups who take so many risks to pursue change, as well as the civil servants who rally against the grain to be as responsive as possible, deserve at least that.

BIBLIOGRAPHY

"2011 Global Study on Homicide." United Nations Office on Drugs and Crime, 2011, http://www.unodc.org/unodc/en/data-and-analysis/statistics/crime/global -study-on-homicide-2011.html. Retrieved September 5, 2013.

"2012 Progress Reports Submitted by Countries." UNAIDS, 2012, http://www .unaids.org/en/dataanalysis/knowyourresponse/countryprogressreports /2012countries/#a_52698. Retrieved September 5, 2013.

"2.9 Million Trapped in Modern-Day Slavery in China, 30 Million Worldwide." *South China Morning Post*, October 17, 2013, http://www.scmp.com/news/world /article/1333894/29-million-trapped-modern-day-slavery-china-30-million -worldwide. Retrieved May 12, 2014.

"Abortion Becomes an Issue in Brazil's Presidential Elections." *World*, October 28, 2010, http://www.theworld.org/2010/10abortion-becomes-an-issue-in-brazil %E2%80%99s-presidential-elections/. Retrieved June 16, 2012.

Abrahamsen, Rita. "The Power of Partnerships in Global Governance." *Third World Quarterly* 25, no. 8: 1453–1467, http://www.tandfonline.com/doi/abs/10.1080 /0143659042000308465. Retrieved May 12, 2015.

Acemoglu, Daron, and James Robinson. *Why Nations Fail*. New York: Random House, 2013.

Ackerman, Spencer. "Internet and Attitude, A Powerful Combination." *New York Times*, August 20, 2012, http://www.nytimes.com/roomfordebate/2012/08/20 /what-makes-protest-effective/internet-and-attitude-a-powerful-combination. Retrieved June 6, 2012.

Adario, Paulo. "Brazil Risks Protection Record by Proposing Changes to Forest Code." *Guardian*, May 27, 2011, http://www.guardian.co.uk/environment/2011 /may/27/brazil-forest-protection-code. Retrieved June 11, 2012.

Adelman, Miriam, and Mariana Correa de Azevedo. "Families, Gender Relations and Social Change in Brazil: Practices, Discourse, Policy." *Journal of Child and Family Studies* 21 (2012): 65–74, http://www.mendeley.com/research/families -gender-relations-social-change-brazil-practices-discourse-policy/. Retrieved April 25, 2012.

Ahnen, Ronald E. "The Politics of Police Violence in Democratic Brazil." Latin American Politics & Society 49, no. 1 (2007): 141–164, http://muse.jhu.edu /journals/latin_american_politics_and_society/v049/49.1ahnen.html. Retrieved May 15, 2014.

"AIDSinfo: China." UNAIDS, June 20, 2012, http://www.unaids.org/en/regionscoun tries/countries/china/. Retrieved July 27, 2013.

Allen, John L., Jr. "Brazil's Bishops Sound Alarm about the Amazon." *National Catholic Reporter* 46, no. 14 (April 30, 2010), http://ncronline.org/blogs/ncr -today/brazils-bishops-sound-alarm-about-amazon. Retrieved May 24, 2012.

Allison, Simon. "Fixing China's Image in Africa, One Student at a Time." *Guardian*, July 5, 2013, http://www.theguardian.com/world/2013/jul/31/china-africa -students-scholarship-programme. Retrieved June 17, 2014.

"Almost 19 Million Urban Brazilians Live with No Access to Drinking Water of Sewage." *MercoPress*, May 25, 2012, http://en.mercopress.com/2012/05/25 /almost-19-million-urban-brazilians-live-with-no-access-to-drinking-water-of -sewage. Retrieved June 10, 2012.

Alonso, Angela, and Débora Maciel. "From Protest to Professionalization: Brazilian Environmental Activism after Rio-92." *Journal of Environment Development* 19 (2010): 300–317, http://jed.sagepub.com/content/19/3/300.full.pdf+html. Retrieved May 30, 2012.

Altman, Daniel. "The Dark Side of Dilma." *Foreign Policy*, October 27, 2014, http:// foreignpolicy.com/2014/10/27/the-dark-side-of-dilma/. Retrieved April 16, 2015.

Alvarez, Sonia E., Evelina Dagnino, and Arturo Escobar. *Culture of Politics, Politics of Culture*. Boulder: Westview, 1998.

Amar, Paul. "Operation Princess in Rio de Janeiro: Policing 'Sex Trafficking', Strengthening Worker Citizenship, and the Urban Geopolitics of Security in Brazil." *Security Dialogue* 40, no. 4–5 (2009): 513–541, http://www.global.ucsb .edu/faculty/amar/SD_OpPrincess_PUBLISHED.pdf. Retrieved April 29, 2012.

"America's Global Image Remains More Positive than China's." Pew Research Global Attitudes Project, July 18, 2013, http://www.pewglobal.org/2013/07/18 /americas-global-image-remains-more-positive-than-chinas/. Retrieved May 6, 2014.

Amorim, Celso. "Brazilian Foreign Policy under President Lula (2003–2010): An Overview." *Revista Brasileira de Política Internacional* 52 (December 2010): 214–240, http://www.scielo.br/scielo.php?pid=S0034–73292010000300013 &script=sci_arttext. Retrieved July 5, 2013.

Apco Worldwide. *China's 12th Five-Year Plan*, December 10, 2010, http://www .apcoworldwide.com/content/pdfs/chinas_12th_five-year_plan.pdf. Retrieved May 10, 2012.

Arias, E. *Drugs & Democracy in Rio de Janeiro: Trafficking, Social Networks, & Public Security*. Chapel Hill: University of North Carolina Press, 2006.

"Around 10 Million People Living with HIV Now Have Access to Antiretroviral Treatment." UNAIDS, June 30, 2013, http://www.unaids.org/en/resources

/presscentre/pressreleaseandstatementarchive/2013june/20130630prtreatment/.
Retrieved December 31, 2013.

Avritzer, Leonardo. "Urban Reform, Participation and the Right to the City in
Brazil." Institute of Development Studies, September 2007, http://www.ids.ac
.uk/ids/Part/proj/pnp.html. Retrieved September 10, 2012.

———. "Civil Society in Brazil: From State Autonomy to Political Inter-
dependency." Paper Presented at the Conference on Citizenship, Democratic
Participation and Civil Society in Global Perspective, May 12, 2009, http://
orecomm.net/wp-content/uploads/2009/05/avritzer-roskilde.pdf. Retrieved
August 14, 2012.

Babones, Salvatore. "The Middling Kingdom." *Foreign Affairs* 90, no. 5 (2011):
79–88.

Badkar, Mamta. "22 Chinese People Who Were Handed the Death Sentence
for White Collar Crime." *Business Insider* (Australia), July 16, 2013, http://
au.businessinsider.com/chinese-white-collar-criminals-death-sentence
-2013–7#zeng-chengjie-executed-1. Retrieved July 26, 2013.

Bai Tiantian and Yan Shuang. "Re-education to Be Reformed." *Global Times*,
January 8, 2013, http://www.globaltimes.cn/content/754403.shtml. Retrieved
July 27, 2013.

Baranov, David. *The Abolition of Slavery in Brazil.* Santa Barbara, CA: Praeger, 2000.

Barbara, Vanessa. 2013a. "Brazil's Vinegar Uprising." *New York Times*, June 21, 2013,
http://www.nytimes.com/2013/06/22/opinion/brazils-vinegar-uprising.html.
Retrieved July 31, 2013.

———. 2013b. "Have a Nice Day, N.S.A." *New York Times*, September 27, 2013,
http://www.nytimes.com/2013/09/27/opinion/have-a-nice-day-nsa.html.
Retrieved December 16, 2013.

———. "Brazil's Unaffordable Homes." *New York Times*, July 30, 2014, http://www
.nytimes.com/2014/07/31/opinion/vanessa-barbara-brazils-unaffordable-homes
.html. Retrieved July 31, 2014.

Barbassa, Juliana. "Brazil Protests Counter Military Coup Celebration." Associated
Press, March 29, 2012, http://news.yahoo.com/brazil-protests-counter-military
-coup-celebration-225153308.html. Retrieved September 18, 2012.

Barboza, David. "Chameleon Mao, the Face of Tiananmen Square." *New York Times*,
May 28, 2006, http://www.nytimes.com/2006/05/28/weekinreview/28barboza
.html?pagewanted=all&_r=0. Retrieved February 20, 2014.

Barboza, David, and Michael Forsythe. "With Choice at Tiananmen, Student Took
Road to Riches." *New York Times*, June 3, 2014, http://www.nytimes.com
/2014/06/04/world/asia/tiananmen-era-students-different-path-to-power-in
-china.html. Retrieved June 5, 2014.

Barchfield, Jenny, and Nicole Winfield. "Pope Francis in Brazil: Beware the
'Ephemeral Idols.'" *Christian Science Monitor*, July 24, 2013, http://www.cs
monitor.com/World/Latest-News-Wires/2013/0724/Pope-Francis-in-Brazil
-Beware-the-ephemeral-idols. Retrieved August 9, 2013.

Barnes, Taylor, and Sara Miller Llana. "Brazil School Massacre Puts Spotlight on
Gun Violence, Rising Firearm Sales." *Christian Science Monitor*, April 8, 2011,

http://www.csmonitor.com/World/Americas/2011/0408/Brazil-school-massacre
-puts-spotlight-on-gun-violence-rising-firearm-sales. Retrieved May 30, 2013.

Barnes, Taylor. "Brazil Election: Why Antigovernment Protesters Are Now Voting Rousseff." *Christian Science Monitor*, October 26, 2014, http://m.csmonitor.com /World/Americas/2014/1026/Brazil-election-Why-antigovernment-protesters -are-now-voting-Rousseff-video. Retrieved October 29, 2014.

Barrionuevo, Alexei. "Stagnation' Made Brazil's Environment Chief Resign." *New York Times*, May 16, 2008, http://www.nytimes.com/2008/05/16/world /americas/16brazil.html?fta=y. Retrieved June 19, 2012.

———. "Bypassing Resistance, Brazil Prepares to Build a Dam." *New York Times*, August 15, 2010, http://www.nytimes.com/2010/08/16/world/americas/16brazil. html. Retrieved May 24, 2012.

———. 2011a. "Brazil Rejects Panel's Request to Stop Dam." *New York Times*, April 5, 2011, http://www.nytimes.com/2011/04/06/world/americas/06brazil.html. Retrieved May 24, 2012.

———. 2011b. "Brazil, After a Long Battle, Approves Amazon Dam." *New York Times*, June 1, 2011, http://www.nytimes.com/2011/06/02/world/americas /02brazil.html. Retrieved May 24, 2012.

———. 2011c. "Brazilian Amazon Groups Invade Site of Dam Project." *New York Times*, October 27, 2011, http://www.nytimes.com/2011/10/28/world/americas /brazilian-amazon-groups-try-to-stop-dam-project.html. Retrieved May 24, 2012.

Bayron, Heda. "China Confronts Rising Crime in a Fast-Track Economy." Voice of America, October 29, 2009, http://www.voanews.com/content/a-13-2005-02 -28-voa9-67378612/382581.html. Retrieved July 26, 2013.

"BBC Country Rating Poll Reveals Positive Views of Brazil on the Rise in 2011." *BBC World Service Poll*, March 7, 2011, http://www.bbc.co.uk/pressoffice /pressreleases/stories/2011/03_march/07/brazil.shtml. Retrieved June 23, 2013.

Beaubien, Jason. "Activists Fear Brazil's Triumph over HIV Has Fizzled." NPR, *Morning Edition*, July 20, 2012, http://www.npr.org/blogs/health/2012/07/20 /157059273/activists-fear-brazils-triumph-over-hiv-has-fizzled. Retrieved August 13, 2012.

Becker, Daniel. "The People Have Awakened." *New York Times*, June 20, 2013, http://www.nytimes.com/roomfordebate/2013/06/19/will-the-protests-in-brazil -lead-to-change/the-people-of-brazil-have-awakened. Retrieved August 14, 2013.

"Beijing Disperses Rain to Dry Olympic Night." *Xinhua*, August 9, 2008, http://news .xinhuanet.com/english/2008-08/09/content_9079637.htm. Retrieved May 23, 2013.

Bevins, Vincent. "Religion Strikes Back at Brazil's Gay Culture, *Guardian*, July 2, 2011, http://www.theguardian.com/commentisfree/belief/2011/jul/02/brazil- gay-rights-evangelical-movement. Retrieved June 24, 2014.

———. "Brazil's Evangelical Churches Rewrite the Rules of Politics." *Los Angeles Times*, October 21, 2012, http://articles.latimes.com/2012/oct/21/world/la-fg -brazil-evangelicals-20121022. Retrieved May 31, 2013.

———. "Homophobic Attacks Increase in Seemingly Gay-Friendly Brazil." *Los Angeles Times*, March 22, 2015, http://www.latimes.com/world/brazil/la-fg-ff-brazil-homophobia-20150322-story.html. Retrieved April 16, 2015.

Biehl, João. "The Activist State: Global Pharmaceuticals, AIDS, and Citizenship in Brazil." *Social Text* 22, no. 3 (Fall 2004): 105–132.

"Birth Defects: Facts about Anencephaly." Centers for Disease Control and Prevention, 2014, http://www.cdc.gov/ncbddd/birthdefects/anencephaly.html. Retrieved May 10, 2015.

Black, Richard. "Climate Targets 'Risk' from Brazil's Forest Changes." *BBC News*, December 7, 2011, http://www.bbc.co.uk/news/science-environment-16074628. Retrieved May 21, 2012.

Blanchette, Thaddeus. "Prostitute Campaigns for a Seat in the Brazilian Federal Congress." *Wagadu* 8 (2010), http://www.docstoc.com/docs/78763237/Prostitute-Campaigns-for-a-Seat-in-the-Brazilian-Federal-Congress. Retrieved April 29, 2012.

Bleisch, William. "China 'Unfairly Seen as Eco-Villain'" *BBC News*, June 16, 2009, http://news.bbc.co.uk/2/hi/science/nature/8100988.stm. Retrieved May 21, 2012.

Blum, Susan D. "China's Many Faces: Ethnic, Cultural, and Religious Pluralism." In *China Beyond the Headlines*, edited by Timothy B. Weston and Lionel M. Jensen, 69–95. Lanham, MD: Rowman & Littlefield, 2010.

Boadle, Anthony. "Brazil's Rousseff Says Extreme Poverty Almost Eradicated." Reuters, February 13, 2013, http://www.Reuters.com/article/2013/02/19/us-brazil-poverty-idUSBRE91I14F20130219. Retrieved May 30, 2013.

Boehler, Patrick. "Dongguan Sex Worker Report Stokes Debate about Legalizing Prostitution." *South China Morning Post*, February 11, 2014, http://www.scmp.com/news/china-insider/article/1425942/dongguan-sex-worker-reports-stoke-debate-about-legalising. Retrieved June 11, 2014.

Borden, Sam. "A Soccer Prodigy, at Home in Brazil." *New York Times*, July 9, 2012, http://www.nytimes.com/2012/07/10/sports/soccer/neymar-soccer-prodigy-is-at-home-in-brazil.html?pagewanted=all. Retrieved July 7, 2014.

———. "For Brazil, Winning Trumps Aesthetics." *New York Times*, July 7, 2014, http://www.nytimes.com/2014/07/08/sports/worldcup/world-cup-2014-brazil-eschews-the-beautiful-game-for-more-rugged-style.html. Retrieved July 14, 2014.

Bourne, Richard. *Lula of Brazil: The Story So Far*. Oakland, CA: University of California Press, 2009.

Bovingdon, Gardner. *The Uyghurs: Strangers in Their Own Land*. New York: Columbia University Press, 2010.

Boynton, Xiaoqing Lu, Olivia Ma, and Molly Claire Schmalzbach. "Key Issues in China's Health Care Reform." Washington, DC: Center for Strategic and International Studies, 2012, http://csis.org/files/publication/121207_Boynton_KeyIssuesChinaHealth_Web.pdf. Retrieved May 12, 2015.

Branigan, Tania. "Chinese Parents Turn to Microblogging in Hunt for Missing Children." *Guardian*, February 9, 2011, http://www.guardian.co.uk/world/2011/feb/09/china-microblogging-missing-children. Retrieved June 24, 2013.

———. "Chinese Environmental Activist Goes on Trial over Books." *Guardian*, October 11, 2012, http://www.theguardian.com/world/2012/oct/11/chinese-activist-trial-books. Retrieved January 8, 2014.

Branigan, Tania, "HIV/Aids Activist Flees China for US." *Guardian*, May 10, 2010, http://www.theguardian.com/world/2010/may/10/aids-activist-flees-china-america. Retrieved July 29, 2013.

"Brazil." *Insight Crime*, April 9, 2013, http://www.insightcrime.org/organized-crime -profile/brazil. Retrieved September 5, 2013.

"Brazil: 9-Year-Old Has Abortion despite Church Objections." *New York Times*, March 5, 2009, http://www.nytimes.com/2009/03/05/world/americas/05briefs -9YEAROLDSABO_BRF.html. Retrieved June 20, 2014.

"Brazil, After a Long Battle, Approves an Amazon Dam." Amazon Watch, June 1, 2011, http://amazonwatch.org/news/2011/0601-brazil-after-a-long-battle -approves-an-amazon-dam. Retrieved July 7, 2014.

"Brazil and Germany to Propose UN Resolution to Propose Anti-Spying Resolution at UN." Reuters, October 25, 2013, http://news.yahoo.com/germany-brazil -propose-anti-spying-resolution-u-n-025753740.html. Retrieved December 16, 2013.

"Brazil at a Crossroads for LGBT Rights." *Nation*, April 5, 2011, http://www. thenation.com/article/159703/brazil-crossroads-lgbt-rights. Retrieved February 24, 2012.

"Brazil: Clashes in Rio Slum Over Death of Youth." Associated Press, August 14, 2013, m/brazil-clashes-in-rio-slum-over-death-of-youth/article/feed/578424. Retrieved August 31, 2013.

"Brazil Court Upholds Law that Protects Torturers." Amnesty International, April 30, 2010, http://www.amnesty.org/en/for-media/press-releases/brazil-court -upholds-law-protects-torturers-2010–04–30. Retrieved August 12, 2013.

"Brazil Drugs Raids: Police Surge into North Rio Slums." *BBC News*, October 14, 2012, http://www.bbc.co.uk/news/world-latin-america-19940440. Retrieved October 26, 2012.

"Brazil Eases Rules on Conserving Amazon Rainforest." *BBC News*, May 25, 2011, http://www.bbc.co.uk/news/world-latin-america-13538578. Retrieved May 21, 2012.

"Brazil Elections: Dilma Rousseff Promises Reform after Poll Win." *BBC News*, October 27, 2014, http://www.bbc.com/news/world-latin-america-29782073. Retrieved October 27, 2014.

"Brazil Entices Tinder Users in Covert Safe-Sex Campaign." *Global Times*, February 11, 2015, www.globaltimes.cn/content/907163.shtml. Retrieved May 10, 2015.

"Brazil Evangelical Christians Hold Huge São Paulo Rally." *BBC News*, July 14, 2012, http://www.bbc.co.uk/news/world-latin-america-18845211. Retrieved July 19, 2012.

"Brazil Farmers Mass in Protest of Forest Regulations." Reuters, April 5, 2011, http://www.trust.org/alertnet/news/brazil-farmers-mass-in-protest-of-forest -regulations. Retrieved May 30, 2012.

"Brazil Fights Crime While Bringing Development to the Favelas." World Bank, March 22, 2013, http://www.worldbank.org/en/news/feature/2013/03/21/brazil-crime-violence-favela. Retrieved September 5, 2013.

"Brazil Fossil-Fuel CO2 Emissions." Carbon Dioxide Information Analysis Center, 2011, http://cdiac.ornl.gov/trends/emis/tre_bra.html. Retrieved May 31, 2012.

"Brazil: Freedom in the World 2011." Freedom House, http://www.freedomhouse.org/report/freedom-world/2011/brazil. Retrieved August 16, 2012.

"Brazil: Freedom in the World 2012." Freedom House, http://www.freedomhouse.org/country/brazil. Retrieved August 15, 2012.

"Brazil: Freedom in the World 2013." Freedom House, http://www.freedomhouse.org/report/freedom-world/2013/brazil-0. Retrieved June 1, 2013.

"Brazil Grants Building Permit for Belo Monte Amazon Dam." *BBC News*, June 1, 2011, http://www.bbc.co.uk/news/world-latin-america-13614684. Retrieved May 24, 2012.

"Brazilian Discontent Ahead of World Cup." Pew Research Global Attitudes Project, June 3, 2014, http://www.pewglobal.org/2014/06/03/chapter-1-views-of-national-conditions-and-the-economy-in-brazil/. Retrieved June 24, 2014.

"The Brazilian Model." *Economist*, November 17, 2011, http://www.economist.com/node/21537004. Retrieved August 14, 2012.

"Brazilians Upbeat about Their Country, Despite Its Problems." Pew Research Center, Global Attitudes Project, September 22, 2010, http://pewresearch.org/pubs/1736/poll-brazil-opinion-national-conditions-rising-power. Retrieved May 29, 2012.

"Brazil Indigenous Guarani Leader Nisio Gomes Killed." *BBC News*, November 18, 2011, http://www.bbc.co.uk/news/world-latin-america-15799712. Retrieved May 21, 2012.

"Brazil: Journalist Escapes Assassination Attempt." *Global Journalist*, April 24, 2012, http://www.globaljournalist.org/freepresswatch/2012/04/brazil/journalist-escapes-assassination-attempt/. Retrieved May 30, 2012.

"Brazil Lawmakers to Propose Referendum on Gun Law." *BBC News*, April 13, 2011, http://www.bbc.co.uk/news/world-latin-america-13060993. Retrieved September 23, 2012.

"Brazil Lifts Ban on Aborting Brain-Damaged Fetuses." Reuters, April 12, 2012, http://www.msnbc.msn.com/id/47036165/ns/health/t/brazil-lifts-ban-aborting-brain-damaged-fetuses/. Retrieved April 29, 2012.

"Brazil Overview." World Bank, 2013, http://www.worldbank.org/en/country/brazil/overview. Retrieved May 30, 2013.

"Brazil Panel Delivers Report on Regime Brutality." Associated Press, December 10, 2014, http://www.nytimes.com/aponline/2014/12/10/world/americas/ap-lt-brazil-truth-commission.html. Retrieved January 29, 2015.

"Brazil Sex Education Material Suspended by President." *BBC News*, May 25, 2011, http://www.bbc.co.uk/news/world-latin-america-13554077. Retrieved September 14, 2013.

"Brazil Summons Canadian Envoy Over Spy Claims." *BBC News*, October 7, 2013, http://www.bbc.co.uk/news/world-latin-america-24438355. Retrieved December 16, 2013.

"Brazil: The World Factbook." Central Intelligence Agency, 2015, https://www.cia.gov/library/publications/the-world-factbook/geos/br.html. Retrieved September 19, 2015.

"Brazil to Fine Chevron $28M for Rio Oil Spill." *BBC News*, November 21, 2011, http://www.bbc.co.uk/news/world-latin-america-15829974. Retrieved May 22, 2012.

"Brazil Truth Commission: Abuse 'Rife' Under Military Rule." *BBC News*, December 10, 2014, http://www.bbc.com/news/world-latin-america-30410741. Retrieved January 29, 2015.

"Brazil's Amazon Deforestation in 2011 Lowest on Record." Environment News Service, December 7, 2011, http://www.ens-newswire.com/ens/dec2011/2011-12-07-02.html. Retrieved May 24, 2012.

"Brazil's Coming Recession: The Crash of a Titan." *Economist*, February 28, 2015, http://www.economist.com/news/finance-and-economics/21645248-brazils-fiscal-and-monetary-levers-are-jammed-result-it-risks-getting-stuck. Retrieved April 14, 2015.

"Brazil's Economy Grows at Twice the Rate Expected." *BBC News*, February 27, 2014, http://www.bbc.com/news/business-26368704. Retrieved May 12, 2014.

"Brazil's Election: Dilma's Fragile Lead." *Economist*, April 30, 2014, http://www.economist.com/blogs/americasview/2014/04/brazils-election. Retrieved May 12, 2014.

"Brazil's March towards Universal Coverage." *Bulletin of the World Health Organization* 88, no. 9 (September 2010): 641–716, http://www.who.int/bulletin/volumes/88/9/10-020910/en/index.html. Retrieved August 20, 2012.

"Brazil's Rousseff to UN: US Surveillance an 'Affront.'" RT.com, September 24, 2013, http://rt.com/news/brazil-roussef-nsa-usa-278/. Retrieved October 29, 2014.

"Bringing the State Back into the Favelas of Rio de Janeiro." World Bank, October 2012, http://wwwwds.worldbank.org/external/default/WDSContentServer/WDSP/IB/2013/03/15/000333037_20130315115010/Rendered/PDF/760110ESW0P12300Rio0de0Janeiro02013.pdf. Retrieved September 5, 2013.

Brink, Susan. "A Chinese Child's Lung Cancer is Linked to Pollution." *National Geographic*, November 8, 2013, http://news.nationalgeographic.com/news/2013/11/131108-lung-cancer-childhood-china-pollution-eight-year-old-girl/. Retrieved December 9, 2013.

Brook, Timothy. *The Confusions of Pleasure: Commerce and Culture in Ming China*. Berkeley: University of California Press, 1998.

Brown, Nathan J. *When Victory is Not an Option: Islamist Movements in Arab Politics*. Ithaca, NY: Cornell University Press, 2012.

Bruschi, Nicholas. "Why Only the Amazonians Can Save the Rainforest." *Ecologist*, May 11, 2010, 2–3, http://www.theecologist.org/investigations/natural_world

/482479/why_only_the_amazonians_can_save_the_rainforest.html. Retrieved May 16, 2012.

Bueno de Mesquita, Bruce, and Alastair Smith. *The Dictator's Handbook: Why Bad Behavior is Almost Always Good Politics*. New York: PublicAffairs, 2012.

Burkitt, Laurie. "Again? Ferrari Struggles with 'Spin' in China." China Real Time Report (blog), *Wall Street Journal*, June 12, 2012, http://blogs.wsj.com/chinareal time/2012/06/12/again-ferrari-struggles-with-spin-in-china/. Retrieved June 24, 2013.

"BTI 2012: Brazil Country Report." Bertelsmann Stiftung's Transformation Index (BTI), 2012, http://www.bti-project.de/fileadmin/Inhalte/reports/2012/pdf/BTI%22012%20Brazil.pdf. Retrieved August 14, 2012.

Butler, Rhett. "Brazil's Plan to Save the Amazon Rainforest." Mongabay.com, June 2, 2009, http://news.mongabay.com/2009/0602-brazil.html. Retrieved August 11, 2014.

———. "Majority of Brazilians Reject Changes in Amazon Forest Code." Mongabay.com, June 11, 2011, http://news.mongabay.com/2011/0611-amazon_code_poll.html. Retrieved May 29, 2012.

Caldeira, Teresa P. R. *City of Walls: Crime, Segregation, and Citizenship in Sao Paulo*. Oakland: University of California Press, 2000.

———. "Democracy and Enclosed Spaces: From Social Movements to Fortified Enclaves to Hip-Hop in Sao Paulo. Conference Prepared for the Symposium '(In)visible Cities. Spaces of Hope, Spaces of Citizenship.'" Centre de Cultura Contemporània de Barcelona, July 25–27, 2003, http://www.publicspace.org/en/text-library/eng/a015-democracy-and-enclosed-spaces-from-social-move ments-to-fortified-enclaves-to-hip-hop-in-s-o-paulo. Retrieved September 10, 2012.

Callahan, William A. *China Dreams: 20 Visions of the Future*. New York: Oxford University Press, 2013.

Canaves, Sky, and Shai Oster. "Chinese Dialogue on Racism Emerges." *Wall Street Journal*, November 17, 2009, http://online.wsj.com/article/SB125830043530149179.html. Retrieved May 3, 2012.

Canaves, Sky. "Gangster Trials Highlight China's Crime Battle." *Wall Street Journal*, December 30, 2009, http://online.wsj.com/article/SB126204784391808331.html. Retrieved July 26, 2013.

Cao, Liqun, and Steven Stack. "Exploring *Terra Incognita*: Family Values and Prostitution Acceptance in China." *Journal of Criminal Justice* 38, no. 4 (2010): 531–537.

Cao, Shixiong, Li Chen, and Zhande Liu. "An Investigation of Chinese Attitudes toward the Environment: Case Study Using the Grain for Green Project." *Ambio* 38, no. 1 (February 2009): 55–64.

Cárdenas, José R. "With Rousseff's Visit Canceled, Where Do US-Brazil Relations Go from Here?" *Foreign Policy*, September 30, 2013, http://shadow.foreign policy.com/posts/2013/09/20/with_rousseffs_visit_canceled_where_do_us _brazil_relations_go_from_here#sthash.eK5Jywjp.dpbs. Retrieved January 8, 2014.

Cardoso, Fernando Henrique. "More Personal Security, Less Inequality." *Economist*, January 19, 2012, http://www.economist.com/blogs/americasview/2012/01/fern ando-henrique-cardoso-brazils-future-0. Retrieved July 7, 2014.

Cardoso, Fernando L. "Political and Sexual Attitudes Concerning Same-Sex Sexual Behavior." *Sexuality & Culture* 14 (2010): 306–326, http://www.springerlink .com/content/x448102651618813/. Retrieved April 29, 2012.

Carneiro, Julia Dias. "Brazil HIV/Aids Strategy Needs New Focus, Campaigners Say." *BBC News*, July 26, 2012, http://www.bbc.co.uk/news/world-latin-amer ica-18980108. Retrieved August 13, 2012.

Carneiro, Julia. "Brazil Election Candidates Stay Silent on Abortion Issue." *BBC News*, October 2, 2014, http://www.bbc.com/news/world-latin-america-294 41299. Retrieved October 28, 2014.

Carrillo, Beatriz Garcia. "China's Welfare Policies: The Future of Welfare?" *China Express*, issue 2, 2012, http://sydney.edu.au/china_studies_centre/china_ express/issue_2/features/chinas_welfare_policies.shtml. Retrieved July 27, 2013.

Carter, Miguel. "The Landless Rural Workers Movement and Democracy in Brazil." *Latin American Research Review*, October 18, 2010, http://lasa-2.univ.pitt.edu /LARR/prot/fulltext/Vol45noSI/Carter_186–217_45-SI.pdf. Retrieved August 17, 2012.

Carvalho, Georgia O. "Environmental Resistance and the Politics of Energy Development in the Brazilian Amazon." *Journal of Environment and Development* 15, no. 3 (September 2006): 245–268, http://www.whrc.org/resources /publications/pdf/CarvalhoEnvDevt.06.pdf. Retrieved May 23, 2012.

Cavatorta, Francesco. "Civil Society Activism under Authoritarian Constraints." In *Civil Society Activism under Authoritarian Rule: A Comparative Perspective*, edited by Francesco Cavatorta, 1–12. New York: Routledge 2013.

Chan, Aris, and Geoffrey Crothall. "Paying the Price for Economic Development: The Children of Migrant Workers in China." *China Labour Bulletin*, November 2009, http://www.clb.org.hk/en/files/share/File/research_reports/Children_of _Migrant_Workers.pdf. Retrieved July 12, 2013.

Chan, Gerald. "China's Compliance in Global Environmental Affairs." *Asia Pacific Viewpoint* 45, no. 1 (April 2004).

Chan, Gerald, Pak K. Lee, and Lai-Ha Chan. "China's Environmental Governance: the Domestic-International Nexus." *Third World Quarterly* 29, no. 2 (2008): 291–314.

Chan, Kam Wing. "The Chinese Hukou System at 50." *Eurasian Geography and Economics* 50, no. 2 (2009): 197–221.

Chan, Kelvin. "Tiananmen Memory Flickers in Tiny Hong Kong Museum." Associated Press, June 3, 2014, http://hosted.ap.org/dynamic/stories/A/AS _HONG_KONG_TIANANMEN_MUSEUM?SITE=AP&SECTION =HOME&TEMPLATE=DEFAULT Retrieved June 4, 2014.

Chan, Yuen. "Out of the Closet in China." *BBC News*, 13 January 13, 2004, http://news.bbc.co.uk/2/hi/asia-pacific/3389767.stm. Retrieved September 2, 2011.

Chang, Jack. "A Great Divide." *Miami Herald*, June 17, 2007, http://www.miamiherald.com/multimedia/news/afrolatin/part3/. Retrieved July 7, 2014.

Chen, Andrea. "China's Confucius Institute Faces Backlash at Prestigious US School." *South China Morning Post*, May 13, 2014, http://www.scmp.com/news/china-insider/article/1511268/chinas-confucius-institute-faces-backlash-prestigious-us-school. Retrieved June 3, 2014.

Chen, Stephen. "The Famous Mao Slogan that He Never Even Used." *South China Morning Post*, September 25, 2009, http://www.scmp.com/article/693526/famous-mao-slogan-he-never-even-used. Retrieved June 3, 2014.

Chenoweth, Erica. "Creative Non-Violence Can Defeat Repression." *New York Times*, August 20, 2012, http://www.nytimes.com/roomfordebate/2012/08/20/what-makes-protest-effective/creative-nonviolence-can-defeat-repression. Retrieved June 6, 2013.

"Chevron Oil Spill: Brazil Workers Sue Oil Company for Environmental, Financial Damages." Reuters, March 28, 2012, http://www.huffingtonpost.com/2012/03/28/chevron-oil-spill-brazil-lawsuit_n_1385437.html. Retrieved May 24, 2012.

Child, Ben. "China Bans Actors with a History of Drug Use from Film or TV Roles." *Guardian*, October 9, 2014, http://www.theguardian.com/film/2014/oct/09/china-bans-actors-with-history-of-drug-use-prostitution. Retrieved November 3, 2014.

"China Becomes More Urban in Historic Population Shift." *BBC News*, January 17, 2012, http://www.bbc.co.uk/news/world-asia-china-16588851. Retrieved January 17, 2012.

"China: Country Summary." Human Rights Watch, January 2012, http://www.hrw.org/sites/default/files/related_material/china_2012_0.pdf. Retrieved July 3, 2012.

China Internet Network Information Center, *Statistical Report on Internet Development in China*, 2013, http://www1.cnnic.cn/IDR/ReportDownloads/201302/P020130221391269963814.pdf. Retrieved May 22, 2013.

"China: NPC Should Scrap State Secrets, Hukou Laws." Human Rights Watch, March 4, 2010, http://www.hrw.org/news/2010/03/04/china-npc-should-scrap-state-secrets-hukou-laws. Retrieved July 18, 2013.

"China Sentences 16 for Violent Protest against Pollution." Reuters, February 7, 2013, http://www.Reuters.com/article/2013/02/07/us-china-protest-sentences-idUSBRE9160BM20130207. Retrieved January 7, 2014.

"China's Evolving 'Core Interests.'" *New York Times*, May 11, 2013, http://www.nytimes.com/2013/05/12/opinion/sunday/chinas-evolving-core-interests.html. Retrieved June 17, 2014.

"China's Politics and Actions for Addressing Climate Change." *Xinhua*, November 22, 2011, http://news.xinhuanet.com/english2010/china/2011–11/22/c_131262368.htm. Retrieved February 6, 2014.

"China's Urban Population Exceeds Countryside for the First Time." Bloomberg, January 17, 2012, http://www.bloomberg.com/news/articles/2012–01–17/china -urban-population-exceeds-rural. Retrieved May 22, 2013.

"China Takes Dispute with Vietnam to UN." Associated Press, June 9, 2014, http:// www.washingtonpost.com/world/asia_pacific/china-takes-dispute-with -vietnam-to-un/2014/06/09/6f987dac-f020–11e3-ba99–4469323d5076_story .html. Retrieved June 16, 2014.

"China to Build School in Contested Paracel Islands." BBC News, June 15, 2014, http://www.bbc.com/news/world-asia-27856082. Retrieved June 17, 2014.

"China to Move 20,000 People at Risk from Three Gorges Landslides." Reuters, April 18, 2012, http://www.reuters.com/article/2012/04/18/china-hydropower -idUSL3E8FI45720120418. Retrieved April 18, 2012.

"Chinese Anger Over Pollution Becomes Main Cause of Social Unrest." Bloomberg, March 6, 2013, http://www.bloomberg.com/news/2013–03–06/pollution-passes -land-grievances-as-main-spark-of-china-protests.html. Retrieved January 7, 2014.

Choi, Susanne Y. P. "State Control, Female Prostitution and HIV Prevention in China." China Quarterly 205 (March 2011): 96–114.

Chu, Samuel C., and Kwang-Ching Liu. Li Hung-chang and China's Early Modern-ization. Armonk: M.E. Sharpe, 1994.

Chua, Lynette J. "Pragmatic Resistance, law, and Social Movements in Authoritarian States: The Case of Gay Collective Action in Singapore." Law & Society Review 46, no. 4 (2012), http://onlinelibrary.wiley.com/doi/10.1111 /j.1540–5893.2012.00515.x/abstract. Retrieved June 16, 2013.

"Classification by Installed Capacity with Energy." International Commission on Large Dams, 2014, http://www.icold-cigb.org/gb/world_register/general_ synthesis.asp?IDA=213. Retrieved June 17, 2014.

Cohen, David. "China's Factional Politics." Diplomat, December 8, 2012, http:// thediplomat.com/2012/12/chinas-factional-politics/. Retrieved May 6, 2014.

Coleman, Robin R. Means. "All Around the World Same Song: Blackness, Racism and Popular Culture in China." Journal of Media Sociology 1, no. 1/2 (Winter /Spring 2009): 5–21.

Collier, David. "The Comparative Method." In Political Science: The State of the Discipline II, edited by Ada W. Finifter, 105–119. Washington, DC: American Political Science Association, 1993.

Colitt, Raymond. "Focus on Brazil's Poor Helps Rousseff's Reelection Chances." Bloomberg Business, January 22, 2014, http://www.bloomberg.com/bw/articles /2014–01–02/brazil-presidents-reelection-chances-social-programs-help. Retrieved April 14, 2015.

Coonan, Clifford. "China's First Cultural Revolution Museum Exposes Mao's War on 'Bourgeois Culture.'" Independent, February 21, 2006, http://www.indepen-dent.co.uk/news/world/asia/chinas-first-cultural-revolution-museum-exposes-maos-war-on-bourgeois-culture-467265.html. Retrieved June 3, 2014.

Cooper, Helene. "During Hagel Visit, China Showed Its Military Might, and Its Frustrations." New York Times, April 10, 2014, http://www.nytimes.com/

2014/04/11/world/asia/during-hagel-visit-china-showed-its-military-might-and
-its-frustrations.html. Retrieved June 14, 2014.

Costa, Claudia. "Brazilian Workers Buck Union Officials to Strike." *Labor Notes*,
June 23, 2014, http://labornotes.org/2014/06/brazilian-workers-buck-union
-officials-strike. Retrieved October 22, 2014.

Cost of Pollution in China: Economic Estimates of Physical Damages, World Bank,
February 1, 2007, http://documents.worldbank.org/curated/en/2007/02/750
3894/cost-pollution-china-economic-estimates-physical-damages. Retrieved
July 3, 2012.

"Country Summary: China." Human Rights Watch, January 2012, http://www.hrw
.org/sites/default/files/related_material/china_2012_0.pdf. Retrieved July 5,
2013.

Covin, David. *The Unified Black Movement in Brazil, 1978–2002*. Jefferson, NC:
McFarland and Co., 2006.

Crago, Anna-Louise. "Our Lives Matter: Sex Workers Unite for Health and Rights."
Open Society Institute, August 2008, http://www.soros.org/initiatives/health
/focus/sharp/articles_publications/publications/ourlivesmatter_20080724.
Retrieved April 27, 2012.

Creamer, Robert. "Reducing Income Inequality Is the Key to Economic Growth."
Huffington Post, July 30, 2012, http://www.huffingtonpost.com/robert-creamer
/reducing-income-inequalit_b_1414602.html. Retrieved August 15, 2012.

Croix, Sarah de Sainte. "Murder Rates Doubled Since 1980: Daily." *Rio Times*,
December 15, 2011, http://riotimesonline.com/brazil-news/rio-politics/brazil
-murder-rates-doubled-since-1980/. Retrieved September 18, 2012.

———. 2012a. "Brazil Strives for Economic Equality." *Rio Times*. February 7, 2012,
http://riotimesonline.com/brazil-news/rio-business/brazil-strives-for-economic
-equality/. Retrieved August 15, 2012.

———. 2012b. "Guanabara Bay Cleanup Plan Launched." *Rio Times*, April 23,
2012, http://riotimesonline.com/brazil-news/front-page/guanabara-bay-clean
up-plan-launched-rio/. Retrieved May 29, 2012.

Custer, Charles. "China's Missing Children." *Foreign Policy*, October 10, 2011,
http://www.foreignpolicy.com/articles/2011/10/06/china_missing_children.
Retrieved October 12, 2011.

———. "Kidnapped and Sold: Inside the Dark World of Child Trafficking in
China." *Atlantic*, July 25, 2013, http://www.theatlantic.com/china/archive
/2013/07/kidnapped-and-sold-inside-the-dark-world-of-child-trafficking-in
-china/278107/. Retrieved July 25, 2013.

Daflon, Veronica Toste. "Lula's Approach to Affirmative Action and Race."
NACLA Report on the Americas 44, no. 2 (March/April 2011): 34–40, https://
nacla.org/article/lula%E2%80%99s-approach-affirmative-action-and-race.
Retrieved March 29, 2012.

Dagnino, Evelina. "We All Have Rights, but . . . Contesting Concepts of Citizenship
in Brazil." In *Inclusive Citizenship: Meanings and Expression*, edited by Naila
Kabeer and Ramya Subrahmanian, 149–163. London: Zed, 2005.

Dahl, Robert. *Democracy and Its Critics*. New Haven: Yale University Press, 1989.

Dalmia, Shikha. "Chinese Environmentalism: Prestige over People?" *Forbes*, June 9, 2010, http://www.forbes.com/2010/06/09/china-pollution-democracy-opinions-columnists-shikha-dalmia.html. Retrieved May 10, 2012.

Daly, John. "Despite Booming Economy, Brazilians Rally against Amazonian Dam." OilPrice.com, October 31, 2011, http://oilprice.com/Alternative-Energy/Hydroelectric/Despite-Booming-Economy-Brazilians-Rally-Against-Amazonian-Dam.html. Retrieved June 11, 2012.

da Motta, Ronaldo Seroa. "Environmental Sustainability in Trade: Evaluation of the Potential Industrial Environmental Impacts of the FTAA." Organization of American States, November 2003, http://www.oas.org/dsd/fida/publications/BrazilFTAA.pdf. Retrieved June 11, 2012.

Daniel, G. Reginald. *Race and Multiraciality in Brazil and the United States: Converging Paths?* University Park, PA: Penn State University Press, 2006.

da Silva, Patricia Pereira, and Franklin Daniel Rothman. "Press Representation of Social Movements: Brazilian Resistance to the Candonga Hydroelectric Dam." *Journal of Latin American Studies* 43 (2011): 725–754, http://www.epjap.org/action/displayAbstract?fromPage=online&aid=8444013. Retrieved May 24, 2012.

"Data: Internet Users." World Bank, 2015, http://data.worldbank.org/indicator/IT.NET.USER.P2. Retrieved September 18, 2015.

Dávila, Jerry. "World Cup Protests Signal Democratic Progress in Brazil." *Huffington Post*, June 13, 2014, http://www.huffingtonpost.com/jerry-davila/world-cup-protests-signal_b_5491968.html. Retrieved June 20, 2014.

"Death Penalty Splits Views in Brazil." Angus Reid Public Opinion, April 12, 2008, http://www.angus-reid.com/polls/31491/death_penalty_splits_views_in_brazil/. Retrieved August 12, 2013.

"Death Sentence over Inner Mongolia Herder Killing." *BBC News*, June 8, 2011, http://www.bbc.co.uk/news/world-asia-pacific-13697612. Retrieved January 9, 2014.

"Defesanet." International Institute for Strategic Studies, September 2, 2011, http://www.defesanet.com.br/toa/noticia/2615/IISS—-Brazil-s-porous-jungle-borders/. Retrieved December 16, 2013.

de la Dehesa, Rafael. *Queering the Public Sphere in Mexico and Brazil: Sexual Rights Movements in Emerging Democracies*. Durham, NC: Duke University Press, 2010.

Demick, Barbara. "How China Kept Lid on Ramadan." *Los Angeles Times*, September 11, 2011, http://articles.latimes.com/2011/sep/11/world/la-fg-china-muslims-20110912. Retrieved January 17, 2012.

Denyer, Simon. "Chinese Families Still at Mercy of Officials Despite Announced Easing of One-child Policy." *Washington Post*, November 22, 2012, http://www.washingtonpost.com/world/chinese-families-still-at-mercy-of-officials-despite-easing-of-one-child-policy/2013/11/21/f5a6db22-5215-11e3-9ee6-2580086d8254_story.html. Retrieved May 14, 2014.

de Oliveira, Jose Antonio Puppim. "Understanding Organizational and Institutional Changes for Management of Environmental Affairs in the Brazilian Petroleum

Sector." *Utilities Policy* 11 (2003): 113–121, http://www.sciencedirect.com
/science/article/pii/S095717870300033X. Retrieved May 21, 2012.

Deomampo, Daisy. "Gender, Sexuality, and AIDS in Brazil: Transformative
Approaches to HIV Prevention." *New Directions in Medical Anthropology* 17,
no. 1 (2008), http://quod.lib.umich.edu/m/mdia/0522508.0017.107?rgn=main;
view=fulltext. Retrieved August 6, 2012.

de Onis, Juan. "Brazil's Big Moment: A South American Giant Wakes Up." *Foreign
Affairs*, November/December 2008, http://www.foreignaffairs.com/articles
/64610/juan-de-onis/brazils-big-moment. Retrieved June 24, 2014.

Diacon, Todd A. "Peasants, Prophets, and the Power of a Millenarian Vision in
Twentieth-Century Brazil." *Comparative Studies in Society and History* 32, no. 3
(July 1990): 488–514, http://www.jstor.org/over/10.2307/179063?uid=373984
0&uid=2129&uid=2&uid=70&uid=4&uid=3739256&sid=21100897796791.
Retrieved July 5, 2012.

Diamond, Larry. *Developing Democracy: Toward Consolidation*. Baltimore: Johns
Hopkins University Press, 1999.

———. *The Spirit of Democracy: The Struggle to Build Free Societies throughout the
World*. New York: Times Books, 2008.

———. "Chasing Away the Democracy Blues." *Foreign Policy*, October 24, 2014,
http://www.foreignpolicy.com/articles/2014/10/24/chasing_away_the_demo
cracy_blues. Retrieved October 27, 2014.

Diamond, Larry, and Marc F. Plattner. "Introduction." In *The Global Resurgence of
Democracy*, edited by Larry Diamond and Marc F. Plattner, ix-xxvi. Baltimore:
Johns Hopkins University Press, 1993.

Diamond, Sara, and Christian Poirier. "Brazil's Native Peoples and the Belo Monte
Dam: A Case Study." *NACLA Report on the Americas* 43, no. 5 (September
/October 2010): 25–70, https://nacla.org/article/brazil%E2%80%99s-native
-peoples-and-belo-monte-dam-case-study. Retrieved May 23, 2012.

Dikötter, Frank. 2010a. *Mao's Great Famine: The History of China's Most Devastating
Catastrophe, 1958–1962*. New York: Walker and Company.

———. 2010b. "Mao's Great Leap to Famine." *New York Times / International Herald
Tribune*, December 15, 2010, http://www.nytimes.com/2010/12/16/opinion
/16iht-eddikotter16.html Retrieved June 2, 2014.

Dip, Andrea. "Brazil World Cup: Forced Evictions Violate Residents' Rights."
Publica, June 28, 2012, http://www.huffingtonpost.com/2012/06/28/brazil
-world-cup-forced-evictions_n_1631885.html. Retrieved May 29, 2013.

Doran, D'Arcy. "Reality TV Show Exposes Racism in China." *Telegraph*, November
13, 2009, http://www.telegraph.co.uk/expat/expatnews/6560168/Reality-TV
-show-exposes-racism-in-China.html. Retrieved May 3, 2012.

Downie, Andrew. "Abortion Debate Heats up Brazil Election." *Christian Science
Monitor*, October 15, 2010, http://www.csmonitor.com/World/Americas
/2010/1015/Abortion-debate-heats-up-Brazil-election. Retrieved May 5,
2014.

Eakin, Marshall. *Brazil: The Once and Future Country*. New York: St. Martins, 1998.

"Economies of Emerging Markets Better Rated During Difficult Times." Pew Research Center, May 23, 2013, http://www.pewglobal.org/2013/05/23/econo mies-of-emerging-markets-better-rated-during-difficult-times/. Retrieved September 19, 2015.

Economy, Elizabeth. "A Land Grab Epidemic: China's Wonderful World of Wukans." *Asia Unbound: Council on Foreign Relations*, February 7, 2012, http://blogs.cfr .org/asia/2012/02/07/a-land-grab-epidemic-chinas-wonderful-world-of-wukans /. Retrieved May 10, 2012.

Eimer, David. "China's Divorce Rule Dubbed 'Law that Makes Men Laugh and Women Cry.'" *Telegraph*, October 30, 2011, http://www.telegraph.co.uk/news /worldnews/asia/afghanistan/8857708/Chinas-divorce-rule-dubbed-Law-that -makes-men-laugh-and-women-cry.html. Retrieved February 24, 2012.

Eisenhammer, Stephen. "Mega-Events May Get Less Ambitious as Brazil Counts World Cup Costs." Reuters, June 13, 2014, http://www.Reuters.com/article /2014/06/13/us-brazil-worldcup-megaevents-analysis-idUSKBN0EO0CJ2014 0613. Retrieved July 14, 2014.

Ekiert, Grzegorz, and Jan Kuik. "Contentious Politics in New Democracies: East Germany, Hungary, Poland, and Slovakia." *World Politics* 50 (July 1998): 547–581, https://muse.jhu.edu/login?auth=0&type=summary&url=/journals /world_politics/v050/50.4ekiert.html. Retrieved May 11, 2015.

Ekstrom, Karin, and Leonardo Miguel Alles. "Brazilian Foreign Policy under Lula: From Non-Intervention to Non-Indifference." *Political Perspectives* 6, no. 2 (2012): 9–29.

Ellerbeck, Alexandra. "Little Change 10 Years After Sister Dorothy Stang Died Fighting For Brazil's Landless." *Huffington Post*, February 15, 2015, http://www .huffingtonpost.com/2015/02/15/sister-dorothy-stang-brazil_n_6679360.html . Retrieved May 10, 2015.

Elvin, Mark. *The Retreat of the Elephants: An Environmental History of China*. New Haven: Yale University Press, 2004.

"Emerging and Developing Economies Much More Optimistic than Rich Countries about the Future." Pew Research Center, October 9, 2014, http://www.pew global.org/2014/10/09/emerging-and-developing-economies-much-more -optimistic-than-rich-countries-about-the-future/. Retrieved April 12, 2015.

Encarnación, Omar. "A Gay Rights Revolution in Latin America." *Americas Quarterly*, May 17, 2011, http://americasquarterly.org/node/2534. Retrieved April 24, 2012.

"Environmental Activists Being Killed in Increasing Numbers, Global Witness Rights Group Warns." *Associated Press*, April 14, 2015, http://www.cbsnews .com/news/environmental-activists-killed-in-increasing-numbers-global -witness-group-warns/. Retrieved September 21, 2015.

"Environmental Issues." Pew Research Global Attitudes Project, June 17, 2010, http://www.pewglobal.org/2010/06/17/chapter-8-environmental-issues-2/. Retrieved June 24, 2014.

Erickson, Ingrid. "Reproduction and Perpetuation of Social Inequality in Brazil: A Study of Civil Society Organizations in Rio de Janeiro and Salvador." Ph.D.

diss., University of Florida, May 2011, http://www.brasa.org/_sitemason/files
/c9d5ok/Ingrid%20Erickson.pdf. Retrieved September 23, 2012.

Errera, Alexandre. "Watch Out: Chinese Contemporary Art is Going Global." *Forbes,*
January 7, 2014, http://www.forbes.com/sites/alexandreerrera/2014/01/07
/chinese-contemporary-art-goes-global-and-for-real/. Retrieved June 17, 2014.

Etim, Bassey. "Reuters Debate Brazil's Protests." *New York Times,* June 19, 2013, http://
thelede.blogs.nytimes.com/author/bassey-etim/. Retrieved August 14, 2013.

Evans, Peter. "Government Action, Social Capital, and Development: Reviewing
the Evidence on Synergy." In *State-Society Synergy: Government and Social
Capital in Development,* edited by Peter Evans, 178–215. UC Berkeley: GAIA
Research Series, January 1, 1997, http://www.escholarship.org/uc/item/8mp
05335#page-184. Retrieved June 6, 2013.

———. *Livable Cities? Urban Struggles for Livelihood and Sustainability.* Oakland:
University of California Press, 2002.

Evans, Peter B., Harold K. Jacobson, and Robert D. Putnam, eds. *Double-Edged
Diplomacy: International Bargaining and Domestic Politics.* Berkeley: University
of California, 1993.

Fallows, James. *China Airborne.* New York: Pantheon, 2012.

Feigenbaum, Evan A. "Who Will Win as China's Economy Changes?" Council
on Foreign Relations, July 24, 2011, http://www.cfr.org/china/win-chinas-
economy-changes/p25531. Retrieved July 25, 2011.

Fellet, Joao. "Indigenous Brazilians Use Web to Fight for Rights." *BBC News,* June
5, 2013, http://www.bbc.co.uk/news/world-latin-america-22787583. Retrieved
June 6, 2013.

Feng, Vicky. "It's the Police's Job to Beat People, Chinese Official Says in Viral
Video." *South China Morning Post,* July 2, 2013, http://www.scmp.com/print
/news/china/article/1273782/its-polices-job-beat-people-chinese-official-says
-viral-video. Retrieved July 26, 2013.

Fernandes, Bernardo Mancano. "The MST and Agrarian Reform in Brazil." *Socialism
and Democracy Online* 23, no. 3 (2009): 90–99, http://sdonline.org/51/the-mst
-and-agrarian-reform-in-brazil/.

"Fernando Henrique Cardoso on Brazil's Future." *Economist,* January 19, 2012,
http://www.economist.com/blogs/americasview/2012/01/fernando-henrique
-cardoso-brazils-future-0. Retrieved June 28, 2012.

Ferreira, Leila da Costa, and Sergio B. F. Tavolaro. "Environmental Concerns in
Contemporary Brazil: An Insight into Some Theoretical and Societal Backgrounds (1970s-1990s)." *International Journal of Politics, Culture and Society* 19
(2008): 161–177, http://www.springerlink.com/content/d162185w32l51x84/.
Retrieved May 16, 2012.

Fewsmith, Joseph. "Rethinking the Role of the CCP: Explicating Jiang Zemin's
Party Anniversary Speech." *China Leadership Monitor* 1, no. 2 (2002).

Fijalkowski, Lukasz, "China's 'Soft Power' in Africa?" *Journal of Contemporary
African Studies* 29, no. 2 (April 2011): 223–232, http://www.tandfonline.
com/doi/abs/10.1080/02589001.2011.555197?journalCode=cjca20#preview.
Retrieved June 23, 2013.

Filho, Paulo Coelho. "Truth Commission in Brazil: Individualizing Amnesty, Revealing the Truth." *Yale Review of International Studies*, February 2012, http://yris.yira.org/essays/440. Retrieved August 27, 2013.

Fincher, Leta Hong. *Leftover Women: The Resurgence of Gender Inequality in China.* New York: Zed Books, 2014.

"Findings from Landesa's Survey of Rural China Published." Landesa Rural Development Institute, February 6, 2012, http://www.landesa.org/news/6th-china-survey/. Retrieved May 10, 2012.

Fisher, Max. "Capital Punishment in China." *Atlantic*, September 22, 2011, http://www.theatlantic.com/international/archive/2011/09/capital-punishment-in-china/245520/. Retrieved June 24, 2013.

———. "China's Tight-Rope Walk: Balancing the Contradictions in Chinese Growth." *Atlantic*, May 4, 2012, http://www.theatlantic.com/international/archive/2012/05/chinas-tight-rope-walk-balancing-the-contradictions-in-chinese-growth/257136/. Retrieved May 15, 2012.

Fiszbein, Ariel, and Norbert Schady. "Conditional Cash Transfers: Reducing Present and Future Poverty." World Bank, 2009, http://siteresources.worldbank.org/INTCCT/Resources/5757608–1234228266004/PRR-CCT_web_noembargo.pdf. Retrieved April 19, 2015.

"Flawed but Fair: Brazil's Health System Reaches Out to Poor." *Bulletin of the World Health Organization* 86, no. 4 (April 2008), http://www.who.int/bulletin/volumes/86/4/08–030408/en/index.html. Retrieved August 20, 2012.

FlorCruz, Jaime. "Divorce Rate Rises in China." *CNN News*, June 18, 2010, http://articles.cnn.com/2010–06–18/world/china.divorces_1_divorce-rate-marriage-law-couples?_s=PM:WORLD. Retrieved February 24, 2012.

Foley, John. "China's Hukou Belongs on History's Scrapheap." Reuters, December 28, 2012, http://blogs.Reuters.com/breakingviews/2012/12/28/chinas-hukou-belongs-on-historys-scrapheap/. Retrieved June 3, 2013.

Foller, Maj-Lis. "The Politics of AIDS: Inclusion and Exclusion in the Brazilian AIDS NGO Politics." *Anales Nueva Época* 13 (2010): 47–90, http://www.gu.se/english/research/publication?publicationId=139491. Retrieved September 20, 2015.

Font, Mauricio A. *Transforming Brazil: A Reform Era in Perspective.* Lanham, MD: Rowman and Littlefield, 2003.

Ford, Peter. "China's 'Para-Police' Brutality under Scrutiny." *Christian Science Monitor*, July 22, 2013, http://www.csmonitor.com/World/Asia-Pacific/2013/0722/China-s-para-police-brutality-under-scrutiny. Retrieved July 26, 2013.

Forero, Juan. "Push to Loosen Abortion Laws in Latin America." *New York Times*, December 3, 2005, http://www.nytimescom/2005/12/03/international/americas/03abortion.html?pagewanted=print. Retrieved July 4, 2012.

———. "In the Hills of Rio, Shantytowns Get a Makeover." NPR, *Morning Edition*, November 1, 2011, http://www.npr.org/2011/11/01/141234680/in-the-hills-of-rio-shantytowns-get-a-makeover. Retrieved September 11, 2012.

———. "Brazil's Oil Euphoria Hits Reality Hard." *Washington Post*, January 6, 2014, http://www.washingtonpost.com/world/brazils-oil-euphoria-hits-reality-hard

/2014/01/05/0d213790–4d4b-11e3-bf60-c1ca136ae14a_story.html. Retrieved April 16, 2015.

Foster, Peter. "Beijing's Hutong Saved after Heritage Groups Campaign." *Telegraph*, September 8, 2010, http://www.telegraph.co.uk/news/worldnews/asia/china /7989545/Beijings-hutong-saved-after-heritage-groups-campaign.html. Retrieved July 18, 2013.

———. "China Suffering from 'Confucian Confusion' Over Sex." *Telegraph*, September 22, 2011, http://www.telegraph.co.uk/news/worldnews/asia/china /8780976/China-suffering-from-Confucian-confusion-over-sex.html. Retrieved September 23, 2011.

Foweraker, Joe, and Todd Landman. *Citizenship Rights and Social Movements: A Comparative and Statistical Analysis*. New York: Oxford University Press, 1997.

Frank, Robert. "Are China's Politicians the Richest in the World?" The Wealth Report (blog), *Wall Street Journal*, February 27, 2012, http://blogs.wsj.com /wealth/2012/02/27/are-chinas-politicians-the-richest-in-the-world/?utm_ source=twitterfeed&utm_medium=twitter. Retrieved February 27, 2012.

Frayssinet, Fabiana. "Brazil: Efforts to Improve Water Quality Falling Short." *Inter Press Service*, August 2, 2011, http://ipsnews.net/news.asp?idnews=56713. Retrieved June 11, 2012.

Fraundorfer, Markus. "Global Solutions from the Tropics. The Brazilian Vision of How to Fight Hunger and Poverty." *Society Breeze*, May 10, 2013, http://www .societybreeze.com/?p=83. Retrieved May 30, 2013.

"Freedom in the World Country Ratings, 1972–2015." Freedom House, https://free domhouse.org/report-types/freedom-world#.VTAP3PPD_cs. Retrieved April 16, 2015.

French, Howard W. "Single Mothers in China Forge a Difficult Path." *New York Times*, April 6, 2008, http://www.nytimes.com/2008/04/06/world/asia/06china .html?pagewanted=all. Retrieved May 4, 2012.

Freyre, Gilberto. *The Masters and the Slaves*. Berkeley: University of California Press, 1933.

———. "Slavery, Monarchy, and Modern Brazil." *Foreign Affairs*, July 1955, http:// www.foreignaffairs.com/articles/71198/gilberto-freyre/slavery-monarchy-and -modern-brazil. Retrieved June 16, 2014.

Friedman, Elisabeth Jay. "Gender, Sexuality and the Latin American Left: Testing the Transformation." *Third World Quarterly* 30, no. 2 (2009): 415–433, http:// www.ingentaconnect.com/content/routledg/ctwq/2009/00000030/00000002 /art00009. Retrieved April 24, 2012.

Friedman, Elisabeth Jay, and Kathryn Hochstetler. "Assessing the Third Transition in Latin American Democratization." *Comparative Politics*, October 2002, http://www.jstor.org/over/10.2307/4146926?uid=2129&uid=2&uid=70&uid=4 &sid=21102359033851. Retrieved June 21, 2013.

Friedman, Lisa. "Brazil Plans a Price on Oil to Accelerate Climate Efforts." *New York Times*, October 25, 2010, http://www.nytimes.com/cwire/2010/10/25/25 climatewire-brazil-plans-a-price-on-oil-to-accelerate-cl-91681.html?page wanted=all. Retrieved May 21, 2012.

Friedman-Rudovsky, Jean. "The Bully from Brazil." *Foreign Policy*, July 20, 2012, http://www.foreignpolicy.com/articles/2012/07/20/the_bully_from_brazil. Retrieved July 7, 2014.

Friedman, Sara L. *Intimate Politics: Marriage, the Market, and State Power in Southeastern China*, Harvard East Asian Monographs 265, Harvard University Asia Center. Cambridge, MA: Harvard University Press, 2006.

Friedman, Thomas L. 2009a. "Our One-Party Democracy." *New York Times*, September 8, 2009, http://www.nytimes.com/2009/09/09/opinion/09friedman.html. Retrieved January 9, 2014.

———. 2009b. "Lost There, Felt Here." *New York Times*, November 14, 2009, http://www.nytimes.com/2009/11/15/opinion/15friedman.html. Retrieved June 9, 2012.

———. "Who's Sleeping Now." *New York Times*, January 10, 2010, http://www.nytimes.com/2010/01/10/opinion/10friedman.html. Retrieved May 10, 2012.

———. "Takin' It to the Streets." *New York Times*, June 29, 2013, http://www.nytimes.com/2013/06/30/opinion/sunday/takin-it-to-the-streets.html. Retrieved July 5, 2013.

Fu, Jing. "Urban-Rural Income Gap Widest since Reform." *China Daily*, March 2, 2010, http://www.chinadaily.com.cn/china/2010–03/02/content_9521611.htm. Retrieved July 27, 2013.

Fullilove, Michael. "Do We Really Want China to be a Responsible Stakeholder in Global Affairs?" *Christian Science Monitor*, December 3, 2010, http://www.brookings.edu/research/opinions/2010/12/03-china-fullilove. Retrieved May 9, 2014.

"Full Text of Hu Jintao's Report at 18th Party Congress." *Xinhua*, November 17, 2012, http://news.xinhuanet.com/english/special/18cpcnc/2012–11/17/c_131981259.htm. Retrieved June 17, 2014.

Garcia, John. "Life-Threatening Abortions: A Frequent Practice in Brazil." Council on Hemispheric Affairs, July 2, 2010, http://www.coha.org/life-threatening-abortions-a-frequent-practice-in-brazil/. Retrieved April 25, 2012.

Garcia-Navarro, Lourdes. 2013a. "Brazilians Keep World Cup Hopes in Check Amid Complications." NPR, *Morning Edition*, April 30, 2013, http://www.npr.org/2013/04/30/179879540/brazil-seeks-to-avoid-own-goal-ahead-of-world-cup. Retrieved June 9, 2013.

———. 2013b. "Criminals Fleeing Rio Crackdown Set Up Shop in the Suburbs." NPR, *Morning Edition*, June 7, 2013, http://www.npr.org/blogs/parallels/2013/06/07/188688574/criminals-fleeing-rio-crackdown-set-up-shop-in-the-suburbs. Retrieved July 31, 2013.

Gardam, Tim. "Christians in China: Is the Country in Spiritual Crisis?" *BBC News*, September 11, 2011, http://www.bbc.co.uk/news/magazine-14838749. Retrieved September 12, 2011.

Gaspari, Elio. "Let Them Eat Soccer." *New York Times*, June 25, 2013, http://www.nytimes.com/2013/06/26/opinion/let-them-eat-soccer.html. Retrieved July 5, 2013.

Gates, Henry Louis. *Black in Latin America*. New York: NYU Press, 2011.

"Gay Groups Urge Boycott of Movies by Lü Liping and Sun Haiying." *Shanghailist*, June 27, 2011, http://shanghaiist.com/2011/06/27/gay_groups_urge_boycott _of_movies_b.php. Retrieved September 2, 2011.

"GDP Ranking 2014." World Bank, 2015, http://data.worldbank.org/data-catalog /GDP-ranking-table. Retrieved September 19, 2015.

"Gendercide: The War on Baby Girls." *Economist*, March 4, 2010, http://www .economist.com/node/15636231. Retrieved April 16, 2012.

Gewirtz, Paul. "What China Means by 'Rule of Law.'" *New York Times*, October 19, 2014, http://www.nytimes.com/2014/10/20/opinion/what-china-means-by -rule-of-law.html?ref=opinion. Retrieved October 20, 2014.

Gill, Bates, J. Stephen Morrison, and Xiaoqing Lu. "China's Civil Society Organizations: What Future in the Health Sector?" Center for Strategic and International Studies, November 2007, http://csis.org/files/media/csis/pubs /071102_chinacivilsociety.pdf. Retrieved July 5, 2013.

Gilley, Bruce. "Meet the New Mao." *National Interest*, September 28, 2011, http:// nationalinterest.org/commentary/meet-the-new-mao-5953. Accessed June 24, 2014.

"Gini: Out of the Bottle." *Economist*, January 26, 2013, http://www.economist.com /news/china/21570749-gini-out-bottle. Retrieved August 19, 2013.

"The Global Gender Gap Report 2013." World Economic Forum, October 24, 2013, http://www.google.com/l?sa=t&rct=j&q=&esrc=s&source=web&cd=1&ved= 0CB8QFjAA&url=http%3A%2F%2Fwww.weforum.org%2Freports%2Fglobal -gender-gap-report-2013&ei=nLqpU5SwNZahyAStlIHIDA&usg=AFQjCNE GKWto54NMaRnn4bLeNQ_lEQ26ag&sig2=FNtZ5A_kPyFwY0EmiYyk0A &bvm=bv.69620078,d.aWw. Retrieved June 22, 2014.

"Global Brazil and U.S.-Brazil Relations." Council on Foreign Relations, July 12, 2011, http://www.cfr.org/brazil/global-brazil-us-brazil-relations/p25407. Retrieved June 24, 2014.

Göbel, Christian, "Authoritarian Consolidation." *European Political Science* 10 (January 2011): 176–190.

"God's Gift to Brazil?" *BBC News*, November 12, 2009, http://news.bbc.co.uk/2/hi /business/8355343. Retrieved May 22, 2012.

Gómez, Eduardo. "Brazil's European Dream." *Foreign Policy*, March 20, 2012, http:// www.foreignpolicy.com/articles/2012/03/20/brazils_european_dream. Retrieved December 28, 2013.

———. "The Politics of Receptivity and Resistance: How Brazil, India, China, and Russia Strategically Use the International Health Community in Response to HIV/AIDS: A Theory." *Global Health Governance* 3, no. 1 (Fall 2009), http://www.ghgj.org/gomez3.1receptivityandresistance.htm. Retrieved April 8, 2015.

González, Mónica Treviño. "Opportunities and Challenges for the Afro-Brazilian Movement." In *Brazil's New Racial Policies*, edited by Bernd Reiter and Gladys L. Mitchell, 123–128. Boulder, CO: Lynne Rienner, 2010.

Goossaert, Vincent, and David A. Palmer. *The Religious Question in Modern China*. Chicago: University of Chicago Press, 2011.

"Graduate Makes Formal Complaint against Local Government for Hukou Discrimination." *China Labour Bulletin*, May 16, 2013, http://www.clb.org .hk/en/content/graduate-makes-formal-complaint-against-local-government -hukou-discrimination. Retrieved July 12, 2013.

Green, James N. "The Emergence of the Brazilian Gay Liberation Movement, 1977– 1981." *Latin American Perspectives* 21, no. 1 (Winter 1994): 38–55, http://lap .sagepub.com/content/21/1/38.extract. Retrieved April 24, 2012.

"Group Plans More Protests against WCup in Brazil." Fox News, April 5, 2012, http://www.foxnews.com/sports/2012/04/05/group-plans-more-protests-against -wcup-in-brazil/. Retrieved September 11, 2012.

"Growing Concerns in China about Inequality, Corruption." Pew Research Center, Global Attitudes Project, October 16, 2012, http://www.pewglobal.org/2012 /10/16/chapter-1-domestic-issues-and-national-problems/. Retrieved August 12, 2013.

"Guangzhou Land Rally Erupts Amid Key Meeting." *South China Morning Post*, January 18, 2012, http://www.scmp.com/article/990414/guangzhou-land-rally -erupts-amid-key-meeting. Retrieved July 29. 2013.

Guez, Olivier. "The Artful Dodgers of Brazil." *New York Times*, June 10, 2014, http:// www.nytimes.com/2014/06/11/opinion/the-artful-dodgers-of-brazil.html?hp &rref=opinion&_r=0. Retrieved June 13, 2014.

Guidry, John A. "The Struggle to Be Seen: Social Movements and the Public Sphere in Brazil." *International Journal of Politics, Culture, and Society* 16, no. 4 (summer 2003), http://www.jstor.org/over/10.2307/20020183?uid=3739840 &uid=2129&uid=2&uid=70&uid=4&uid=3739256&sid=21101022706403. Retrieved September 4, 2012.

Guijt, Irene. "Rethinking Monitoring in a Complex Messy Partnership in Brazil." *Development in Practice* 20, no. 8 (November 2010), http://www.tandfonline .com/doi/abs/10.1080/09614524.2010.513729#preview. Retrieved June 9, 2012.

Guilhem, Dirce, and Anamaria Ferreira Azevedo. "Brazilian Public Policies for Reproductive Health: Family Planning, Abortion, and Prenatal Care." *Developing World Bioethics* 7, no. 2 (2007): 68–77, http://www.ncbi.nlm.nih .gov/pubmed/17614992. Retrieved April 25, 2012.

Guy, Peters. *Comparative Politics: Theory and Method*. New York: New York University Press, 1998.

Hagopian, Frances. "Paradoxes of Democracy and Citizenship in Brazil." *Latin American Research Review* 46, no. 3 (2011): 216–227, https://muse.jhu.edu /login?auth=0&type=summary&url=/journals/latin_american_research_review /v046/46.3.hagopian.pdf. Retrieved October 31, 2014.

Hakim, Peter. "Two Ways to Go Global." *Foreign Affairs*, January/February 2002, http://www.foreignaffairs.com/articles/57628/peter-hakim/two-ways-to-go -global. Retrieved June 24, 2014.

Hall, Rodney Bruce. *Reducing Armed Violence with NGO Governance*. New York: Routledge, 2014.

Hancock, Tom. "Activist Silenced as China Island Forests Destroyed." *Agence France-Presse*, April 11, 2013.

Harding, Harry. *China's Second Revolution: Reform after Mao*. Washington, DC: Brookings Institution, 1987.

Hargis, Victoria, and John He. "Brazil on the World Stage." *Harvard Political Review*, December 20, 2009, http://hpronline.org/world/brazil-on-the-world-stage/. Retrieved August 15, 2012.

Harvey, Fiona. "Climate Talks: China Calls on Developing Countries to 'Step Up.'" *Guardian*, November 3, 2011, http://www.theguardian.com/environment/2011/nov/03/climate-talks-china-developing-countries. Retrieved February 6, 2014.

Hayes, Anna. "AIDS, Bloodheads and Coverups: the 'ABC' of Henan's AIDS Epidemic." *AQ: Australian Quarterly* 77, no. 3 (2005): 12–16.

Hayford, Charles W. "The Open Door Raj: Chinese-American Cultural Relations 1900–1945." In *Pacific Passage: The Study of American-East Asian Relations on the Eve of the 21st Century*, edited by Warren I. Cohen. New York: Columbia University Press, 1996.

Hayoun, Massoud. "Islam with Chinese Characteristics." *Atlantic*, January 28, 2012, http://www.theatlantic.com/international/archive/2012/01/islam-with-chinese-characteristics/251409/. Retrieved February 15, 2012.

He, Baogang, and Mark E. Warren. "Authoritarian Deliberation: The Deliberative Turn in Chinese Political Development." *Perspectives on Politics* 9, no. 2 (June 2011): 269–289.

Heckenberger, Michael, and Eduardo Góes Neves. "Amazonian Archaeology." *Annual Review of Anthropology* 38 (October 2009): 251–266, http://www.annualreviews.org/doi/abs/10.1146/annurev-anthro-091908-164310. Retrieved July 19, 2012.

Henry, Laura A. "Complaint-making As Political Participation in Contemporary Russia." *Communist and Post-Communist Studies*, September-December 2012, 45 (nos. 3–4) (September-December 2012): 243–254.

———. *Red to Green: Environmental Activism in Post-Soviet Russia*. Ithaca, NY: Cornell University Press, 2010.

Hess, Steve. "Nail-Houses, Land Rights and Frames of Injustice on China's Protest Landscape." *Asian Survey* 50, no. 5 (September 2010): 908–926.

Hildebrandt, Timothy. *Social Organizations and the Authoritarian State in China*. Cambridge: Cambridge University Press, 2013.

Himmelman, Jeff. "A Game of Shark and Minnow." *New York Times*, October 27, 2013, http://www.nytimes.com/newsgraphics/2013/10/27/south-china-sea/. Retrieved June 6, 2014.

Hinchberger, Bill. "Brazilian Sex Workers Don't Mourn, They Organize." Brazilmax.com, October 19, 2005, http://www.brazilmax.com/news.cfm/tborigem/fe_society/id/23. Retrieved April 29, 2012.

———. "Carnaval Is Over." *Foreign Policy*, April 7, 2012, http://www.foreignpolicy. com/articles/2012/04/07/carnaval_is_over. Retrieved August 15, 2012.

Hinsch, Bret. *Passions of the Cut Sleeve: The Male Homosexual Tradition in China.* Berkeley: University of California Press, 1990.

Hirsch, Tim. "Brazil's Carbon Challenge." *World Watch* 22, no. 4 (July/August 2009): 30–35, http://www.worldwatch.org/node/6162. Retrieved May 24, 2012.

"HIV & AIDS in Brazil." *Avert*, 2012, http://www.avert.org/aids-brazil.htm#content Table0. Retrieved May 31, 2013.

Hochstetler, Kathryn. "Brazil as an Emerging Environmental Donor." *Triple Crisis*, April 13, 2012, http://triplecrisis.com/brazil-as-an-emerging-environmental -donor/print/. Retrieved May 24, 2012.

Hoelscher, Kristian. "Politics and Social Violence in Developing Democracies: Theory and Evidence from Brazil." *Political Geography* 44, no. 1 (2015): 29–39, http://www.sciencedirect.com/science/article/pii/S0962629814000742. Retrieved May 12, 2015.

Hochstetler, Kathryn. "Democratizing Pressures from Below? Social Movements in New Brazilian Democracy." Paper presented at the Latin American Studies Association International Congress, Guadalajara, Mexico, April 17–19, 1997, http://lasa.international.pitt.edu/LASA97/hochstetler.pdf. Retrieved September 20, 2015.

———. "After the Boomerang: Environmental Movements and Politics in the La Plata River Basin." *Global Environmental Politics* 2, no. 4 (November 2002): 35–57, http://www.mitpressjournals.org/doi/abs/10.1162/152638002320980614. Retrieved May 31, 2012.

———. "Civil Society in Lula's Brazil." Working Paper CBS-57-04, Centre for Brazilian Studies, University of Oxford, September 11, 2003, http://lac-live .nsms.ox.ac.uk/sites/sias/files/documents/Kathryn%2520Hochstedler%252057 .pdf. Retrieved December 15, 2013.

Hochstetler, Kathryn, and Margaret E. Keck. *Greening Brazil: Environmental Activism in State and Society.* Durham, NC: Duke University Press, 2007.

Hogg, Chris. "China Ends Death Penalty for 13 Economic Crimes." *BBC News*, February 25, 2011, http://www.bbc.co.uk/news/world-asia-pacific-12580504. Retrieved July 26, 2013.

Hood, Johanna. "Between Entitlement and Stigmatization: The Lessons of HIV/ AIDS for China's Medical Reform." In *Unequal China: The Political Economy and Cultural Politics of Inequality*, edited by Wanning Sun and Yingjie Guo, 139–153. New York: Routledge, 2013.

"How to Reduce Poverty: A New Lesson from Brazil for the World?" World Bank, March 22, 2014, http://www.worldbank.org/en/news/feature/2014/03/22 /mundo-sin-pobreza-leccion-brasil-mundo-bolsa-familia. Retrieved April 12, 2015.

Htun, Mala. "From "Racial Democracy" to Affirmative Action: Changing State Policy on Race in Brazil." *Latin American Research Review* 39, no. 1 (February 2004).

————. "Racial Quotas for a "Racial Democracy." *NACLA Report on the Americas* 38, no. 4 (January/February 2005): 20–25, http://news-business.vlex.com/vid /racial-quotas-for-democracy-62245617. Retrieved March 29, 2012.

Hudson, R. "Terrorist and Organized Crime Groups in the Tri-Border Area (TBA) of South America." Federal Research Division, US Library of Congress, 2003, http://www.loc.gov/rr/frd/pdf-files/TerrOrgCrime_TBA.pdf. Retrieved September 15, 2012.

"Human Trafficking, HIV/AIDS, and the Sex Sector: Human Rights for All." Center for Human Rights and Humanitarian Law, October 2010, http://www .genderhealth.org/files/uploads/change/ publications/hivaidsandthesexsector .pdf/. Retrieved April 29, 2012.

Hunter, Jane. *The Gospel of Gentility: American Women Missionaries in Turn-of-the -Century China*. New Haven, CT: Yale University Press, 1989.

Hunter, Wendy. *Eroding Military Influence in Brazil: Politicians against Soldiers*. Chapel Hill: University of North Carolina Press, 1997.

Huntington, Samuel P. *The Third Wave: Democratization in the Late 20th Century*. Norman: University of Oklahoma, 1991.

Hutchings, Graham. *Modern China: A Guide to a Century of Change*. Cambridge, MA: Harvard University Press, 2001.

"In Brief: Fact Sheet." Guttmacher Institute, January 2012, http://www.guttmacher .org/pubs/fb_IAW.html. Retrieved May 3, 2012.

"Inequality-adjusted Human Development Index." *Human Development Report 2014*, United Nations Development Program, 2014, http://hdr.undp.org/en/data. Retrieved April 12, 2015.

"Introduction: Lula's Legacy in Brazil." *NACLA Report*, March 1, 2011, https:// nacla.org/article/introduction-lula%E2%80%99s-legacy-brazil. Retrieved August 14, 2012.

Isacson, Adam. "Rio de Janeiro's Pacification Program." Washington Office on Latin America, January 5, 2011, http://www.wola.org/rio_de_janeiro_s_pacification _program. Retrieved September 5, 2013.

Ituassu, Arthur. "Brazil's Revolution Isn't Leading to a Welfare State." *Guardian*, August 10, 2011, http://www.guardian.co.uk/commentisfree/2011/aug/10 /brazil-democracy-welfare-state. Retrieved June 11, 2012.

Ivanova, Nadya. "China's Dirty Water Leads to Protests, Some Reform." *Circle of Blue*, September 9, 2009, http://www.circleofblue.org/waternews/2009/world /chinas-dirty-water-leads-to-protests-some-reform/. Retrieved July 4, 2012.

Jacobs, Andrew. "China Pushes to End Public Shaming." *New York Times*, July 27, 2010, http://www.nytimes.com/2010/07/28/world/asia/28china.html. Retrieved February 23, 2012.

————. 2011a. "Confucius Statue Vanishes Near Tiananmen Square." *New York Times*, April 22, 2011, http://www.nytimes.com/2011/04/23/world/asia/23 confucius.html. Retrieved February 20, 2014.

————. 2011b. "Village Revolts Over Inequities of Chinese Life." *New York Times*, December 14, 2011, http://www.nytimes.com/2011/12/15/world/asia/chinese

-village-locked-in-rebellion-against-authorities.html?pagewanted=all. Retrieved May 10, 2012.

———. 2013a. "Plans to Harness Chinese River's Power Threaten a Region." *New York Times*, May 4, 2013, http://www.nytimes.com/2013/05/05/world /asia/plans-to-harness-chinas-nu-river-threaten-a-region.html?_r=0. Retrieved May 7, 2013.

———. 2013b. "Reporters for Reuters Won't Receive China Visa." *New York Times*, November 9, 2013, http://www.nytimes.com/2013/11/10/world/asia/reporter -for-Reuters-wont-receive-china-visa.html?_r=0. Retrieved April 21, 2014.

Jacobs, Andrew, and Chris Buckley. "Tales of Army Discord Show Tiananmen Square in a New Light." *New York Times*, June 2, 2014, http://www.nytimes .com/2014/06/03/world/asia/tiananmen-square-25-years-later-details-emerge -of-armys-chaos.html. Retrieved June 4, 2014.

Jaffe, Gabrielle. "Performing *The Vagina Monologues* in China." *Atlantic*, November 29, 2013, http://www.theatlantic.com/china/archive/2013/11/performing-em -the-vagina-monologues-em-in-china/281924/. Retrieved June 12, 2014.

"Japanese Public's Mood Rebounding, Abe Highly Popular." Pew Research Global Attitudes Project, July 11, 2013, http://www.pewglobal.org/2013/07/11 /japanese-publics-mood-rebounding-abe-strongly-popular/ Retrieved June 5, 2014.

Jebsen, Kristian. "Brazil's Surge in Violence against Gays Is Just Getting Worse." *Daily Beast*, April 8, 2012, http://www.thedailybeast.com/articles/2012/04/08 /brazil-s-surge-in-violence-against-gays-is-just-getting-worse.html. Retrieved April 16, 2012.

Jeffrey, Paul. "Brazilian Prostitutes Lobby for Respect." *National Catholic Reporter*, November 14, 1997, http://findarticles.com/p/articles/mi_m1141/is_n4_v34 /ai_20005294/. Retrieved June 14, 2012.

Jeffreys, Elaine. "Exposing Police Corruption and Malfeasance: China's Virgin Prostitute Cases." *China Journal* no. 63 (January 2010): 127–149.

Johnson, Keith. "Dilma's Power Problem." *Foreign Policy*, February 19, 2014, http:// www.foreignpolicy.com/articles/2014/02/19/dilmas_power_problem. Retrieved June 19, 2014.

Jolly, Richard, and Deepayan Basu Ray. "The Human Security Framework and National Human Development Reports." U.N. Development Programme, National Human Development Report Occasional Paper No. 5, May 2006, http://hdr.undp.org/docs/nhdr/thematic_reviews/Human Security_Guidance _Note.pdf. Retrieved September 19, 2015.

Johnson, Ian. "China's Great Uprooting: Moving 250 Million into Cities." *New York Times*, June 15, 2013, http://www.nytimes.com/2013/06/16/world/asia/chinas -great-uprooting-moving-250-million-into-cities.html?pagewanted=all&_r=0. Retrieved July 10, 2013.

Jordan, Lucy. "Brazilians Support *Bolsa Família* Welfare." *Rio Times*, January 15, 2013, http://riotimesonline.com/brazil-news/front-page/brazilians-support-bolsa -familia-welfare/#. Retrieved May 30, 2013.

Joseph, Richard. "Africa: The Rebirth of Political Freedom." In *The Global Resurgence of Democracy*, edited by Larry Diamond and Marc F. Plattner, 307–320. Baltimore: Johns Hopkins University Press, 1993.

Kahn, Joseph. "China's Communist Party Opens Its Doors to Capitalists." *New York Times*, November 4, 2002, http://www.nytimes.com/2002/11/04/international /asia/04CHIN.html. Retrieved May 1, 2014.

———. "In China, a Lake's Champion Imperils Himself." *New York Times*, October 14, 2007, http://www.nytimes.com/2007/10/14/world/asia/14china.html?page wanted=all&_r=0. Retrieved January 28, 2014.

Kaiman, Jonathan. "Razing History: The Tragic Story of a Beijing Neighborhood's Destruction." *Atlantic*, February 9, 2012, http://www.theatlantic.com/interna tional/archive/2012/02/razing-history-the-tragic-story-of-a-beijing-neighbor hoods-destruction/252760/. Retrieved July 28, 2013.

Kao, Ernest. "Guangzhou May Reverse Ban on People with Sexually-transmitted Diseases from Teaching." *South China Morning Post*, May 29, 2013, http://www .scmp.com/news/china/article/1248859/guangzhou-may-reverse-ban-people -sexually-transmitted-diseases-teaching. Retrieved July 5, 2013.

Kapstein, Ethan B. "Is Realism Dead? The Domestic Sources of International Politics." *International Organization*, 49, no. 4 (Autumn 1995): 751–774.

Kasfir, Nelson. "Civil Society, the State and Democracy in Africa." In *Society in Democratization*, edited by Peter Burnett and Peter Calvert, 115–142. Portland, OR: Frank Cass, 2004.

Katzenstein, Peter J. "International Relations and Domestic Structures: Foreign Economic Policies of Advanced Industrialized States." *International Organization* 30, no. 1 (Winter 1976): 1–45.

Keating, Joshua E. "The Bedroom State." *Foreign Policy*, May/June 2012, http://www .foreignpolicy.com/articles/2012/04/23/the_bedroom_state. Retrieved April 23, 2012.

Keck, Margaret. "Social Equity and Environmental Politics in Brazil: Lessons from the Rubber Tappers of Acre." *Comparative Politics* 27, no. 4 (July 1995): 409–424, http://www.jstor.org/stable/10.2307/422227. Retrieved June 8, 2012.

Keck, Zachary. "China's Former Leaders Tell Xi to Halt Anti-Corruption Campaign." *Diplomat*, April 4, 2014, http://thediplomat.com/2014/04/chinas -former-leaders-tell-xi-to-halt-anti-corruption-campaign/. Retrieved May 1, 2014.

Kent, Jo Ling. "Faking Their Way to a Perfect Olympics." *ABC News*, August 12, 2008, http://abcnews.go.com/International/China/story?id=5565191. Retrieved June 17, 2014.

Kepp, Michael. "Digging Deep: Lula Promises Economic Growth. He's Looking at the Amazon to Get It." *CBS Business Library*, April 2004, http://findarticles .com/p/articles/mi_m0BEK/is_4_12/ai_n6013602/pg_2/?tag=content;col1. Retrieved May 16, 2012.

Khazan, Olga. "Brazil's Government Gives Money to Women 'Because They're More Reliable,'" *The Atlantic*, April 8, 2014, http://www.theatlantic.com

/international/archive/2014/04/brazils-government-gives-money-to-women
-because-theyre-more-reliable/360336/. Retrieved April 14, 2015.

Kiernan, Paul, and Rogerio Jelmayer. "Labor Strikes Roil Brazil Ahead of World
Cup." *Wall Street Journal*, May 29, 2014, http://online.wsj.com/articles/labor
-strikes-roil-brazil-ahead-of-world-cup-1401398941. Retrieved October 22,
2014.

Kingstone, Steve. "Amazon Destruction Accelerating." *BBC News*, May 19, 2005,
http://news.bbc.co.uk/2/hi/americas/4561189.stm. Retrieved May 21, 2012.

Kinosian, Sarah. "Brazil's Military Police: Calls for Demilitarization." *InSight Crime*,
September 4, 2013, http://www.insightcrime.org/news-analysis/brazils-military
-police-calls-for-demilitarization. Retrieved September 5, 2013.

Kohrman, Matthew. "Why Am I Not Disabled? Making State Subjects, Making
Statistics in Post-Mao China." In *Disability in Local and Global Worlds*,
edited by Benedicte Instad and Susan Reynolds Whyte, 212–236. Berkeley:
University of California, 2003.

Kolesnikov-Jessop, Sonia. "China's New Rich Turning to High Life at Sea." *New
York Times*, September 20, 2011, http://www.nytimes.com/2011/09/21/business
/global/chinas-new-rich-turning-to-high-life-at-sea.html?pagewanted=all&
_r=0. Retrieved February 27, 2012.

Kristeva, Julia. "Feminism under Pressure in China." *Guardian*, June 21, 2011, http://
www.guardian.co.uk/global/2011/jun/21/comment. Retrieved May 3, 2012.

Kulczyncki, Andrzej. "A Comparative Study of the Determinants of Abortion
Policymaking in Brazil and South America." *Public Policy: Brazil in Comparative Perspective*, November 18–19, 2011, http://eaesp.fgvsp.br/sites/eaesp.fgvsp
.br/files/Kulczycki_Abortion%20Policymaking%20in%20Brazil%20and%20
South%20America.pdf. Retrieved April 25, 2012.

Kupchan, Charles A. "America's Place in the New World." *New York Times*, April 7,
2012, http://www.nytimes.com/2012/04/08/opinion/sunday/americas-place
-in-the-new-world.html?pagewanted=all&_r=0. Retrieved December 16, 2013.

LaFraniere, Sharon, and Alan Cowell. "French and Chinese Leaders Meet to End
Tibet Friction." *New York Times*, April 1, 2009, http://www.nytimes.com/2009
/04/02/world/europe/02france.html. Retrieved June 16, 2014.

Lai, Alexis. "'One Party, Two Coalitions' – China's Factional Politics." CNN, November 8, 2012, http://www.cnn.com/2012/10/23/world/asia/china-political
-factions-primer/. Retrieved May 6, 2014.

Landertinger, Laura. "Brazil's Landless Workers Movement (MST)." Unpublished
paper, York University, July 2009, http://www.yorku.ca/cerlac/documents
/Landertinger.pdf. Retrieved December 15, 2014.

Lang, Chris. "Indonesia Re-enters the Guinness Book of Records for the World's
Fastest Rate of Deforestation." Redd-monitor.org, October 7, 2008, http://www
.redd-monitor.org/2008/10/07/indonesia-re-enters-the-guinness-book-of-records
-for-the-worlds-fastest-rate-of-deforestation/. Retrieved January 29, 2015.

Larson, Christina. "The Green Leap Forward." *Washington Monthly*, July/August
2007, http://www.washingtonmonthly.com/features/2007/0707.Larson.html.
Retrieved May 10, 2012.

———. 2011a. "The Green Leap Forward." *Foreign Policy*, July 19, 2011, http://www
.foreignpolicy.com/articles/2011/07/06/the_green_leap_forward. Retrieved
May 14, 2012.

———. 2011b. "A Once-Polluted Chinese City Is Turning from Gray to Green."
Yale Environment 360, October 17, 2011, http://e360.yale.edu/feature/shenyang
_a_once-polluted_china_city_is_turning_from_gray_to_green/2454/. Retrieved
May 21, 2012.

———. "How to Clean Up China's Environment." *Fast Company: The 100 Most
Creative People in Business 2012*, April 27, 2012, http://www.fastcompany.com
/most-creative-people/2012/ma-jun. Retrieved May 29, 2012.

———. "China Begins to Get Serious about Water Conservation." *The Wilson
Center: China Environment Forum*, January 22, 2014, http://www.scribd.com
/doc/201548961/China-Begins-to-Get-Serious-about-Water-Conservation
Retrieved January 27, 2014.

"Latinobarómetro Report 2011." *Latinobarómetro*, October 28, 2011, http://www
.latinobarometro.org/latino/latinobarometro.jsp. Retrieved August 4, 2014.

"The Latinobarómetro Poll: Listen To Me." *Economist*, November 2, 2013, http://
www.economist.com/news/americas/21588886-slightly-brighter-picture-demo
cracy-not-liberal-freedoms-listen-me. Retrieved May 12, 2014.

Laurence, Caramel. "China at Centre of Illegal Timber Trade." *Guardian*, December
11, 2012, http://www.theguardian.com/environment/2012/dec/11/china-illegal
-logging-deforestation. Retrieved January 9, 2014.

Leal, Pedro Enrique. "Homophobia, Fire and Terror in Brazil." Open Democracy,
October 21, 2014, https://www.opendemocracy.net/pedro-henrique-leal/homo
phobia-fire-and-terror-in-brazil. Retrieved April 16, 2015.

Lee, Cheol-Sung. "Associational Networks and Welfare States in Argentina, Brazil,
South Korea, and Taiwan." *World Politics* 64, no. 3 (July 2012): 507–554,
http://journals.cambridge.org/action/displayAbstract?fromPage=online&aid=
8624681. Retrieved September 11, 2012.

Leland, John. "For Adoptive Parents, Questions without Answers." *New York Times*,
September 16, 2011, http://www.nytimes.com/2011/09/18/nyregion/chinas
-adoption-scandal-sends-chills-through-families-in-united-states.html?page
wanted=all. Retrieved July 25, 2013.

Lester, David. "Suicide and the Chinese Cultural Revolution." *Archives of Suicide
Research* 9, no. 1 (2005): 99–104.

Levin, Dan. "Many in China Can Now Have 2nd Child, But Say No." *New York
Times*, February 25, 2014, http://www.nytimes.com/2014/02/26/world/asia
/many-couples-in-china-will-pass-on-a-new-chance-for-a-second-child.html?
_r=0. Retrieved June 11, 2014.

Levine, Jill. "From the Shadows: China's Growing Tolerance of Transgender Rights."
Atlantic, August 9, 2013, http://www.theatlantic.com/china/archive/2013/08
/from-the-shadows-chinas-growing-tolerance-of-transgender-rights/278540/.
Retrieved June 11, 2014.

Levitsky, Steven, and Lucan A. Way. *Competitive Authoritarianism: Hybrid Regimes
after the Cold War*. New York: Cambridge University Press, 2010.

Levitt, Tom. "Liu Jianqiang: Fighting for Environmental Justice in China." *Ecologist*, May 11, 2012, http://www.theecologist.org/News/news_analysis/1366233 /liu_jianqiang_what_its_like_being_an_enemy_of_the_state_in_china.html. Retrieved May 15, 2012.

Levy, Charmain. "Brazilian Urban Popular Movements: The 1997 Mobilization of the Inner-City Slum Movement in Sao Paulo." *Studies in Political Economy* 85 (Spring 2010), http://www.synergiescanada.org/journals/ont/spe/994. Retrieved September 20, 2012.

Lewis, Charlton. "China's Dam Boom Is an Assault on Its Great Rivers." *Guardian*, November 4, 2013, http://www.theguardian.com/environment/2013/nov/04 /china-dam-hydropower-boom-rivers. Retrieved January 8, 2014.

Lewis, David. "Civil Society and the Authoritarian State: Cooperation, Contestation and Discourse." *Journal of Civil Society* 9, no. 3 (2013): 325–340, http://www .researchgate.net/publication/263247770_Civil_Society_and_the_Authoritarian_State_Cooperation_Contestation_and_Discourse. Retrieved May 12, 2015.

Liang, Wei. "Changing Climate? China's New Interest in Global Climate Change Negotiations." In *China's Environmental Crisis: Domestic and Global Political Impacts and Responses*, edited by Joel Jay Kassiola and Sujian Guo, 61–84. New York: Palgrave Macmillan, 2010.

Lieberthal, Kenneth. *Governing China: From Revolution Through Reform*. 2nd ed. New York: W.W. Norton, 2004.

Li, Hui, Nana Taona Kuo, Hui Liu, Christine Korhonen, Ellenie Pond, Hayouan Guo, Liz Smith, Hui Xue, and Jiangping Sun. "From Spectators to Implementers: Civil Society Organizations Involved in AIDS Programmes in China." *International Journal of Epidemiology* 29, no. 2 (2010): ii 65 – ii 71, http://ije .oxfordjournals.org/content/39/suppl_2/ii65.full. Retrieved July 5, 2013.

Lijphart, Arend. "Comparative Politics and the Comparative Method." *American Political Science Review* 65, no. 3 (September 1971): 682–693.

Lim, Louisa. *People's Republic of Amnesia: Tiananmen Revisited*. New York: Oxford University Press, 2014.

Linz, Juan J. "An Authoritarian Regime: The Case of Spain." In Erik Allardt and Yrjö Littunen (Ed.s), *Cleavages, Ideologies and Party Systems* (Helsinki: Transactions of the Westermark Society, 1964), 291–342. Reprinted in Erik Allardt and Stein Rokkan (Ed.s), *Mass Politics: Studies in Political Sociology* (New York: Free Press, 1970), 374–381.

Linz, Juan J., and Alfred Stepan. *Problems of Democratic Transition and Consolidation: Southern Europe, South America, and Post-Communist Europe*. Baltimore: Johns Hopkins University Press, 1996.

Li, Raymond. "Li Keqiang's Meeting with NGOs Injects New Life into HIV/Aids Fight." *South China Morning Post*, December 2, 2012, http://www.scmp.com /news/china/article/1095245/li-keqiangs-meeting-ngos-injects-new-life-hivaids -fight. Retrieved July 5, 2013.

Liu, Melinda. "Where Poor is a Poor Excuse." *Newsweek*, June 28, 2008, http://www .thedailybeast.com/newsweek/2008/06/28/where-poor-is-a-poor-excuse.html. Retrieved May 10, 2012.

Li, Wei, Melanie Beresford, and Guojun Song. "Market Failure or Governmental Failure? A Study of China's Water Abstraction Policies." *China Quarterly* 208 (December 2011): 951–969.

Logan, Samuel. "Brazil: Ten Years of Viva Rio." *Brazzil*, December 14, 2003, http://www.samuellogan.com/articles/brazil-ten-years-of-viva-rio.html. Retrieved September 19, 2012.

Longman, Jeré. "Success for Brazil, Just Not on the Field." *New York Times*, July 13, 2014, http://www.nytimes.com/2014/07/14/sports/worldcup/world-cup-2014-brazil-was-a-good-host-but-poor-competitor.html?hp&action=click&pgtype=Homepage&version=HpHeadline&module=second-column-region&region=top-news&WT.nav=top-news. Retrieved July 14, 2014.

Lubman, Stanley. "Re-examining Re-education through Labor." China Real Time Report (blog), *Wall Street Journal*, September 11, 2012, http://blogs.wsj.com/chinarealtime/2012/09/11/examining-chinas-re-education-on-labor-camps/. Retrieved July 27, 2013.

Luft, Gal. "China's Pollution Revolution." *Foreign Policy*, December 16, 2013, http://in.Reuters.com/article/2014/01/17/column-russell-china-coal-idINL3N0KR11Y20140117 Retrieved January 23, 2014.

Lu, Horace. "Cross-Dressing Garbage Collector Wins National Sympathy after Fire." *Shanghailist*, January 17, 2012, http://shanghaiist.com/2012/01/17/cross-dress_garbage_collector_wins.php. Retrieved January 17, 2012.

Luoma, Jon R. "China's Reforestation Programs: Big Success or Just an Illusion?" *Yale Environment 360*, January 17, 2012, http://e360.yale.edu/content/print.msp?id=2484. Retrieved May 21, 2012.

Lu, Yiyi. *Non-Governmental Organizations in China: The Rise of Dependent Autonomy.* New York: Routledge, 2009.

Lyons, Charles. "Suicides Spread Through a Brazilian Tribe." *New York Times*, January 2, 2015, http://www.nytimes.com/2015/01/04/opinion/sunday/suicides-spread-through-a-brazilian-tribe.html. Retrieved January 29, 2015.

Macaulay, Fiona. "Civil Society-State Partnerships for the Promotion of Citizen Security in Brazil." *Sur. Revista Internacional de Direitos Humanos* 2, no. 2 (2005), http://www.scielo.br/scielo.php?pid=S1806-64452005000100007&script=sci_arttext&tlng=en. Retrieved September 23, 2012.

Mackey, Robert, and Tom Zeller Jr. "George Soros and the Clean-Energy Economy." *New York Times*, October 14, 2008, http://green.blogs.nytimes.com/2008/10/14/george-soros-on-the-green-energy-economy/. Retrieved May 25, 2012.

Magistad, Mary Kay. "China Past Due: Hukou 'Economic Apartheid.'" Public Radio International, *World*, April 30, 2013, http://www.theworld.org/2013/04/china-past-due-hukou/. Retrieved June 5, 2013.

Makinen, Julie. "China TV Expose on Sex Workers Sparks Angry Backlash." *Los Angeles Times*, February 10, 2014, http://www.latimes.com/world/worldnow/la-fg-wn-china-sex-workers-20140210-story.html. Retrieved June 11, 2014.

Makley, Charlene. "Minzu, Market, and the Mandala: National Exhibitionism and Tibetan Buddhist Revival in Post-Mao China." In *Faiths on Display: Religion,*

Tourism, and the Chinese State, edited by Tim Oakes and Donald S. Sutton, 127–156. Lanham, MD: Rowman and Littlefield, 2010.

Mance, Henry. "Obama Buoys Black LatAm Politics." *BBC News*, September 23, 2008, http://news.bbc.co.uk/2/hi/americas/7596087.stm. Retrieved July 7, 2014.

———. "Acronym Alert: The Eagles Rock," Beyondbrics (blog), November 15, 2010, http://blogs.ft.com/beyond-brics/2010/11/15/acronym-alert-the-eagles-rock/?#axzz2U2xfp43X. Retrieved May 22, 2013.

Martin, Christopher, and Ehren Goossens. "China Solar Boom Erodes Technology Edge Backed by U.S. Loans." *Bloomberg*, November 3, 2011, http://www.bloomberg.com/news/2011-11-03/china-solar-boom-erodes-technology-edge-backed-by-5-5-billion-u-s-loans.html. Retrieved November 3, 2011.

Martine, George, and Gordon McGranahan. "Brazil's Early Urban Transition: What Can It Teach Urbanizing Countries." International Institute for Environment and Development (IIED) and UN Population Fund (UNFPA), 2010, http://www.citiesalliance.org/sites/citiesalliance.org/files/IIED_Brazil%27sEarlyUrbanTransition.pdf. Retrieved September 14, 2013.

Massarani, Luisa. "Brazilians top Biodiversity and Rio+20 Awareness Poll." Science and Development Network, May 23, 2012, http://www.scidev.net/en/agriculture-and-environment/biodiversity/news/brazilians-top-biodiversity-and-rio-20-awareness-poll.html. Retrieved May 29, 2012.

"Mass Evictions at Pinheirinho: Favela Residents Confront Brazil's Development Boom." North American Congress on Latin America, January 27, 2012, https://nacla.org/blog/2012/1/27/mass-evictions-pinheirinho-favela-residents-confront-brazil%E2%80%99s-development-boom. Retrieved September 10, 2012.

"Mass Favela Eviction Highlights Squatters' Fight in Brazil." Pan-American Post (blog), January 24, 2012, http://panamericanpost.blogspot.com/2012/01/mass-favela-eviction-highlights.html. Retrieved September 10, 2012.

McAdam, Doug, Sidney Tarrow, and Charles Tilly. *Dynamics of Contention*. New York: Cambridge University Press, 2001.

———. "Comparative Perspectives on Contentious Politics." In *Comparative Politics: Rationality, Culture, and Structure*, edited by Mark Irving Lichbach and Alan S. Zuckerman, 260–290. New York: Cambridge University Press, 2009.

McCormick, Sabrina. "The Governance of Hydro-Electric Dams in Brazil." *Journal of Latin American Studies* 39, no. 2 (May 2007): 227–261, http://journals.cambridge.org/action/displayAbstract?fromPage=online&aid=1005116. Retrieved May 23, 2012.

———. "Damming the Amazon: Local Movements and Transnational Struggles over Water." *Society and Natural Resources* 24 (2011): 34–48, http://www.tandfonline.com/doi/abs/10.1080/08941920903278129?journalCode=usnr20#preview. Retrieved May 23, 2012.

McGivering, Jill. "Sex Is Prime Cause of China's HIV." *BBC News*, August 20, 2007, http://news.bbc.co.uk/2/hi/6954859.stm. Retrieved July 27, 2013.

McGregor, James. *One Billion Customers: Lessons from the Front Lines of Doing Business in China*. New York: Free Press, 2005.

Meisner, Maurice. *Mao's China and After: A History of the People's Republic*. New York: Free Press, 1986.

Mendonca, Patricia. "Decentralization of Social Policies, State and Civil Society Relationships in Brazil: Toward Synergy?" Paper presented at the ISTR 6th International Conference, Toronto, July 11–14, 2004, http://atlas-conferences .com/cgi-bin/abstract/caml-44. Retrieved September 11, 2012.

Meng, Lin. "Debate: Death Penalty," *China Daily*, September 13, 2010, http://www .chinadaily.com.cn/opinion/2010–09/13/content_11291205.htm. Retrieved October 31, 2012.

Merkel, Wolfgang. "Embedded and Defective Democracies." *Democratization* 11, no. 5 (December 2004): 33–58, http://homepage.univie.ac.at/vedran.dzihic /merkel_embedded_democracies_2004.pdf. Retrieved October 31, 2014.

Migdal, Joel. "Researching the State." In *Comparative Politics: Rationality, Culture, and Structure*, edited by Mark Alan Lichbach and Alan S. Zuckerman, 162–192. New York: Cambridge University Press, 2009.

"The Millennium Development Goals Report 2012." United Nations, 2013, http:// www.un.org/millenniumgoals/pdf/MDG%20Report%202012.pdf. Retrieved May 23, 2013.

Milliband, Ed. "The Road from Copenhagen." *Guardian*, December 20, 2009, http:// www.theguardian.com/commentisfree/2009/dec/20/copenhagen-climate -change-accord. Retrieved January 9, 2014.

Minter, Adam. "China's Microbloggers Take on Re-education Camps." *Bloomberg*, August 25, 2012, http://www.bloomberg.com/news/2012–08–15/china-s-micro bloggers-take-on-re-education-camps.html. Retrieved July 27, 2013.

Misse, Michel, and Joana D. Vargas. "Drug Use and Trafficking in Rio de Janeiro: Some Remarks on Harm Reduction Policies." *Vibrant: Virtual Brazilian Anthropology* 7, no. 2 (July-December 2010), http://www.vibrant.org.br/issues /v7n2/michel-misse-and-joana-d-vargas-drug-use-and-trafficking-in-rio-de -janeiro/. Retrieved August 27, 2013.

"Missing Children Spark Outcry." *Radio Free Asia*, May 4, 2009, http://www.rfa.org /english/news/china/missing-05042009111344.html. Retrieved July 29, 2013.

"Model Gisele Slams Church, Asks 'Who's a Virgin?'" Reuters, June 5, 2007, http:// www.Reuters.com/article/2007/06/05/us-brazil-sex-gisele-idUSN05279247200 70605. Retrieved October 28, 2014.

Mollman, Marianne. "Fatal Consequences: Women, Abortion, and Power in Latin America." International Planned Parenthood Foundation, March 13, 2012, http://www.ippfwhr.org/en/blog/fatal-consequences-women-abortion-and -power-latin-america. Retrieved April 29, 2012.

Moody, Andrew, and Lan Lan. "Focusing on Future Urbanization." *China Daily*, March 22, 2010, http://www.chinadaily.com.cn/bizchina/2010–03/22/content _9621374.htm. Retrieved September 13, 2011

Mu Chunshan. "Why the CCP Won't Abandon Mao Zedong Thought." *Diplomat*, November 1, 2012, http://thediplomat.com/2012/11/why-the-ccp-wont- abandon-mao-zeodong-thought/. Retrieved April 21, 2014.

Muello, Peter. "Brazilian Pols Support IMF Deal." Associated Press, August 20, 2002, http://www.apnewsarchive.com/2002/Brazilian-Pols-Support-IMF-Deal/id-c8eae28e84603e61eed388695415010b. Retrieved July 20, 2012.

Mulvenney, Nick. "China Plants Trees to Hold Back Desertification." Reuters, June 17, 2007, http://www.Reuters.com/article/2007/06/18/us-deforestation-china-desert-idUSPEK12318820070618. Retrieved January 29, 2014.

"Murder Mysteries." *Economist*, April 6, 2013, http://www.economist.com/news/china/21575767-official-figures-showing-sharp-drop-chinas-murder-rate-are-misleading-murder-mysteries. Retrieved July 26, 2013.

"Murder Rate among World's Lowest, Most Solved: Report." *Global Times*, February 27, 2013, http://www.globaltimes.cn/content/764415.shtml. Retrieved September 5, 2013.

Murray, Laura R., Jonathan Garcia, Miguel Muñoz-Laboy, and Richard G. Parker. "Strange Bedfellows: The Catholic Church and Brazilian National AIDS Program in the Response to HIV/AIDS in Brazil." *Social Science & Medicine* 72 (2011): 945–952, http://www.ncbi.nlm.nih.gov/pubmed/21324573. Retrieved August 10, 2012.

Nathan, Andrew J. "Authoritarian Resilience." *Journal of Democracy* 14 no. 1 (January 2003): 6–17.

Nauta, Wiebe. "Mobilizing Brazil as Significant Other in the Fight for HIV/AIDS Treatment in South Africa: The Treatment Action Campaign (TAC) and Its Global Allies." *African Engagements* (2011): 133–162, http://booksandjournals.brillonline.com/content/10.1163/ej.9789004209886.i-390.45. Retrieved August 10, 2012.

Ness, Robert. "Thief Map Lets Netizens Fight Crime." Danwei (blog), February 9, 2007, http://www.danwei.org/internet/thief_maps_lets_netizens_fight.php. Retrieved July 11, 2013.

Neuhouser, Kevin. "'If I had Abandoned My Children': Community Mobilization and Commitment to the Identity of Mother in Northeast Brazil." *Social Forces* 77, no. 1 (September 1998): 331–358.

———. *Modern Brazil*. Boston: McGraw-Hill, 1999.

New, William. "Brazil HIV Drug Patent Ruling Allows Generics, Sends Pipeline Process into Doubt." Intellectual Property Watch, March 21, 2012, http://www.ip-watch.org/2012/03/21/brazil-hiv-drug-patent-ruling-allows-generics-sends-pipeline-process-into-doubt/. Retrieved August 10, 2012.

Nie, Jingbao. *Behind the Silence: Chinese Voices on Abortion*. Lanham, MD: Rowman and Littlefield, 2005.

Niemi, R. G., and B. I. Sobieszek. "Political Socialization." *Annual Review of Sociology* 3 (August 1977): 209–233, http://www.annualreviews.org/doi/abs/10.1146/annurev.so.03.080177.001233. Retrieved June 28, 2012.

Nunn, Amy. *The Politics and History of AIDS Treatment in Brazil*. New York: Springer Verlag, 2010.

Nye, Joseph S. "Soft Power." *Foreign Policy* 80 (Autumn 1990): 153–171.

———. "What China and Russia Don't Get About Soft Power." *Foreign Policy* (April 29, 2013), http://www.foreignpolicy.com/articles/2013/04/29/what _china_and_russia_don_t_get_about_soft_power. Retrieved June 21, 2013.

Oakes, Tim, and Donald S. Sutton, eds. *Faiths on Display: Religion, Tourism, and the Chinese State.* Lanham, MD: Rowman and Littlefield, 2010.

O'Brien, Kevin J., and Lianjiang Li. *Rightful Resistance in Rural China.* Cambridge: Cambridge University Press, 2006.

O'Brien, Thomas. "Human (In)Security and Democracy in Central America." *Democracy and Security* 11, no. 1 (March 9, 2015): 44–59.

Ogland, Curtis, and Ana Paula Verona. "Religion and Attitudes toward Abortion and Abortion Policy in Brazil." *Journal for the Scientific Study of Religion* 50, no. 4 (December 2011): 812–821, http://onlinelibrary.wiley.com/doi/10.1111/j.14 68–5906.2011.01602.x/abstract. Retrieved April 25, 2012.

Olesen, Alexa. "Young Women Tied to Abortion Rise in China." Associated Press, January 9, 2011, http://www.msnbc.msn.com/id/40967081/ns/health-womens _health/t/young-women-tied-abortion-rise-china/#.T6nw_8WNmSo. Retrieved April 16, 2012.

O'Neill, Shannon K. "Brazil as an Emerging Power: The View from the United States." Council on Foreign Relations, February 2010, http://www.cfr.org /brazil/brazil-emerging-power-view-united-states/p21503. Retrieved June 19, 2014.

Ortiz, Fabiola. "Brazil: Fight for Gay Rights Making Strides." *Inter Press Service*, August 25, 2011, http://www.ipsnews.net/2011/08/brazil-fight-for-gay-rights -making-strides/. Retrieved June 24, 2014.

———. "Where Law Enforcement Goes Bad." *Inter Press Service*, May 23, 2013, http://www.ipsnews.net/2013/05/where-law-enforcement-goes-bad/. Retrieved May 31, 2013.

Osava, Mario. 2007a. "Rights-Brazil: Homeless Join Month of Protests." *Inter Press Service*, April 25, 2007, http://www.ipsnews.net/2007/04/rights-brazil-home less-join-month-of-protests/. Retrieved September 11, 2012.

———. 2007b. "Brazil: Homeless Take Fate into Their Own Hands." *Inter Press Service*, May 31, 2007, http://www.ipsnews.net/2007/05/brazil-homeless-take -fate-into-their-own-hands/. Retrieved September 11, 2012.

Osnos, Evan. "Meet Dr. Freud." *New Yorker*, January 10, 2011, 54–63.

Ozug, Matt. "Brazil's Effective HIV Prevention Strategies." Public Radio International, January 11, 2010, http://www.pri.org/stories/2010–01–11/brazils-effec tive-hiv-prevention-strategies. Retrieved December 28, 2013.

Pagano, Anna. "The 'Americanization' of Racial Identity in Brazil: Recent Experiments with Affirmative Action in a 'Racial Democracy.'" *Journal of IPS* 5 (Spring 2006), http://www.mixedracestudies.org/wordpress/?tag=ana-pagano. Retrieved March 29, 2012.

Pan, Philip P. "Who Controls the Family? Blind Activist Leads Peasants in Legal Challenge to Abuses of China's Population-Growth Policy." *Washington Post*,

August 27, 2005, http://www.washingtonpost.com/wp-dyn/content/article/2005/08/26/AR2005082601756.html. Retrieved May 2, 2012.

Paquette, Gabriel. "Empire of Exceptions." *History Today* 61, no. 6 (June 2011): 39–46, http://www.historytoday.com/gabriel-paquette/empire-exceptions-making-modern-brazil. Retrieved July 11, 2012.

Parker, Richard G. "Civil Society, Political Mobilization, and the Impact of HIV Scale-up on Health Systems in Brazil." *Journal of Acquired Immune Deficiency Syndrome* 52 (November 2009), http://www.ncbi.nlm.nih.gov/pmc/articles/PMC3157647/. Retrieved August 10, 2012.

Parshley, Lois Farrow. "Why Are Tibetan Monks Setting Themselves on Fire?" *Atlantic*, January 17, 2012, http://www.theatlantic.com/international/archive/2012/01/why-are-tibetan-monks-setting-themselves-on-fire/251342/. Retrieved January 17, 2012.

Patience, Martin. "China Officials Warns of 300-year Desertification Fight." *BBC News*, January 4, 2011, http://www.bbc.co.uk/news/world-asia-pacific-12112518. Retrieved June 27, 2012.

Peale, John S. *The Love of God in China: Can One Be Both Chinese and Christian?* New York: iUniverse, 2005.

Pearlman, Alex. "Right Groups: One Gay Brazilian Murdered Per Day." *GlobalPost*, April 13, 2012, http://www.globalpost.com/dispatches/globalpost-blogs/rights/one-hate-crime-day-brazils-lgbt-community. Retrieved June 15, 2012.

Pei, Minxin. "China's Income Gap Solution: Too Little, Too Late?" Fortune.cnn.com, February 15, 2013, http://management.fortune.cnn.com/2013/02/15/chinas-income-gap-solution-too-little-too-late/. Retrieved May 22, 2013.

Peixoto, Paulo. "'I Faced Death and Loneliness,' Says Dilma about the Dictatorship." *Folha de S. Paulo*, June 22, 2012, http://www1.folha.uol.com.br/internacional/en/national/1108764-i-faced-death-and-loneliness-says-dilma-about-the-dictatorship.shtml. Retrieved June 28, 2012.

"People in Emerging Markets Catch Up to Advanced Economies in Life Satisfaction." Pew Research Center, October 30, 2014, http://www.pewglobal.org/2014/10/30/people-in-emerging-markets-catch-up-to-advanced-economies-in-life-satisfaction/. Retrieved April 12, 2015.

Perkowski, Jack. "China Leads the World in Renewable Energy Investment." Forbes.com, July 27, 2012, http://www.forbes.com/sites/jackperkowski/2012/07/27/china-leads-the-world-in-renewable-energy-investment/. Retrieved May 8, 2014.

Perruci, Gamaliel. "'Green McWorld versus 'Gold Jihad: The Clash of Ideas in the Brazilian Amazon." *Global Society* 13, no. 2 (1999).

Perry, Elizabeth J. "'Sixty is the New Forty' (Or is it?): Reflections on the Health of the Chinese Body Politic." In *The People's Republic of China at 60: An International Assessment*, edited by William C. Kirby, 133–144. Cambridge, MA: Harvard University Press, 2011.

Philippou, Styliane. "Modernism and National Identity in Brazil, or How to Brew a Brazilian Stew." *National Identities* 7, no. 3 (September 2005): 245–264, http://

www.tandfonline.com/doi/abs/10.1080/14608940500201771?journalCode
=cnid20#preview. Retrieved July 5, 2013.

Phillips, Tom. "Street Gang Spreads Fear across Brazil's Biggest City." *Guardian*,
August 11, 2006, http://www.theguardian.com/world/2006/aug/12/brazil.main
section. Retrieved September 18, 2015.

———. "Poor Brazilians Rejoice as Loggers Return to Pillage the Rainforest."
Guardian, February 14, 2009, http://www.guardian.co.uk/environment/2009
/feb/15/amazon-deforestation-brazil. Retrieved June 1, 2012.

———. 2011a. "Brazilian Census Shows African-Brazilians in the Majority for the
First Time." *Guardian*, November 17, 2011, http://www.guardian.co.uk/world
/2011/nov/17/brazil-census-african-brazilians-majority. Retrieved April 29,
2012.

———. 2011b. "Guns for Goalposts? Fifa Mulls Brazilian Plans for World Cup Disarmament Drive." *Guardian*, December 14, 2011, http://www.guardian.co.uk
/world/2011/dec/14/guns-goalposts-fifa-brazil-disarmament. Retrieved September 19, 2012.

———. "With No Enemies in Sight, Brazil Eyes Defense Boom." *Bloomberg*, March
1, 2012, http://www.bloomberg.com/news/articles/2012–03–01/with-no-ene
mies-in-sight-brazil-eyes-defense-boom-dom-phillips. Retrieved May 14, 2015.

Pierson, David. "Wealth Rises in China with Increasing Social Cost." Money and
Company (blog), *Los Angeles Times*, September 13, 2011, http://latimesblogs
.latimes.com/money_co/2011/09/economic-conditions-around-the-world-may
-be-deteriorating-but-you-couldnt-tell-by-the-headlines-in-chinathe-latest
-list-o.html. Retrieved June 24, 2013.

Pimenta, Cristina, Sonia Correa, Ivia Maksud, Soraya Dominicis, and Jose Miguel
Olivar. "Sexuality and Development: Brazilian National Response to HIV/
AIDS Amongst Sex Workers." Associacão Brasileira Interdisciplinar de
AIDS, 2010, http://www.abiaids.org.br/_img/media/Relatorio%20prost%20
feminina%20INGLES.pdf. Retrieved April 29, 2012.

Pines, Yuri. *Everlasting Empire: The Political Culture of Ancient China and Its Imperial
Legacy*. Princeton, NJ: Princeton University Press, 2012.

Pitanguy, Jacqueline. "Bridging the Local and the Global: Feminism in Brazil and
the International Human Rights Agenda." *Social Research* 69, no. 3 (Fall
2002), http://findarticles.com/p/articles/mi_m2267/is_3_69/ai_94227142/.
Retrieved April 24, 2012.

"Police Pledge to Fight Child Trafficking." *Xinhua*, July 7, 2012, http://news.xin
huanet.com/english/china/2012–07/07/c_131700671.htm. Retrieved July 25,
2012.

Portela, Samantha Rebelo. "Brazil: The Hypersexualization of a Nation." *Pulsa
Merica*. April 3, 2014, http://www.pulsamerica.co.uk/2014/04/03/brazil-the
-hypersexualisation-of-a-nation/. Retrieved August 11, 2014.

Porter, Eduardo. "In Latin America, Growth Trumps Climate." *New York Times*,
December 10, 2014, http://www.nytimes.com/2014/12/10/business/in-latin
-america-growth-trumps-climate.html. Retrieved January 29, 2015.

Pothuraju, Babjee. "Backgrounder: UNASUR and Security in South America." Institute for Defence Studies and Analyses, October 30, 2012, http://idsa.in /backgrounder/UNASURandSecurityinSouthAmerica. Retrieved June 19, 2014.

"Prostitution Crackdown Restores Morality." *China Daily*, February 18, 2014, http:// www.chinadaily.com.cn/china/2014–02/18/content_17290280.htm. Retrieved November 3, 2014.

"Protecting Brazil's Forests: Fiddling While the Amazon Burns." *Economist*, December 3, 2011, http://www.economist.com/node/21541033. Retrieved May 21, 2012.

Przeworski, Adam, and Henry Teune. *The Logic of Comparative Social Inquiry*. New York: Wiley, 1970.

Purdom, Rebecca, and Kelly Nokes. "Brazil Repeals Forest Code and Deforestation Accelerates." *Top Ten Environmental Watch List 2014*, Vermont Law School, 2014, http://watchlist.vermontlaw.edu/brazil-repeals-forest-code-and-deforest ation-accelerates/. Retrieved June 12, 2014.

Putnam, Robert D. "Diplomacy and Domestic Politics: The Logic of Two-Level Games." *International Organization*, 42, no. 3 (Summer 1988): 427–460.

Rajagopalan, Mesha. "China's Debate on the Death Penalty Becomes Increasingly Open." *Christian Science Monitor*, September 28, 2011, http://www.csmonitor .com/World/Asia-Pacific/2011/0928/China-s-debate-on-the-death-penalty -becomes-increasingly-open. Retrieved July 27, 2013.

Ramos, Silvia, and Julita Lemgruber. "Urban Violence, Public Safety Policies and Responses from Civil Society." Social Watch, 2004, http://old.socialwatch.org /en/informesNacionales/408.html. Retrieved September 23, 2012.

Ramzy, Austin. "Heroes of the Environment: Wang Canfa." *Time*, October 17, 2007, http://www.time.com/time/specials/2007/article/0,28804,1663317 _1663320_1669921,00.html. Retrieved July 6, 2012.

———. "Chinese Dissident Bao Tong Speaks Out." *Time*, January 27, 2009, http:// content.time.com/time/world/article/0,8599,1874164,00.html Retrieved June 4, 2014.

Rapoza, Kenneth. "Over A Million People Sign Petition against Brazil's 'Pandora Dam,'" *Forbes*, December 20, 2011, http://www.forbes.com/sites/kenrapoza /2011/12/20/over-a-million-people-sign-petition-against-brazils-pandora-dam/. Retrieved January 1, 2012.

———. "Was Brazil's Belo Monte Dam a Bad Idea?" *Forbes*, March 7, 2014, http:// www.forbes.com/sites/kenrapoza/2014/03/07/was-brazils-belo-monte-dam-a-bad -idea/. Retrieved June 16, 2014.

Ravallion, Martin. "A Comparative Perspective on Poverty Reduction in Brazil, China and India." *World Bank Observer* 26, no. 1 (2011): 71–104.

Recuero, Raquel. "Social Media and Public Sphere: The #VetaDilma Movement and Brazil's Forests." DMLCentral, May 25, 2012, http://dmlcentral.net/blog /raquel-recuero/social-media-and-public-sphere-vetadilma-movement-and -brazils-forests. Retrieved May 31, 2012.

Reiter, Bernd, and Gladys L. Mitchell. "After the Racial Democracy." In *Brazil's New Racial Politics*, edited by Bernd Reiter and Gladys L. Mitchell, 217–225. Boulder, CO: Lynne Rienner, 2010.

"Render unto Caesar." *Economist*, February 11, 2012, http://www.economist.com /node/21547287. Retrieved February 10, 2012 (one day before print).

"Restrictions on AIDS Activists in China." Human Rights Watch, June 14, 2005, http://www.hrw.org/reports/2005/06/14/restrictions-aids-activists-china. Retrieved July 5, 2013.

Reynolds, James. "Olympic Evictions." *BBC News*, July 19, 2008, http://www.bbc .co.uk/blogs/thereporters/jamesreynolds/2008/07/olympic_evictions.html. Retrieved December 13, 2014.

Richardson, Lydia, and Adele Kirsten. "Armed Violence and Poverty in Brazil." Center for International Cooperation and Security, University of Bradford, March 2005, http://www.researchgate.net/publication/27312871_Armed_ violence_and_poverty_in_Brazil_a_case_study_of_Rio_de_Janeiro_and_ assessment_of_Viva_Rio_for_the_Armed_Violence_and_Poverty_Initiative. Retrieved September 18, 2012.

Richburg, Keith B. "Chinese Environmental Activist Faces Prison Sentence for Publishing Books." *Washington Post*, October 12, 2012, http://www.washing tonpost.com/world/chinese-environmental-activist-faces-prison-sentence-for -publishing-books/2012/10/12/86e56f90–145a-11e2–9a39–1f5a7f6fe945_story .html. Retrieved January 8, 2014.

"Rights Activists Share Alternative Nobel." Associated Press, September 30, 2010, http://article.wn.com/view/2010/09/30/Rights_activists_share_Alternative_ Nobel_h/. Retrieved June 11, 2012.

"Rio +20: Behind Brazil's Amazing Success against Hunger and Poverty, Questions Remain." Oxfam, 2012, http://www.oxfam.org/sites/www.oxfam.org/files /oxfam-rioplus20-case-study-brazil-jun2012.pdf. Retrieved May 30, 2013.

Roett, Riordan. *Brazil: Politics in a Patrimonial Society*. Westport, CT: Praeger, 1999.

Roberts, Dexter. "A Courageous Voice for a Greener China." *BusinessWeek*, July 11, 2005, http://www.businessweek.com/stories/2005–07–10/a-courageous-voice -for-a-greener-china. Retrieved May 15, 2012.

———. "China's Income-Inequality Gap Widens Beyond U.S. Levels." *Businessweek*, April 30, 2014, http://www.businessweek.com/articles/2014–04–30/chinas-in come-inequality-gap-widens-beyond-u-dot-s-dot-levels. Accessed June 22, 2014.

Robinson, Kaleigh. "Brazil's Global Warming Agenda." World Resources Institute, March 1, 2010, http://www.wri.org/stories/2010/03/brazils-global-warming -agenda. Retrieved May 31, 2012.

Rohter, Larry. 2005a. "Brazil, Bowing to Protests, Reopens Logging in Amazon." *New York Times*, February 13, 2005, http://query.nytimes.com/gst/fullpage .html?res=9A03E2DF153AF930A25751C0A9639C8B63&pagewanted=all. Retrieved May 21, 2012.

———. 2005b. "Brazil's Lofty Promises After Nun's Killing Prove Hollow." *New York Times*, September 23, 2005, http://www.nytimes.com/2005/09/23

/international/americas/23nun.html?pagewanted=print. Retrieved June 9, 2012.

———. 2005c, "A Record Amazon Drought, and Fear of Even Wider Ills." *New York Times*, December 11, 2005, http://query.nytimes.com/gst/fullpage.html ?res=9D06E0D71131F932A25751C1A9639C8B63&pagewanted=all. Retrieved May 21, 2012.

———. 2007a. "In the Amazon: Conservation or Colonialism?" *New York Times*, July 27, 2007, http://www.nytimes.com/2007/07/27/world/americas/27amazon .html. Retrieved December 16, 2013.

———. 2007b. "Brazil, Alarmed, Reconsiders Policy on Climate Change." *New York Times*, July 31, 2007, http://www.nytimes.com/2007/07/31/world/amer icas/31amazon.html?pagewanted=all. Retrieved May 31, 2012.

———. "Brazilian President's Attempts to Placate Protesters Backfire." *New York Times*, July 14, 2013, http://www.nytimes.com/2013/07/14/world/americas /brazils-leader-is-on-the-defensive-as-attempts-to-placate-protesters-misfire .html?pagewanted=all&_r=0. Retrieved July 31, 2013.

Romero, Simon. "New Fields May Propel Americas to Top of Oil Companies' Lists." *New York Times*, September 20, 2011, http://www.nytimes.com/2011/09/20 /world/americas/recent-discoveries-put-americas-back-in-oil-companies-sights .html. Retrieved May 21, 2012.

———. 2012a. "Slum Dwellers Are Defying Brazil's Grand Design for Olympics." *New York Times*, March 4, 2012, http://www.nytimes.com/2012/03/05/world /americas/brazil-faces-obstacles-in-preparations-for-rio-olympics.html?page wanted=all. Retrieved September 10, 2012.

———. 2012b. "Brazil Bars Oil Workers from Leaving After Spill." *New York Times*, March 18, 2012, http://www.nytimes.com/2012/03/19/business/energy -environment/brazil-bars-17-at-chevron-and-transocean-from-leaving-after -spill.html. Retrieved May 24, 2012.

———. 2012c. "Amid Brazil's Rush to Develop, Workers Resist." *New York Times*, May 5, 2012, http://www.nytimes.com/2012/05/06/world/americas/brazils-rush -to-develop-hydroelectric-power-brings-unrest.html?pagewanted=all. Retrieved June 13, 2012.

———. 2012d. "Brazil: President Vetoes Major Parts of Bill to Open up Forests." *New York Times*, May 25, 2012, http://www.nytimes.com/2012/05/26/world /americas/brazil-president-vetoes-parts-of-bill-to-open-forests.l?module=Searc h&mabReward=relbias%3As%2C[%22RI%3A5%22%2C%22RI%3A14%22]. Retrieved June 24, 2014.

———. 2012e. "Brazil Gains Business and Influence as It Offers Aid and Loans in Africa." *New York Times*, August 7, 2012, http://www.nytimes.com/2012/08/08 /world/americas/brazil-gains-in-reaching-out-to-africa.html. Retrieved June 24, 2014.

———. 2013a. "Brazilian Court Council Removes a Barrier to Same Sex Marriage." *New York Times*, May 14, 2013, http://www.nytimes.com/2013/05/15/world /americas/brazilian-court-council-removes-a-barrier-to-same-sex-marriage .html. Retrieved October 4, 2013.

———. 2013b. "Public Rapes Outrage Brazil, Testing Ideas of Image and Class." *New York Times*, May 24, 2013, http://www.nytimes.com/2013/05/25/world /americas/rapes-in-brazil-spur-class-and-gender-debate.html?pagewanted =all&_r=0. Retrieved June 3, 2013.

———. 2013c. "Protests Widen as Brazilians Chide Leaders." *New York Times*, June 18, 2013, http://www.nytimes.com/2013/06/19/world/americas/brazilian -leaders-brace-for-more-protests.html?pagewanted=all. Retrieved August 14, 2013.

———. 2013d. "Troupe, Taking to YouTube, Tickles Brazil and Ruffles Feathers." *New York Times*, September 1, 2013, http://www.nytimes.com/2013/09/01 /world/americas/on-youtube-comedy-troupe-tickles-brazil- and-ruffles-fea thers.html?pagewanted=all&module=Search&mabReward=relbias%3Aw%2C. Retrieved July 17, 2014.

———. 2013e. "Brazil's Leader Postpones State Visit to Washington over Spying." *New York Times*, September 17, 2013, http://www.nytimes.com/2013/09/18 /world/americas/brazils-leader-postpones-state-visit-to-us.html. Retrieved December 16, 2013.

———. 2013f. "Brazilian Officers Will Face Charges of Torture and Murder." *New York Times*, October 3, 2013, http://www.nytimes.com/2013/10/03/world/amer icas/brazilian-officers-will-be-charged-with-torture-and-murder.html. Retrieved October 3, 2013.

———. "Brazil Releases Report on Past Rights Abuses." *New York Times*, December 10, 2014, http://www.nytimes.com/2014/12/11/world/americas/torture-report -on-brazilian-dictatorship-is-released.html. Retrieved January 29, 2015.

———. 2015a. "'Bullet Caucus' in Brazil Signals Political Shift to the Right." *New York Times*, January 14, 2015, http://www.nytimes.com/2015/01/15/world/amer icas/bullet-caucus-in-brazil-signals-a-shift-to-the-right.html. Retrieved January 29, 2015.

———. 2015b. "Brazilian Protests Return as Scandals Intensify." *New York Times*, April 12, 2015, http://www.nytimes.com/2015/04/13/world/americas/brazilian -protests-return-as-scandals-intensify.html?_r=0. Retrieved April 14, 2015.

Roney, Tyler. "The Shanghai Cooperation Organization: China's NATO?" *The Diplomat*, September 11, 2013, http://thediplomat.com/2013/09/the-shanghai -cooperation-organization-chinas-nato-2/. Retrieved June 7, 2014.

Rosenberg, Adrienne. "The Brazilian Paradox: The Lesbian, Gay, Bisexual, and Transgender Battle for Human Rights." *Digest: Human Rights in Latin America*, 2011, http://www.du.edu/korbel/hrhw/researchdigest/latinamerica2/digest -human%20rights%20in%20latin%20america%20vol%202-brazil.pdf. Retrieved April 19, 2012

Rosato, Sebastian. "The Flawed Logic of Democratic Peace Theory." *American Political Science Review* 97, no. 4 (November 2003): 585–602, http://www.jstor .org.ezproxy.libraries.wright.edu:2048/stable/3593025?&seq=1#page_scan_ tab_contents. Retrieved May 11, 2015.

Rossi, Marina, Pedro Marcondes de Moura, and Talita Bedinelli, "Brazilian Government Makes Concessions to Quell Protests before World Cup." *El País*,

June 10, 2014, http://elpais.com/m/elpais/2014/06/10/inenglish/1402409059
_811070.html. Retrieved October 27, 2014.

Rothkopf, Davis. "The BRICs and What the BRICs Would Be Without China."
Foreign Policy, June 15, 2009, http://rothkopf.foreignpolicy.com/posts/2009/06
/15/the_brics_and_what_the_brics_would_be_without_china. Retrieved June
18, 2012.

Rowlatt, Justin. "Saving the Amazon: Winning the War on Deforestation." *BBC
News*, January 1, 2012, http://www.bbc.co.uk/news/magazine-16295830. Retrieved May 16, 2012.

Rudolf, John Collins. "After Killings, Brazil Vows to Confront Amazon Violence."
New York Times, June 1, 2011, http://green.blogs.nytimes.com/2011/06/01
/after-killings-brazil-vows-to-confront-amazon-violence/. Retrieved June 1,
2012.

Russar, Juliana. "Flashmob for Sao Paulo Mobility Plan." 350.org, November 24,
2011, http://planetsave.com/2011/11/24/flashmob-for-sao-paulo-mobility-plan/.
Retrieved May 31, 2012.

Russell, Clyde. China Moves to Cut Coal Use Look Bearish for Imports, May Not Be."
Reuters, January 17, 2014, http://in.Reuters.com/article/2014/01/17/column
-russell-china-coal-idINL3N0KR11Y20140117. Retrieved January 29, 2014.

Rustow, Dankwart. "Modernization and Comparative Politics: Prospects in Research
and Theory." *Comparative Politics* 1, no. 1 (October 1968): 37–51.

Safreed-Harmon, Kelly. "Human Rights and HIV/AIDS in Brazil." The Body: The
Complete HIV-AIDS Resource, April 2008, http://www.thebody.com/content
/art52667.html. Retrieved August 10, 2012.

"Same-Sex Marriage: Global Comparisons." Council on Foreign Relations, July
31, 2013, http://www.cfr.org/society-and-culture/same-sex-marriage-global-
comparisons/p31177. Retrieved April 16, 2015.

"São Paulo Gay March Urges Action on Homophobia." *Agence France-Presse*, May
4, 2014, http://www.globalpost.com/dispatch/news/afp/140504/sao-paulo-gay
-march-urges-action-homophobia. Retrieved June 20, 2014.

Schedler, Andreas. *The Politics of Uncertainty: Sustaining and Subverting Electoral
Authoritarianism*. New York: Oxford University Press, 2013.

Schiavenza, Matt. "Meet the 'Chengguan': China's Violent, Hated Local Cops."
Atlantic, July 22, 2013, http://www.theatlantic.com/china/archive/2013/07
/meet-the-chengguan-chinas-violent-hated-local-cops/277975/. Retrieved July
27, 2013.

Schmitter, Phillippe C. "Civil Society East and West." In *Consolidating Third World
Democracies: Themes and Perspectives*, edited by Larry Diamond, 239–262.
Baltimore: Johns Hopkins University Press, 1997.

Schmitter, Phillippe C., and Terry Lynn Karl. "What Democracy Is . . . and Is Not."
In *Global Resurgence of Democracy*, edited by Larry Diamond and Marc F.
Plattner, 39–52. Baltimore: Johns Hopkins University Press, 1993.

Scholz, Emme. "Environmental Policy Cooperation among Organized Civil Society,
National Public Actors and International Actors in the Brazilian Amazon."
European Journal of Development Research 17, no. 4 (December 2005): 681–

705, http://www.palgrave-journals.com/ejdr/journal/v17/n4/abs/ejdr200538a .html. Retrieved May 23, 2012.

Schultz, Kirsten. *Tropical Versailles: Empire, Monarchy, and the Portuguese Royal Court in Rio de Janeiro, 1808–1821*. New York: Routledge, 2001.

Schwartz, Stuart B. "Brazil: Ironies of the Colonial Past." *Hispanic American Historical Review* 80, no. 4 (2000), http://www.deepdyve.com/lp/duke-university-press /brazil-ironies-of-the-colonial-past-mVcYXvokBu. Retrieved July 14, 2012.

Seltzer, Sarah. "A Bit of Drama Stirs Attention, Without Anger." *New York Times*, August 20, 2012, http://www.nytimes.com/roomfordebate/2012/08/20/what -makes-protest-effective/a-bit-of-drama-stirs-attention-without-anger. Retrieved June 6, 2013.

Serva, Leão. "An Assault on the Amazon." *New York Times*, November 16, 2011, http://www.nytimes.com/2011/11/17/opinion/an-assault-on-the-amazon.html. Retrieved July 7, 2014.

Shambaugh, David. *China Goes Global: The Partial Power*. New York: Oxford University Press, 2013.

Shallcross, David, and Nana Taona Kuo. "The Expectations and Realties of NGO Registration: A Study of HIV/AIDS Groups in Sichuan and Yunnan." *China Development Brief*, December 12, 2012, http://www.chinadevelopmentbrief.cn /?p=1353. Retrieved July 7, 2013.

Shan, Juan. "Millions of Wives Wed to Gay Men: Expert." *China Daily*, February 3, 2012, http://www.chinadaily.com.cn/china/2012–02/03/content_14528838 .htm. Retrieved May 3, 2012.

Shankland, Alex, and Leonardo Hasenclever. "Indigenous Peoples and the Regulation of REDD+ in Brazil: Beyond the War of the Worlds?" *IDS Bulletin* no. 3 (May 2011), http://onlinelibrary.wiley.com/doi/10.1111/j.1759–5436.2011.00 225.x/abstract. Retrieved June 1, 2012.

Sharma, Ruchir. "Brazil: The Un-China." *Time*, July 18, 2011, http://www.time.com /time/magazine/article/0,9171,2081831,00.html. Retrieved July 5, 2013.

Shifter, Michael. "Brazil's Election Illusion." *Foreign Policy*, October 20, 2014, http:// www.foreignpolicy.com/articles/2014/10/20/brazils_election_illusion_rousseff _neves. Retrieved October 27, 2014.

Shirk, Susan L. *China: Fragile Superpower*. New York: Oxford, 2007.

Sibaja, Marco. "Brazil Vows New Crackdown on Amazon Deforestation." Associated Press, January 25, 2008, http://articles.boston.com/2008–01–25/news/292704 99_1_amazon-deforestation-environment-minister-marina-silva-rain-forest. Retrieved June 20, 2012.

Silk, Richard. "China Weighs Environmental Costs." *Wall Street Journal*, July 23, 2013, http://online.wsj.com/news/articles/SB10001424127887324879504578597462908226052. Retrieved February 6, 2014.

Simões, Solange, and Marlise Matos. "Modern Ideas, Traditional Behaviors, and the Persistence of Gender Inequality in Brazil." *International Journal of Sociology* 38, no. 4 (Winter 2008–2009): 94–110, http://mesharpe.metapress.com/app /home/n.p?referrer=parent&backto=issue,6,8;journal,14,33;linkingpublication results,1:110910,1. Retrieved April 25, 2012.

Simon, Rita J., and Alison Brooks. *Gay and Lesbian Communities the World Over.* Lanham, MD: Lexington Books, 2009.

Skidmore, Thomas E. *Brazil: Five Centuries of Change.* New York: Oxford University Press, 1999.

Skidmore, Thomas E., and Peter H. Smith. *Modern Latin America.* New York: Oxford University Press, 2005.

Skocpol, Theda. *States and Social Revolutions: A Comparative Analysis of France, Russia, and China.* New York: Cambridge University Press, 1979.

"Slavery's Legacy." *Economist*, April 26, 2013, http://www.economist.com/blogs /americasview/2013/04/affirmative-action-brazil. Retrieved June 20, 2014.

Smith, Amy Erica. "Affirmative Action in Brazil." *Americas Quarterly*, October 21, 2010, http://www.americasquarterly.org/node/1939. Retrieved March 23, 2012.

Soares, Gilberta, and Cecilia Sardenberg. "Campaigning for the Right to Legal and Safe Abortion." *IDS Bulletin* 39, no. 3 (July 2008), http://www.mendeley.com /research/campaigning-right-legal-safe-abortion-brazil/. Retrieved April 25, 2012.

"Social Spending in Brazil: The End of Poverty?" *Economist*, February 28, 2013, http://www.economist.com/blogs/americasview/2013/02/social-spending-brazil. Retrieved May 30, 2013.

Sokoloff-Rubin, Emma. "Breaking the Silence in Brazil: The Playwrights Who Came Before the Protesters." *Foreign Affairs*, July 1, 2013, http://www.foreignaffairs .com/articles/139548/emma-sokoloff-rubin/breaking-the-silence-in-brazil. Retrieved January 8, 2014.

Sola, Lourdes. "Brazil: A Spring in Autumn?" International IDEA, July 16, 2013, http://www.idea.int/americas/brazil-spring-in-autumn.cfm. Retrieved May 12, 2014.

Somin, Ilya. "Brazil Forcibly Displaced Thousands of People to Make Way for the World Cup." *Washington Post*, June 18, 2014, http://www.washingtonpost.com /news/volokh-conspiracy/wp/2014/06/18/brazil-forcibly-displaced-thousands -of-people-to-make-way-for-the-world-cup/. Retrieved July 16, 2014.

Souza, Marcelo Lopes de. "Social Movements in the Face of Criminal Power." *City* 13, no. 1 (March 2009), http://1mundoreal.org/wp-content/uploads/2012/03 /Marcelo-Lopes-de-Souza-Social-Movements-in-the-face-of-Criminal-Power -2009.pdf. Retrieved September 20, 2012.

"'Soya King' Wins Golden Chainsaw Award." Greenpeace International, June 19, 2005, http://www.greenpeace.org/international/en/news/features/soya-king -wins-chainsaw/. Retrieved June 11, 2012.

Speelman, Tabitha. "Tiptoeing Out of the Closet: The History and Future of LGBT Rights in China." *Atlantic*, August 21, 2013, http://www.theatlantic.com /china/archive/2013/08/tiptoeing-out-of-the-closet-the-history-and-future-of -lgbt-rights-in-china/278869/. Retrieved November 3, 2014.

Spence, Jonathan D. *The Search for Modern China.* New York: W.W. Norton, 1990.

Stalcup, Travis. "What is Brazil Up to with its Nuclear Policy?" *Georgetown Journal of International Affairs*, October 10, 2012, http://journal.georgetown.edu/2012

/10/10/what-is-brazil-up-to-with-its-nuclear-policy-by-travis-stalcup/. Retrieved June 3, 2013.

Stalley, Phillip. "Can Trade Green China? Participation in the Global Economy and the Environmental Performance of Chinese Firms." *Journal of Contemporary China* 18, no. 61 (September 2009): 567–590.

"Statement by Mr. Liang Heng of the Chinese delegation at the Third Committee of the 68th Session of the General Assembly on Agenda Item 66: Rights of Indigenous Peoples." Permanent Mission of the People's Republic of China to the UN, October 21, 2013, http://www.china-un.org/eng/hyyfy/t1091938.htm, Retrieved June 17, 2014.

Steinberg, David A., and Victor C. Shih. "Interest Group Influence in Authoritarian States: The Political Determinants of Chinese Exchange Rate Policy." *Comparative Political Studies* 45, no. 1 (November 2012): 1405–1434.

Stolte, Christina. "Brazil in Africa: Just another BRICS Country Seeking Resources?" Briefing paper, Chatham House, November 2012, http://www.chathamhouse .org/publications/papers/view/186957. Retrieved June 3, 2013.

"Stop the Belo Monte Monster Dam!" Amazon Watch, n.d., http://amazonwatch.org /take-action/stop-the-belo-monte-monster-dam. Retrieved May 24, 2012.

Stuenkel, Oliver. "Leading the Disenfranchised or Joining the Establishment? India, Brazil, and the UN Security Council." Carta Internacional, March 2010, http://www.postwesternworld.com/2011/08/07/new-article-leading-the-dis enfranchised-or-joining-the-establishment-india-brazil-and-the-un-security -council/. Retrieved June 20, 2014.

Stepan, Alfred. "On the Tasks of a Democratic Opposition." In The Global Resurgence of Democracy, edited by Larry Diamond and Marc F. Plattner, 61–69. Baltimore: Johns Hopkins University Press, 1993.

Stout, Kristie Lu. "China's Great Migration from 'Hukou Hell.'" *CNN News*, February 8, 2013, http://www.cnn.com/2013/02/07/world/asia/china-lu-stout -great-migration. Retrieved June 5, 2013.

"Straight Talk: Brazil and HIV." PBS, *NewsHour*, July 16, 2003, http://www.pbs.org /newshour/bb/health/july-dec03/brazil_7-16.html. Retrieved August 11, 2012.

Strange, Hannah. "Troops Deployed to Contain Brazilian Protests." *Telegraph*, June 19, 2013, http://www.telegraph.co.uk/news/worldnews/southamerica/10129269/ Troops-deployed-to-control-Brazil-protests.html. Retrieved September 14, 2012.

"Street Children of Brazil." *Religion and Ethics Newsweekly*, June 15, 2007, http://www .pbs.org/wnet/religionandethics/2007/06/15/june-15-2007-street-children-of -brazil/3563/. Retrieved August 19, 2013.

"Submission Prepared by Centre on Housing Rights and Evictions (COHRE) for United Nations Committee on Economic, Social and Cultural Rights Concerning Brazil." Centre on Housing Rights and Evictions, April 2008, http:// www2.ohchr.org/english/bodies/cescr/docs/info-ngos/COHRE_BRAZIL.pdf. Retrieved September 11, 2012.

Subramanian, Arvind. "The Inevitable Superpower: Why China's Dominance Is a Sure Thing." *Foreign Affairs* (September/October 2011): 66–78.

"Summary of 2011 17-Province Survey's Findings." Landesa Rural Development Institute, 2012, http://www.landesa.org/china-survey-6/. Retrieved May 10, 2012.

Sun, Yun. "BRICS and China's Aspiration for the New 'International Order.'" Brookings Institution, March 25, 2013, http://www.brookings.edu/blogs/up-front/posts/2013/03/25-xi-jinping-china-brics-sun. Retrieved June 17, 2014.

"Survey of the Ethno-Racial Characteristics of the Population: A Study on the Classification Categories of Color or Race." Instituto Brasileiro de Geografia e Estatística, July 22, 2011, http://www.ibge.gov.br/english/presidencia/noticias/noticia_visualiza.php?id_noticia=1933&id_pagina=1. Retrieved April 18, 2012.

Sweig, Julia E. "A New Global Player." *Foreign Affairs* 89, no. 6 (November/December 2010): 173–184, http://www.foreignaffairs.com/articles/66868/julia-e-sweig/a-new-global-player. Retrieved September 18, 2012.

Swiebel, Joke. "Lesbian, Gay, Bisexual and Transgender Human Rights: The Search for an International Strategy." *Contemporary Politics* 15, no. 1 (March 2009): 19–35, http://www.ingentaconnect.com/content/routledg/ccpo/2009/00000015/00000001/art00002. Retrieved June 16, 2013.

"Tackling Building Energy Waste." *China Daily*, January 19, 2007, http://www.china.org.cn/english/environment/196623.htm. Retrieved May 22, 2012.

Taddeia, Renzo, and Ana Laura Gamboggi. "Gender and the Semiotics of Political Visibility in the Brazilian Northeast." *Social Semiotics* 19, no. 2 (June 2009): 149–164, http://web.ebscohost.com.ezproxy.libraries.wright.edu:2048/ehost/pdfviewer/pdfviewer?vid=3&hid=12&sid=7a80de69-f8bb-4ab7-906e-20000caff4e0%40sessionmgr11. Retrieved July 4, 2012.

Tan, Kenneth. "Blogger-Activist Liumang Yan Turns Prostitute for a Day to Speak Up for Sex Workers." *Shanghailist*, January 16, 2012, http://shanghaiist.com/2012/01/16/bloggeractivist_liumang_yan_turns.php?utm_source=twitterfeed&utm_medium=twitter. Retrieved January 15, 2012.

Tarrow, Sidney. *Power in Movement: Social Movements, Collective Action and Politics.* Cambridge: Cambridge University Press, 1994.

Tatlow, Didi Kirsten. "For China, A New Kind of Feminism." *New York Times,* September 17, 2013, http://www.nytimes.com/2013/09/18/world/asia/for-china-a-new-kind-of-feminism.html?_r=0. Retrieved June 12, 2014.

Tavener, Ben. "Brazil Anti-Corruption Protests Stay Active." *Rio Times*, October 28, 2011, http://riotimesonline.com/brazil-news/front-page/brazil-anti-corruption-protests-stay-active/. Retrieved June 4, 2013.

"Thousands Take Part in Brazil Slut Walks." *Sky News*, May 27, 2012, http://www.skynews.com.au/world/article.aspx?id=754463&vId=. Retrieved May 31, 2012.

"Tibetan Nomads Resist Relocation, Are Stripped of Personal Documents." *Radio Free Asia*, November 7, 2014, http://www.rfa.org/english/news/tibet/resist-11072014165412.html. Retrieved May 9, 2015.

Tiezzi, Shannon. "The Maritime Silk Road v. The String of Pearls." *Diplomat*, February 13, 2014, http://thediplomat.com/2014/02/the-maritime-silk-road-vs-the-string-of-pearls/. Retrieved June 6, 2014.

Tilly, Charles, and Tarrow, Sidney. *Contentious Politics*. Boulder, CO: Paradigm Press, 2007.

Toh, Han Shih. "China's formula to reduce poverty could help developing nations," *South China Morning Post*, March 29, 2013, http://www.scmp.com/news/china /article/1202142/chinas-formula-reduce-poverty-could-help-developing -nations. Retrieved May 9, 2013.

Tollefson, Jeff. "A Light in the Forest." *Foreign Affairs* 92, no. 2 (March/April 2013): 141–151.

Trennepohl, Natascha. "Brazil's Policy on Climate Change: Recent Legislation and Challenges to Implementation." *Carbon and Climate Law Review* (March 2010): 271–277, http://www.lexxion.de/en/verlagsprogramm-shop/details/1898 /70/cclr/cclr-3/2010/brazil%E2%80%99s-policy-on-climate-change—recent -legislation-and-challenges-to-implementation.html. Retrieved June 1, 2012.

Vallance, Monique M. "Prostitution." In *Brazil Today: An Encyclopedia of Life in the Republic*, edited by John J. Crocitti, 505–509. Santa Barbara, CA: ABC-CLIO, 2012.

Vallikappen, Sanat. "China May Become Home to Half the Millionaires in 10 Major Asian Economies." *Bloomberg Online*, August 31, 2011, http://www.bloomberg .com/news/2011–08–31/china-to-have-half-of-asia-s-millionaires-by-2015-baer -says.html. Retrieved July 26, 2013.

Vasconcellos, Pedro Lima. "Apocalypses in the History of Brazil." *Journal for the Study of the New Testament* 25, no. 2 (December 2002): 235–254, http://web .ebscohost.com.ezproxy.libraries.wright.edu:2048/ehost/pdfviewer/pdfviewer?vi d=3&hid=10&sid=4a4331ba-1496–4e2d-91f1-e4a5d7f93dcf%40sessionmgr13. Retrieved July 5, 2012.

Verbeek, Esmee. "Rousseff Works for Wealth Equality: Daily." *Rio Times*, April 13, 2012, http://riotimesonline.com/brazil-news/rio-politics/rousseff-works-for- wealth-equality/. Retrieved August 14, 2012.

Vianna, A. R. B., S. Carrara, and P. Lacerda. "Sexual Politics and Sexual Rights in Brazil: An Overview." *Global Public Health* 3 no. 2 (2008): 5–21, http://www .ncbi.nlm.nih.gov/pubmed/19288350. Retrieved April 25, 2012.

"Viewpoint: The Powerful Factions among China's Rulers." *BBC News*, November 5, 2012, http://www.bbc.com/news/world-asia-china-20203937. Retrieved May 6, 2014.

"Views of US Continue to Improve in 2011 BBC Country Rating Poll." *BBC News*, March 7, 2011, http://www.worldpublicopinion.org/pipa/articles/views_on _countriesregions_bt/680.php. Retrieved December 28, 2013.

Villarreal, Diego. "World Climate Policies: Substantial Progress but Enormous Challenges Remain." State of the Planet (blog), Earth Institute, May 1, 2012, http://blogs.ei.columbia.edu/2012/05/01/world-climate-policies-substantial -progress-but-enormous-challenges-remain/Retrieved May 29, 2012.

Vincent, Jon S. *Culture and Customs of Brazil*. Westport, CT: Greenwood Press, 2003.

"Violence on the Basis of Sexual Orientation, Gender Identity and Gender Expression against Non-Heteronormative Women in Asia." *International Gay and Lesbian Human Rights Commission Summary Report, 2010*, http://iglhrc.org/ sites/default/files/386–1_0.pdf. Retrieved May 14, 2014.

"Viva Rio: Farewell to Arms in Brazil." *Peace News* no. 2452 (September/November 2003), http://peacenews.info/node/3761/viva-rio-farewell-arms-brazil. Retrieved September 19, 2012.

"Viva Rio Launches Campaign to Change Drug Law in Brazil." *Viva Rio*, July 7, 2012, http://vivario.org.br/en/viva-rio-launches-campaign-to-change-drug-law-in -brazil/. Retrieved September 18, 2012.

"Volunteers Take Search for China's Missing Children Online." *Agence France -Presse*, May 24, 2013, http://www.rawstory.com/rs/2013/05/24/volunteers -take-search-for-chinas-missing-children-online/. Retrieved July 26, 2013.

Wagner, F. E., and John O. Ward. "Urbanization and Migration in Brazil." *American Journal of Economics and Sociology* 39, no. 3 (July 1980), http://www.jstor.org /stable/3486104?seq=10. Retrieved September 14, 2013.

Waiselfisz, Julio Jacobo. "Map of Violence, 2013: Homicides and Youth in Brazil." Center for Latin American Studies (Cebela), 2013, http://www.mapada violencia.org.br/pdf2013/mapa2013_homicidios_juventude.pdf. Retrieved September 5, 2013.

Walder, Andrew G. "Popular Protest and Party Rule: China's Evolving Policy." In *The People's Republic of China at 60: An International Assessment*, edited by William C. Kirby, 145–52. Cambridge, MA: Harvard University Asia Center, 2011.

Walker, Derek. "California's Carbon Market Could Help Stop Brazil's Deforest- ation." Environmental Defense Fund, February 7, 2014, http://blogs.edf.org /climatetalks/category/brazil/. Retrieved March 4, 2014.

Walzer, Robert P. "Brazilian Wind Power Gets a Boost." *New York Times*, November 9, 2008, http://green.blogs.nytimes.com/2009/11/09/brazilian-wind-power-gets-a -boost/. Retrieved May 25, 2012.

Wan, William. "Pollution in China's Tai Lake Worse Despite National Push for Environmentalism." *Washington Post*, October 29, 2010, http://www.washing tonpost.com/wp-dyn/content/article/2010/10/28/AR2010102806796.html. Retrieved May 22, 2012.

Wang, Alex. "China Environmental Law Group Partners with Leading U.S. Environmental Organization to Meet Rising Pollution Challenge." Press release, Natural Resource Defense Council, February 14, 2006, http://www .nrdc.org/media/pressreleases/060214.asp. Retrieved July 6, 2012.

Wang, Hairong. "Modifying Weather." *Beijing Review*, September 24, 2012, http://www .bjreview.com.cn/nation/txt/2012–09/24/content_485942_2.htm. Retrieved June 20, 2014.

Wang, Yiqing. "The Economic Roots of China's Crimes." *China Daily*, March 4, 2010, http://www.chinadaily.com.cn/opinion/2010–03/04/content_9534912. htm. Retrieved July 26, 2013.

Wang, Zheng. *Never Forget National Humiliation: Historical Memory in Chinese Politics and Foreign Relations*. New York: Columbia University Press, 2012.

Wassener, Bettina. "New Term for Emerging Economies Is Suggested." *New York Times,* November 15, 2010, http://www.nytimes.com/2010/11/16/business /global/16eagles.html?_r=0. Retrieved May 28, 2013.

Watson, James L. "Chattel Slavery in Chinese Peasant Society: A Comparative Analysis." *Ethnology* 15, no. 4 (October 1976): 361–375.

Watson, Rubie. "Afterword." In *Faiths on Display: Religion, Tourism and the Chinese State,* edited by Tim Oakes and Donald S. Sutton, 265–270. Lanham, MD: Rowman and Littlefield Publishers, 2010.

Watts, Jonathan. "The New China: A Hunger Eating Up the World." *Guardian,* November 10, 2005, http://www.guardian.co.uk/business/2005/nov/10/environ ment.china. Retrieved May 21, 2012.

———. "China's Loggers Down Chainsaws in Attempt to Regrow Forests." *Guardian,* March 11, 2009, http://www.guardian.co.uk/environment/2009 /mar/11/china-forests-deforestation. Retrieved July 5, 2012.

———. *When a Billion Chinese Jump: How China Will Save Mankind—or Destroy It.* New York: Scribner, 2010.

———. "Herder's Death Deepens Tensions in Inner Mongolia." *Guardian,* May 27, 2011, http://www.theguardian.com/world/2011/may/27/tensions-herders -miners-inner-mongolia. Retrieved January 9, 2014.

———. 2012a. "NGOs Upbeat over China's Environmental Transparency Progress." *Guardian,* January 16, 2012, http://www.guardian.co.uk/environment/2012/jan /16/green-transparency-china. Retrieved January 17, 2012.

———. 2012b. "Citizen Journalism Triumphs at China Environmental Press Awards." *Guardian,* April 11, 2012, http://www.theguardian.com/environment /2012/apr/11/china-environmental-press-awards. Retrieved January 8, 2014.

———. 2013a. "Brazilian Riot Police Evict Indigenous People near Rio's Maracanã Stadium." *Guardian,* March 22, 2013, http://www.guardian.co.uk/world/2013 /mar/22/brazilian-police-evict-indigenous-people. Retrieved May 29, 2013.

———. 2013b. "Head of Brazil's Equality Body Accused of Homophobia and Racism." *Guardian,* April 5, 2013, http://www.theguardian.com/world/2013 /apr/05/brazil-equality-body-homophobia-racism. Retrieved October 28, 2014.

———. 2013c. "Brazil Protests Take to the Pitch as People's Cup Highlights Evictions." *Guardian,* June 18, 2013, http://www.theguardian.com/global -development/2013/jun/18/brazil-protests-peoples-cup-evictions. Retrieved August 9, 2013.

———. 2013d. "Brazil's Ninja Reporters Spread Stories from the Streets." *Guardian,* August 29, 2013, http://www.theguardian.com/world/2013/aug/29/brazil-ninja -reporters-stories-streets. Retrieved August 31, 2013.

———. 2014a. "Brazilian Green Activist Marina Silva Announces Unlikely Election Alliance." *Guardian,* April 15, 2014, http://www.theguardian.com/world/2014 /apr/15/marina-silva-eduardo-campos-brazil-election. Retrieved May 13, 2014.

———. 2014b. "Brazil's 'Chainsaw Queen' Appointed New Agriculture Minister." *Guardian,* December 24, 2014, http://www.theguardian.com/world/2014/dec/24 /brazil-agriculture-katia-abreu-climate-change. Retrieved January 29, 2015.

Waugh, Rob. "Brazil First Country to Try and Use Twitter's New Censorship Policy to Silence Its Citizens," *MailOnline*, February 10, 2012, http://www.dailymail.co.uk/sciencetech/article-2099391/Brazil-country-use-Twitters-new-censorship-policy-silence-citizens.html. Retrieved April 16, 2012.

Wells, Miriam. "Report Maps Three Decades of Violence in Brazil." *InSight Crime*, August 12, 2013, http://www.insightcrime.org/news-analysis/report-maps-three-decades-of-murders-in-brazil. Retrieved September 5, 2013.

Wergin, Clemens. "Is Obama's Foreign Policy Too European?" *New York Times*, July 8, 2014, http://www.nytimes.com/2014/07/09/opinion/clemens-wergin-is-obamas-foreign-policy-too-european.html. Retrieved July 14, 2014.

"WFP Centre of Excellence." Global Child Nutrition Forum, May 20–24, 2013, http://gcnf2013.org/views/index.php?pg=pagina&cat=about_the_event&id=18. Retrieved May 30, 2013.

"What the US Can Learn from Upbeat Brazil." NPR, *Tell Me More*, November 30, 2011, http://www.npr.org/templates/story/story.php?storyId=142943026. Retrieved August 14, 2012.

White, Ben. "Taking Shelter." *New Statesman*, March 24, 2008, http://www.newstatesman.com/society/2008/03/brazil-movement-sao-campaign. Retrieved September 4, 2012.

Whiteman, Hilary. "Deaths in Dumpster Expose Plight of China's Street Kids." *CNN News*, November 21, 2012, http://www.cnn.com/2012/11/21/world/asia/china-boys-dead-dumpster. Retrieved July 12, 2013.

Whyte, Martin King. "Myth of the Social Volcano: Popular Responses to Rising Inequality in China." In *The People's Republic of China at 60: An International Assessment*, edited by William Kirby, 273–290. Cambridge, MA: Harvard University Asia Center, 2011.

Wilkinson, Francis. "How Brazil Exploited Sexual Insecurity to Curb Guns: An Interview with Antonio Bandeira." *Bloomberg*, March 8, 2013, http://www.bloomberg.com/news/2013-03-08/how-brazil-exploited-sexual-insecurity-to-curb-guns-an-interview-with-antonio-bandeira.html. Retrieved May 31, 2013.

Williamson, Theresa, and Mauricio Hora. "In the Name of the Future, Rio is Destroying Its Past." *New York Times*, August 12, 2012, http://www.nytimes.com/2012/08/13/opinion/in-the-name-of-the-future-rio-is-destroying-its-past.html. Retrieved September 4, 2012.

Wines, Michael. 2011a. "Bystanders' Neglect of Inured Toddler Sets Off Soul-Searching on Web Sites in China." *New York Times*, October 19, 2011, http://www.nytimes.com/2011/10/19/world/asia/toddlers-accident-sets-off-soul-searching-in-china.html?pagewanted=all. Retrieved June 22, 2014.

———. 2011b. "Police Fire Tear Gas at Protesters in Chinese City." *New York Times*, December 23, 2011, http://www.nytimes.com/2011/12/24/world/asia/china-jails-rights-activist-chen-wei-for-9-years.html. Retrieved July 29, 2013.

Winter, Brian. "Analysis: Brazil and US, Like Star-Crossed Lovers, Foiled Again." Reuters, September 18, 2013, http://www.Reuters.com/article/2013/09/18/us-brazil-us-diplomacy-analysis-idUSBRE98H11G20130918. Retrieved December 16, 2013.

————. "Brazil's Rousseff's Popularity Tumbles in New Poll." Reuters, March 18, 2015, http://www.Reuters.com/article/2015/03/18/us-brazil-rousseff-poll-idUS KBN0ME12J20150318. Retrieved April 16, 2015.

Winter, Brian, and Anthony Boadle. "Brazil's Rousseff, Neves Race for Support in Election Runoff." Reuters, October 6, 2014, http://www.Reuters.com /article/2014/10/06/us-brazil-election-idUSKCN0HU03C20141006. Retrieved October 29, 2014.

Wish, Valdis. "Brazil: Climate Fact Sheet." *Allianz*, August 26, 2010, http://know ledge.allianz.com/climate/country_profiles/?194/climate-profile-brazil-facts. Retrieved June 1, 2012.

Womack, Brantley. *China Among Unequals: Asymmetric Foreign Relationships in Asia.* Hackensack, NJ: World Scientific Publishing, 2010.

Wong, Edward. 2011a. "Chinese Director's Path from Rebel to Insider." *New York Times*, August 14, 2011, http://www.nytimes.com/2011/08/14/world/asia/14 filmmaker.html?pagewanted=all. Retrieved July 7, 2013.

————. 2011b. "Pushing China's Limits on Web, if Not on Paper." *New York Times*, November 6, 2011, http://www.nytimes.com/2011/11/07/world/asia/murong -xuecun-pushes-censorship-limits-in-china.html?pagewanted=all. Retrieved November 7, 2011.

"World Development Indicators." World Bank, 2012, http://data.worldbank.org /country/brazil. Retrieved August 15, 2012.

"World Development Indicators." World Bank, 2015, http://data.worldbank.org /country/china. Retrieved April 14, 2015.

"World Directory of Minorities and Indigenous Peoples: Brazil Overview." Minority Rights Group International, 2007, http://www.minorityrights.org/?lid=5289. Retrieved May 17, 2012.

"World Directory of Minorities and Indigenous Peoples: China Overview." Minority Rights Group International, October 2009, http://www.refworld.org/cgi-bin /texis/vtx/rwmain?docid=4954ce5b23. Retrieved May 10, 2012.

"The World Factbook." Central Intelligence Agency, 2014, https://www.cia.gov /library/publications/the-world-factbook/. Retrieved June 24, 2014.

"The World in 2050: Will the Shift in Global Economic Power Continue?" PWC .com, February 2015, http://www.pwc.com/gx/en/issues/the-economy/assets /world-in-2050-summary-report-february-2015.pdf. Retrieved September 18, 2015.

"Worldwide Protests against Amazon Mega-Dam." Survival International, August 22, 2011, http://www.survivalinternational.org/news/7602. Retrieved May 31, 2012.

Wright, Angus, and Wendy Wolford. *To Inherit the Earth: The Landless Movement and the Struggle for a New Brazil.* Oakland, CA: Food First! Publications, 2003.

Wyler, Grace. "What It Is Like to Get an Abortion in Brazil, One of the Most Restrictive Countries in the World." *Business Insider*, May 4, 2013, http://www .businessinsider.com/illegal-abortions-2013–5. Retrieved June 21, 2014.

"Xi Jinping and the Chinese Dream." *Economist*, May 4, 2013, http://www.economist .com/news/leaders/21577070-vision-chinas-new-president-should-serve-his -people-not-nationalist-state-xi-jinping. Retrieved June 5, 2014.

Xue, Zaixing. "Urban Street Children in China: A Social Exclusion Perspective." *International Social Work* 52, no. 3 (2009): 401–408.

Xu, Jianchu. "China's New Forests Aren't as Green as They Seem." *Nature* 477, no. 371 (September 21, 2011), http://www.nature.com/news/2011/110921/full /477371a.html. Retrieved July 5, 2012.

Yan, Alice, and Blum, Jeremy. "Pollutants' Effect on Infertility Rates in China to Be Examined." *South China Morning Post*, September 4, 2013, http://www.scmp .com/news/china/article/1303303/pollutants-effect-infertility-rates-china-be -examined. Retrieved December 9, 2013.

Yang, Fang. "On the Justice of Policy of Adding Points in the University Entrance Examination Applying to Minority Nationalities in China." *Ethno-National Studies* 6 (2010), http://www.cnki.net/kcms/detail/detail.aspx?dbcode=cjfq &dbname=cjfq2010&filename=mzyj201006002&uid=&p=. Retrieved May 8, 2012.

Yang, Guobin. "Environmental NGOs and institutional Dynamics in China." *China Quarterly* 181 (2005): 46–66.

Yan, Hairong. *New Masters, New Servants: Migration, Development, and Women Workers in China*. Durham, NC: Duke University Press, 2008.

Yan, Xuetong. "How China Can Defeat America." *New York Times*, November 20, 2011, http://www.nytimes.com/2011/11/21/opinion/how-china-can-defeat -america.html?_r=0, Retrieved December 28, 2013.

Yardley, Jim. "Today's Face of Abortion in China is a Young, Unmarried Woman." *New York Times*, May 13, 2007, http://www.nytimes.com/2007/05/13/world /asia/13abortion.html?pagewanted=all. Retrieved April 16, 2012.

Yoon, Sangwon. "Biggest Emitter China Best on Climate, Figures Says." *Bloomberg*, January 14, 2014, http://www.bloomberg.com/news/2014-01-13/top-global -emitter-china-best-on-climate-change-figueres-says.html. Retrieved April 6, 2014.

Yu, Daniela, and Anita Pugliese. "Majority of Chinese Prioritize Environment Over Economy." Gallup.com, June 8, 2012, http://www.gallup.com/poll/155102/ma jority-chinese-prioritize-environment-economy.aspx. Retrieved June 10, 2012.

Yuen, Lotus. "Communist Party Membership is Still the Ultimate Resume Booster." *Atlantic*, May 29, 2013, http://www.theatlantic.com/china/archive/2013/05 /communist-party-membership-is-still-the-ultimate-resume-booster/276347/. Retrieved May 6, 2014.

Yun, Lisa. *The Coolie Speaks: Chinese Indentured Laborers and African Slaves in Cuba*. Philadelphia: Temple University Press, 2008.

Zainulbhai, Hani. "Brazil's Corruption Scandal, Economy Drive Rousseff's Ratings to Record Low." Pew Research Center, August 17, 2015. http://www.pew research.org/fact-tank/2015/08/17/brazils-corruption-scandal-economy-drive -rousseffs-ratings-to-record-low/. Retrieved September 19, 2015.

Zanini, Fábio. "Foreign Policy in Brazil: A Neglected Debate." *Harvard International Review*, October 23, 2014, http://hir.harvard.edu/archives/7486. Retrieved April 16, 2015.

Zhai, Keith. "Rape Victim's Mother Tang Hui Wins Damages over Labour Camp Sentence." *South China Morning Post*, July 15, 2013, http://www.scmp.com/news/china/article/1283035/rape-victims-mother-tang-hui-wins-appeal-landmark-labour-camp. Retrieved May 7, 2014.

Zhang, Daqing, and Paul U. Unschuld. "China's Barefoot Doctor: Past, Present and Future." *Lancet* 372, no. 9653 (2008): 1865–1867.

Zhang, Lijia. "China's Death-Penalty Debate." *New York Times*, December 29, 2014, http://www.nytimes.com/2014/12/30/opinion/chinas-death-penalty-debate.html?emc=eta1&_r=0. Retrieved February 6, 2015.

Zhao, Litao, and Lim Tin Seng. "Introduction." In *China's New Social Policy: Initiatives for a Harmonious Society*, edited by Zhao Litao and Lim Tin Seng, 11–22. Hackensack, New Jersey: World Scientific, 2010.

Zheng, Caixiong. "Guangzhou Moves to Abolish Rural Hukou." *China Daily*, May 10, 2013, http://europe.chinadaily.com.cn/china/2013–05/10/content_16488985.htm. Retrieved June 4, 2013.

Zheng, Tiantian. *Red Lights: The Lives of Sex Workers in Postsocialist China*. Minneapolis: University of Minnesota Press, 2009.

Zhou, Bo. "The String of Pearls and the Maritime Silk Road." *China-US Focus*, February 11, 2014, http://www.chinausfocus.com/foreign-policy/the-string-of-pearls-and-the-maritime-silk-road/. Retrieved June 20, 2014.

Zi, Heng Lim. "Why China Executes So Many People." *Atlantic*, May 19, 2013, http://www.theatlantic.com/china/archive/2013/05/why-china-executes-so-many-people/275695/. Retrieved July 27, 2013.

Zimmerman, A. "In Brazil, Many Laws Are for Englishmen's Eyes Only." *Brazzil*, September 25, 2008, http://brazzil.com/articles/196-september-2008/10116-in-brazil-many-laws-are-for-englishmens-eyes-only.html. Retrieved September 15, 2011.

Zylberman, Joris. "School's Out Forever for Migrant Workers' Children." *France24*, September 15, 2011, http://www.france24.com/en/20110914–2011-china-migrant-workers-beijing-schools-shut-down-closed-exclusion-real-estate-demography. Retrieved June 24, 2013.

INDEX

"3 Separations," 176

abertura, 56, 59, 114, 154, 169
abortion, 192–196 (fig 4.1), 200
　Brazil, 160, 162–165
　China, 183–185
absolute poverty, 31, 94–95, 261
accommodation, 30, 45, 49–50, 63, 87,
　176, 196, 216, 260, 263
accountability, 58, 82, 122, 132
　environmental, 204, 228, 260
　police, 105, 131, 135, 145
acts of commission and acts of
　omission, 144, 237
affirmative action, 198
　Brazil, 153, 155–159
　China, 174
Africa, 11, 67, 92, 156, 278
　Brazilian heritage, 41–42, 44–48, 83,
　　151–152, 155–156, 192 (fig 4.1)
　Brazilian investment, 251, 263
　Chinese investment, 118, 272, 279
Afro-Brazilian, 54, 101, 153–154,
　156–157, 170, 197
　religious traditions, 46, 115, 194
Agenda 21, 276
agrarian reform, 22, 31, 61
agribusiness, 259, 294
Ai Xiaoming, 181
AIDS. See HIV-AIDS
All China Women's Federation, 139,
　181

Amazon, 22, 42, 107, 255
　Belo Monte, 212–213
　core issue, 34, 262, 286
　deforestation, 202, 206–208, 211,
　　235, 256–257
Amnesty, 58, 85, 107
Andean Community, 246–247
anti-AIDS movements, 114, 116–118,
　142, 146
anti-dam movements, 213–216, 223
anti-violence movements, 107–110,
　118.
anti-retroviral therapy (ART), 117,
　137, 251–252
Argentina, 56, 58, 247, 285
ARV. See anti–retroviral therapy
Association of Southeast Asian
　Nations (ASEAN), 269, 271
authoritarian, 3–4, 6–12, 16, 18, 24,
　35, 84–86, 199, 281–282, 289, 293
　regime type, 6–7
　Brazil, 40–43, 48, 52–53, 56, 118,
　　161, 169
　partnerships, 21, 28–29, 31, 292
　China, 72, 79, 144–145, 148–149,
　　237–240, 292, 296–297
　　Beijing Consensus, 34, 286, 294

Bali Conference, 277
Ban Ki-Moon, 275
Beijing Consensus, 34, 286. See also
　authoritarian

Belo Monte, 212–218, 235, 239
biodiversity 1, 207, 213, 255
biofuels, 257, 261
bipolarity, 275, 284
"black jails," 31, 133
"blue sky days," 223, 231
Bo Xilai, 135
Bolsa Escola (The School Stipend), 93.
    See also conditional cash transfers
Bolsa Família (The Family Stipend),
    31, 93–95, 159, 257. *See also*
    conditional cash transfers
    soft power, 291, 251
boycott, 17, 190
branding, 245, 259, 267
    global brand, 244, 250, 262, 282
Brasilia Consensus, 34, 286
"the Brazilian way," 40–54, 157, 196.
    See also exceptionalism, Brazil
BRIC (Brazil, Russia, India and
    China), 27–28, 250, 272
BRICS (Brazil, Russia, India, China
    and South Africa), 272
Buddhism, 174, 176, 184
Bush, George W., 167

capital punishment,
    Brazil, 106, 145
    China, 128, 134, 141 (fig 3.1)
Cardoso, Fernando Henrique, 48, 60
    economics, 93, 155
    racial policies, 153, 157, 170, 192
        (fig. 4.1), 198
Catholic, 33, 146, 194–197
    Brazil, 46, 59, 97, 160
        abortion, 164–165, 192 (fig 4.1)
        capital punishment, 145
        environmentalism, 208, 215
        homosexuality, 168–170
    China, 174, 179
"Century of Shame," 68, 178
Chen Guangcheng, 199
chengguan (urban management law
    enforcement bureau), 132

Chinese Communist Party (CCP), 38,
    67, 72, 131, 133, 189, 191, 272
    challenges to, 82–87, 91, 141 (fig
        3.1), 221, 239, 293, 274, 296
    ideology, 23, 33, 66, 71–81, 125,
        172, 180, 281
    officials, 30, 76, 79, 120, 127
    policies on religion, 175–176, 178,
        194
    revolutionary legacy of, 69–70, 124
Chinese communist revolution, 64, 78,
    130, 178, 265
Chinese People's Political Consultative
    Conference (CPPCC), 82–83
CIMI. *See* Indigenous Missionary
    Council
civil disobedience, 17, 62, 210
civil society, 14–19
    military dictatorship, 57, 59
    environmentalism, 204–206, 239
    healthcare, 112–114, 117–118, 147,
        189, 251–252
    heterogeneity of, 97, 202
    authoritarian regimes, 6–7, 9, 56
    democracies, 5–6
    international, 156–157, 215
    partnerships, 109–110
    religion, 46, 107
    sexual minorities, 139, 166, 169
    synergy with the state, 19, 28,
        93–94, 97–98, 249
civil war, 4, 10, 20, 70
    Brazil, 30, 45, 49
    China, 72, 274
clientelism, 15, 61
climate change, 235–236, 284–285
    Brazil, 255–260
    China, 222, 229, 231, 276–279
coal, 219–220, 232, 278
Cold War, 22, 55, 248
colonialism,
    Brazil, 42, 46–47, 50–52, 92,
        104–105, 160
    China, 150

"color," 192 (fig 4.1)
 Brazil, 32, 52, 57, 150–155, 158, 207
 China, 173
Communist Youth League (CYL), 81
comparative politics, 4, 10, 12–13,
 27–28, 242–243, 298
concubinage, 68, 185
conditional cash transfers (CCTs),
 93–94, 143, 251, 257. *See also*
 Bolsa Família
Confucianism, 185
 impact on social relations, 74, 181,
 184, 197
 spiritual identity, 176, 178
 virtues, 71, 77, 172, 265
Confucius Institutes, 71, 280
Congress
 Brazil, 56, 105, 163–164, 167, 171,
 193, 216–217.
 China. *See* National People's
 Congress
conservationists, 208, 257, 260
conservative, 4, 21, 193–194
 Brazil, 16, 55, 61, 97, 146, 151, 162,
 193, 207, 217
 religious conservatism, 164–165,
 168, 171
 China, 33, 75, 79, 81, 119, 181
consolidation, 5–6
 Brazil, 11, 20, 31, 58, 62, 85, 296
 China 292
constitution, 1982 (China), 122, 173,
 175, 180, 219
constitutions (Brazil), 55
 (1824), 52–53
 (1891), 164
 (1988), 93, 112, 117, 158, 161, 170,
 193
 environment, 210, 214
contested issues, 21, 98, 147, 151, 290,
 292–293
co-optation, 8, 13, 26, 287
 Brazil, 16, 18, 47, 54, 60, 294
 China, 82

Copenhagen negotiations, 258, 277
core issues, 8, 12, 25–26, 29, 150, 293,
 297. *See also* "red line" issues
 Brazil, 192 (fig 4.1), 233, 234 (fig
 5.1), 256
 China, 191, 286
corruption, 12, 86, 91, 145, 147–148,
 196, 295–296
 Brazil, 55, 59, 61–63, 102–107, 119,
 164, 167, 171, 261
 China, 67, 80, 83, 128, 130, 133–
 134, 141 (fig 3.1), 181, 187, 193,
 227, 294
counterhegemonic, 34, 243–244,
 250–252, 273, 283–286
counterrevolutionary, 71, 78, 85
countervailing pressures (or protests),
 15, 19, 201, 240
 Brazil, 109, 141 (fig 3.1), 151, 158,
 162, 192 (fig 4.1), 203, 234 (fig
 5.1), 255
 China, 125, 138, 141–142 (fig 3.1),
 189, 193, 224
coup, 53, 55–56
crime, 141 (fig 3.1), 145–148
 Brazil, 58, 85, 96, 104–111, 162,
 168, 171–172
 China, 24, 31–32, 91, 128–134, 274
criminal syndicates, 106, 130
critical junctures, 12–13, 62, 86, 114,
 166, 202
Cuba, 55, 66, 253
Cubatão, 203, 238
cultural dilution, 176, 191
Cultural Revolution, 12, 70–75, 77–79,
 83–85, 175

Dai Qing, 222
Dalai Lama, 176–177, 274–275
dams, 226–229, 236, 239
 Brazil, 206–216
 China, 222–223
"dangerous" issues. *See* core issues, red
 line issues

Daoism, 174, 176, 184
da Silva, Luiz Inácio "Lula," 41, 59,
    106, 157, 167, 198
    abortion, 163–165, 192 (fig. 4.1)
    civil society, 61–62, 194, 210,
        259–260
    dictatorship, 58, 60
    election, 59–60, 86, 295
    environment, 209–210, 212, 216,
        256–257, 259–260
    foreign policy, 244–245, 253–257,
        260–261, 263
    LGBT rights, 170–171, 193 (fig.4.1)
    pragmatism, 58–61, 63, 93, 164,
        294–295
    social programs, 61, 94, 96, 295
debt, 47, 50, 57, 62, 66, 261
decentralization, 42–43, 112
deforestation, 15, 29, 201, 233–235,
    234 (fig 5.1)
    Brazil, 202–203, 206–217, 256–260
    China 218, 230–233
Democracy Wall, 75–76
democratic transition, 12, 22, 57, 85,
    255
Deng Xiaoping, 70, 74–75, 79, 119,
    185
desertification, 231–233
developmentalist policy, 202, 205, 209,
    212, 215, 237
Diaoyu Islands, 267–268
dibao, (minimum livelihood guarantee
    scheme), 136
"differentiated responsibilities," 258, 284
Dilma. See Rousseff, Dilma
Ding Zilin, 77
diplomacy, 283–286
    Brazil, 245, 249–253
    China, 264, 270, 272
direct action, 17, 61–62, 98–99,
    209–210, 225
Diretas Ja! Movement, 57
Dirty War, 12, 56, 84–85
divorce, 162, 181–182
drugs, drug trafficking

Brazil, 97, 105–107, 109, 214, 252
China, 130, 133, 136–137, 139, 186

East China Sea, 268, 275
eco-tourism, 208
elections, 5, 280
    Brazil, 38, 53, 56, 60, 63, 165, 194,
        209, 239
    China, 127
empires
    Brazil, 50, 84
    China, 65–68. See also imperial
        system
environment, 16, 201–241, 284–287
    Brazil, 62
        climate change, 255–260
        dangers, 22, 34, 108.
    China, 11, 34, 82, 118
        climate change, 276–279
environmental justice, 203, 208
Environmental Justice Network, 204
environmental refugees, 222, 231
evangelicals, 194
    Brazil, 33, 146, 160, 164, 168, 171,
        192 (fig 4.1), 197
    China, 178
exceptionalism, 83–85
    Brazil, 39–40, 42, 48–49, 54, 106,
        152, 167, 202, 244, 258, 261, 264
    China, 265
extrajudicial, 145–146
    Brazil, 102, 105–106, 141 (fig 3.1)
    China, 31
extraterritoriality, 67–68
extrovert, 283, 290

Facebook, 23–24, 182
family planning, 135, 183–184, 195.
    See also reproductive rights
favelas, 96, 100, 108, 110, 144
feminism, 195–197
    Brazil, 57, 161–163, 170
    China, 180–182, 185
feudal system, 43
Five Year Plans, 122, 137, 144

flash mobs, 17, 19, 24
"floating population," 122, 124, 137, 144
fome zero (zero hunger), 94–95, 251
food security, 94, 251
Forest Code, 216–218, 234 (fig 5.1)
"Four frees, one care" program, 137
Freedom House,
    Brazil, 32, 107, 263–264
    China, 269
"Friends of Nature," 225

gangs
    Brazil, 97, 111
    China, 129–132
Gao Yaojie 138–139
Global Gender Gap (reports), 161–162,
    180
GMD. *See* Nationalist Party
Goulart, João, 55, 60
Great Leap Forward, 83, 118
"Green Great Wall," 230–231, 277
Group of 8 (G8), 250, 272
Group of 20 (G20), 272
Group of 77 (G77), 250, 278
guerilla, 60, 106
gun control, 20, 109, 128
Guo Jianming, 181
G2, 272, 276

Han, 33, 72, 173–178, 191, 232
    Han Dynasty, 3, 71
harm-avoidance approach, 116
harm-reduction approach, 109, 146
hate crimes, 168, 171–172. *See also*
    homophobia, transphobia
health care, 1, 14, 148
    Brazil, 93–94, 104, 163
    China, 68, 176
    See also HIV-AIDS
hegemon,
    Brazil, 247
    China, 271–273, 278, 280
    counter-hegemonic, 34–35, 243–244,
        250–252, 283–286
    United States, 2, 269

hegira, 48. *See also* exceptionalism,
    Brazil
HIV-AIDS, 13, 142, 146–147, 193, 197
    Brazil, 18, 31, 93, 112–118, 165–167,
        198, 251–252, 263, 182, 187, 291,
        295
    China, 135–140, 181, 186, 189, 196,
        233, 292
Homeless Workers Movement
    (*Movimento dos Trabalhadores
    sem Teto*, MTST), 98–103,
    144–145
homicide rates, 32, 105, 111, 145
homophobia, 168, 171, 193
Hong Kong, 68, 77, 130–131, 231
"hooliganism," 188
"house churches," 175, 179
housing,
    Brazil, 94, 97–104, 112, 115
    China, 121, 124
Hu Jia, 138
Hu Jintao, 80–81, 272, 275
hukou, 121–127, 136, 188.
hutong, 126
Human Development Index (HDI),
    92, 153
human rights, 34, 147, 282–284
    Brazil, 248
        abortion, 165
        democratic transition, 32
        dictatorship, 22
        environmental, 215
        human security, 83, 112
        LGBT, 114, 171–172
        foreign policies, 253
        race relations, 156, 162
    China. *See also* Beijing Consensus
        LGBT, 198
        sex workers, 185–187
        foreign policies, 269, 280–282
human trafficking, 33, 129–132, 213
hybrid, 152
    analytical approaches, 14, 25, 26 (fig
        1.1), 234 (fig 5.1)
    regimes, 7

hydropower (or hydro-electricity)
  Brazil, 212, 216, 257–258, 261
  China, 226, 229

impeachment, 62, 91, 104, 294
imperial system, 246–247
  China, 23, 65–71, 77, 185
      collapse, 83
      regional rivalries, 265, 268
      sexual identity, 185, 188
      social relations, 121, 173
impunity, 141 (fig 3.1), 146
  Brazil, 58, 104–112, 211
  China, 83, 128–135
India, 277
  BRIC/BRICS, 13, 27–28, 250
  regional relations, 267, 269, 285
  United Nations Security Council
      bid, 273
Indigenous Missionary Council
  (CIMI), 107, 214
indigenous rights, 22, 208, 214–216
inequality, 1, 4, 12, 31, 90–91, 145,
  191
  Brazil. See also Bolsa Familia; land
      reform
          economic, 95–96, 98, 104, 111,
              261, 282
          environmental, 203
          foreign policies, 251
          gender, 161–162
          legal impunity, 105–108, 295
          racial, 155–159. See also color
          social, 40–43, 54, 61, 84
  China
          economic, 91–92, 120, 128
Inner Mongolia, 232
Inter-American Human Rights Court,
  215
interdependence, 18, 247, 266
international civil society, 151,
  156–157, 215
International Monetary Fund (IMF),
  60, 250, 254, 276

Internet, 19, 236. See also social
  media
  Brazil, 165, 170, 210, 248
  China, 23–24, 69, 77, 134, 182,
      187, 190, 198–199, 291. See also
      netizens
introvert, 283, 290
Iran, 11, 219, 253, 269, 285
"iron rice bowl," 119, 143
Israel, 246, 254
issue salience, 29, 147, 199, 288, 297.
  See also core issues

Japan, 128, 173, 228, 231
  animosity with China, 266–269,
      285
  economy, 27, 118, 276
  influence over Imperial China, 68,
      84, 178
  United Nations Security Council
      bid, 254, 273
jeito (little fix), 58, 87, 105
Jesuits, 46, 68, 178, 187
Jiang Zemin, 79–81
journalists, journalism, 22, 236
  Brazil, 102–103, 209
  China, 76, 124, 222–227, 232, 280
judiciary, 15, 86, 170, 229

kidnappings, 106, 129–133
"kowtow," 65
Kyoto Protocols, 276–277

land,
  core issue, 44–45, 54–55, 61, 141
      (fig. 3.1), 211, 233, 234 (fig. 5.1),
      293–297
  concentration, 30, 42–45, 92, 96,
      98, 194
  land grabs, 23, 126–127, 145, 294
land reform,
  Brazil, 54–55, 98, 194, 234 (fig. 5.1),
      293–297
  China, 74

Landless Workers Movement
(*Movimento dos Trabalhadores
Rurais sem Terra*, MST), 61–62,
98–99, 101, 213
Latinobarómetro, 2, 62, 262
leftist, 16, 31, 59, 61, 99, 236
legislature, 15, 52, 125, 190, 222, 229
See also National People's Congress
legitimacy, 7, 17, 29, 172, 292, 297
economy, 31, 62
environment, 238, 260
China, 67, 73, 82, 122, 125
lesbian, gay, bisexual and transgender
(LGBT), 21, 33, 193, 196–198
Brazil, 159–172
China, 33, 179–189
lesbians, 188–189, 191
Li Keqiang, 31, 81, 137, 272
liberation theology, 97, 207
Liu Jianqiang, 227, 236
Liu Xiaobo, 82
local officials, 126, 128, 182, 194, 199
crime, 128, 132
environment, 221, 224, 229, 232,
238
HIV-AIDS, 137, 140
population planning, 183–184
Lula. *See* da Silva, Luiz Inácio "Lula"

Ma Jun, 223–224, 228, 236
machismo, 109, 159
Maoist, 78–79, 81, 128, 135
economic policy, 143, 218
forms of struggle, 75, 77–78
Mao Zedong, 37, 69, 80, 118, 135, 218
Chinese Communist Party, 80–81,
296
Chinese history, 67 69
Cultural Revolution, 74, 78–78
legacy, 69–70, 75
revolution, 73, 77–78, 84
succession, 70, 283
United Nations, 273
women, 180, 199

"marginals," 48, 144
Marriage Law of 1950, 180–182
marriage, 66,68, 171, 179–184, 197
equal, 33, 170–171, 188–191
interracial, 151, 154
Marxist, 73, 78
mass conflicts, 127
May Fourth Movement of 1919,
180–181
media, 15, 126, 155–156, 160, 163–164
crime, 109, 111
official, 180, 129
relations with state, 86, 103, 295
traditional media, 23–24, 102–103,
111
violence, 102–103, 132–133
See also social media
men who have sex with men (MSM),
116, 138, 146
Mercosul, 246–247
"messy middle," 7, 11, 27, 289, 293, 297
middle class, 143, 162
Brazil, 56, 61, 91, 95, 212, 261
China, 120, 175, 180, 230
Middle Kingdom, 178, 188, 265, 282
Midia Ninja, 102–103
migrants, 144–145, 196
Brazil, 44, 96, 144, 206, 213
China, 119, 122–125, 128, 144
migration, 140–141 (fig. 3.1), 144, 147,
96
China, 33, 119, 121, 176, 181, 191
military, 244, 80, 103, 206, 256
Brazil, 91, 105, 109, 254, 261–262,
282
amnesty, 58, 85, 107
colonial, 51–53
dictatorship, 22, 55–56, 58–59,
154
Vargas, 53, 55
China, 69, 264–267, 269, 274, 281
comparison, 282, 285, 290
Millennium Development Goals, 31,
93, 279

Ming Dynasty, 67
Ministry of Environmental Protection, 224, 228
minzu, 174
missionaries, 68–69, 107, 178, 187, 214
    Jesuits, 46, 68
mobility, 67, 122–123, 128, 184
mobilization, 6, 16, 22, 78
    Brazil, 62, 98, 118, 153
Mongolia, Mongolians, 65, 126, 231–232
most-different cases, 10, 28–29, 290
Movement of People Affected by Dams (Movimento dos Atingidos por Barragens, MAB), 214, 216
Movement for Sanitary Reform (Movimento para Reforma Sanitaria), 112–113
"mulatto escape hatch," 154, 191
multilateralism, 35, 246–247, 250
multipolar, 2, 34, 242, 284
    Brazil, 250, 287
    China, 271, 275, 284
Muslim, 33, 175, 177–178
"My House, My Life" (Minha Casa, Minha Vida), 94–95
"nail house," 126

National AIDS Program (NAP), 114–115
national character, 42, 48–49, 152
National People's Congress (NPC), 83, 125, 184, 190, 222
national security, 107, 109, 154, 216
nationalism, 215, 255–256
    Brazil, 47, 53–54, 158, 164
    China, 84, 178, 266, 268, 273
Nationalist Party (GMD), 69, 70, 73, 274
negotiations, 249, 253, 277–278
    Brazil, 16, 100–101, 114, 210
    China, 127, 268, 270–271, 275, 287
neo-Confucian. See Confucianism
nepotism. See corruption
new media. See social media

netizens, 129, 132, 187, 190, 291
non-governmental organizations (NGOs), 15, 19–20
    Brazil, 108, 164, 197, 263–264
        HIV-AIDS, 117, 166, 197
        environment, 202–210, 237–238
        dams, 210, 213, 217, 236
    China, 124, 137, 139, 181, 190, 197
        environment, 224–226, 234 (fig. 5.1)
non-indifference, 245–246, 250
non-interference
    Brazil, 245, 253, 285
    China, 271, 274–275, 287
North Korea, 269–271, 285
nouveaux riches, 120, 129, 143
Nu River, 226, 239

Obama, Barack, 167, 247–248
occupations, 17, 62, 99, 100, 111, 256
official histories, 37–38, 65
    Brazil, 40, 42, 45, 47
oil,
    Brazil, 92, 202, 205–206, 238, 259, 261
    China, 219, 230, 268, 278
old media. See media
oligarchic, 43, 51, 53, 284, 287
Olympics,
    Brazil (2016), 100, 110, 144, 235
    China (2008), 144, 223, 280
"one child" policy, 183
oppositional movement, 20–21, 16, 18, 86, 141 (fig.3.1)
oppositional politics,
    Brazil, 99, 62–63, 141 (fig 3.1), 234 (fig 5.1), 287
    prodemocracy movement, 57, 59, 97, 112, 161, 169
organized crime, 106, 130, 237
    See also gangs

pacification, 110–112
Pan Yue, 201, 224

para inglês ver, 44–45, 48
  dictatorship, 56, 87, 158, 294, 296
Paraguay, 52, 212, 222, 246–247, 262
party, 6, 8, 56, 79
patriarchal, 159–160
patronage, 43–44, 54, 280, 296
patron-client relations, 81, 84
peasant,
  Brazil, 52, 61, 208
  China, 67, 72–74, 78–79, 137, 218
    revolution, 73, 85, 265
People's Armed Police (PAP), 131
People's Liberation Army (PLA), 69,
  80, 85
personalist politics, 57, 76
Petrobrás, 205, 212, 261
Philippines, 268, 275, 281
PM 2.5, 220, 223, 228
poder moderador (moderating power),
  52, 55
Police Pacification Units (UPPs),
  110–111, 145
political culture, 23, 84
  Brazil, 49, 59, 61, 104, 118
  China, 69, 71
political opportunity structures, 9, 19,
  21, 39, 83, 100, 286
polls, 86, 165
  Brazil, 60, 63, 158, 195, 236, 257
  China, 187, 190, 236
pollution, 23, 233, 234 (fig. 5.1)
  Brazil, 202–203, 238
    air, 202, 218
    activism, 203–204
    water, 204, 295
  China, 202–203, 238–239, 292,
    294–295
    activism, 219, 221, 228–229,
      294–295
    air, 118, 220–224, 238
    data, 223–224, 226
    health effects, 220, 225
    spiritual, 128
    state efforts, 221, 238–239, 292
    water, 34, 118, 220–224, 226

Pope Benedict, 164, 215
populist, 53–55, 81, 120
Portugal, 41–32, 47, 49–50, 84, 170
positive discrimination, 157, 192 (fig.
  4.1)
poverty, 16, 52, 31, 63, 73, 76, 143
  Brazil, 31, 61, 92, 60, 96, 153
    environment, 203, 209, 256
    inequality, 61, 91–92, 261
  /model, 251, 263, 282, 286, 295
  China, 225, 229, 236, 286
  programs, 93–95, 293, 295
prevention, 137–139
  HIV-AIDS, 116–117, 142 (fig. 3.1),
    166, 170, 252
pro-democracy movement, 97, 112,
  207
prostitution, 33, 146–147
  Brazil, 114, 116, 160, 165–167, 196,
    252
  China, 68, 130, 133, 139, 149,
    185–187, 196, 198
protest as opposition, 17–18, 177
protest as pressure, 17–19, 25–26 (fig.
  1.1)
  Brazil, 108, 161, 192–193 (fig. 4.1)
    HIV-AIDS, 115, 142 (fig. 3.1)
    sex workers, 166, 193 (fig. 4.1)
  China, 133, 141 (fig. 3.1), 234 (fig.
    5.1)
public opinion, 11, 158, 164, 187, 190,
  195, 205
Public Security Bureau (PSB), 131
public services, 91, 94, 102

Qing Dynasty, 66, 69, 72–73, 126, 131,
  174
Qinghai–Xizang Railway, 176

recession, 89–90, 93, 100, 260–261
reciprocal multilateralism, 35, 250
Red Army, 89
Red Guards, 70
red-line issues, 22, 140, 256, 286, 290,
  293, 295, 297. *See also* core issues

referendum, 101, 108–109
reforestation, 230, 277
"reform through labor" (RTL), 133
religious activists, 16, 115
religious groups, 16, 33, 151, 162, 164,
    193
remittances, 122, 125, 186
renewable energy, 216, 222, 235, 239,
    258–260
repertoire, 4–5, 9, 14, 23, 140, 240
    Brazil, 62, 98, 116, 165, 210
    China, 77, 190, 192 (fig.4.1), 221,
        294
    regime type, 11–12, 280, 297
responsiveness, 2, 10, 80, 98, 112, 238,
    298
reproductive rights, 151, 163–165,
    183–185, 195
    See also abortion, "one child" policy,
        population planning
Republic of China, 67, 73
"responsible stakeholder," 254, 270,
    276
"rights to the city," 97–98, 118
Rousseff, Dilma, 22, 60, 85
    election, 63, 165, 209
    environmental policies, 216–217,
        259–260
    international relations, 245, 263
    racial policies, 157, 198
    sexuality and sexual identity
        (policies), 171, 194
    social welfare programs, 94–96, 100
rule of law, 5–6, 8
    Brazil, 104–105, 108–109,
        146–147
    China, 146–147, 291

safe sex, 115–116, 186
Sandberg, Sheryl, 182
sanitation, 94, 97–98, 204
Sarney, José, 117, 255
scandals, 146
    Brazil, 55, 59, 62, 90–91, 164, 171,
        261

schools, 144
    China, 20, 71, 122–123, 128, 138,
        218
self-determination, 191, 284
sex work. *See* prostitution
"shame parades," 187
Shang Dynasty, 66
Shanghai Cooperation Organization
    (SCO), 269
"Shanghai gang," 81
Shanghai pride, 190
"sharp" mobilizations, 98
slavery, 30, 32, 40–45, 66, 58, 152
    legacy, 41, 56, 84, 92, 104–105
    official history, 40, 152, 154
social contract, 244, 296
social media, 23–24, 86, 295
    Brazil, 102–103, 217
    China, 132–133, 141 (fig. 3.1), 182
social movement, 4, 10, 15, 19, 23, 38,
    86
    Brazil, 53, 59, 61, 97, 114, 155, 209
social stratification, 43, 66, 72
social welfare programs, 14, 147
    Brazil, 54, 60, 93–94, 112, 206, 251
    China, 136–137, 143
soft power, 244, 290
    Brazil, 51, 198, 249, 252, 259–64,
        291
    China, 71, 269, 274, 280–282, 287
Song Dynasty, 185
South, 34, 286–287
    Brazil's relations with, 245, 249–250,
        254, 260, 263, 283
South China Sea, 267–268, 275
South–North Water Transfer Project,
    230
sovereignty, 34, 233, 286
    Brazil, 167, 252–253, 256, 284–285
    China, 273–275, 285, 293
spiritual pollution, 128
Spratley Islands, 268
squatters' movement, 62, 97–98
Stang, Dorothy, 34, 107–108, 211, 237
state-owned enterprises, 119, 136, 224

street children, 16, 93, 124, 129
Sun Yatsen, 67, 73
superpowers, 147
    Brazil, 31, 93–94, 250–252, 257,
        259–261, 264, 282, 287
    China, 219, 244–246, 267, 279,
        282–283
synergy, 18
    Brazil, 113, 142 (fig. 3.1), 165, 286,
        290
    China, 132, 139, 141 (fig. 3.1), 142
        (fig. 3.1), 234 (fig. 5.1)

Tai Lake, 228
Taiwan, 27, 131, 179, 273, 275
    history, 68, 70–71, 130
    core issue, 35, 274–275, 286
"Tank Man," 77, 291
    See also Tiananmen Square
television, TV, 109
    China, 128, 181, 185–188, 190, 229,
        280
territorial integrity, 34, 174, 274–275,
    286
theory-infirming, 10–11, 28–29, 201,
    290, 297
"thief maps,"132
Three Gorges Dam, 222, 239
"Tiananmen Mothers," 77, 85
Tiananmen Square, 38, 70–86
    post-Tiananmen, 119–120, 138, 223,
        296
Tibet, Tibetan, 24, 33, 191, 286, 274,
    295
    core issue, 35, 84, 173–177, 229–230
torture, 229
    Brazil's democracy, 111, 146
    Brazil's dictatorship, 54, 56, 58, 60,
        85, 154
totalitarian, 12, 54, 289
traditional family, 160, 162, 169
traditional media. *See* media
transgender,
    Brazil, 114, 166, 168–169, 197
    China, 33, 187–188, 190

transnational, 4, 243
    Brazil, 153, 209, 249, 255,
    China, 271–272, 275–276
transparent, transparency,
    Brazil, 57, 109–110, 118–119, 145
    China, 131, 137, 228, 238, 269,
        291
transphobia, 168, 193 (fig. 4.1)
transportation, 97, 132, 219
travestis. *See* transgender
"Treaty Ports," 66–68, 84
triads, 131
truth commission, 56, 58, 85
Twitter, 23–24, 103, 129, 186, 217

Uighurs, 173–174, 176–178, 274, 295
Unified Black Movement (*Movimento
    Negro Unificado*, MNU), 154–155,
    157, 161
Unified Health System (*Sistema Único
    de Saude*, SUS), 112
unions (trade), 16, 121
    Brazil, 24, 41, 59–60, 205
United Nations (UN),
    Brazil, 105, 153, 156, 163, 251, 254,
        284
    environment, 217, 255
    China, 230, 270–273, 275, 278
United Nations Educational,
    Scientific, and Cultural
    Organization (UNESCO), 32,
    101, 156, 226
United Nations Security Council
    (UNSC), 3, 35, 253
United States, 2, 23, 27, 107, 131, 167,
    181, 243
    Chinese exiles, 76, 138, 199
    comparisons to Brazil, 202, 218, 262,
        282, 294
    comparisons to Brazil on race, 32,
        44–45, 152–154, 156
    comparisons to Brazil on sex and
        gender, 164, 168, 170, 190
    comparisons to China, 276–277,
        287, 291

United States (*continued*)
    relations with Brazil, 32, 167, 245,
        247–254, 259, 277, 284
    relations with China, 68, 70–71,
        264–276, 280, 284–285
urban reform movement, 97–98
urbanization,
    Brazil, 54, 96, 160
    China, 125, 141 (fig. 3.1), 184, 218,
        231

Vargas, Getúlio, 53–55
Vatican, 195–196
vigilante, 105, 108
"virgin prostitutes," 187
Viva Rio, 108–109

Wan Yanhai, 138–139
Weibo, 190, 232
Wen Jiabao, 81, 120
white collar crimes, 128, 134
women,
    Brazil, 53, 161–165, 197
        activism, 99, 109, 154, 160–161,
            163
        gender ideologies, 159–161
        HIV–AIDS, 114, 116
        status, 161–162, 172
    China, 68, 85, 130, 139, 181,
        186–191
        activism, 181, 187

gender ideologies, 180–181
    status, 180, 182, 199
See also reproductive rights
Workers' Party (*Partido dos
    Trabalhadores*, PT),
    environment, 209, 214, 216–218,
        256
    foreign policy, 245, 256
    history, 16, 31, 59–63, 86
    human security, 61, 95–99, 143, 165,
        171
    state, 60, 86, 103, 293–295
World Bank, 2
    Brazil, 92, 94, 110, 114, 213, 250
    China, 118, 222, 276–278
World Cup, 100–101, 109–110, 144
    protests, 22, 62–63, 91, 103, 289,
        290–291
World War II, 254, 266
"Wukan model" of engagement, 127

Xi Jinping, 31, 81, 228, 265, 272
    corruption, 80, 296
    foreign policy, 242, 267, 273
Xinjiang, 84, 174, 220, 231
    core issue, 35, 177–178, 274
    cultural dilution, ix, 33, 191

Zhang Xianling, 77
Zhao Liang, 138

CPSIA information can be obtained at www.ICGtesting.com
Printed in the USA
LVOW07§0300130116

469818LV00009B/19/P